*Unionism
and Relative Wages
in the United States*

This volume is a publication of the
Workshop in Labor and Industrial Relations

★

STUDIES IN ECONOMICS
of the
ECONOMICS RESEARCH CENTER
of the
UNIVERSITY OF CHICAGO

Unionism
and Relative Wages
in the United States

AN EMPIRICAL INQUIRY

By

H. G. LEWIS

THE UNIVERSITY OF CHICAGO PRESS

CHICAGO AND LONDON

Library of Congress Catalog Card Number: 63-20915

THE UNIVERSITY OF CHICAGO PRESS, CHICAGO & LONDON
The University of Toronto Press, Toronto 5, Canada

Printed in the United States of America

To my parents

Preface

I was initially encouraged to undertake the preparation of this book by a series of discussions of empirical studies of unionism and relative wages held in 1955–56 in the Labor Workshop at the University of Chicago. My earlier somewhat casual reading of these studies had given me the impression of considerable disagreement among them in their findings. Our review suggested, however, that much of the seeming disagreement might be the result of conceptual differences in the wage effects of unionism that were examined, variations over time in the relative wage effects of unionism and differences in the dates to which the estimated effects pertained, and lack of uniformity among the authors in their choice of adjectives to describe their findings. These suggestions played a key part in the growth of this book.

The intervening years have afforded me many opportunities to benefit from discussion of my work on the book—with colleagues at the University of Chicago, especially those in the Labor Workshop; with members of the Columbia University Labor Workshop; and with most of the authors of the studies reviewed in the book. Gary S. Becker, Milton Friedman, Albert E. Rees, and George J. Stigler read and commented on large portions of the manuscript.

I am also indebted to the American Enterprise Institute for Public Policy Research for a grant supporting my research on unionism and relative wages and to Joseph L. Craycraft, Robert Evans, Claire Friedland, Robert W. Fuller, Thomas D. Harris, John C. Hause, Florence I. Jaffy, Ethel B. Jones, Millard F. Long, Jacob P. Meerman, Thomas G. Moore, Sherwin H. Rosen, and Edgardo P. Zialcita for their research assistance.

My secretary, Mrs. Alyce G. Monroe, typed the draft and final manuscripts of the book and in many other ways gave me invaluable help.

H. G. L.

Chicago
August, 1963

vii

Contents

III
Earlier Studies of Unions and Wage Differentials: The Industry Studies

IV
Earlier Studies of Unions and Wage Differentials: The "Economy-wide" Studies

V
The Impact of Unionism on the Average Wage of All Union Labor Relative to the Average Wage of All Nonunion Labor

VI

Wage Rigidity and the Relative Wage Effects of Unionism

VII

*Dispersion in the Extent of Unionism among
Industries in the United States*

VIII

*Dispersion in the Relative Wage Effects of
Unionism among Industries*

Contents

IX

Effects of Unionism on Relative Wage Inequality

Tables

Tables

I

The Scope of the Inquiry

I.1. INTRODUCTION

THIS IS an empirical study of labor unions and relative wages in the United States. Its main purpose is to estimate the magnitude of the impact of unionism on percentage (relative) wage differentials among groups of labor. The principal questions for which the study attempts to give quantitative answers are:

By how much has unionism increased the average wage of union labor relative to the average wage of all labor, both union and nonunion? Reduced the average wage of nonunion labor relative to the average wage of all labor?

To what extent has unionism affected, in different proportions, the average wages of different industries?

How variable were the effects of unionism on relative wages from one date to another during the last forty years? How much of this variability can be explained by changes in the rate of inflation of the general price level or general money wage level? By changes in the degree of unionization of the labor force?

How much higher or lower is the relative inequality in average wages among industries than it would be in the absence of relative wage effects of unionism? The amount of relative inequality in the distribution of wages among all workers?

I.2. RELATIVE AND ABSOLUTE WAGE EFFECTS OF UNIONISM

Labor unions may have three different kinds of "wage" effects that are often confused with each other. Unionism may change (a) the economy-wide average or general level of money wages per hour; (b) the economy-wide average or general level of real wages per hour; and (c) relative wages—the ratios of the wages per hour of particular groups of labor to the average wage per hour of all labor. The first two, (a) and (b), are *absolute* wage effects of unionism. This study deals only with (c), the *relative* wage effects of unionism.

Unionism can affect the relative wages of different groups of labor only if it changes the wages of the groups by percentage amounts which differ from one group to another, that is, changes the percentage differences in wages among the groups. Furthermore, neither unionism nor anything else can raise (or, alternatively, lower) the wage of every

1

different group of labor relative to the average wage of all labor. Therefore, all of the following statements have the same meaning:

Unionism has raised the average relative wage of union workers.
Unionism has lowered the average relative wage of nonunion workers.
Unionism has raised the average wage of union workers relative to the average wage of nonunion workers.
Unionism has lowered the average wage of nonunion workers relative to the average wage of union workers.

On the other hand, that unionism has raised the average *relative* wage of union workers—lowered the average *relative* wage of nonunion workers—does not mean that unionism has raised the average *absolute* wage (money or real) of union workers or lowered the average *absolute* wage of nonunion workers or changed in either direction the average *absolute* wage of all workers taken together. The effects of unionism on the general level of either money or real wages cannot be deduced from knowledge only of the *relative* wage effects of unionism.

Chapter ii treats more precisely the concepts of relative and absolute wage effects of unionism and demonstrates the propositions of the preceding paragraph.

The effect of unionism on the average relative wage of a particular group of labor (the labor employed in a particular industry, occupation, city, etc.) is a weighted average of corresponding relative wage effects for (a) the union workers and (b) the nonunion workers in the group, where the relative weight for the union workers is the degree of unionization of the group. For example, if the degree of unionization were 50 per cent and if unionism had raised the relative wage of union workers in the group by 10 per cent and lowered the relative wage of the nonunion workers by 2 per cent, the effect of unionism on the average relative wage of the group would be a plus 4 per cent. Thus the differences among groups in the impact of unionism on their relative wages will be larger, the greater are the corresponding differences in degree of unionization and in the effects of unions on the relative wages of union workers and of nonunion workers. Chapter ii analyzes the arithmetic and economic relationships between the degree of unionization of a group of labor and the average relative wage effect of unionism for the group. Chapter ii also describes the methods used in this study to estimate the relative wage effects of unionism.

I.3. Empirical Studies of Unionism and Wages

Our knowledge of the relative wage impact of unionism in the United States stems almost entirely from research reported in the last decade and a half. Before 1945 there were, to be sure, many serious studies of wages and of unionism containing statements regarding the effects of unions on wage differentials, but in none of these studies, to the best of my knowledge, are there numerical estimates of the relative wage effects of unions.[1] Since World War II, on the other hand, a substantial amount of empirical research on one or another facet of unionism and wages has been performed by economists; the findings given in this volume are based chiefly on the evidence presented in twenty of these recent studies.[2]

Twelve of them focus on relatively small segments of the U.S. labor force, ranging from barbers to steel workers. In addition, there are eight global studies dealing with large segments of the labor force. Chapter iii reviews each of the twelve "industry" studies, chapter iv the eight global studies. From the evidence presented in each study and from supplementary data, I have drawn estimates of the impact of unionism on the relative wage of the union workers covered in the study. Table 49 in chapter v displays these estimates in detail.

At first glance the amount of dispersion in the estimates appears to be enormous: the figures range from zero to more than 100 per cent. Bituminous coal mining is the extreme case. The data for this industry indicate that in 1921–22 the wages of coal miners in unionized mines may have been more than twice as high as they would have been in the absence of unionization in coal mining. In contrast, it appears that about

[1] Mention should be made, however, of Paul H. Douglas' *Real Wages in the United States, 1890–1926* (Boston and New York: Houghton Mifflin Co., 1930). This work was devoted almost entirely to the construction of historical statistics on wages and hours of work by industry, but in a brief discussion of unionism as a possible cause of the increase in real wages which occurred in the United States between 1890 and 1926, Douglas observed (p. 564): "Unionism, in other words, very probably does give an appreciable increase in earnings during the early period of effective organization, but during the later and more mature years of union development, the relative rate of further progress seems, to say the least, to be no more rapid on the whole for unionists than for nonunionists. Judging by our indexes, indeed, the nonunion trades have made slightly greater relative progress since 1914 than the union trades, although their average absolute earnings are still below those of the unionist." Nowhere in his study does Douglas replace the adjective "appreciable" in the above statement by a number or a set of numbers.

[2] I have endeavored to cover all of the reports of empirical research on unionism and wage differentials from which I could take directly or compute numerical estimates of relative wage effects of unionism or of directions of change in these effects. I have excluded, therefore, a good many studies in which there is evidence that unionism may have caused relative wage changes, but the evidence was of such nature that I could not estimate the size or direction of change of the wage effects. Much of the postwar research on unions and wage differentials has been reported only in unpublished or little-known papers and dissertations, some of which, no doubt, I have not covered simply because they were not known to me.

1945 the wages of unionized miners on the average were *no* higher than they would have been in the absence of miner unionization. Neither of these two extremes lasted very long. By the mid-1920's the estimated relative wage effect had fallen to about 50 to 60 per cent. Similarly, after 1945 the relative wage effect rose to a level in 1956–57 which was about the same as that in 1924–26.

Few of the studies of other groups of union labor, however, yielded estimates above 25 per cent. The relative wage effects of 50 per cent or more observed for union coal miners in part of the 1920's and 1930's and again in recent years, therefore, truly deserve to be called "extremely large." On the other hand, the zero relative wage effect for union coal miners near the end of World War II was not exceptionally low compared to the effects estimated from studies of other industries. Rather, the period was exceptional: during much of 1944–49, unionism apparently had little impact on the U.S. relative wage structure.

I.4. The Impact of Unionism on the Average Wage of Union Labor Relative to the Average Wage of Nonunion Labor

In chapter v, I estimate the percentage amount by which unionism raised the *average* wage of union labor relative to the *average* wage of nonunion labor. There is much uniformity in the evidence provided by the studies reviewed in chapters iii and iv that the impact of unionism on the average union/nonunion relative wage varied markedly from one date to another. The peak impact of the last forty years occurred, I judge, about 1932–33, near the bottom of the Great Depression. At the peak, the effect of unionism on the average wage of union workers relative to the average wage of nonunion workers may have been above 25 per cent. In the ensuing inflation the relative wage effect declined sharply to a level between 10 per cent and 20 per cent, I estimate, by the end of the 1930's.

The decline in the average union/nonunion relative wage effect of unionism continued until about 1947 or 1948, near the peak of the inflation immediately following World War II. At the trough, the impact of unionism on the average wage of union labor relative to the average wage of nonunion labor was close to zero—under 5 per cent. (There is much less evidence for the similar period following World War I, but what there is suggests that then, too, the relative wage impact of unionism was unusually low.)

The near-zero relative wage effect of unionism observed shortly after World War II did not persist, however, through the following decade. I estimate that in recent years the average union/nonunion relative wage was approximately 10 to 15 per cent higher than it would have been in the absence of unionism. During the 1950's, the extent of unionization of the labor force was close to 25 per cent. These figures imply that recently the average wage of union workers was about 7 to 11 per cent higher relative to the average wage of all workers, both union and nonunion, than it would have been in the absence of unionism. Similarly, the average wage of nonunion workers was about 3 to 4 per cent lower relative to the average wage of all workers than in the absence of unionism.

I.5. Unionism and Money Wage Rigidity

The finding that the relative wage impact of unionism was greatest near the bottom of the Great Depression and was least during the periods of unusually rapid inflation and low unemployment following both world wars is not new. The authors of several of the studies reviewed in chapters iii and iv noted the phenomenon and commented on it. Albert E. Rees, Milton Friedman, Walter A. Morton,[3] and a number of other economists have attributed the phenomenon to rigidities or lags in the adjustment of money wages introduced by collective bargaining: the collective-bargaining contract running for a year or more, the reluctance of unions to accept wage cuts during periods of deflation lest the deflation not continue, and the similar reluctance of employers of union labor to agree to unusually large money wage increases during periods of unusually rapid inflation.

In chapter vi, I report on a quantitative study in which I have attempted to measure the separate effects of changes in the general price level and changes in the rate of unemployment in the labor force on the average union/nonunion relative wage. The resulting estimates of the impact of unionism on the average wage of union workers relative to the average wage of nonunion workers agree fairly well, both in level and in directions of change over time, with those derived from the earlier studies. More importantly, the study indicates that during 1920–58, abnormally high rates of inflation strongly tended to reduce—and abnormally low rates of inflation to increase—the effect of unionism on the average

[3] Albert E. Rees, "Postwar Wage Determination in the Basic Steel Industry," *American Economic Review*, XLI, No. 3 (June, 1951), 395–99. Milton Friedman, "Some Comments on the Significance of Labor Unions for Economic Policy," in David McCord Wright (ed.), *The Impact of the Union* (New York: Harcourt, Brace & Co., 1951), pp. 226–31. See also Friedman's "Discussion" in Industrial Relations Research Association, *Proceedings of the Eleventh Annual Meeting* (1958), pp. 212–16. Walter A. Morton, "Trade Unionism, Full Employment and Inflation," *American Economic Review*, XL, No. 1 (March, 1950), 18.

union/nonunion relative wage. The study provides weaker evidence that changes in the rate of unemployment caused changes in the same direction in the relative wage impact of unionism.

I.6. THE EXTENT AND LOCUS OF UNIONISM IN THE UNITED STATES

To a significant extent, the differences among industries in the effects of unionism on their average relative wages stem from corresponding differences in their degree of unionization. Chapter vii presents annual data, 1900 to 1960, on the degree of unionization of the U.S. labor force and for selected dates estimates of degree of unionization by industry.

In 1897, eleven years after the founding of the American Federation of Labor, union membership comprised less than 2 per cent of the labor force. By 1904 the proportion had risen to about 7 per cent, where it remained until 1917. From 1917 to 1920, union membership grew rapidly, but the increment in membership was short lived. In 1923 about one-twelfth of the labor force was unionized; a decade later the fraction was almost the same as in 1904.

In the decade beginning in 1935 the degree of unionization of the labor force approximately quadrupled to a level of about 25 per cent in 1945. The percentage rose slightly from 1945 to 1953 and since 1953 has declined by a small amount.

Before 1934 the degree of unionization was appreciable only in coal mining, contract construction, printing, men's and women's outerwear manufacturing, the railroads, local transit and trucking, the stage and theater, and the postal service, yet in 1929 only one-third of the persons engaged in this group of industries were union members. In 1929 these industries employed one-sixth of the U.S. labor force and three-fourths of all union members.

Since 1944 roughly half the work forces in mining, contract construction, manufacturing, and communications and public utilities (except transportation) have been represented by unions in collective bargaining. In transportation the degree of unionization has been about 75 per cent. However, within each of these broad industry divisions there are wide differences in degree of unionization among detailed industries.

Both before and after 1934 the degree of unionization has been close to zero in agriculture, wholesale and retail trade, finance and insurance, and government (except government enterprises). The same is true of the service industries except for hotels and eating and drinking places in large cities, the entertainment industries, and some of the personal service industries. The agriculture, trade, finance, service, and government industry divisions have employed about half the labor force.

Between 1933 and 1945 the amount of inequality among industries in degree of unionization doubled. Since 1945 the inequality in the distribution of unionism by industry has been approximately half as large as it could conceivably be. Thus, *as a matter of arithmetic*, another doubling, or close to it, of inequality in degree of unionization among industries is possible. For this extreme to occur, however, the extent of unionization of the labor force would have to rise to 50 per cent and, more importantly, all of the union workers would have to be employed in industries that were 100 per cent unionized.

Since 1945 there has been no persistent tendency for the degree of unionization of the labor force to increase, but even if it were to rise to 50 per cent, the dispersion among industries in degree of unionization would not increase substantially unless the growth of unionism were to consist much more largely than it has in the past of the unionization of supervisory and staff (nonproduction) employees in industries in which the production workers were already highly unionized.

I.7. UNIONISM AND THE INTERINDUSTRIAL RELATIVE WAGE STRUCTURE

Chapter viii deals mainly with the relative wage effects of unionism among industries. The studies reviewed in chapter iii provide estimates for various dates of relative wage effects for only a short list of industries. Moreover, it is not possible to deduce from these estimates and from other data presented in this study the relative wage effects, industry by industry, for the rest of the industries in the economy.

Nevertheless, some of the over-all characteristics of the distribution of the relative wage effects of unionism among industries can be gauged from the data on degree of unionization by industry given in chapter vii and the relative wage effect estimates drawn from earlier studies. The majority of workers, I judge, are employed in industries whose average relative wages have been raised or lowered by unionism by no more than about 4 per cent. However, in industries employing a quite small fraction of the labor force—considerably less than 6 per cent—the relative wage effect is 20 per cent or more.

I cannot, for lack of information, give a complete list of the industries in which the relative wage effects recently have been as high as 20 per cent. The studies covered in chapter iii suggest that the list includes bituminous coal mining, some of the building trades in some cities in which the trades are highly unionized, and possibly barbering in a few cities. The inclusion of the building trades, however, rests chiefly on data for 1939 and for both these trades and other industries the estimates of the relative wage effects of unionism may contain substantial errors.

It is likely that the industries which should be added to the list are highly unionized. However, a high degree of unionization does not guarantee that the relative wage effect of unionism is also large. For example, the manufacturing of men's and boys' suits and coats is a highly unionized industry, yet according to a study discussed in chapter iii the relative wages of union workers in the industry have been affected very little by unionism since World War II.

Only about 15 per cent of the females in the labor force are union members. The corresponding figures for males is 30 per cent. If there were no differences by sex in the average relative wage effects of unionism among either union workers or nonunion workers, I estimate that in recent years unionism has lowered the average relative wage of females by about 1 to 1.5 per cent and raised that of males by less than 1 per cent. However, in the occupations in which the impact of unionism on relative wages apparently has been greatest—coal miners, airline pilots, skilled building tradesmen, and seamen, for example—the ratio of female to male employees is very close to zero. For this reason, the above figures may underestimate somewhat the difference in relative wage effects by sex. But even if the effect for women were the same as that estimated for *nonunion* workers—a minus 3 per cent to a minus 4 per cent—the corresponding effect for males would be no more than a plus 2 per cent.

I.8. The IMPACT OF UNIONISM ON THE DISTRIBUTION OF WAGE AND SALARY INCOME

Unionism has tended to raise relative wages most in industries with above-average relative wages. Therefore, unionism has been a factor making the relative inequality of wages *among industries* greater than it otherwise would be. In chapter ix, I estimate that in 1958, unionism increased the relative inequality of average wages among industries by about 6 to 10 per cent compared to what the inequality would have been in the absence of relative wage effects of unionism.

It does not follow, however, that unionism must have increased the relative inequality of the distribution of wages *among all individual workers in the labor force*. The latter inequality depends on both (a) the relative inequality of average wages *among* industries and (b) the average relative inequality of wages of individual workers *within* industries. Therefore, unionism could have reduced the all-worker inequality by reducing the average inequality *within* industries by more than enough to offset the increase in inequality *among* industries.

Unfortunately, numerical evidence of the kind and quantity needed to estimate closely the magnitude of the impact of unionism on the average inequality of wages among individual workers within industries is not available. Nevertheless, I think it is improbable that unionism has changed this within-industry inequality by as much as 5 per cent. The majority of employees, I judge, work in industries within which unionism has had a trivial effect on relative wage inequality. The remaining minority of employees are divided in uncertain ratio between industries (a) within which unionism has increased relative wage inequality and industries (b) within which unionism has decreased relative wage inequality. But this implies that the average increase in relative wage inequality within industries (a) or, alternatively, the average decrease in relative wage inequality within industries (b) would have to be quite large in order to change the average within-industry inequality by as much as 5 per cent for all industries taken together.

If unionism has increased the inequality of average relative wages *among industries* by 8 per cent and has changed the average relative wage inequality *among workers within industries* by no more than 5 per cent, then unionism has changed the relative wage inequality *among all workers* by less than 6 per cent.

I conclude tentatively that unionism has had a small impact on the relative inequality of the distribution of wages among all workers. The direction of the effect, on presently available evidence, is ambiguous.

II

The Relative Wage Impact of Unionism: Concepts and Methods

II.1. INTRODUCTION

THE AVERAGE relative wage of a group of labor is the ratio of the group's average absolute wage to the average absolute wage of all labor in the economy. The effect of unionism on the group's average relative wage at a particular date is the percentage difference between the average relative wage of the group in the presence of unionism at the date and the corresponding average in the absence of unionism. The average relative wage of the group "in the presence of unionism" is the group's actual average relative wage at the date.[1] The "corresponding average in the absence of unionism" is the average relative wage that would have been observed for the group at the same date in the absence of unionism.

The "unionism" to which I refer in the expressions "in the presence of unionism" and "in the absence of unionism" is *all* of the unionism in the economy at the specified date and earlier; that is, the effect of "unionism" on a group's average relative wage is the total effect of any unionism in the group and of any unionism elsewhere in the economy. Of course, if the group is nonunion, the total effect for the group contains only the "indirect" effect of unionism elsewhere. On the other hand, if the group is completely unionized, the total effect need not be the same as the "direct" effect of the unionism present in the group. Section ii.5 deals with some of the problems of estimating "direct" effects from "total" effects.

The average relative wage of a group of labor in the presence of unionism can be observed directly.[2] What the corresponding average would have been in the absence of unionism, however, can be inferred only uncertainly from observable data. Broadly speaking, two different types of approaches have been used to estimate relative wage effects of unionism.

1. The *indirect* approach estimates the effect of unionism on the average relative wage of a group of labor from estimates of the effects of unionism on other economic magnitudes pertaining to the group, such as its relative employment, relative quit rate, excess supply ("queuing")

---

[1] But see pp. 49–52.
[2] See pp. 49–52 for exception.

of labor or excess demand ("shortage") of labor, the relative price of the commodity produced by the group, and so on. Evidence that the latter effects are absent is usually strong evidence that the corresponding relative wage effect is also absent. Similarly, a finding that the non-wage effects of unionism are not zero can often be taken as evidence that unionism has affected the average relative wage of the group. However, when the non-wage effects of unionism are not zero, it is usually difficult to estimate from them the *size* of the implied relative wage effect of unionism for the group. I discuss the problems of translating non-wage effects of unionism into corresponding relative wage effects in the reviews of the studies using the indirect approach.

2. In the *direct* approach, the relative wage effects of unionism are estimated from comparisons of the wages or wage changes of two or more groups of labor differing in degree of unionization or in the changes of degree of unionization. The estimates of relative wage effects presented in later chapters are based mainly on this approach.

In essence, the direct (or wage comparison) approach estimates the effects of unionism on relative wages by correlating average wages or changes in average wages with degree of unionization or changes in degree of unionization across the covered groups of labor. The percentage differences in actual average wages among several groups of labor, however, reflect not only the relative wage effects of unionism but also the effects of other factors that may be correlated with the degree of unionization of the groups. In the common measures of average wages these factors usually include (a) the composition of the working forces of the groups by such characteristics as sex, race, age, and training; (b) the attractiveness of the work and working conditions offered employees; (c) the rates of change over time of underlying demand and supply conditions; and (d) the responsiveness of wages to changes in these conditions. Similarly, the differences in wage *changes* among several groups of labor also reflect in part the effects of factors other than unionism. Therefore, the central problem in this approach is adjusting the wage data used for the effects of factors other than unionism that are correlated with the wage effects of unionism.

Because the studies reviewed in chapters iii and iv differ substantially in the details of the adjustments of their wage data for effects of factors other than unionism, I defer discussion of these details to the individual reviews. However, all of the studies have in common the problem of holding constant both the "quality" of the labor services and the "quality" of working conditions in their wage comparisons. Unfortunately, the required data on these two quality aspects are generally unavailable and therefore, typically, the adjustments for them have been incomplete. Section ii.10 discusses the biases in the relative wage effect estimates resulting from such incomplete adjustment of the wage data.

The wage comparison approach also presents another problem. Suppose that the average wages of several groups of labor at a particular date are perfectly adjusted for effects of factors other than unionism[3] and that the adjusted wage figures are correlated with the corresponding figures on the degree of unionization of the groups. One or more summary numbers, measures of the "relative wage impact of unionism" in the covered groups, emerge from the correlation. The meaning of each number depends on both the manner of its calculation and the particular groups of labor covered. Differences among the numbers in either of these respects may make them conceptually incomparable. Moreover, the meaning of some types of summary numbers is not obvious. These problems of interpretation of the relative wage effect estimates are usually even more serious when wage *changes* over time, instead of wage *levels* at a given time, are correlated with degree of unionization or changes in degree of unionization. This chapter is chiefly devoted to exploring the meaning of the common types of measures of relative wage effects of unionism and finding ways of dealing with the incomparabilities among them.

II.2. Types of Wage Comparisons

The studies reviewed in chapters iii and iv use two different types of wage comparison approaches to estimate wage differential effects of unionism. In the Type *A* approach the wage figures compared are the adjusted wage *levels* at a particular date of two or more groups of labor; in the Type *B* approach the adjusted *changes* in wages from a base date to a given date are compared. Within each of the two broad types of wage comparisons, three variant procedures may be distinguished.

A. The Adjusted Wage Differential Approach

Variant A-I compares the average wage of a given group at a particular date with the average wage at the same date of *all labor in the economy*. The gross percentage difference in average wage between the given group and all labor in the economy is adjusted to eliminate effects of factors that would produce a difference in average wages in the absence of unionism. It is this adjusted wage differential that is attributed to

---

[3] In the sense that the adjusted wages contain no effects of factors other than unionism that are correlated with the degree of unionization of the groups.

unionism. The relative wage effect estimated by Variant A-I is the effect of unionism on the average relative wage of the given group.

Variant A-II differs from Variant A-I in that the comparison or benchmark group is not all labor in the economy, but usually a nonunion group of labor considered "comparable" to the given group. Thus Variant A-II estimates the effect of unionism on the average wage of the given group relative to the average wage of the benchmark group.

Variant A-III deals simultaneously with three or more groups differing in degree of unionization. This variant adjusts the average wages of the groups for factors other than unionism and correlates the adjusted averages with degree of unionization. The adjustment and the correlation may take place at the same time in a multivariate analysis of wages, degree of unionization, and variables reflecting the effects of factors other than unionism. In general, this procedure does not yield estimates of the relative wage effects of unionism for the individual groups of labor covered, but under certain circumstances the variant provides an unbiased estimate of the effect of unionism on the average wage of all union labor employed in the covered groups relative to the corresponding average wage of all nonunion labor.

B. *The Adjusted Change-in-Wage Differential Approach*

Variant B-I adjusts the percentage *change* from a base date to a given date in the average relative wage of a given group for factors other than unionism and attributes to unionism the adjusted change in the average relative wage. This variant therefore estimates the percentage *change* from the base date to the given date in the effect of unionism on the average relative wage of the given group. Of course, if the unionism effect at the base date was negligible, the *change* in effect *from the base date to the given date* is approximately the same as the *level* of the effect *at the given date*.

Variant B-II is like Variant B-I except that the benchmark group is usually a nonunion group "comparable" to the given group. The relative wage effect estimated by this variant is the percentage change from the base date to the given date in the effect of unionism on the average wage of the given group relative to the average wage of the benchmark group.

Variant B-III has two sub-variants. In both, the percentage changes from a base date to a given date in the average wages of several groups of labor are adjusted for factors other than unionism. The two sub-variants differ as follows:

Variant B-IIIa correlates the adjusted wage *changes* with the corresponding *changes*, in percentage points, in degree of unionization of the groups. Under some conditions this method yields an unbiased estimate of the impact of unionism *at the given date* on the average wage of all union labor employed in the covered groups relative to the corresponding average wage of all nonunion labor.

Variant B-IIIb correlates the adjusted wage *changes* of the groups with their *absolute levels* of degree of unionization at the base date or the given date or some intermediate date. This variant may yield:

1. An unbiased estimate of the effect of unionism *at the given date* on the average wage of all union labor in the covered groups relative to the average wage of all nonunion labor in the groups.

2. An unbiased estimate of the *change* from the base date to the given date in the union/nonunion relative wage effect in the covered groups.

As these brief descriptions suggest, the two different approaches and the variants of each yield measures of "relative wage effects of unionism" which in general are not strictly comparable in concept. Furthermore, in some of the variants the meaning of the relative wage effect that is measured is uncertain. Sections ii.3–ii.9 examine these incomparabilities and ambiguities in more detail and develop procedures for coping with some of them.

II.3. Indexes of Absolute and Relative Wage Effects of Unionism

Classify all of the labor employed in the economy into a set of mutually exclusive groups. Let w_i be the weighted geometric[4] mean wage, in money or real units,[5] of the labor employed in the ith group at a particular date in the presence of unionism; $w_{i,o}$ is the corresponding weighted geometric mean wage, with the same weights as in w_i, that would have been observed in the group in the absence of unionism.

Both w_i and $w_{i,o}$ are geometric means of the wages per man-hour of the various detailed kinds, grades, or qualities of labor services em-

---

[4] Nothing of importance in this chapter hinges on the use of geometric rather than arithmetic means. I use the geometric form only because it leads to slightly simpler exposition.

[5] In the definitions of various indexes of the effects of unionism on relative wages that follow I do not distinguish between relative *money* wages and relative *real* wages. The effects of unionism on relative money wages are the same as the effects of unionism on relative real wages only if the effects of unionism on the cost of living of employees in different groups are the same. I assume that any differences among groups in the effects of unionism on the cost of living of their employees are negligible and, therefore, interpret the relative wage findings of this study as applying equally to relative money wages and relative real wages.

ployed in the group. I include in "wages" not only what is conventionally regarded as "wages and salaries" in the United States but also "wage supplements"[6] and other payments "in kind."[7] The relative weight for each labor grade in the averages w_i and $w_{i,o}$ is the ratio of the aggregate compensation per unit period of time of employees in the grade to the total compensation of all employees in the group, the compensation ratios being calculated in the presence of unionism.[8]

Denote the counterparts of w_i and $w_{i,o}$ for the economy as a whole by $\bar{w}$ and $\bar{w}_o$, respectively. The economy-wide averages are defined in the same manner as the group averages w_i and $w_{i,o}$: both are weighted geometric means of the wages per man-hour of the various grades of labor employed in the economy, the weight for each grade in both $\bar{w}$ and $\bar{w}_o$ being the ratio of the aggregate compensation of employees in the grade to the aggregate compensation of employees in all grades. The economy-wide averages $\bar{w}$ and $\bar{w}_o$ are also weighted geometric means over all groups of the group averages w_i and $w_{i,o}$, with a weight for each group equal to the ratio of the aggregate compensation of employees in the group to the aggregate compensation of employees in all groups.

For a particular group, the average *relative* wage, denoted by v, is the ratio of the group's average absolute wage to the all-group average absolute wage. Thus the ith group's average relative wage in the presence of unionism is $v_i = w_i/\bar{w}$; in the absence of unionism it is $v_{i,o} = w_{i,o}/\bar{w}_o$. These *relative* wage averages are weighted geometric means, with the same weights as in w_i and $w_{i,o}$, of the corresponding *relative* wages of the various grades of labor employed in the group.

Let $\bar{v}$ and $\bar{v}_o$ be the economy-wide analogues of $\bar{w}$ and $\bar{w}_o$, respectively. That is, $\bar{v}$ and $\bar{v}_o$ are weighted geometric means of:

1. The group relative wage averages v_i and $v_{i,o}$, respectively, with weights by group in $\bar{v}$ and $\bar{v}_o$ equal to those in $\bar{w}$ and $\bar{w}_o$.
2. The relative wages, in the presence of unionism and in the absence of unionism, respectively, of the various grades of labor employed in the economy, with weights by grade the same as in $\bar{w}$ and $\bar{w}_o$.

---

[6] Employer contributions to public and private unemployment insurance, retirement insurance, health and accident insurance, and other employee benefit programs.

[7] That is, the difference between w_i and $w_{i,o}$ should include the effect of unionism on both the pecuniary and the nonpecuniary terms of employment.

[8] If the aggregate production function for the group were a Cobb-Douglas function of the rates of employment of the various grades of labor and of other productive services and were independent of unionism, then the set of relative compensation weights would be the same in the presence of unionism as in its absence and the ratio of w_i to $w_{i,o}$ would be the true index of the effect of unionism on the absolute level of wages in the group as seen by employers.

It follows that both economy-wide relative wage averages, $\bar{v}$ and $\bar{v}_o$, are always equal to unity. In other words, unionism cannot raise—or, alternatively, lower—the average wage of every group relative to the average wage in all groups taken together.

The ratio, denoted by A_i, of the average absolute wage in the ith group in the presence of unionism to the corresponding average absolute wage in the absence of unionism is the index of the effect of unionism on the absolute wage level of the group:

$$A_i = w_i/w_{i,o}.$$

The size of this absolute wage effect in per cent is $100(A_i - 1)$. The index A_i is the weighted geometric mean, with the same weights as in w_i and $w_{i,o}$, of similar indexes for each of the grades of labor employed in the group. The economy-wide counterpart of the A_i, defined as $\bar{A} = \bar{w}/\bar{w}_o$, is the index of the effect of unionism on the absolute wage level of the economy as a whole. $\bar{A}$ is the weighted geometric mean of the:

1. A_i, with weights by group the same as in $\bar{w}$ and $\bar{w}_o$.
2. Corresponding indexes of effects of unionism on the absolute wages of the grades of labor employed in the economy, with weights as in $\bar{w}$ and $\bar{w}_o$.

The index, denoted by R_i, of the effect of unionism on the average *relative* wage of the ith group is the ratio of the group's average relative wage in the presence of unionism to the group's average relative wage in the absence of unionism. That is, $R_i = v_i/v_{i,o}$. R_i is the weighted geometric mean, with weights the same as in w_i and $w_{i,o}$, of corresponding relative wage effect indexes for each of the labor grades in the group. The size of the relative wage effect of unionism in per cent is $100(R_i - 1)$.

The economy-wide weighted geometric mean, $\bar{R}$, with weights as in $\bar{w}$ and $\bar{w}_o$, of the relative wage effect indexes by group or by labor grade is the ratio of $\bar{v}$ to $\bar{v}_o$. Since $\bar{v} = \bar{v}_o = 1$, $\bar{R} = 1$.

Since by definition

$$R_i = \frac{v_i}{v_{i,o}} = \frac{w_i/\bar{w}}{w_{i,o}/\bar{w}_o} = \frac{w_i/w_{i,o}}{\bar{w}/\bar{w}_o} = \frac{A_i}{\bar{A}},$$

the indexes (R's) of the effects of unionism on relative wages can be deduced from the set of indexes (A's) of the effects of unionism on absolute wages. The converse proposition, however, does not hold: the effects of unionism on absolute wages cannot be deduced from the effects of unionism on relative wages. Of course, if unionism has no effect on the general wage level, so that $\bar{A} = 1$, then $R_i = A_i$. However, not even the algebraic sign of $\bar{A} - 1$ can be deduced from knowledge only of the R's.

II.4. Variant A-I, A-II, B-I, and B II Indexes of
the Relative Wage Effects of Unionism

The index R_i measures the effect of unionism at a particular date on the average wage of the ith group relative to the average wage of all groups. This is the type of index estimated by Variant A-I. Let $R_{i:g}$ and $R_{i:b}$ be the values of R_i at a given date and a base date, respectively. Variant B-I estimates $R_{i:g}/R_{i:b}$. If the base date is chosen so that $R_{i:b} = 1$ (there is no effect of unionism on the relative wage of the ith group at the base date), then, of course, $R_{i:g}/R_{i:b} = R_{i:g}$.

Variant A-II compares the adjusted average wage of a given (ith) group with the adjusted average wage of a benchmark (jth) group that is not all groups taken together. Hence define:

$v_{i/j} = w_i/w_j$, the average wage of the given group relative to the average wage of the benchmark group in the presence of unionism;

$v_{i/j,o} = w_{i,o}/w_{j,o}$, the corresponding ratio in the absence of unionism; and

$R_{i/j} = \dfrac{v_{i/j}}{v_{i/j,o}}$, the index of the effect of unionism on the average wage of the given group relative to the average wage of the benchmark group.

$R_{i/j}$ is the index estimated by Variant A-II. By definition,

$$R_{i/j} = \frac{w_i}{w_{i,o}} \frac{w_{j,o}}{w_j} = \frac{A_i}{A} \frac{\overline{A}}{A_j} = \frac{R_i}{R_j}.$$

Although $R_{i/j}$ can be deduced from R_i and R_j, neither of the latter can be deduced from knowledge only of $R_{i/j}$.

Let $R_{i/j:g}$ and $R_{i/j:b}$ be the values of $R_{i/j}$ at a given date and a base date, respectively. Then Variant B-II estimates $(R_{i/j:g})/(R_{i/j:b})$.

The benchmark group in Variants A-II and B-II is usually a nonunion group.

II.5. Direct and Indirect Effects of Unionism
on Relative Wages

The Variant A-I index measures the total effect of all of the unionism in the economy on the average relative wage of a particular group of labor. For some purposes, however, the relevant index is one that measures the effect of only part of the unionism in the economy. In particular, for a unionized group of labor, very often what is sought is the index measuring only that part of the total effect attributable to *unionism in the group*, that is, to the unionization of the employees in the group. I shall call such indexes "direct effect" indexes.

Denote the unionized group for which the direct effect index is to be estimated by the number 1, the group comprising the rest of the labor force by -1, and let group k be any part of group -1. For group 1, define the following measures:

$v_{1,k}$, the average relative wage in group 1 in the presence of all the unionism in the economy except that in group k;

$v_{1,1k}$, the average relative wage in group 1 in the presence of all the unionism in the economy except that in groups 1 and k;

$D_1 = v_{1,k}/v_{1,1k}$, the index of the (direct) effect of unionism in group 1 on the average relative wage of that group in the presence of all the unionism outside group 1 except the unionism in group k; and

$I_1 = R_1/D_1$, the index of the (indirect) effect of unionism outside group 1 on the average relative wage of group 1.

If group 1 comprises all the unionized labor in the economy, then $D_1 = R_1$, and I_1 is unity. In order to avoid approximating this analytically trivial case, I assume that group 1 covers only a relatively small fraction of the unionized labor force.

D_1, as defined above, is a *family* of direct effect indexes for group 1. The members of this family all measure the same direct effect if and only if the impact of unionism in group 1 on the average relative wage of that group is independent of unionism elsewhere in the economy. In that event, the specification of the unionism content of group k is irrelevant to the measurement of D_1.

In general, however, the direct effect depends on the "level" at which the unionism outside the group is held constant while D_1 is being measured. For example, suppose that group 1 covers a small segment of the bituminous coal mining industry. Then the direct effect in the presence of unionism elsewhere in the industry is likely to be much greater than the direct effect in the absence of unionism elsewhere in the industry.

Thus the division of the total effect for group 1 between a direct effect and an indirect effect is ambiguous unless (a) the unionism outside group 1 at which D_1 is to be measured is specified or (b) D_1 is independent of unionism elsewhere.[9] In what follows I assume that one of these provisos is fulfilled.

Usually, the approach followed in estimating a direct effect index for a unionized group of labor is Variant A-II, which estimates the index

$$R_{1/j} = R_1/R_j = D_1 \cdot I_1/R_j.$$

[9] Usually, the specification of the unionism outside group 1 in the presence of which D_1 is to be measured is *all* the unionism in the economy outside group 1. This is the specification I use in later chapters in all references to the effects of unionism in a given group on the average relative wage of that group.

The given (numerator) group is the unionized group for which the direct effect is to be estimated. The benchmark (denominator) group consists of nonunion employees having characteristics similar to those in the given group. Since the benchmark (jth) group is nonunion, R_j measures only *indirect* effects of unionism outside that group on the group's average relative wage. Under what circumstances will R_j neatly cancel I_1 so that $R_{1/j} = D_1$?

For group j define measures similar to those defined above for group 1:

$v_{j,k}$, the average relative wage of the group in the presence of all the unionism in the economy except that in group k;

$v_{j,1k}$, the average relative wage of the group in the presence of all the unionism in the economy except that in groups 1 and k;

$R_j(1) = v_{j,k}/v_{j,1k}$, the index of the (indirect) effect of unionism in group 1 on the average relative wage of group j in the presence of all the unionism outside group 1 except that in group k; and

$R_j(-1) = R_j/R_j(1)$, the index of the effect of unionism outside group 1 on the average relative wage of group j.

These measures are defined in the same manner as their counterparts—v_j and $v_{j,o}$ for $v_{j,k}$ and $v_{j,1k}$ and R_j for $R_j(1)$ and $R_j(-1)$—in section ii.3. In particular is it true by definition that the economy-wide averages (over all values of j, including 1) of $v_{j,k}$, $v_{j,1k}$, $R_j(1)$ and $R_j(-1)$[10] are all unity.

The division of R_j into $R_j(1)$ and $R_j(-1)$, like the similar division of R_1 into D_1 and I_1, is generally ambiguous unless the content of group k is clearly specified.

In the Variant A-II index, substitute $D_1 \cdot I_1 = D_1 \cdot R_1(-1)$ for R_1 and $R_j(1)R_j(-1)$ for R_j, obtaining

$$R_{1/j} = R_1/R_j = D_1 \frac{I_1}{I_j} = D_1 \frac{R_1(-1)}{R_j(1)R_j(-1)}. \tag{1}$$

Thus the Variant A-II index is approximately equal to D_1 if the benchmark group is chosen so that both $R_j(1)$ and $R_1(-1)/R_j(-1)$ are approximately equal to unity.

A. Indirect Effects of Unionism in the Given Group on the Average Relative Wages of Other Groups

Consider first the effect of unionism in the given group on the average relative wage of the benchmark group, indexed by $R_j(1)$. I assume that the given group is wholly unionized and employs a quite small fraction of the labor force. Let c_1 be the ratio of the total compensation of em-

[10] $R_1(1)$ is D_1 and $R_1(-1)$ is I_1.

ployees in the given group to the total compensation of all employees in the economy. This ratio, by assumption, is a small number, say 0.03 or less.

$R_{-1}(1)$ is the average of the $R_j(1)$ over all groups in the economy except the given group; $\overline{R}(1)$ is the average of the $R_j(1)$ over all groups in the economy, including the given group. Since $\overline{R}(1) = 1$, $R_1(1) = D_1$, and $\overline{R}(1)$ is the weighted geometric mean of $R_1(1)$ and $R_{-1}(1)$, with weights c_1 and $1 - c_1$, respectively, it follows that $\log R_{-1}(1) = -(c_1 \log D_1)/(1 - c_1)$. If c_1 does not exceed 0.03 and D_1 is greater than unity but less than 1.38,[11] then $R_{-1}(1)$ is between 0.99 and unity, that is, the indirect effect of unionism in the given group on the average relative wage of all other groups taken together is less than 1 per cent numerically and is in opposite direction to the direct effect. In the light of the evidence presented in later chapters, I doubt that there is any small group of labor (with c_1 less than 0.03) in the United States for which the index, $R_{-1}(1)$, of the average indirect effect of unionism is less than 0.99. Therefore, I judge that if D_1 exceeds unity and if the benchmark group is a large, broadly based sample of nonunion employees in the United States, the value of $R_j(1)$ will be very slightly smaller than unity. On the other hand, if the benchmark group is a small, nonrandom sample of nonunion employees and if the dispersion of the $R_j(1)$ among such groups is appreciable, $R_j(1)$ may differ significantly from unity. Hence it is necessary to examine the factors that might cause such dispersion.

The impact of unionism in the given group on the relative wages of other groups will tend to differ among these groups if they are dissimilarly related in labor demand or supply to the given group or if the unions in the given group present greater threats to some employers than to others to organize their employees and gain wage increases for them. To begin with, I shall ignore the effects of unionization threats from the given group.

It is conceivable, though very unlikely, that unionism in the given group might cause *no* changes in the labor demand and supply schedules of other groups relative to each other, even though D_1 exceeds unity and the various groups are not similarly related in labor demand and supply to the given group. This could occur if firms in the given group employed a non-labor resource useful only in the given group, whose supply to the given group was fixed, and which was combined in a fixed ratio with labor in the given group. Wage increases in the given group that were not so large as to create an excess supply of the resource would then have only

[11] A value of D_1 equal to 1.38 means that the direct effect of unionism in the given group on the average relative wage of that group is 38 per cent.

the effect of lowering the price of the resource. In general, however, the incidence of the wage increase resulting from unionism in the given group will not be confined to some complementary, non-labor resource.

Let y_j be the index of the effect of unionism in the given group on the quantity of labor demanded by the jth group (at specified wages in the jth group relative to the average wage in all groups except group 1) relative to total employment in all groups except the given group; x_j is the corresponding index for the relative supply of labor to the jth group, and Ey_j and Ex_j are the numerical values of the elasticities of relative labor demand and relative labor supply, respectively, in the jth group. Then the difference, in logarithmic terms, between the indirect effect of unionism in the given group on the average relative wage of the jth group and the corresponding average effect for all groups except the given group is

$$\log R_j(1) - \log R_{-1}(1) = (\log y_j - \log x_j)/(Ey_j + Ex_j). \qquad (2)$$

The relative demand for labor in the jth group will increase—that is, $\log y_j$ will be positive—if labor in the given group is more substitutable (less complementary) in demand for labor in the jth group than it is on the average for other groups of labor. The relative supply of labor to the jth group will increase—that is, $\log x_j$ will be positive—if labor in the given group is more mobile to the jth group than to other groups on the average.[12] Therefore, $R_j(1)$ will exceed $R_{-1}(1)$ if the relative substitutability in labor demand between the jth group and the given group is larger than the corresponding relative substitutability (mobility) in labor supply. The numerical value of the difference between $R_j(1)$ and $R_{-1}(1)$ will be smaller, the larger the sum of the elasticities of demand and supply, Ey_j and Ex_j. Indeed, if the mobility of labor among groups were so great that the elasticity of relative supply, Ex, to every group was very high, then the dispersion of the $R_j(1)$ among nonunion groups would be small.

If, on the other hand, mobility of labor among groups were low, the dispersion of the indirect effects could be large compared to $R_{-1}(1)$. For example, suppose that the labor in a nonunion group, call it group 2, is combined in production in a fixed ratio with the labor in group 1 and that at all levels of relative wages in group 2 the relative supply of labor to group 2 is a fixed quantity. Then the whole brunt of the indirect effects of unionism in group 1 will be borne by labor in group 2.

---

[12] If labor in the given group is more *mobile* to the jth group than to others on the average, then employment in the jth group is a better than average *substitute in supply* to employees in the given group.

In this example, as in the one discussed above in which the perfect complement to labor in group 1 was a non-labor resource, the elasticity of relative demand for labor in group 1 is zero. Therefore, D_1 may be large, since the unions in the given group can obtain relative wage increases for their members in the group without reducing their relative employment.[13]

If the labor in group 2 were a better than average *substitute*, rather than *complement*, in demand for the labor in group 1 and if there were no group with a low relative elasticity of labor supply that was highly complementary in labor demand to the given group, then $R_2(1)$ might exceed $R_{-1}(1)$ substantially. Furthermore, in this case the average value of the $R_j(1)$ for all groups except groups 1 and 2 would be less than $R_{-1}(1)$.

A strong interrelation in labor demand between groups 1 and 2, however, is not a necessary condition for a large difference between $R_2(1)$ and $R_{-1}(1)$. Suppose that unionism in the given group has no effect on the demand for labor by group 2 relative to the demand for labor by other groups except group 1 (that is, log y_2 is zero), the relative mobility of labor between groups 1 and 2 is very high, and the relative mobility of labor out of groups 1 and 2 to other groups is zero. In this situation, all of the relative *supply* effects of unionism in the given group fall on group 2.

As the preceding examples indicate, the indirect effects of unionism in the given group on the relative labor demand and relative labor supply schedules of the benchmark group will tend to cause the Variant A-II index $R_{1/j}$—see equation (1)—to overestimate D_1 appreciably if the mobility of labor out of the benchmark group to groups other than group 1 is low and if the benchmark group is a strong complement in labor demand or a strong substitute in labor supply to the given group. Conversely, $R_{1/j}$ will tend to understate D_1 appreciably if the relative mobility of labor to the benchmark group from the given group and other groups is low and the benchmark group is a strong substitute in labor demand to the given group.

Typically, users of the Variant A-II procedure have chosen benchmark groups whose employees strongly resemble those in the given group in terms of such characteristics as sex, occupation, training and experience, and locality of employment.[14] Such comparability increases the likelihood that the relative mobility of labor from the given group to the benchmark group is above average and, therefore, that $R_{1/j}$ is an overestimate of D_1.

---

[13] As long as $R_2(1)$ exceeds zero.

[14] Choosing a benchmark group that is highly comparable to the given group simplifies the problem of adjusting the gross wage differential between the two groups for factors other than unionism.

However, if the workers in the two groups are employed in the same industry, so that the two groups are substitutes in labor demand as well as in labor supply, the relative supply and relative demand effects will tend to offset each other.

The dispersion among nonunion groups of labor in the indirect effects of unionism on their average relative wages cannot be large if the mobility of labor among the groups is high—that is, if the elasticities of relative labor supply to the groups are high. For some small, specialized groups of labor, strongly related in labor demand or supply to unionized groups, the indirect relative wage effects on some occasions may have been substantial. However, I am strongly convinced that elasticities of relative labor supply to nonunion groups of labor typically have been large and that, therefore, the dispersion among nonunion groups in the indirect relative wage effects has not been large compared to the average of these effects. Assume that during the last forty years, mobility of labor has been low in the U.S. labor force. Then wages in the sectors which experienced large growth in relative labor demand—for example, air transportation; airplane manufacturing; radio and television broadcasting; professional, scientific, and business services; and the federal government—should have increased greatly relative to wages in such declining sectors as farming, domestic service, and tobacco, textiles, and lumber and wood products manufacturing. However, despite the large differences between the rapidly growing and the declining sectors in trends of employment and value of output, there has been no really significant trend in wages in the rapidly growing sectors relative to wages in the declining sectors.[15]

B. The Threat Effect

The existence of unionism in the given group may present to some nonunion employers a real threat to unionize employees and gain wage increases for them. Generally speaking, the threat is likely to be real and present if and only if

1. The nonunion employers are within the organizing jurisdiction of the national union or unions in the given group, and especially if the output of these nonunion employers competes strongly with that of employers in the given group, that is, if the labor employed by the nonunion employers is a good substitute in demand for that employed in the given group; and

2. The unions have threatened to organize the establishments of the nonunion employers and have recently demonstrated their capacity to carry out

[15] See chap. ix, pp. 287 and 289, Tables 81 and 82, and the data on employment, wages, and national income in the sources underlying these tables.

their threats by organizing comparable establishments in the same communities as those in which the nonunion establishments are located, or in communities of similar size and attitude toward unionism, and by winning wage increases in these newly unionized establishments.

If, as I have assumed, employment in the given group is a quite small percentage of the labor force, then the establishments for which the above conditions will hold also will tend to employ a small fraction of the labor force. I presume, therefore, that the unionization threats emanating from the given group will produce negligible effects on the relative wages of all but a small minority of nonunion employees. As I noted above, however, users of the Variant A-II approach have commonly chosen benchmark groups whose employees are comparable to those in the given group in terms of sex, occupation, training and experience, industry, and locality of employment. Strong comparability of the benchmark and given groups in these respects greatly raises the likelihood that the first of the above conditions will hold.

The unionization threat to a nonunion employer within the organizing jurisdiction of the unions in the benchmark group will tend to be greater, the higher the relative rate at which these unions have organized nonunion employees in the recent past. The decade beginning about 1934 was one of rapid growth in the degree of unionization of the U.S. labor force, but since 1945, and especially since 1953, the rate of growth of unionism in the United States has been low.[16] I judge, therefore, that among threatened employers the average subjective probability that their employees would be unionized was substantially greater in the late 1930's and early 1940's than it has been in recent years.

The existence of a threat to unionize the employees of a nonunion employer will induce him to increase the average relative wage of his employees only if (a) he cannot avoid the threat by taking less costly actions and (b) by raising the relative wages of his employees he reduces substantially the subjective probability that his employees will be unionized in the future. Let P be the probability, as he sees it, that his employees will be unionized in the future as a result of unionism in the given group, where $0 \leq P < 1$. He expects that if his employees are unionized, their average relative wage would be approximately $100(D_1 - 1)$ per cent higher than in the absence of both their unionization and the unionization threat. I assume that D_1 exceeds unity and that employment in the employer's establishment is small relative to employment in the given group so that he takes D_1 as a datum. I also assume that the employer has taken all such non-wage actions that increase his expected (mathe-

[16] See chap. vii.

matical expectation of) future profits and that even after these actions P is not negligible.

Denote by T the index of the average (current and future) effect of the threat on the average relative wage of his employees. T measures his planned relative wage response, averaged over the current and future dates, to the unionization threat from the given group. The index, call it C, of the effect of the threat on his *expected* (mathematical expectation of) future relative labor cost per unit of labor—the expected average relative wage of his employees—then, is

$$C = T + P(D_1 - T) = D_1 - (1 - P)(D_1 - T) \qquad (3)$$

Let C_o and P_o be the values of C and P when T equals unity—that is, when the employer makes no relative wage response to the threat—so that

$$C_o = 1 + P_o(D_1 - 1) = D_1 - (1 - P_o)(D_1 - 1) < D_1. \qquad (4)$$

The employer, I postulate, will not choose a value of T greater than unity unless by doing so he reduces his expected cost C below C_o.

Equations (3) and (4) imply that

$$\frac{D_1 - C}{D_1 - C_o} = \frac{1 - P}{1 - P_o} \frac{D_1 - T}{D_1 - 1}. \qquad (5)$$

The left-hand side cannot be greater than unity—C cannot be less than C_o—unless there is some value of T greater than unity at which the decline in ratio terms from $D_1 - 1$ to $D_1 - T$ in the excess of D_1 over T is less than the corresponding increase from $1 - P_o$ to $1 - P$ in the probability that the employees will *not* be unionized.

Thus a nonunion employer who judges that increases in the relative wages of his employees will reduce but little the probability that they will be unionized will not attempt to counter the unionization threat by *wage* actions. In the light of the history of unionism in the United States, such judgments are not absurd. I suspect, therefore, that commonly among groups of nonunion employers for whom both P_o and D_1 are substantial there are some employers who do not try to forestall the unionization of their employees by increasing relative wages.

Furthermore, for an employer who does respond to the threat by increasing his employees' relative wages, the ratio of the planned average threat effect, $T - 1$, to the increase, $D_1 - 1$, expected from unionization will tend to be less than P_o. For if C_o is greater than C, equation (5) implies that

$$\frac{T - 1}{D_1 - 1} < \frac{P_o - P}{1 - P} < P_o.$$

$T - 1$ is an average of the employer's actual current relative wage response and of his planned future relative wage responses to the unionization threat emanating from the given group. Thus the inequality $(T - 1) < P_o(D_1 - 1)$ does not imply that the actual current response is less than $D_1 - 1$. However, the current response cannot be large compared to $D_1 - 1$ unless (a) the extent of the threat as measured by P_o is substantial and (b) the employer judges that he can greatly reduce the threat by a temporary increase in the relative wages of his employees.

The annals of unionism contain a good deal of circumstantial evidence, especially during periods in which the extent of unionism in the economy was growing, that some nonunion employers threatened with unionization raised the relative wages of their employees. For this reason I think it is unsafe to assume that the average wage effect of the unionization threats for a benchmark group which is highly comparable to the given group is negligible. Unless the threat effect is negligible or is offset by other indirect effects discussed earlier, the Variant A-II index of equation (1),

$$R_{1/j} = D_1 \frac{R_1(-1)}{R_j(1)R_j(-1)},$$

will be less than the index of the direct effect, D_1, in the given group.

C. Indirect Effects of Unionism Outside the Given Group on the Average Relative Wages of the Given and Benchmark Groups

The analysis of the indexes $R_1(-1)$ and $R_j(-1)$ of the effects of unionism outside the given group on the average relative wages of the given and benchmark groups is, in the main, the same as that for the index $R_j(1)$ given in the preceding pages, unionism in the given group now being replaced by unionism outside the given group. Since $R_{1/j} = D_1 \cdot R_1(-1)/R_j(1) \cdot R_j(-1)$, the critical question regarding $R_1(-1)$ and $R_j(-1)$ is not their absolute size compared to unity, but the extent to which their ratio differs from unity.

If the two groups were quite dissimilar in their economic interrelations with union labor outside the given group, then $R_1(-1)/R_j(-1)$ might differ sufficiently from unity to produce a significant bias in $R_{1/j}$ as an estimate of D_1. For example, suppose that the labor in group 1 is a considerably worse than average substitute in labor supply and a substantially better than average substitute in labor demand for union labor outside the given group and is within the organizing jurisdiction of strong unions, while the reverse of these is true of the benchmark group. Then even with high mobility of labor among groups, $R_1(-1)/R_j(-1)$ might exceed unity by enough to make $R_{1/j}$ overestimate D_1 significantly. Such results are unlikely, however, if the employees in the benchmark group are similar to those in the given group in sex, occupation, experience, locality of employment, and industry; that is, such comparability will tend to make $R_1(-1)$ and $R_j(-1)$ approximately equal.

In summary:

1. The Variant A-II index $R_{1/j} = D_1 \cdot R_1(-1)/R_j(1) \cdot R_j(-1)$ is in general a biased estimate of D_1, the index of the direct effect of unionism in the given group on the average relative wage of that group.

2. For some pairs of given and benchmark groups, the indirect relative labor demand and relative labor supply effects of unionism in the given group or elsewhere may cause $R_1(-1)/R_j(1) \cdot R_j(-1)$ to differ sufficiently from unity to make $R_{1/j}$ a seriously biased estimate of D_1. In my judgment, if the given and benchmark groups are comparable, such cases are probably atypical.

3. However, if the two groups are comparable, there is a danger during periods of rapid growth of unionism that threats of unionization emanating from the given group may cause $R_j(1)$ to exceed unity by enough to make $R_{1/j}$ underestimate D_1 significantly.

II.6. THE STATISTICAL AND ARITHMETIC RELATIONS BETWEEN DEGREE OF UNIONIZATION AND THE RELATIVE WAGE EFFECTS OF UNIONISM

Divide the labor services employed in the ith group at a particular date between (a) unionized labor services—that is, those covered by collective-bargaining arrangements—and (b) all other labor services. Let p_i be the corresponding ratio of the aggregate compensation of unionized labor to the aggregate compensation of all labor employed in the group. This ratio, which is a measure of the degree of unionization of the group, I shall call the group's "extent of unionism." The economy-wide counterpart of p_i, denoted by $\bar{p}$, is a weighted arithmetic mean of the p's over all groups, the p for each group being weighted by the aggregate compensation of labor employed in the group. The difference, $U_i = p_i - \bar{p}$, between the extent of unionism of the group and the extent of unionism in the labor force as a whole I shall call the group's "excess extent of unionism." The weighted arithmetic mean of the U_i over all groups, with the same weights as in $\bar{p}$, is zero.

Variant A-III correlates the average wages, adjusted for effects of factors other than unionism, of several mutually exclusive groups at a particular date with the degree of unionization of these groups at the same date. In the following analysis I measure degree of unionization by extent of unionism, p. Let $\hat{w}_{i,o}$ be the estimate of $w_{i,o}$ yielded by the adjustment procedure. I assume that the adjustment error

$$d_i = \log \hat{w}_{i,o} - \log w_{i,o} \qquad (6)$$

has a weighted arithmetic mean of zero over the groups covered and is uncorrelated among these groups with extent of unionism, p. The "adjusted" average wage for the ith group is

$$\hat{A}_i = w_i/\hat{w}_{i,o} = A_i e^{-d_i},$$

where $\hat{A}_i$ is the estimate of A_i, the index of the effect of unionism on the average absolute wage of the group.

I use the symbol G to denote the weighted geometric mean and M the weighted arithmetic mean over the covered groups of whatever variable is indicated by the attached subscript. β is the weighted simple regression coefficient of $\log \hat{A}$ on p across the covered groups. Then

$$\log \hat{A}_i = \log G_A + \beta(p_i - M_p) + \lambda'_i, \qquad (7)$$

where λ'_i is the residual from the regression equation. Add d_i to and subtract $\log \overline{A}$ from both sides of equation (7) and substitute $\log A_i$ for $\log \hat{A}_i + d_i$, $\log R_i$ for $\log A_i - \log \overline{A}$, $\log G_R$ for $\log G_A - \log \overline{A}$, and λ_i for $\lambda'_i + d_i$. The result is

$$\log R_i = \log G_R + \beta(p_i - M_p) + \lambda_i. \qquad (8)$$

Since both λ' and d are uncorrelated with p, λ is also uncorrelated with p. Therefore, the regression coefficient β of $\log \hat{A}$ on p is also the regression coefficient of $\log R$ on p if the procedure for adjusting the average wages of the covered groups for effects of factors other than unionism is unbiased.

In the special case in which the covered groups comprise the whole economy, $\log G_R = \log \overline{R} = 0$, $M_p = \overline{p}$, $U_i = p_i - \overline{p}$, and equation (8) becomes

$$\log R_i = \beta U_i + \lambda_i. \qquad (8')$$

What information about the relative wage effects of unionism is provided by the regression coefficient β? The answer to this question is critical for interpreting the results yielded by Variants A-III and B-III.

Let R_{i_u} and R_{i_n} be the counterparts of R_i for the union and nonunion labor in the ith group. R_i is a weighted geometric mean of R_{i_u} and R_{i_n} with weights p_i and $1 - p_i$, respectively. That is,

$$\log R_i = p_i \log R_{i_u} + (1 - p_i) \log R_{i_n}. \qquad (9)$$

Similarly,

$$\log G_R = M_p \log G_{R_u} + (1 - M_p) \log G_{R_n}. \qquad (10)$$

Subtract equation (10) from equation (9). The result, after slight rearrangement of terms, is

$$\log R_i = \log G_R + B(p_i - M_p) + L_i, \qquad (11)$$

where

$$B = \log G_{R_u} - \log G_{R_n} = \log (G_{R_u}/G_{R_n}),$$
$$L_i = p_i(\log R_{i_u} - \log G_{R_u}) + (1 - p_i)(\log R_{i_n} - \log G_{R_n}). \tag{12}$$

Thus the coefficient B in equation (11) is the logarithm of the index of the effect of unionism on the average wage of all union labor in the covered groups relative to the corresponding average wage of all non-union labor. L_i is the weighted arithmetic mean of the deviations of log R_{i_u} and log R_{i_n} from their respective means.

Let $\bar{R}_u$ and $\bar{R}_n$ be the economy-wide counterparts of the R_{i_u} and R_{i_n}, respectively. Then if the covered groups comprise the whole economy, $G_{R_u} = \bar{R}_u$, $G_{R_n} = \bar{R}_n$, and $B = \bar{B} = \log(\bar{R}_u/\bar{R}_n) = \log\bar{R}_{u/n}$, where $\bar{R}_{u/n}$, is the index of the effect of unionism on the average wage of all union labor in the economy relative to the average wage of all nonunion labor in the economy. ($\bar{R}_{u/n}$ is one of the major statistics I seek to estimate in this study.) In this case, equation (10) simplifies to

$$\log \bar{R}_n = -\bar{p} \log \bar{R}_{u/n} \text{ or to } \log \bar{R}_u = (1 - \bar{p}) \log \bar{R}_{u/n}, \tag{10'}$$

and equation (11) becomes

$$\log R_i = \bar{B}U_i + L_i. \tag{11'}$$

It follows from equations (11) and (12) that

$$\beta = B + b_{Lp} = B + M_p b_{R_u p} + (1 - M_p)b_{R_n p}, \tag{13}$$

where b_{Lp}, $b_{R_u p}$, and $b_{R_n p}$ are the weighted simple regression coefficients across the covered groups of L, log R_u, and log R_n, respectively, on p. Thus the regression coefficient β is the sum of two components:

B, the logarithm of the union/nonunion relative wage effect index in the covered groups, the component reflecting the purely *arithmetic* dependence of a weighted mean on its weights; and

$b_{Lp} = M_p b_{R_u p} + (1 - M_p)b_{R_n p}$, reflecting the *economic* dependence of the relative wage effect indexes R_u for union labor and R_n for nonunion labor on extent of unionism p.

Equation (13) shows that in general it is incorrect to interpret a positive correlation between log $\hat{A}$ and p as evidence that the greater the extent of unionism in a group, the greater are the relative wage effect indexes R_u and R_n for the group. If the differences among groups in the indexes R_u and R_n did not depend at all upon corresponding differences in extent of unionism—that is, if R_u and R_n were distributed among groups independently of p—then L would be uncorrelated with p, and b_{Lp} would be zero. In that event, β would be positive if B were positive.

II.7. ECONOMIC DEPENDENCE OF THE RELATIVE WAGE EFFECTS OF
UNIONISM ON EXTENT OF UNIONISM

In this study I interpret the regression coefficient, β, of adjusted wages (log $\hat{A}$) on extent of unionism across the covered groups at a moment of time as an estimate of B, the logarithm of the index of the effect of unionism on the average wage of covered union workers relative to the corresponding average wage of nonunion workers. β is an unbiased estimate if there is no covariation among the groups between extent of unionism and either the effects (log R_u) of unionism on the average relative wages of union workers or the corresponding effects (log R_n) for nonunion workers.[17]

Divide the covered groups into three categories: (a) those with p equal to or very close to zero, (b) those with p equal to or very close to unity, and (c) all others. If the employee compensation weight for category (c) is quite small compared to the corresponding weights for categories (a) and (b) taken separately, then there cannot be an appreciable bias in β as an estimate of B.[18] I therefore exclude such cases from the following discussion.

For the nonunion labor in each group, the relative wage effect (R_n) is the indirect result of unionism present in the group, in other covered groups, and elsewhere in the economy. These indirect effects, discussed in section ii.5, stem from union-caused shifts in relative labor demand and supply schedules to groups of nonunion employers and from threats to unionize their employees and gain wage increases for them. In section ii. 5, I argued that because of generally high elasticities of relative labor supply to groups of nonunion employers, the shifts in labor demand and supply schedules probably produce little dispersion in the relative wage effects of unionism among groups of nonunion labor. Therefore, except in the instance especially noted later in which there may be significant covariation between threat effects and extent of unionism, I assume that b_{R_np} differs negligibly from zero. Thus the following analysis deals chiefly with the effects of unionism on the relative wages of union labor.

---

[17] It is not strictly necessary, of course, that both log R_u and log R_n be uncorrelated with p. However, I suspect that

$$\beta - B = b_{Lp} = M_p b_{R_up} + (1 - M_p) b_{R_np}$$

rarely will be zero if both log R_u and log R_n are correlated with p.

[18] When the weight for category (c) is small compared to the weights of categories (a) and (b), Variant A-III is approximately the same as Variant A-II, the given group consisting of category (b) and the benchmark group of category (a).

A. Upward Bias in β

Divide the labor in each group into occupations, grouping together in the same occupation all labor services that are close substitutes in demand. I begin with the case in which:

1. Each group includes only one occupation.
2. There is little or no interrelation in demand between the labor in each group and the labor in other groups.
3. The occupation is similar from group to group.
4. If each group excludes labor which is a good substitute or a good complement of the covered labor, there is little correlation among the groups between the extent of unionism, p, of the covered labor and the extent of unionism of either the excluded substitutes or the excluded complements.

Conditions 1 and 2 imply that the nonunion labor in each group is a considerably better substitute in demand for the union labor in the same group than for the union labor in other groups; conditions 3 and 4 that the differences between groups in the demand conditions for union labor do not depend strongly upon dissimilarities between the groups in the characteristics of the covered labor or in the interrelations in demand between covered labor and excluded labor. Although, as I show later, these conditions are stronger than those required for upward bias in β, there are many examples of groups that fit the conditions rather well.

For example, suppose that the groups cover barbers classified by the city of their employment. This example is suggested by Joseph L. Craycraft's study of barbers in twenty lareg U.S. cities in 1948 and 1954, which I discuss in the next chapter (pp. 86 ff.). The services of nonunion barbers in a particular city tend to be good substitutes in demand for the services of union barbers in the same city but poor substitutes for the services of both nonunion and union barbers in other cities. Furthermore, both the chief labor substitutes ("do-it-yourself") and the chief labor complements (barbershop cashiers, manicurists, bootblacks, janitors, etc.) of barber labor are generally nonunion.[19]

The index, R_u, for the union barbers in a particular city reflects the demand conditions for the services of these barbers and other factors. Some of the demand variables may differ considerably in size from city to city—for example, the output of union barbershops relative to the output of nonunion barbershops. Others, however, have more or less

---

[19] It is not surprising, therefore, that in barbering, the local unions are organized by city areas and that in the main, the locals act independently of each other and of other unions in collective bargaining.

common values in all of the cities, and in some periods these factors common to the cities may be of such overwhelming importance that there is little dispersion in the R_u's among cities.

The years 1945–48, I judge, made up such a period, Craycraft's estimate of β for 1948 was negligibly different from zero; I doubt that this is a seriously biased estimate of B for large-city barbers in 1948. The next four chapters contain much evidence that in 1945–48 unionism generally had little effect on relative wages in the United States. In this period the rate of inflation was unusually great and all unions had in common the problem of trying to respond to the rapid increases in money demand prices through collective-bargaining arrangements that were poorly designed for this task.

Craycraft's estimate of β for 1954 was about 20 per cent. In 1951–54 the rate of inflation was quite low. I think it is likely, therefore, that in 1954, differences in demand factors and other factors among cities caused substantial intercity differences in the R_u's. Furthermore, these differences were probably positively correlated with corresponding differences in extent of unionism.

Denote by D the index of the direct effect of barber unionism on the average relative wage of union barbers in a particular city; I_u is the index of the indirect effect of other unionism on the average relative wage of these barbers. The factors affecting I_u are much the same as those affecting R_n, and I shall assume, as for R_n, that there is little covariation among cities between I_u and p—that is, the covariation between R_u and p consists chiefly of covariation between D and p.

The direct effect, D, in a city will be greater, the lower is the elasticity of demand, η, for the services of *union* barbers in the city.[20] Thus D will tend to be negatively correlated with η. Since nonunion barbershops in a given city are substantially more competitive with union barbershops in the same city than with union barbershops in other cities, and since the chief labor substitutes and labor complements of barber labor are generally nonunion, the elasticity of demand for the services of union barbers in the city will tend to be lower, the higher the extent of unionism of barbers in the city.[21] Thus η and p will tend to be negatively correlated, and, therefore, D will tend to be positively correlated with p.[22] Hence in

[20] See Albert Rees, *The Economics of Trade Unions* (Chicago: University of Chicago Press, 1962), pp. 70–73.

[21] *Ibid.*

[22] The correlation between D and p is likely to be substantially less than unity, since the correlations linking D and p will generally be imperfect, for D depends not only on η but also on the relative weight in the barber-union "utility function" of high relative

1954 the direct relative wage effects of barber unionism on the average relative wages of union barbers were probably positively correlated among cities with the extent of unionism of barbers, causing β to overestimate B for large-city barbers in that year.

Of the two links in the correlation of D with p—negative correlation of D with η, negative correlation of η with p—the second is the crucial one, for in general, D and η will tend to be negatively correlated. Thus the sign of the bias in β as an estimate of B is opposite to the sign of the correlation of η with p. The correlation of η with p will tend to be negative and, therefore, $\beta - B$ will tend to be positive if nonunion labor is substantially more competitive with union labor within each of the covered groups than between them and if other factors affecting η are poorly correlated with the extent of unionism, p.

In the barber situation, each group includes only one occupation and the occupation is similar from group to group. Although these characteristics of the case simplify its analysis, they are not the root of the upward bias in β, as the following examples indicate.

Example 1, in which the occupation varies from group to group: Each group covers a single occupation in a particular city. In each city, independently of the other covered cities, the occupation is selected at random from a list of occupations, the same for all cities, in local market industries. Thus in one city the selected occupation may be barbers; in a second city, taxicab drivers; in a third city, elementary school teachers; and so on. In this example, nonunion labor is considerably more competitive with union labor within groups than between groups, so that η and p will tend to be negatively correlated. To be sure, the heterogeneity of occupations between groups will tend to increase the dispersion in D among groups and lower the correlation between D and p, but these do not imply that the regression coefficient of D on p, will be smaller, compared to B, than in the barber example.[23]

Example 2, in which each group covers several occupations: The groups cover the production workers, classified by city, in a local market industry that is the same from city to city. The industry is one characterized by industrial unionism among production workers: either all or none of the production

---

wages as compared to high relative employment, the capacities of the union leaders, the attitude of the community toward unionism, and other factors. Similarly, η depends not only on p but also on the homogeneity of the output of union and nonunion barbershops, elasticities of supply of non-labor complements of union labor, elasticities of substitution between union labor and other productive services combined with it in barbershops, and the elasticity of demand for the output of union and nonunion barbershops taken together.

[23] However, a positive correlation between the extent of unionism of the included occupations and the extent of unionism of excluded, complementary occupations would tend to reduce the regression coefficient of D on p.

workers in each firm are unionized. The output of the industry in each city is not closely related in demand to the output of other industries. This example is essentially the same as the barber example, the single occupation being replaced by a package of occupations.

B. Downward Bias in β

Suppose that each group covers a collection of occupations that are good complements in demand. The collection is similar from one group to another, does not exclude any labor that is a good substitute or complement of included labor, but there is little interrelation in labor demand between groups. Within each group the extent of unionism of each *occupation* is either zero or unity. Then in each group, nonunion labor is a good *complement* rather than a good substitute for union labor, but between groups there is little complementarity or substitution between union and nonunion labor. Therefore, the higher the extent of unionism in each group, the greater the elasticity of demand for the union labor in the group will tend to be. Thus η and p will tend to be positively correlated and $\beta - B$ will tend to be negative. This example illustrates the essential feature of the case in which β tends to underestimate B: there is substantially greater complementarity (less substitution) in demand between union and nonunion labor within groups than there is on the average between groups.

What if the extent of unionism figures for some or all of the complementary occupations in each group were to differ slightly from zero and unity in such a way as to keep the extent of unionism, p, of each group constant? Then to a small extent the nonunion labor in each group would be a substitute instead of a complement of the union labor in the group, and the downward bias would be slightly less.

Therefore, it is not necessary for downward bias in β that the *interoccupational* dispersion in extent of unionism within each group be as large as it could be, given p in the group. On the other hand, complementarity among the *occupations* within each group is not sufficient for downward bias. What is required is that *nonunion labor* within groups be a complement rather than a substitute on balance for *union labor*. As the interoccupational dispersion in each group falls from the maximum toward zero, nonunion labor becomes increasingly a substitute instead of a complement of union labor and the downward bias in β diminishes. At the point where nonunion labor is as much a substitute as a complement of union labor within each of the groups, the bias in β is zero. At still lower values of the interoccupational dispersion, the bias is upward rather than downward.

C. No Bias in β

At the point where the bias is zero, in this example, there is little or no interrelation in demand between union and nonunion labor either within groups or between them. There will also tend to be no bias in β if the interrelation in demand between nonunion and union labor within groups is strong, provided that the between-group interrelation is equally strong and in the same direction.

Example: The segment studied covers production workers, grouped by city of employment, employed in a manufacturing industry whose output is sold on the national market. In each firm in the industry, either all or none of the production workers are unionized. Then nonunion labor in each group is about as good a substitute for union labor in other cities as for union labor in the same city. Therefore, the extent of unionism figure that is relevant to the elasticity of demand for the union labor in each group is the average extent of unionism of all the groups taken together rather than the extent of unionism of the group.

D. Problems in Estimating the Sign of the Bias

In applications of Variant A-III in which

1. Each group excludes unionized occupations that are good complements of the covered occupations, or

2. Each group covers an exhaustive collection of occupations that are good complements in demand, but interoccupational dispersion in extent of unionism within each group is not zero or as large as it could be, given the extent of unionism of the group,

the sign of the bias in β is usually not obvious. Stephen Sobotka's study of the building trades is an example (see pp. 63 ff.). This study covered a composite of five of the most important skilled building occupations (carpenters, masons, painters, plasterers, and plumbers), classified by city, in thirty-two large cities in 1939. The study also dealt separately with each of these occupations and with common labor employed in building construction.

Building construction is local market industry. That is, to buyers of the services of, say, carpenters, the chief labor substitutes for the services of union carpenters in a particular city are the services of nonunion carpenters in the same city, and the chief labor complements of the services of union carpenters are the services of workers, both union and nonunion, in other building construction occupations in the same city. Thus the nonunion labor in a particular building construction occupation and city is a relatively good substitute for union labor in the same occupation and city and a complement of the labor in other building occupations in the same city, but is poorly related in demand to union construction labor in other cities.

I examine first the problem of estimating the sign of the bias in β when each group covers all of the building construction occupations in a city. Let k be the ratio of the actual interoccupational variance (squared standard deviation) of extent of unionism in building construction in a city to the largest value that the variance could take, given the extent of unionism, p, of building construction labor and the relative (employee compensation) weight of each construction occupation in the city.[24] By definition, $0 \leq k \leq 1$. η is the elasticity of demand for union construction labor in the city taken as a group. The elasticity of demand, η, in general depends upon k as well as p:

$$\eta = f(p, k). \tag{14}$$

I shall write the partial derivatives of $f(p, k)$ in the form f_p, f_k, and f_{pk}, where f_p and f_k are the first partial derivatives with respect to p and k, respectively, and f_{pk} is the second (cross) partial derivative with respect to p and k. The function $f(p, k)$ has the following properties:

1. When $k = 1$, nonunion labor in each group (city) is a complement of union labor in the same group. As k falls toward zero, given the value of p, nonunion labor in each group becomes increasingly a substitute instead of a complement of union labor in the same group, and, therefore, η rises as k falls—that is, f_k is negative.

2. The sign of f_p depends on the magnitude of k. When $k = 1$ and, therefore, union and nonunion labor are complements within groups, η rises as p rises—that is, f_p is positive at $k = 1$. When $k = 0$, union and nonunion labor are substitutes within groups and, therefore, f_p is negative. Hence f_p rises as k increases (f_{pk} is positive) and at some value of k, call it $\overset{*}{k}$, the value of f_p is zero. Thus f_p has the sign of $k - \overset{*}{k}$.

A simple function with these properties is

$$\eta = a[(1 - \overset{*}{k}) - (1 - p)(k - \overset{*}{k})], \tag{15}$$

[24] If the relative weights of the occupations were variable, the largest possible variance, given p, would be $p(1 - p)$. However, when the weights are fixed, the maximum variance for a given p may be less than $p(1 - p)$. For example, if there were six occupations with relative weights equal to 0.04, 0.06, 0.08, 0.20, 0.31, and 0.31 and if p or $1 - p$ were equal to any of the following numbers, the maximum value of the variance would be $p(1 - p)$: 0.04; 0.06; 0.08; 0.10; 0.12; 0.14; 0.18; 0.20; 0.24; 0.26; 0.28; 0.30; 0.31; 0.32; 0.34; 0.35; 0.37; 0.38; 0.39; 0.41; 0.43; 0.45; 0.49. For other values of p or $1 - p$, the maximum value of the variance would be slightly less than $p(1 - p)$.

where a and $\overset{*}{k}$ are positive constants and $0 < \overset{*}{k} < 1$.[25] I use equation (15) as an approximation of equation (14). It follows from equation (15) that

$$b_{\eta p} = -a[b_{k(1-p),p} + \overset{*}{k}], \tag{16}$$

where $b_{\eta p}$ and $b_{k(1-p),p}$ are the regression coefficients across the groups of η and $k(1-p)$, respectively, on p. Since $b_{\eta p}$ and $\beta - B$ tend to have opposite signs, $\beta - B$ tends to have the sign of $b_{k(1-p),p} + \overset{*}{k}$.

For the six occupations (carpenters, masons, painters, plasterers, plumbers, and common labor) included in Sobotka's study, $b_{k(1-p),p}$ was positive in 1939. These six occupations together comprised a large fraction of all building-construction labor employed in large cities in 1939. Thus I judge that the regression coefficient, β, computed across large cities for building construction employees in 1939 would over-estimate the corresponding value of B.

A positive value of $\beta - B$ for all building construction occupations taken together does not imply that the values of β computed for the individual occupations or subsets of occupations also overestimate the corresponding values of B. Let η_m be the elasticity of demand for union labor in the mth occupation[26] in a city; p_m is the extent of unionism of the occupation in the city, and p is the extent of unionism of all building occupations in the city. The elasticity of demand, η_m, will tend to be higher, the higher is the extent of unionism of other occupations complementary to the mth occupation and the lower is the extent of unionism in the mth occupation.

[25] The function $f(p, k)$ has the form given in equation (15) under the following conditions:

In each city and each trade—plumbing, carpentry, etc.—the output of nonunion employers is a perfect substitute for the output of union employers; labor inputs are in fixed ratios to outputs, and neither these ratios nor other supply conditions (except, of course, wage differences between union and nonunion labor) vary systematically within trades between union and nonunion employers, between trades in a city, or between cities.

In each city the outputs of the various building construction trades are combined in fixed proportions in producing "buildings." These proportions and the demand conditions for buildings are distributed among cities independently of k and p.

These conditions do not imply that $\overset{*}{k}$ and a must be constant, but only that both be distributed among groups independently of k and p.

[26] The elasticity of demand, η_m, for the union labor in the mth occupation takes into account the changes in wages of *union* labor in other building construction occupations. That is, along the demand schedule for union labor in the mth occupation, the wages of union labor in other occupations change in the same ratio as wages of union labor in the mth occupation.

The counterparts of equations (15) and (16) for the mth occupation are

$$\eta_m = a[(1 - \overset{*}{k})p + (1 - p_m)] \tag{17}$$

$$b_{\eta_m p_m} = a[(1 - \overset{*}{k})b_{p p_m} - 1], \tag{18}$$

where a and k are the same constants that appear in equations (15) and (16) and $b_{\eta_m p_m}$ and $b_{p p_m}$ are the regression coefficients of η_m and p, respectively, on p_m. (The assumptions underlying these equations are the same as those on which equation (15) is based.)[27] Since $1 - \overset{*}{k}$ is positive and less than unity, $b_{\eta_m p_m}$ cannot be positive, and, therefore, $\beta - B$ will tend to be positive if $b_{p p_m}$ is less than unity. In Sobotka's study, the estimated values of $b_{p p_m}$ were less than unity for each of the six individual building construction occupations.[28]

Let the subscript s denote a subset of the building construction occupations (one such subset, for example, is Sobotka's composite of five skilled building trades); η_s is the elasticity of demand for the union labor in the subset in a particular city; p_s is the corresponding value of the extent of unionism of the subset; k_s, the counterpart for the subset of k for all building occupations, is the ratio of the actual interoccupational variance of extent of unionism in the subset and city to its corresponding maximum value; as before, p is the extent of unionism of all building occupations in the city taken together. The elasticity of demand, η_s, is the weighted average of the η_m for all occupations in the subset, each η_m being weighted by the compensation of union labor in the occupation. The weighted average of equation (17) for all occupations in the subset is

$$\eta_s = a[(1 - \overset{*}{k})p + (1 - p_s) - k_s(1 - p_s)]. \tag{17'}$$

Notice that if the subset comprises all of the building construction occupations, $p_s = p$, $k_s = k$, and equation (17') becomes equation (15).

It follows from equation (17') that

$$b_{\eta_s p_s} = a[(1 - \overset{*}{k})b_{p p_s} - 1 - b_{k_s(1 - p_s),\, p_s}], \tag{18'}$$

where $b_{\eta_s p_s}$, $b_{p p_s}$, and $b_{k_s(1 - p_s),\, p}$ are the regression coefficients across the covered cities of η_s, p, and $k_s(1 - p_s)$ on p_s. For Sobotka's building trades composite, $b_{p p_s}$ was smaller than unity and $b_{k_s(1 - p_s), p_s}$ was positive. Thus for this composite, $b_{\eta_s p_s}$ was probably negative and, therefore, $\beta - B$ was probably positive.[29]

[27] See n. 25 above.

[28] However, the estimates of the $b_{p p_m}$ undoubtedly contain large errors; see pp. 68 ff.

[29] See n. 28 above.

Eight of the studies discussed in chapter iv apply Variant A-III or Variant B-III to data classified by industry. Two of the eight cover almost all industries in the economy and both wage-earners and salaried employees. The other six cover only wage-earners (production workers) and deal mainly or exclusively with the manufacturing sector.

Classify all labor in the economy by detailed industry, grouping together in the same detailed industry all labor employed in the production of commodities or services that are close substitutes in demand. If unionism in the United States followed a pattern of pure "industrial" unionism—unionism along industry lines in which either all or none of the employees, both production workers and others, of each firm in the industry were unionized—then union and nonunion labor would tend to be substantially better substitutes in demand within detailed industries than between them and β computed across the whole set of industries would tend to overestimate the value of $\bar{B}$ in the economy. Although degree of unionization data are not available for each detailed industry in the United States and, within industries, for each establishment and occupation, there is a good deal of evidence, though it is imprecise and fragmentary, that this model does not fit U.S. unionism well. In the first place, industrial unionism in this country generally pertains to the production workers rather than to all employees in an industry. Nonproduction workers, who tend to be complements instead of substitutes of production workers in demand, commonly are nonunion, even in industries in which the production workers are highly unionized. Moreover, the ratio of nonproduction-worker to production-worker employment varies substantially among industries. Second, in many industries the production workers are organized by craft rather than industrial unions and the extent of unionism of the production-worker occupations varies from occupation to occupation. Thus among equally (and partially) unionized industries, the interrelation in demand between union and nonunion labor is typically a mixture of substitution and complementarity. In this study I assume that in the last two decades the mixture has been one of roughly equal proportions of substitution and complementarity and, therefore, that the regression coefficient β computed across all industries for all employees was not appreciably biased as an estimate of the value of $\bar{B}$ for the whole labor force.

Industrial unionism (of production workers) is probably more prevalent relative to craft unionism in the manufacturing sector than elsewhere in the economy. Furthermore, the six studies that deal mainly or exclusively with manufacturing industries do not cover nonproduction workers. For these reasons, upward bias in β is more likely in these six studies than in the two studies with economy-wide coverage of both production and nonproduction workers by industry.

E. *Bias in β Resulting from Unionization Threat Effects on the Average Relative Wages of Nonunion Workers*

If the nonunion labor in each group is a good substitute in demand for the union labor in the same group, then the nonunion labor is likely to be within the organizing jurisdiction of the national union or unions representing the union labor. In this event, the relative wage indexes, R_n, for nonunion labor may be affected by threats emanating from these unions to organize the nonunion workers and gain wage increases for them. If so, the threat effects are likely to be positively correlated with extent of unionism, p, across the covered groups, for the threat effects will tend to be positively correlated with the direct effects (see sec. ii.5). In turn, the direct effects will tend to be positively correlated with extent of unionism, unless the nonunion labor in each group is as good a substitute in demand for the union labor in other groups as it is for union labor in the same group. Thus when the direct effects produce an upward bias in $β$, threat effects may magnify the bias.[30]

II.8. THE VARIANT B-III INDEXES

Variant B-IIIa correlates the adjusted (for factors other than unionism) percentage changes in the average wages of several groups of labor with the corresponding *changes*, in per cent or decimals, in degree of unionization of the groups. Variant B-IIIb correlates the adjusted wage changes of the groups with their *absolute levels* of degree of unionization at the base date or the given date or some intermediate date.

Return to equation (11) for the ith group:

$$\log R_i = Bp_i + L_i.$$

(I have omitted all terms that are the same for all groups.) Write equation (11) for a base date, b, and a given date, g:

$$\left. \begin{aligned} \log R_{i:b} &= B_b p_{i:b} + L_{i:b} \\ \log R_{i:g} &= B_g p_{i:g} + L_{i:g} \end{aligned} \right\} \tag{19}$$

Subtract the first equation from the second:

$$\Delta \log R_i = \mu_B \Delta p_i + \mu_{p_i} \Delta B + \Delta L_i, \tag{20}$$

---

[30] I doubt that threat effects also tend to magnify downward bias in $β$, for $β$ will tend to be biased downward when nonunion labor is a good *complement* of union labor within groups, but then the nonunion labor is unlikely to be within the organizing jurisdiction of the unions representing the union labor in the same group.

where

$$
\begin{aligned}
\Delta \log R_i &= \log R_{i:g} - \log R_{i:b}; \\
\Delta p_i &= p_{i:g} - p_{i:b}; \\
\Delta B &= B_g - B_b; \\
\Delta L_i &= L_{i:g} - L_{i:b}; \\
\mu_B &= \tfrac{1}{2}(B_b + B_g); \\
\mu_{p_i} &= \tfrac{1}{2}(p_{i:b} + p_{i:g}).
\end{aligned}
\right\} \tag{21}
$$

Let $\beta_{\Delta R, \Delta p}$ and $b_{\Delta L, \Delta p}$ be the regression coefficients of $\Delta \log R$ and ΔL, respectively, on the changes in extent of unionism, Δp; σ_b^2 and σ_g^2 are the variances of the $p_{i:b}$ and $p_{i:g}$, respectively, and σ_{bg} is the covariance between the $p_{i:b}$ and $p_{i:g}$. It follows from equations (20) and (21) that

$$
\beta_{\Delta R, \Delta p} = \mu_B + \Delta B \frac{\tfrac{1}{2}(\sigma_g^2 - \sigma_b^2)}{\sigma_b^2 + \sigma_g^2 - 2\sigma_{bg}} + b_{\Delta L, \Delta p}. \tag{22}
$$

Usually, in applications of Variant B-IIIa the base date is one at which the extent of unionism figures for each of the covered groups and for the economy as a whole are close to zero. In that event, Variants B-IIIa and B-IIIb are approximately the same, Δp_i is approximately equal to $p_{i:g}$, ΔL_i is approximately equal to $L_{i:g}$, and equation (22) becomes

$$
\beta_{\Delta R, \Delta p} \cong B_g + b_{Lp:g} = \beta_g, \tag{23}
$$

where $b_{Lp:g}$ and β_g are the values of b_{Lp} and β, respectively, at the *given* date. That is, in this case, the regression coefficient of the adjusted wage *changes* on either the *change* in extent of unionism or the *level* of extent of unionism at the given date is approximately the same conceptually as the regression coefficient of the adjusted wage *level* at the given date on the extent of unionism *level* at the given date.

Let $\beta_{\Delta R, \mu_p}$ and $b_{\Delta L, \mu_p}$ be the regression coefficients of ΔR and ΔL, respectively, on the average, μ_p, of the extent of unionism figures at the base and given dates. Equations (20) and (21) imply that

$$
\beta_{\Delta R, \mu_p} = \Delta B + \mu_B \frac{2(\sigma_g^2 - \sigma_b^2)}{\sigma_b^2 + \sigma_g^2 + 2\sigma_{bg}} + b_{\Delta L, \mu_p}. \tag{24}
$$

Three of the studies reviewed in chapter iv (see pp. 172 ff.) apply Variant B-IIIb to industry data in the period following World War II. In this period the relative distribution of unionism among industries was quite stable, so that μ_{p_i} was approximately the same as $p_{i:b}$, $p_{i:g}$, and values of p_i between the base and given dates. Under these circumstances, equation (24) reduces to the following approximation:

$$
\beta_{\Delta R, \mu_p} \cong \beta_g - \beta_b. \tag{25}
$$

That is, when the relative distribution of unionism among the covered groups is stable during the period studied, Variant B-IIIb estimates the difference between the value of β at the given date and the value of β at the base date.

In all of the applications of Variants B-IIIa and B-IIIb reported in this study, the assumptions underlying equation (23), or, alternatively, equation (25), are satisfied. When these assumptions do not hold, the B-III procedures in general do not yield either the level of β at the given date or the change in β from the base date to the given date.

II.9. A Common Denominator for the Indexes

The Variant A-III "index" is the regression coefficient, β, across three or more groups of labor of the logarithm of adjusted wages on extent of unionism. The unit of measurement of β is *per cent per percentage* (*or decimal*) *point*—that is, per cent relative wage effect per percentage (or decimal) point of extent of unionism.

The Variant A-I index, R_i, and the Variant A-II index, $R_{i/j} = R_i/R_j$, in general are not regression coefficients of adjusted wages on extent of unionism, and the unit of measurement of both is per cent. However, it is simple to convert both to regression coefficients of the logarithm of adjusted wages on extent of unionism, although for both variants only two, rather than three or more, groups are involved. The conversion gives both the same unit of measurement as β. Thus to convert the Variant A-II index, express the index in logarithmic form and divide by the excess, $p_i - p_j$, of the extent of unionism of the given group over the extent of unionism of the benchmark group:

$$\frac{\log R_{i/j}}{p_i - p_j} = \frac{\log R_i - \log R_j}{p_i - p_j}.$$

Usually, the benchmark group in Variant A-II is completely nonunion, so that the converted Variant A-II index is $(\log R_i - \log R_{j_n})/p_i$.

Variant A-I may be considered the special case of Variant A-II in which the benchmark group is the whole labor force. The relative wage effect index, $\overline{R}$, for the whole labor force is unity and the extent of unionism is $\overline{p}$. Therefore, the converted A-I index is $(\log R_i)/(p_i - \overline{p}) = (\log R_i)/U_i$.

In section ii.7, I showed that β may be interpreted as an estimate of $B = \log (G_{R_u}/G_{R_n})$, the logarithm of the index of the effect of unionism on the average wage of all union labor in the covered groups relative to the corresponding average wage of nonunion labor. The converted A-I and A-II indexes may be interpreted in the same way. However, the special character of the A-I and A-II versions of β permit alternative interpretations. Since $\log R_i = p_i \log R_{i_u} + (1 - p_i) \log R_{i_n}$, the A-II version of β may be written

$$\frac{\log R_{i/j}}{p_i - p_j} = \log (R_{i_u}/R_{i_n})$$

$$+ \frac{p_j \log (R_{i_u}/R_{j_u}) + (1 - p_j) \log (R_{i_n}/R_{j_n})}{p_i - p_j} \qquad (26)$$

$$= B_i + p_j b_{R_u p} + (1 - p_j) b_{R_n p},$$

where B_i is $\log (R_{i_u}/R_{i_n})$ and $b_{R_u p}$ and $b_{R_n p}$ are the regression coefficients across the covered groups of R_u and R_n, respectively, on extent of unionism. Thus the converted A-II index is in general a biased estimate of the logarithm of the index, R_{i_u}/R_{i_n}, of the effect of unionism on the average wage of union labor in the given group relative to the average wage of nonunion labor in the same group.

When the benchmark group is nonunion, $p_j = 0$, and equation (26) reduces to

$$\frac{\log R_{i/j}}{p_i - p_j} = B_i + b_{R_n p}. \qquad (27)$$

I would expect the regression coefficient, $b_{R_n p}$, normally to be small. When the given group is completely unionized and the benchmark group is nonunion, equation (26) becomes, simply,

$$\frac{\log R_{i/j}}{p_i - p_j} = \log (R_{i_u}/R_{j_n}). \qquad (28)$$

Similarly, the A-I version of β may be written

$$\frac{\log R_i}{U_i} = B_i + \frac{\bar{p}}{U_i} (B_i - \bar{B}) + \frac{1}{U_i} \log (R_{i_n}/\bar{R}_n), \qquad (29)$$

where $\bar{B}$ is $\log (\bar{R}_u/\bar{R}_n)$. The chief source of bias in the converted A-I index as an estimate of B_i, in my judgment, is the term $\bar{p}(B_i - \bar{B})/U_i$. Assume that R_{i_n} is approximately equal to $\bar{R}_n$. Then

$$\frac{\log R_i}{U_i} \cong B_i + \frac{\bar{p}}{U_i} (B_i - \bar{B}). \qquad (30)$$

If the difference between B_i and $\bar{B}$ is large, the converted A-I index may err considerably as an estimate of B_i. For example, the converted A-I index for wage-earners in bituminous coal mining in 1956–57 was approximately 0.5.[31] In 1956–57 the corresponding value of U was about 0.7[32] and $\bar{p}$ was about 0.25. I doubt that $\bar{B} = \log (\bar{R}_u/\bar{R}_n)$ was greater

[31] This is the approximate value of the logarithm of the 1956–57 figure (plus unity) in col. 5, Table 9, p. 77. The estimate of U, given in col. 3 of the same table, is 0.70.
[32] See n. 31 above.

than 0.15 in 1956–57 (see chap. v, p. 193). These figures and equation (30) suggest that the converted A-I index for bituminous coal mining wage-earners in 1956–57 overestimated $B_i = \log (R_{i_u}/R_{i_n})$ for that group by about 25 per cent.

The unit of measurement of the Variant B-III coefficients is the same as that for the A-III coefficient, β. (Indeed, all of the B-III coefficients reported in this study are estimates, across specified groups of labor, of the value of β at a given date or of the change in the value of β from one date to another.) On the other hand, the B-I and B-II indexes, like their A-I and A-II counterparts, are in different units and must be adjusted to make their unit of measurement that of β.

The B-I index is $R_{i:g}/R_{i:b}$, the ratio of the A-I index at the given date to the A-I index at the base date. The B-II index is $R_{i/j:g}/R_{i/j:b}$, the ratio of the A-II index at the given date to the A-II index at the base date. If the base date is in a period in which $p_{i:b}$, $p_{j:b}$, and $\bar{p}_b$ are all close to zero, then $R_{i:b}$ and $R_{j:b}$ are likely to differ negligibly from unity. In that event, the B-I index and the B-II index are approximately the same as the A-I and A-II indexes, respectively, and the B-I and B-II indexes may be converted to β form by dividing their logarithms by $U_{i:g}$ and $p_{i:g} - p_{j:g}$, respectively. The interpretation of the resulting converted indexes is the same as that for their Variant A counterparts.

If the period covered is such that $R_{i:b}$ may differ significantly from unity but $U_{i:g}$ differs little from $U_{i:b}$, then the B-I index may be converted to β form by dividing its logarithm by $U_{i:g}$ or $U_{i:b}$ or an average of the two. The converted index is then an estimate of the *change*, $B_{i:g} - B_{i:b}$, in B_i from the base date to the given date:

$$\frac{\log (R_{i:g}/R_{i:b})}{U_i} = (B_{i:g} - B_{i:b}) + \frac{\bar{p}_g}{U_i} [(B_{i:g} - B_{i:b})$$

$$- (\bar{B}_g - \bar{B}_b)] + \frac{\bar{p}_g - \bar{p}_b}{U_i} (B_{i:b} - \bar{B}_b), \qquad (29')$$

where U_i is valued at $U_{i:g}$, or $U_{i:b}$, or their average. Similarly, if $p_{i:g} - p_{j:g}$ is close to $p_{i:b} - p_{j:b}$, the B-II index may be converted to β form by dividing its logarithm by the value of $p_i - p_j$ at the base date, or the given date, or by an average of these two, obtaining

$$\frac{\log (R_{i/j:g}/R_{i/j:b})}{p_i - p_j} = (B_{i:g} - B_{i:b}) + p_{j:g}b_{R_up:g} + (1 - p_{j:g})b_{R_np:g}$$

$$- p_{j:b}b_{R_up:b} - (1 - p_{j:b})b_{R_np:b}. \qquad (26')$$

In the usual case in which the benchmark group is nonunion, equation (26') is

$$\frac{\log (R_{i/j:g}/R_{i/j:b})}{p_i} = (B_{i:g} - B_{i:b}) + (b_{R_np:g} - b_{R_np:b}). \qquad (27')$$

Notice that the converted B-I and B-II indexes in equations (26'), (27'), and (29') are likely to be biased estimates of $B_{i:g} - B_{i:b}$. However, the bias in equation (27') is probably small.

I have converted all of the Variant A-I, A-II, B-I, and B-II estimates of relative wage effects of unionism reported in later chapters to their respective β equivalents in order to make these estimates comparable conceptually to the Variant A-III and B-III estimates.

II.10. Wage Adjustment Biases

Although conceptual biases of the kinds discussed in the preceding sections are important in interpreting the estimates of relative wage effects of unionism given in the next four chapters, the principal causes of bias in the estimates are errors of measurement in the underlying data and errors of adjustment of the wage comparisons for the effects of factors other than unionism. I discuss most of these error problems, which differ considerably from study to study, in the reviews of the individual studies. This section deals only with systematic biases in the estimates caused by imperfect adjustment of the wage data for effects of unionism on the relative quality of the labor employed in unionized segments of the labor force and on the relative nonpecuniary terms of employment in these segments. These biases are common to most of the studies.

The true relative wage effect index, R_i, measures the effect of unionism on the average relative wage of a group of labor of given relative quality at given relative nonpecuniary terms of employment. Truly detailed data on the quality of labor and its nonpecuniary aspects of employment are not available for any segment of the labor force. Furthermore, even if such information were at hand there would remain the exceedingly difficult problem of translating it into corresponding adjustments of the wage data.

If the differences between groups of labor in relative labor quality and relative nonpecuniary terms of employment were uncorrelated with the true effects of unionism on relative wages, failure to adjust fully the gross wage differences for these factors would not lead to bias on the average in the estimates of the relative wage effects of unionism. However, unionism itself may have effects on relative labor quality and relative nonpecuniary terms of employment that are correlated with its relative wage effects.

For example, a 25 per cent greater relative wage for commercial airline pilots than would be true in the absence of their unionization, with pilot quality not tightly specified in collective bargaining, would probably be accompanied by substantial increases in hiring standards for pilots by the airlines. Newly hired pilots would have to meet higher standards of physical fitness, flight training and experience, and the like. The average quality of pilots employed would thus rise over time, reducing the true relative wage effect of the unionization of pilots to less than 25 per cent.

Union rules of various kinds restrain employers from taking full advantage of collectively bargained higher relative wages to raise the average quality of their working forces. Indeed, in some cases the rules may be so restrictive as to cause the average quality of labor employed to fall. Nevertheless, I doubt that on the average the union rules have completely prevented increases in the relative quality of labor employed from taking place. If this judgment is correct, the estimates of relative wage effects of unionism presented in this study contain an upward bias on the average resulting from incomplete adjustment of the wage data for the labor quality factor.

Incomplete adjustment of the pecuniary wage data, for nonpecuniary terms of employment, on the other hand, tends to produce a downward bias in the estimates. The relative wage gains won by unions probably consist partly of relative improvements in the nonpecuniary aspects of employment of union labor. Omission of the nonpecuniary part leads to understatement of the true relative wage effects of unionism. The direction of the combined effect of the two biases is thus unclear.

III

Earlier Studies of Unionism and Wage Differentials: The Industry Studies

III.1. INTRODUCTION

THE ESTIMATES of the relative wage impact of unionism given in this volume rest largely on evidence drawn from twenty earlier studies of unionism and wage differentials. In this chapter and the next, I review each of these studies.[1] The twelve studies reviewed in this chapter focus on small portions of the labor force, the employees in individual industries or occupations. Chapter iv covers eight global studies dealing with large segments of the U.S. economy.

Really thorough review of each of these studies would inquire into the accuracy and relevance of the evidence used in the study, assemble relevant data not brought to bear on the findings, and analyze critically the specific techniques used to isolate unionism from other factors affecting wage differentials. I have not attempted such thorough review of any of the twenty studies. On the other hand, few of the estimates of the relative wage effects of unionism that I have derived from these studies are simply transcriptions of estimates made by the authors. In the first place, the statistical work in some of the studies was not carried to the point of providing numerical estimates of the relative wage effects of unionism in per cent per percentage point of extent of unionism. For these studies I have made the additional calculations, data permitting, required to reach such numerical estimates. Second, in a number of instances I have made alternative or additional estimates that were prompted by disagreements with the procedures used in some of the studies or by the present availability of superior or more recent data.[2]

---

[1] Most of these studies were contained in larger works covering other subjects in addition to unionism and wage differentials. The reviews in this chapter and chap. iv refer only to the portions of these works which are pertinent to the subject of this volume.

[2] Although in the main I have performed these calculations on the data and within the analytical framework of each study, the responsibility for the numbers emerging from these calculations, of course, is mine rather than that of the authors.

47

III.2. ALBERT REES: BASIC STEEL MANUFACTURING IN 1945–48[3]

The principal object of Professor Rees's study[4] was to assess the role of collective bargaining in the postwar inflation from 1945 to 1948 as exemplified by the experience of the basic steel manufacturing and bituminous coal mining industries. In this context, estimation of the level in 1945–48 of the relative wage effect of unionism in basic steel and bituminous coal mining was of secondary importance. Although Rees judged that after the summer of 1946 the United Mine Workers may have made the relative wages of coal miners somewhat higher than they would have been in the absence of collective bargaining in bituminous coal mining,[5] he did not attempt to estimate the magnitude of this effect. On the other hand, Rees estimated that throughout most of the period 1945–48 the average wages of basic steel wage-earners were approximately the same as they would have been in the absence of collective bargaining in this industry:

> The available evidence and the logic of the situation lend as much support to the contention that collective bargaining in the basic steel industry has kept wages below the level which they would otherwise have reached as to the contention that it has raised wages above such levels.[6]

His finding was based largely on evidence (pp. 38–42) of shortages of labor in the industry during 1945–48, but was supported by the comparisons of wage changes summarized below in Table 2.

[3] Albert E. Rees, "The Effect of Collective Bargaining on Wage and Price Levels in the Basic Steel and Bituminous Coal Industries, 1945–1948" (unpublished Ph.D. dissertation, University of Chicago, 1950); Lloyd Ulman, "The Union and Wages in Basic Steel: A Comment," *American Economic Review*, XLVIII, No. 3 (June, 1958), 408–26; Albert E. Rees, "Reply," *American Economic Review*, XLVIII, No. 3 (June, 1958), 426–33. In preparing this review, I have benefited from discussions with Professor Rees.

[4] All textual references to Rees's steel study are to his unpublished dissertation. For published statements of the principal findings of the study, see his "Postwar Wage Determination in the Basic Steel Industry," *American Economic Review*, XLI, No. 3 (June, 1951), 389–404, and his "The Economic Impact of Collective Bargaining in the Steel and Coal Industries during the Post-war Period," Industrial Relations Research Association, *Proceedings of the Third Annual Meeting* (1950), pp. 203–12. Professor Ulman's "Comment" is directed to the first of these published articles.

[5] Rush V. Greenslade's study of the relative wage effects of unionism in bituminous coal mining tends to confirm this finding; see Table 9, p. 77.

[6] P. 140. In the opening paragraph of his "Reply" to Ulman, Rees stated his conclusion in numerical terms, "If Ulman feels that I implied that collective bargaining depressed wages substantially—say 10 percent—he has misread me. If his own conclusion is that it raised wages substantially—say 10 percent—I do not think the evidence supports him."

Rees adduced two kinds of evidence of labor shortages in basic steel in the period 1945–48: (1) U.S. Employment Service, newspaper, and trade-journal reports of unfilled positions or difficulties in recruiting labor (pp. 39–40), and (2) the decline in the average layoff rate and the increase in the average quit rate in basic steel from 1940–41 to 1945–48 (p. 41).

Consider first the reports of labor shortages. Four problems arise in using the reports to estimate the effects of collective bargaining in steel on steel wages.

1. It is difficult to gauge the labor shortages quantitatively, since most of the reports cited by Rees characterized the shortages in terms of adjectives rather than numbers. One would like to know the numerical size of each of the shortages (separately by area and occupation) expressed as the ratio of the number (or man-hours or compensation) of unfilled positions to the number of filled positions. Only one of the reports provided such information (p. 40): in September 1947 the Youngstown Sheet and Tube Company reported a shortage of one thousand employees, about 4 per cent of its filled positions. The plants of this company were located disproportionately in the two steel producing areas—Youngstown and Gary-Chicago—in which reports of labor shortages were most persistent, and in August 1947 the manpower shortage in Youngstown steel plants was described as "acute" (p. 40). These data suggest that shortages as large as 5 per cent probably were very uncommon.

2. It is unsafe to attribute the labor shortages in 1945–48 entirely to the presence of collective bargaining in steel. Indeed, Rees cites reports of labor shortages in the industry during the period 1913–23 in which relatively few steel workers were represented by unions. However, the reports for the earlier period show no tendency for labor shortages to persist, whereas in 1945–48 the reports indicate that labor shortages in the important Gary-Chicago and Youngstown areas continued for two years or more. This contrast and the preceding paragraph suggest that in these two steel producing centers the labor shortages in 1945–48 were larger, by somewhat less than five percentage points, than they would have been in the absence of collective bargaining in steel.

3. There is the problem of translating labor shortages attributed to collective bargaining in steel into corresponding effects on steel wages in the shortage areas. The translation requires information on the elasticity of demand for steel labor and the elasticity of supply of labor to steel producers. Furthermore, the translation can be carried out in two rather different ways. In the following analysis I assume for simplicity that there would be no steel labor shortages in the absence of collective bar-

gaining in steel. I also assume that in the presence of collective bargaining, the shortages, chiefly in the Youngstown and Gary-Chicago areas, were less than 5 per cent.

In the diagram below, *DD* is the demand curve for labor by steel pro-

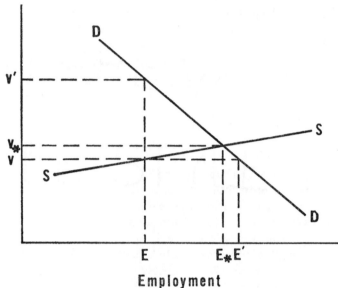

Relative Wage

Employment

ducers in a particular shortage area and *SS* is the supply curve of labor to these producers. In the absence of collective bargaining in steel the relative wage would be v_* and employment would be E_*.[7] In the presence of collective bargaining in steel, however, the relative wage is v and employment is E. At this relative wage there is a labor shortage (excess demand for labor) amounting to $100(E' - E)/E$ per cent. The percentage increase in relative wages required to eliminate the shortage, equal to the amount by which collective bargaining in steel depressed wages in the area, is

$$100(v_* - v)/v_* = (\textit{excess demand in \%})/(\eta_s + \eta_d) < (5\%)/(\eta_s + \eta_d),$$

[7] In the preceding chapter (sec. ii.3) I used the symbol v_0 to denote a relative wage in the absence of unionism, that is, in the absence of all unionism in the economy. The relative wage v_* in the absence of collective bargaining or unionism *in the steel industry* does not assume that unionism is absent elsewhere in the economy. It seems reasonable to suppose that in the presence of unionism elsewhere in the economy, v_* is less than v_0 for a particular steel producing area. However, it appears likely that in 1945–48 the impact of unionism on relative wages in the economy was small enough (see chap. v, p. 190) to make the difference between v_* and v_0 of negligible importance.

where η_s and η_d are the numerical values of the elasticities of supply and of demand, respectively. For individual steel producing areas, such as Youngstown and Gary-Chicago, both of these elasticities probably exceeded unity.[8] But then the depressing effect of steel collective bargaining

[8] I judge that in both Youngstown and Gary-Chicago the elasticity of supply of labor to basic steel producers was considerably greater than unity, since in both places there were many alternative employers competing with the steel mills for labor. The following data are consistent with the view that the elasticity of supply of labor to the steel industry was high. During 1948 the labor shortages in basic steel manufacturing disappeared. Yet the ratio of average hourly earnings in basic steel to average hourly earnings in all manufacturing industries rose only 0.6 per cent from 1947 to 1948 (annual averages) and 1.7 per cent from 1947 (average) to December 1948. The table indicates that the shortages were not eliminated by declines in employment in steel relative to all manufacturing.

DATE	AVERAGE HOURLY EARNINGS (1947 = 100)			PRODUCTION WORKERS (1947 = 100)		
	Basic Steel (1)	All Manufacturing (2)	(1)/(2) (3)	Basic Steel (4)	All Manufacturing (5)	(4)/(5) (6)
1946 average........	89.3	88.3	101.1	89.9	94.5	95.1
1947 average........	100.0	100.0	100.0	100.0	100.0	100.0
1948 average........	109.8	109.1	100.6	103.3	99.4	103.9
December 1948......	115.0	113.1	101.7	105.8	98.2	107.7

Source: U.S. Bureau of Labor Statistics, *Employment and Earnings Statistics for the United States, 1909–1960* (Washington, 1961), Bulletin 1312, pp. 30–32, 95–97.

My belief that the demand for labor by steel producers in Youngstown and Gary-Chicago was elastic in 1946–48 stems mainly from the unusual price policies of the steel industry in this period: steel prices received by steel manufacturers were below the corresponding demand prices of steel buyers. Thus steel producers could have sold a *larger* quantity of steel at *higher* prices than they actually received.

Refer to the diagram in the text. An increase of relative wages of $100(v_* - v)/v$ per cent would have increased employment of steel labor in the labor-short plants by $100(E_* - E)/E$ per cent. Such an increase of employment in the short run would have led, I speculate, to a decline in the marginal *physical* product of steel labor in these plants and to an increase in plant output of *less than* $100(E_* - E)/E$ per cent. (I approximate the short-run production function crudely by $x = AE^\alpha$, where x is steel output, E is production-worker employment, and A and α are constants, α being less than unity. In this approximation, the increase in output and the decline in marginal physical product of labor are smaller in ratio terms than the increase in employment.) I strongly doubt that the increase in output of the labor-short plants would have led to a fall in steel prices. Indeed, the wage increases required to eliminate the labor shortages might have led to *increases* in steel prices. (In this connection see Rees, pp. 121–29, 144). Increases in steel prices, of course, would have raised the value of the marginal product of steel labor, tending to offset the decline in the marginal physical product, thus making for greater elasticity of demand for labor.

The preceding reasoning assumes that the self-imposed price ceilings on steel by steel producers were not the result of unionism in the industry. If the ceilings were

on relative steel wages in these shortage areas would have been less than half as large as the labor shortages. That is, in these areas it seems likely that $100(v_* - v)/v_*$ was considerably less than 5 per cent.

In the preceding paragraph the labor shortage effect of collective bargaining was translated as a *reduction* in the supply price of labor along the supply schedule. The creation of a labor shortage, however, also *raises* the demand price of labor along the demand schedule. The percentage increase in the demand price is

$$100(v' - v_*)/v_* = (excess\ demand\ in\ \%)/(\eta_d + \eta_d^2/\eta_s),$$

a quantity that is less than the labor shortage if, as I think likely, the elasticity of demand for steel labor in the shortage area exceeded unity.

The first quantity, $100(v_* - v)/v_*$, measures the effect of collective bargaining on relative wages actually paid and on the supply price of labor in a shortage area. The second, $100(v' - v_*)/v_*$, measures the corresponding effect of collective bargaining on the demand price or value productivity of labor in the area. The first measure is thus relevant to study of the impact of unionism on the dispersion among industries of wages actually paid. The second measure is the correct one, however, for study of the impact of unionism on relative wages, the latter being viewed as indexes of relative labor productivity.

4. It appears that during much of 1945–48, collective bargaining may have depressed relative steel wages actually paid (and raised the relative demand price of steel labor) by less than 5 per cent in the Youngstown and Gary-Chicago areas. But what of the other steel producing areas? That labor shortages were reported in the Pittsburgh area in late 1945 (p. 39) makes it unlikely that collective bargaining had made relative steel wages appreciably *higher* in that area and at that time than they would have been in the absence of unionism. That the reports of shortages did not recur after the wage increase of February, 1946, makes it improbable that collective bargaining had *depressed* relative steel wages appreciably, if at all, in the Pittsburgh area during 1945 and later. Thus the picture that emerges for 1945–46 for these leading steel producing centers is one of small (less than 5 per cent) effects of steel collective bargaining on relative steel wages.

Had there been similar shortages of steel labor in other steel manufacturing areas or evidence that steel producers in these areas experienced

---

wholly or partly a result of unionism, the observed labor shortages are lower than those that would have occurred at the actual relative wage v in the absence of unionism in the steel industry. But then the estimates in the text of the effects of unionism on the demand price of steel labor and on the supply price of steel labor may be too low.

ncither labor shortages nor labor *surpluses* of significant size in 1945–48, then the preceding finding for the leading steel areas could stand for the whole industry. The other steel producing areas apparently did *not* experience *shortages* of steel labor, at least any serious enough to warrant reporting in the publications cited by Rees. However, information on *surpluses* of steel labor in these areas is lacking. Thus the labor *shortage* reports, since they were not universal in the steel industry at any time in the period 1945–48, provide incomplete evidence on the relative wage effects of steel collective bargaining in this period.

I turn now to the voluntary quit rate and layoff rate data for basic steel manufacturing. Rees interpreted the increase from 1940–41 to 1945–48 in the excess of the voluntary quit rate over the layoff rate in basic steel as evidence supporting his finding of labor shortages in steel in 1945–48. In Table 1, I compare quit and layoff rates in 1940–41 and in

TABLE 1

Quit and Layoff Rates, Selected Manufacturing Industries, 1940–47*

INDUSTRY[a]	Quit Rate[b]		Layoff Rate[b]	
	1940–41[c]	1945–47[c]	1940–41[c]	1945–47[c]
Blast furnaces, steel works, and rolling mills..	0.88	2.88	0.75	0.33
All manufacturing......................	1.55	4.45	1.70	1.23
Sawmills..............................	2.25	6.93	2.20	0.67
Furniture, including mattresses and bedsprings	2.12	7.00	1.62	0.58
Brick, tile, and terra cotta................	1.52	5.43	2.55	0.38
Cotton textiles.........................	2.62	5.87	1.50	0.32
Silk and rayon goods....................	2.40	4.63	3.20	0.67
Boots and shoes........................	1.28	4.80	2.20	0.40
Paints, varnishes, and colors..............	1.32	2.42	0.90	0.40
Industrial chemicals, except explosives.......	1.38	2.50	0.62	0.57

* Source: U.S. Bureau of Labor Statistics, *Handbook of Labor Statistics* (1947 ed.; Washington, 1948) Tables B-1 and B-2.
a Includes all industries in source tables for which turnover data were available for April and October, 1940 and 1941, and in which the extent of collective-bargaining coverage of production workers in 1946, according to the Bureau of Labor Statistics, did not exceed 59 per cent.
b Monthly rates per 100 employees.
c Mean of April and October figures.

1945–47[9] in basic steel manufacturing, all manufacturing, and in eight other industries for which the turnover data were available and in which, according to the U.S. Bureau of Labor Statistics,[10] production workers were less than 60 per cent unionized in 1946. Notice that in *all* of the industries in the table the quit rate increased and the layoff rate declined

[9] I have chosen 1945–47 rather than 1945–48, since Rees cited few reports of steel labor shortages in 1948.

[10] "Extent of Collective Bargaining and Union Recognition, 1946," *Monthly Labor Review*, LXIV, No. 5 (May, 1947), 765–69.

from 1940–41 to 1945–47, suggesting that in all of these industries, reports of labor shortages were more likely in 1945–47 than in 1940–41. There were differences among the industries, of course, in the excess of the quit rate over the layoff rate and in the change of this excess from 1940–41 to 1945–47. (For example, in absolute terms the excess of the quit rate over the layoff rate in 1945–47 and the increase of the excess from 1940–41 to 1945–47 were less for basic steel than for all manufacturing and for six of the eight less-unionized industries.) These differences, however, were the result not only of unionism but also of other demand and supply factors.

Factors other than unionism the same, the quit rate will tend to be negatively correlated with the relative wage effects of unionism. In 1940–41 the quit rate in basic steel was less than that for any of the other industry groups in the table, and in 1945–47 only two of the less-unionized industry groups had lower voluntary quit rates. These comparisons suggest that at both dates, unionism may have made relative wages in steel higher than they otherwise would have been, though by less in 1945–47 than in 1940–41. However, the quit rate data have not been adjusted for factors other than unionism that may explain the differences among industries in quit rates observed in the table.

Rees used the wage change comparisons in Table 2 mainly in support of his finding that unionism had not *increased* wages in steel significantly from 1939 to 1945 and from 1945 to 1948. Indeed, even if the changes in wage differentials shown in Table 2 were entirely the result of unionism, the *level* of the effect of unionism on relative wages in steel in 1945–48 could not be estimated even roughly from the table without some knowledge of the corresponding effect at the base date, 1939, and some knowledge of the changes in relative wage effects in other industries.

Table 2 indicates that between 1939 and 1945–48, wages (as measured by average hourly and average annual earnings) in basic steel manufacturing fell at least 7 per cent relative to wages in all manufacturing industries. In both 1939 and 1945–48 the extent of unionism of production workers in basic steel exceeded that for production workers in all manufacturing by about twenty-five percentage points. Assume that (1) the relative wage effect of unionism per percentage point of excess extent of unionism at both dates was the same in basic steel as in all manufacturing and (2) the decline of 7 per cent or more in steel wages relative to manufacturing wages was the result of unionism. Then between 1939 and 1945–48 the effect of unionism on relative wages in basic steel declined by at least 0.28 per cent per percentage point difference in extent of unionism. In 1939 the extent of unionism of wage-earners in basic steel

TABLE 2

COMPARISON OF CHANGES IN HOURLY AND ANNUAL EARNINGS,
SELECTED INDUSTRIES, 1939–48*

INDUSTRY	PER CENT UNIONIZED 1946ᵃ (1)	AVERAGE HOURLY EARNINGS, WAGE-EARNERS, SEPTEMBER 1948	
		1939 = 100 (2)	May 1945 = 100 (3)
Basic steel........................	80–100	199	139
All manufacturing.................	69	215	131
Crude petroleum..................	20–39	196	146
Non-metallic mining...............	20–39	233	146
Cotton textiles....................	20–39	289	169
Silk and rayon textiles............	20–39	281	165
Confectionery....................	20–39	221	141
Non-alcoholic beverages	20–39	193	132
Butter...........................	20–39	223	146
Ice cream........................	20–39	187	142
Power laundries..................	20–39	199	125
Cleaning and dyeing...............	20–39	197	126
Wholesale trade..................	1–19	193	135
Retail trade.....................	1–19	203	142

INDUSTRY	PER CENT UNIONIZED 1946ᵃ (1)	AVERAGE ANNUAL EARNINGS PER FULL-TIME EQUIVALENT EMPLOYEE, 1948	
		1939 = 100	1945 = 100
Basic steel	80–100	208	118
All manufacturing.................	69	223	121
Crude petroleum..................	20–39	212	129
Non-metallic mining...............	20–39	254	135
Personal services.................	1–39	204	124
Wholesale and retail trade..........	1–19	210	134
Finance, insurance, real estate.......	1–19	168	125
Federal government, general.........	1–19	257	139
Public education..................	1–19	192	143
Private households	. . .ᵇ	272	114
Agriculture.......................	<1	360	120

* Source: Rees dissertation, Tables 12 and 13; these data (except for all manufacturing) are published in his "Postwar Wage Determination in the Basic Steel Industry," pp. 399–400, Tables IV and V.
ᵃ Data refer to unionization of production and related workers.
ᵇ Not available, but probably negligible.

exceeded that for all workers in the economy by roughly fifty-five percentage points. Hence if unionism had no effect on the relative wages of steel wage-earners in 1945–48, the preceding calculation suggests that in 1939 unionism had made the average relative wage of these workers at least 15 per cent higher than it would have been in the absence of unionism. In this sense, these data are consistent with the view that the level of the relative wage effect of unionism in basic steel was small in 1945–48.

However, the wage indexes in Table 2 have not been adjusted to allow for the effects of factors other than unionism.[11] Between 1939 and 1945–48 the standard deviation of relative wages among industries declined by roughly one-fourth to one-third.[12] In my judgment, most of this decline in relative wage dispersion must be attributed to factors other than unionism.[13] Hence to make a crude adjustment for factors other than unionism, I assume that in the absence of unionism the relative wage differential in 1945–48 between steel and all manufacturing would have been only three-fourths as large as that in 1939. In 1939, average hourly earnings in basic steel manufacturing exceeded average hourly earnings in all manufacturing by 32.4 per cent.[14] Since $(1.324)^{.75} = 1.234$, the projected differential in 1945–48 after this rough adjustment for factors other than unionism is 23.4 per cent.[15] The actual differential in 1945–48 was 16.7 per cent,[16] about 5.4 per cent below the projected differential. These calculations, too, suggest that the impact of unionism on relative wages of basic steel workers declined considerably between 1939 and 1945–48.

In summary, the evidence in Rees's study, although incomplete in a number of respects, rather consistently tends to two findings: (1) relative

[11] In his "Reply" to Ulman's "Comment," however, Rees presented data indicating that the observed decline in the relative wage position of basic steel was not caused by (a) a decline in relative productivity per man-hour of basic steel workers (indeed, their relative productivity apparently increased from 1939 to 1948 [see "Reply," p. 427]) or (b) differences among industries in the sex composition of their labor forces in the presence of a decline in relative wage differentials between males and females ("Reply," pp. 428–29).

[12] See chap. iv, p. 141, and chap. ix, p. 287.

[13] See chap. ix, pp. 288–92.

[14] Computed from average hourly earnings data given in multilithed "employment, hours, and earnings," releases of the U.S. Bureau of Labor Statistics.

[15] If I had assumed that factors other than unionism would have reduced the differential by one-third rather than one-fourth, the projected differential in 1945–48 would have been 20.6 per cent, about 3.3 per cent above the actual differential.

I have omitted discussion of Rees's comparisons of changes in wages during 1914–20 with the corresponding changes during 1939–48 (pp. 82–84) because of his comment (p. 82) that these comparisons "prove little in themselves, but are highly useful as a check against more direct evidence." During 1914–20, wages of production workers in basic steel rose about 10 per cent relative to wages of production workers in all manufacturing industries, although the extent of unionism of both groups of workers was low. Hence, assume that in the absence of unionism, wages of steel workers would have *risen* by 10 per cent relative to wages of manufacturing workers during the World War II inflationary period. Then the projected wage differential in 1945–48 would have been 45.6 per cent, or 25 per cent above the actual differential. This calculation implies an absurdly large decline from 1939 to 1945–48 in the effect of unionism on the relative wages of steel workers.

[16] See n. 14 above.

wages of basic steel production workers were about the same in 1945–48 as they would have been in the absence of unionism and (2) in 1939 there was a positive and perhaps substantial effect of unionism on the relative wages of steel wage-earners.

III.3. JOSEPH SCHERER: HOTELS IN LARGE CITIES, 1939 AND 1948[17]

Although the principal union in the hotel industry, the Hotel and Restaurant Employees and Bartenders International Union, was founded in 1891, there was little unionization of hotel employees until the latter half of the 1930's. Between 1935 and 1948, however, this and other unions with jurisdictions in the hotel industry succeeded in unionizing the employees of large hotels in many of the large cities outside the South. Mr. Scherer's study estimates the effects of unionization of these employees on their relative wages in 1939 and 1948.

From data in the hotel censuses for 1929, 1935, 1939, and 1948, Scherer estimated indexes (1929 = 100) of average annual earnings of all hotel employees (except employees of small hotels for which data were not reported in the censuses) in each city with a population of 250,000 or more. Using fragmentary information from a variety of sources, he classified the cities according to their extent of unionism of hotel employees as follows:

Union Cities: The estimated extent of unionism was at least 35 per cent in 1948.
Nonunion Cities: The estimated extent of unionism was less than 10 per cent in 1948.
Other Cities: The estimated extent of unionism was 10 to 34 per cent in 1948.

The union and nonunion cities were:

Union Cities: Buffalo, Chicago, Cincinnati, Cleveland, Detroit, Kansas City, Milwaukee, Minneapolis, Newark, New York, Oakland, Philadelphia, Pittsburgh, Rochester, St. Louis, San Francisco, Seattle, Toledo, and Washington, D.C.
Nonunion Cities: Atlanta, Baltimore, Birmingham, Columbus, Dallas, Denver, Houston, Indianapolis, Louisville, Memphis, New Orleans, and Providence.

[17] Joseph Scherer, "Collective Bargaining in Service Industries: A Study of the Year-Round Hotels" (unpublished Ph.D. dissertation, University of Chicago, 1951). All references in the text to Mr. Scherer's study of the hotel industry are to his unpublished dissertation. The essential portions of his dissertation are contained in his "The Union Impact on Wages: The Case of the Year-Round Hotel Industry," *Industrial and Labor Relations Review*, IX, No. 2 (January, 1956), 213–24. Mr. Scherer wrote his dissertation under a faculty committee of which I was a member.

In all four years, according to Scherer, the average extent of unionism of hotel employees in the *nonunion* cities was essentially zero. In 1948, hotel employees in many of the union cities were much more than 35 per cent unionized and the average extent of unionism of these employees surely was substantially greater than 35 per cent. In 1929 and 1935 the extent of unionism of hotel employees in the "union" cities was probably close to zero. The average extent of unionism of hotel employees in the union cities in 1939, however, is unclear; presumably it was significantly above zero, yet also well below the average for 1948. Scherer excluded the "other" cities from his study.

For each of the two groups of cities, union and nonunion, Scherer calculated the unweighted mean index (1929 = 100) of average annual earnings in 1935, 1939, and 1948. Lines 1 and 2 of Table 3 give the values of these indexes for the union and nonunion cities. (These indexes are from his "The Union Impact on Wages: The Case of the Year-Round Hotel Industry," pp. 216–17, Tables II, III, and IV.) Line 3 shows the ratios of the indexes for the union cities to the corresponding indexes for the nonunion cities.

The ratios on line 3 led Mr. Scherer tentatively to conclude that in 1939 and 1948, unionization of hotel employees in union cities had made their average relative wage about 10 per cent higher than it otherwise would have been, with all or most of the relative wage effect arising during the period 1935–39.

TABLE 3

INDEXES OF AVERAGE ANNUAL EARNINGS OF HOTEL EMPLOYEES IN
UNION AND NONUNION CITIES, 1935, 1939, AND 1948

Line Number and Statistic	1929	1935	1939	1948
1. Unweighted mean index, 19 union cities......	100	79	90	188
2. Unweighted mean index, 12 nonunion cities....	100	76	81	169
3. Ratio of line 1 to line 2ᵃ	1.00	1.03	1.11	1.11
4. Weighted mean index, 19 union cities.........	100	81	88.4	188
5. Weighted mean index, 12 nonunion cities......	100	76	80	168
6. Ratio of line 4 to line 5ᵃ..................	1.00	1.06	1.10	1.12
7. Weighted mean index, 4 nonsouthern, nonunion cities	100	79	88.7	178
8. Ratio of line 4 to line 7ᵃ..................	1.00	1.02	1.00	1.06

ᵃ Computed from the indexes before rounding.

From the data in Scherer's study and data by cities in the 1948 hotel census[18] on the number of hotel employees for the workweek ending

[18] U.S. Bureau of the Census, *United States Census of Business: 1948* (Washington, 1951), VII, Tables 103C by city.

nearest November 15, 1948, I have computed *weighted* mean indexes (using these 1948 employment figures as weights) corresponding to Scherer's unweighted indexes. These weighted indexes are on lines 4 and 5 and their ratios are on line 6. The weighted indexes and their ratios on lines 4, 5, and 6 differ little from their unweighted counterparts on lines 1, 2, and 3.

It is very doubtful that the increase from 1929 to 1935 (estimated as 3 per cent on line 3 and 6 per cent on line 6) in earnings in union cities relative to earnings in nonunion cities was a result of unionization of hotel employees in the union cities. The unionization of these employees occurred almost entirely after 1935. But if the increase in the union/ nonunion earnings ratio from 1929 to 1935 was the result of factors other than unionism, there is a considerable danger that the later changes in the ratio were also effects chiefly of these other factors. For this reason I suspect that the ratios on lines 3 and 6 overstate the effects of unionism on the wages of hotel workers in union cities relative to the wages of hotel workers in nonunion cities.

Eight of the twelve nonunion cities covered in Table 3 are southern cities. Almost all of the union cities, on the other hand, are outside the South. The ratios on lines 3 and 6, therefore, may reflect differences between the North and South in movements of the wage differentials between white and nonwhite workers and of the ratio of white persons to nonwhite persons employed in hotels. Accordingly, I have computed the weighted mean earnings index separately for the four nonsouthern, nonunion cities (Columbus, Providence, Indianapolis, and Denver) included in Table 3. This index is on line 7; the ratio of the index for the 19 union cities to the index on line 7 is on line 8. The ratios on line 8 indicate that there was *no* relative wage effect of hotel unionization before 1940 and, perhaps, an effect of about 6 per cent on the average wage of hotel employees in union cities relative to that for nonunion cities in 1948.

Scherer dealt differently with the problem of controlling for factors other than unionism. In 1948 and earlier years the extent of unionism of employees in the personal services, business services, automobile repair services and garages, and miscellaneous repair service industries was low in both union and nonunion cities. Furthermore, census data from which the average annual earnings of these employees could be estimated by city were available for both 1939 and 1948, but not for 1929 and 1935. Since these service trade employees were nonunion in the main, the differences among cities in their earnings at least roughly index the effects of factors other than unionism that would cause the earnings of hotel employees also to vary among cities. Accordingly, Scherer divided the average annual earnings of hotel employees in each city by the corresponding average annual earnings of the service trade employees. He then averaged (unweighted mean) these hotel/service earnings ratios for 1939 and 1948, expressed as index numbers with 1939 = 100, separately for union and nonunion cities.

TABLE 4

MEAN HOTEL/SERVICE TRADE EARNINGS RATIOS IN UNION AND
NONUNION CITIES, 1939 AND 1948

Line Number and Statistic	1939	1948
1. Unweighted mean hotel/service ratio, 24 union cities........	0.74	0.76
2. Unweighted mean hotel/service ratio, 28 nonunion cities......	0.72	0.68
3. Unweighted mean hotel/service ratio, 10 nonsouthern, non-union cities..	0.77	0.73
4. Ratio of line 1 to line 2[a].................................	1.03	1.11
5. Ratio of line 1 to line 3[a].................................	0.97	1.04

[a] Computed from the unrounded values of the mean hotel/service ratios.

Table 4 compares the mean hotel/service earnings ratio in union cities with the corresponding means for the nonunion cities and the nonsouthern, nonunion cities.[19] Table 4 covers all of the cities included in Table 3 and the following additional ones:

Union Cities: Peoria, San Diego, Springfield (Massachusetts), Spokane, and Syracuse.

Nonunion Cities: Chattanooga, Des Moines, Fort Worth, Grand Rapids, Hartford, Jacksonville, Knoxville, Miami, Nashville, Oklahoma City, Salt Lake City, San Antonio, Tampa, Tulsa, Wichita, and Wilmington.

The figures on lines 4 and 5 of Table 4 tend to confirm the estimates yielded by line 8 of Table 3: unionization of hotel employees had little effect on their relative wages until after 1939; in 1948 the ratio of the average wage of hotel employees in union cities to the average wage of hotel employees in nonunion cities may have been about 6 to 8 per cent higher than it would have been in the absence of unionism. Since the hotel employees in union cities in 1948 were somewhat less than 100 per

[19] Mr. Scherer presented the data in Table 4 only in the form of index numbers, with 1939 = 100. Comparison of the *level* of the mean hotel/service earnings ratio in union cities in 1939 with that for nonunion cities, however, yields a crude estimate of the size of the effect of hotel unionization on relative wages of hotel employees in 1939. I have computed the figures in Table 4 from the average annual earnings data in Tables 25 and 26 of Scherer's study.

cent unionized, the corresponding relative wage effect *per percentage point difference in extent of unionism between union and nonunion cities* may have been greater than 0.06 to 0.08 per cent, perhaps as large as 0.10 per cent.

III.4. IRVIN SOBEL: RUBBER TIRES MANUFACTURING, 1936–49[20]

Unionization of production workers in rubber tires manufacturing began in 1935 with the formation of the United Rubber Workers of America, an industrial union affiliated with the CIO. The union won its first large strike in the industry in March, 1936, and collective bargaining between the union and major tire producers began shortly thereafter. Professor Sobel's dissertation is a study of the impact of unionism in the industry upon the industry's wages, labor costs and labor productivity, hours of work, and the location of its manufacturing facilities. Although Sobel cited evidence that led him to conclude that unionism in the industry had made the industry's relative wages higher than they otherwise would have been, he did not make numerical estimates of the relative wage effects. In this summary of the relevant portions of his study I have attempted to make such estimates.

The major tire manufacturing plants in the 1920's and 1930's were located in and near Akron, Ohio, and Detroit, Michigan. These were the plants which became unionized in the period 1935–38. During the interval from May, 1936, to February, 1938, the average hourly earnings of Ohio-Michigan tire production workers exceeded the corresponding earnings of tire workers in other areas by 42 to 51 per cent, according to figures given by Sobel (p. 15, Table 2). Most of this difference, however, cannot be attributed to the unionization of the Ohio-Michigan workers, for the pre-union difference in earnings between Ohio-Michigan and other tire workers was both persistent and large. The size of the pre-union difference can be only roughly estimated from available data. Bureau of Labor Statistics data for 1924, cited by Sobel (pp. 13–14), indicate that the difference was about one-fourth to one-third. The differential in January, 1936 (p. 15), was 34 per cent. These comparisons suggest that unionization of the Ohio-Michigan tire workers may have raised their wages by about 10 to 18 per cent relative to the wages of other tire workers in the period 1936–38.

[20] Irvin Sobel, "Economic Impact of Collective Bargaining upon the Rubber Tire Industry" (unpublished Ph.D. dissertation, University of Chicago, 1951). Mr. Sobel wrote his dissertation under a faculty committee of which I was a member. A portion of it is contained in his "Collective Bargaining and Decentralization in the Rubber-Tire Industry," *Journal of Political Economy*, LXII, No. 1 (February, 1954), 12–25.

Data on the extent of unionism and average hourly earnings of production workers in tire manufacturing and in all manufacturing industries support the preceding estimate. In 1933–34 the tire industry was nonunion and about one-sixth of manufacturing wage-earners were unionized.[21] In 1936–38 the degree of unionization of tire workers exceeded that of manufacturing workers by roughly twenty-five percentage points.[22] Thus between 1933–34 and 1936–38 the extent of unionism of tire workers grew by about forty percentage points more than that of production workers in all manufacturing industries. During the same interval, average hourly earnings of tire workers rose by about 6 per cent relative to average hourly earnings of manufacturing wage-earners,[23] or roughly 0.15 per cent per percentage point excess of the change in extent of unionism of tire workers over that for all manufacturing workers.

During the World War II inflationary period from 1939 to 1948, wages in tire manufacturing behaved in much the same manner as wages in the basic steel industry (see the discussion of Rees's study on pp. 54–56). In 1939, average hourly earnings of tire production workers exceeded the average hourly earnings of production workers in all manufacturing industries by about 50 per cent.[24] In 1945–48 the differential in earnings was 27 per cent,[25] only 60 per cent as large in ratio terms as that in 1939. As for basic steel, it is likely that most, but not all, of this narrowing of the wage differential was caused by factors other than unionism. If, as in basic steel (see p. 56), it is assumed that these other factors would have reduced the wage differential by one-fourth to one-third, the projected differential in 1945–48 would have been 31 to 35 per cent, or about 3 to 6 per cent larger than the actual differential. This calculation suggests that the impact of unionism on wages of tire workers relative to wages of all manufacturing workers declined considerably between 1939 and 1945–48 to a level well below 0.10 per cent per percentage point difference in extent of unionism.

In contrast to the labor shortages in the steel industry reported by Rees, Sobel presented evidence indicating a surplus of labor supply to tire producers in Ohio. In 1947 the average hours worked per week of Ohio tire production workers was 35.6, although tire workers in other areas averaged 42.6 hours per week and production workers in all manu-

[21] Leo Wolman, *Ebb and Flow in Trade Unionism* (New York: National Bureau of Economic Research, 1936), pp. 116–18 and 224–28.

[22] Florence Peterson, "Industrial Relations in 1938," *Monthly Labor Review*, XLVIII, No. 3 (March, 1939), 493–508.

[23] See n. 14 above.

[24] *Ibid.*

[25] *Ibid.*

facturing industries averaged 40.4 hours per week.[26] The short workweek of tire workers in the Akron area was the direct result of the six-hour day, thirty-six-hour week employment rationing ("work-sharing") practice of tire manufacturing plants in the area. Although these data evidence a positive effect of unionism on the relative wages of Akron tire workers, the size of the effect cannot be estimated from the data.

In summary, from the evidence in Sobel's study and related data I estimate that the effect of unionism on the relative wages of wage-earners in tire manufacturing was roughly 0.10 to 0.18 per cent per percentage point of extent of unionism in 1936–38 and was less than half that large in 1945–48.

III.5. STEPHEN SOBOTKA: THE CONSTRUCTION INDUSTRY, 1914–50[27]

Mr. Sobotka's chief findings regarding union influence on relative wages in the construction industry group derive from a cross-section study of wages of construction workers in 1939 in thirty-two cities with populations of 250,000 or more. The study covered male workers in six groups of occupations: carpenters; masons, tilesetters, and stonecutters; painters (construction), paperhangers, and glaziers; plasterers and cement finishers; plumbers and steamfitters; and common labor. From 1940 *Census of the United States* data he estimated the following statistics for males in each of the thirty-two cities in 1939:

1. Average annual wage and salary income for each of the six occupational groups and the weighted average ("composite") annual wage and salary income of the five skilled occupational groups taken together.

2. Average annual wage and salary income of common labor in all industries except construction, farming, and mining. These common labor averages were standardized (by using fixed weights, the same for all cities) for differences among the thirty-two cities in the distribution of common labor among industries.

3. The ratios of 1 to 2, which he termed "annual earnings ratios." By expressing earnings in the construction trades as ratios to earnings of common labor in the same city, Sobotka hoped to control for the effects of factors other than unionism having a more or less common impact in a given city on the wages of all members of the city's labor force.

[26] The figures for the tire industry are from Sobel's dissertation, p. 59; the figure for all manufacturing is the Bureau of Labor Statistics annual average for 1947.

[27] Stephen Sobotka, "The Influence of Unions on Wages and Earnings of Labor in the Construction Industry" (unpublished Ph.D. dissertation, University of Chicago, 1952). Mr. Sobotka wrote his dissertation under a faculty committee of which I was a member. For a compact version of his study, see his "Union Influence on Wages: The Construction Industry," *Journal of Political Economy*, LXI, No. 2 (April, 1953), 127–43.

4. The average annual number of full-time equivalent months worked per employee in the construction industry as a whole.

5. The corresponding average for all employees in manufacturing, transportation, communications, and other public utilities.

6. The ratio of 4 to 5, which he called the "working ratio."

7. The ratios of 3 to 6. These ratios were rough approximations of the ratios of average hourly earnings in the construction occupational groups to average hourly earnings of common labor except that in construction, farming, and mining.

8. Ratios by region of the average annual wage and salary income of urban nonwhite males to average annual wage and salary income of urban white males.

9. For each of the construction occupational groups and for common labor (other than mining, farming, and construction), the fraction of employees who were nonwhite.

10. By means of 8 and 9 he adjusted the full-time earnings ratios (7) roughly for differences among the thirty-two cities in nonwhite/white wage differentials and in the proportions of nonwhite employees in the construction trades and in the common labor base of the earnings ratios. These adjusted earnings ratios were his basic wage variable, Y.

11. The number of persons employed in each of the six construction occupational groups.

The Bureau of Labor Statistics supplied him with unpublished estimates for the thirty-two cities of union membership in the selected building trades. The ratios of these membership figures to the corresponding employment figures (11) were his estimates of the extent of unionism, X, in each of the construction trade groups.

To estimate the influence of unions on wages, Sobotka computed regressions across the thirty-two cities of the adjusted earnings ratios, Y, on the extent of unionism estimates, X, for each of the six occupational groups and the composite of the five skilled groups. Table 5 summarizes the results of these correlations, together with some related data from the study that are required for interpretation of the correlations. (The averages in column 7, which Sobotka did not compute, are weighted means, with 1940 Census employment weights, of the corresponding figures in columns 1–5.)

For common labor (col. 8) the correlation (l. 9) was so low that Sobotka concluded that unionism had not affected the relative wages of this group. A low correlation coefficient, however, need not imply a low average relative wage effect of unionism. Therefore, I have computed from Sobotka's data (his Table 4) the regression coefficient of Y on X for common labor (col. 8, l. 1) and the corresponding mean of Y (col. 8, l. 2).

The ratio of the first to the second (col 8, l. 3) is an estimate of the effect of unionism on relative wages of common building labor in per cent per percentage point difference in extent of unionism. However, this estimate, 0.04 per cent, is subject to the same biases, discussed below, that affect Sobotka's estimates for the five skilled trades.

For the five skilled building trades, however, he estimated substantial relative wage effects of unionism. Line 1 shows the regression coefficients of Y on X for each of the five skilled trades and their composite and the weighted average of the first five regression coefficients. Line 2 gives the corresponding mean values of Y. The ratios, on line 3, of the regression coefficients on line 1 to the means on line 2 are estimates of the thirty-two-city average *percentage* effects of unionism on relative wages per percentage point difference in extent of unionism. (The ratios on line 3 are my calculations, not Sobotka's.) Notice that these estimates, averaging 0.24 per cent, differ greatly among the trades, ranging from 0.12 for plasterers to 0.46 for plumbers. For reasons given below, I suspect that these differences greatly distort the real differences among the trades in the impact of unionism on their relative wages.

If the intercity differences in Sobotka's adjusted earnings ratios (Y's) reflect only random factors and intercity differences in effects of unionism, then the regression coefficients on line 1 and, therefore, also the coefficients on line 3 are probably biased downward for two reasons:

First, Sobotka's cross-section regressions will estimate the relative wage effects of unionism for the *building trades* only if the effects of unionism on the relative wages of the common labor base group, whose wages are the denominators of the earnings ratios, were uncorrelated among cities with extent of unionism in the building trades.[28] Roughly two-thirds of the common labor base group was employed in the manufacturing and transportation industry divisions in 1939. By 1939 the extent of unionism in these industry divisions in some of the large cities outside the South was surely well above the average for the labor force as a whole. Further-

[28] Denote by R_b the index of the effect of unionism on the relative wage of a building occupational group in a city;

R_c the corresponding index for the common labor base group;

X the extent of unionism of the building occupational group in the city;

b_{YX} the regression coefficient among cities of log Y on X;

b_{R_bX} the regression coefficient among cities of log R_b on X; and

b_{R_cX} the regression coefficient among cities of log R_c on X.

Assume that log $Y =$ log $R_b -$ log R_c plus a random factor uncorrelated among cities with X. Then it follows that

$$b_{YX} = b_{R_bX} - b_{R_cX}.$$

Thus b_{YX} will be smaller than b_{R_bX} if R_c was positively correlated among cities with X.

TABLE 5

Summary of Sobotka Cross-Section Study of Selected Building Trades in 32 Large Cities in 1939*

Line Number and Statistic	Occupation Group[a]							
	Carpenters (1)	Masons (2)	Painters (3)	Plasterers (4)	Plumbers (5)	Composite (6)	Average (7)	Labor (8)
1. Regression coefficient of Y on X	0.23	0.21	0.455	0.18	0.853	0.37	0.36	0.042
2. 32-city mean of Y	1.54	1.67	1.29	1.54	1.86	1.52	1.51	1.02
3. Line 1 divided by line 2	0.15	0.13	0.35	0.12	0.46	0.24	0.24	0.041
4. Largest X among 32 cities (per cent)	195	162	96	175	89	98	....	71
5. Smallest X among 32 cities (per cent)	21	32	8	24	14	19	....	4
6. Line 4 minus line 5	174	130	88	151	75	79	....	67
7. 32-city mean of X (per cent)	74	63	35	67	42	53	....	22
8. 32-city variance of X (per cent squared)	1,970	715	401	1,241	284	585	....	170
9. Correlation coefficient of Y and X	0.44	0.25	0.50	0.32	0.51	0.46	....	0.06

* Sources: All figures in Tables 5 and 6 were transcribed or computed from Sobotka's dissertation, pp. 43–46, Tables 4, 5, and 6; the figures on l. 1 (except col. 7 and col. 8) and l. 9 are shown in his "Union Influence on Wages: The Construction Industry," pp. 134, 136, Tables 1 and 2.

[a] Complete titles of the occupation groups (or columns) are: (1) carpenters; (2) masons, tilesetters, and stonecutters; (3) painters, paperhangers, and glaziers; (4) plasterers and cement finishers; (5) plumbers, gas and steamfitters; (6) composite of five skilled trades; (7) weighted average of figures for five skilled trades; and (8) common labor.

more, evidence from other studies indicates that in 1939 the relative wage effects of unionism for these industry divisions may have been substantial. Moreover, the differences among the thirty-two cities in extent of unionism of the common labor base group, and hence in the effects of unionism on the relative wages of this group, were probably positively correlated with differences in extent of unionism of the building trades. The figures on line 3 thus underestimate the effects of unionism on relative wages of building tradesmen by that part of the corresponding effects of unionism on relative wages of the common labor base group that is correlated with extent of unionism in the building trades.[29]

Second, Sobotka's estimates of extent of unionism in the building occupational groups and in their composite contain some large errors. The most obvious evidence of error is shown in lines 4 and 6 of Table 5. For carpenters, masons, and plasterers the extent of unionism estimates exceeded 100 per cent in some cities and for each of these groups the range of extent of unionism among cities exceeded one hundred percentage points.

In my judgment, the negative correlations between the figures on lines 1 and 3, on the one hand, and the figures on lines 4 and 6, on the other, are not coincidences. Each of the regression coefficients on line 1 is inversely proportional to the corresponding measured variance (squared standard deviation) of X. Consequently, if these variances are overestimated, the corresponding regression coefficients will tend to be underestimated.[30]

[29] For carpenters and plasterers, Sobotka computed earnings figures similar to the adjusted earnings ratios, Y, except that they did not involve the division (deflation) by the earnings of the common labor base group (for description of the alternative earnings figures, see his dissertation, pp. 48–49).

The alternative earnings figures yielded estimates of the relative wage effects of unionism for carpenters and plasterers that were about one and one-half times as large as the corresponding figures on l. 3 of Table 5. Part of this difference between the two pairs of estimates surely reflects the effects of factors other than unionism that were caught in the common labor earnings deflator. These data thus suggest that the bias discussed in the text depressed the relative wage effect estimates on l. 3 by less than one-third.

[30] Let X be the measured value and p the true value of extent of unionism of an occupational group in a city. Then if the errors of measurement, $X - p$, are uncorrelated with the dependent variable, Y,

$$b_{YX} = b_{Yp} \frac{\sigma_p^2}{\sigma_X^2},$$

where b_{YX} is the regression coefficient of Y on X, b_{Yp} is the regression coefficient of Y on p, and σ_p^2 and σ_X^2 are the true and measured values, respectively, of the variance of extent of unionism among cities.

The measured variances, shown on line 8, differ greatly among the occupational groups and except for painters, plumbers, and common building labor are quite large. (Indeed, if the true mean of X for carpenters really were 74 per cent, as on line 7, the variance of X for carpenters could not be larger than 1,924 per cent squared, in contrast to the measured variance of 1,970 per cent squared.) I strongly suspect that the errors in the extent of unionism estimates have led to overestimation of the variances of X and to underestimation of the regression coefficients of Y on X, particularly for carpenters and plasterers, but also for masons and the skilled trades composite. I think it is likely that the differences among the skilled trades in the estimates on line 3 of Table 5 are more largely the result of errors of estimation than of real differences in the relative wage impact of unionism.

In the terminology of chapter ii (see secs. ii.6 and ii.7), the coefficients on line 3 of Table 5 are Variant A-III coefficients, β's. If these coefficients were free of the above biases[31] and if the effects of unionism on the relative wages of both union workers and nonunion workers in each occupation and occupational group were uncorrelated among cities with the extent of unionism in the occupation or occupational group, then each β would measure the coefficient B, defined in chapter ii as the logarithm of the index of the effect of unionism on the average wage of union labor relative to the average wage of nonunion labor in the occupation.[32] In general, however, the β's are biased estimates of the B's.[33]

Refer to equations (18) and (18') in chapter ii (p. 38):

$$b_{\eta_m p_m} = a[(1 - \overset{*}{k})b_{p p_m} - 1] \tag{18}$$

and

$$b_{\eta_s p_s} = a[(1 - \overset{*}{k})b_{p p_s} - 1 - b_{k_s(1-p_s),p_s}], \tag{18'}$$

where

η_m is the elasticity of demand for union labor in an (mth) occupation;

η_s is the elasticity of demand for union labor in a set of occupations, such as the composite of the five skilled building trades;

p_m, p_s, and p are the extent of unionism figures for the mth occupation, the sth set of occupations, and *all* building construction occupations, respectively;

k_s is the ratio of the interoccupational variance of extent of unionism in the sth set of occupations to its maximum value;

---

[31] That is, if each coefficient were the true regression coefficient among cities of (a) the percentage effects of unionism on the relative wages of workers in the occupation on (b) extent of unionism in the occupation.

[32] See chap. ii, sec. ii.7.

[33] *Ibid.*

a and $1 - \overset{*}{k}$ are positive constants, $1 - \overset{*}{k}$ being less than unity;

$b_{\eta_m p_m}$ and $b_{p p_m}$ are regression coefficients across the covered cities of η_m and p respectively on p_m; and

$b_{\eta_s p_s}$, $b_{p p_s}$, and $b_{k_s(1-p_s),p_s}$ are regression coefficients across the covered cities of η_s, p, and $k_s(1 - p_s)$ on p_s.

Equation (18) is the appropriate one for testing for bias in β as an estimate of B in the individual building construction occupations and (18') for estimating the direction of the bias in the β for the skilled trades composite. $\beta - B$ tends to have the opposite sign of $b_{\eta_m p_m}$ for the individual occupations and of $b_{\eta_s p_s}$ for the composite.

For each of the six occupations $b_{p p_m}$ was less than unity:

VALUE OF $b_{p p_m}$

Occupation	32 Cities	19 Cities
Carpenters........	0.42	0.42
Masons..........	0.40	0.32
Painters..........	0.70	0.42
Plasterers........	0.30	0.50
Plumbers	0.94	0.75
Common labor.....	0.54	0.39

The first column of figures shows the value of $b_{p p_m}$ for each occupation, computed from the data for all of the thirty-two cities covered by Sobotka. In thirteen of these cities, the value of p_m in one or more of the six occupations exceeded unity. The values of $b_{p p_m}$ in the second column exclude the thirteen cities. These estimates of the $b_{p p_m}$ indicate that the coefficients on line 3 of Table 5 for each of the six occupations are biased upward conceptually as estimates of the effects of unionism on the average wage of union labor relative to the average wage of nonunion labor in the individual occupations.

For the skilled building trades composite the estimates of $b_{p p_s}$ and $b_{k_s(1-p_s)p_s}$ were:

$b_{p p_s}$: 0.71 in thirty-two cities; 0.73 in nineteen cities.

$b_{k_s(1-p_s),p_s}$: 0.20 in thirty-two cities; 0.14 in nineteen cities.

These figures indicate that, probably, the value of β for the composite was also biased upward as an estimate of the value of B. (The estimates of the test criteria, $b_{p p_m}$, $b_{p p_s}$, and $b_{k_s(1-p_s),p_s}$, were computed from Sobotka's extent of unionism figures in his Table 4.)

The preceding tests for conceptual bias in the β's on line 3 of Table 5 are subject to considerable uncertainty for two reasons: (1) the estimates of p for each city were based on the extent of unionism data for only the six occupations covered by Sobotka rather than data for all building construction occupations; (2) Sobotka's extent of unionism estimates for some of the occupations contain large errors.

The relative wage effect estimates on line 3 of Table 5 thus contain biases in opposite directions: the statistical downward biases noted earlier and the conceptual upward bias just discussed. The statistical downward biases are probably greatest for carpenters, masons, and plasterers. Unless the conceptual bias for these three occupations is large, it seems likely to me that the estimates on line 3 for these occupations are underestimates of the effect of unionism on the average wage of union labor relative to the average wage of nonunion labor. On the other hand, the reverse may be true for painters and plumbers.

In summary, Sobotka's cross-section data suggest to me that in 1939 in large cities, unionization of building construction workers made the relative wages of unionized skilled building tradesmen about 25 per cent higher and the relative wages of unskilled building workers about 5 per cent higher than they would have been in the absence of their unionization.[34] (That is, I estimate that the value of B was about 0.25 per cent

[34] As noted earlier, Sobotka estimated that building trades unionism had not affected the relative wages of common construction labor in 1939. He estimated that unionization of the skilled trades had raised the relative wages of unionized craftsmen by about 10 to 20 per cent. Table 6, a continuation of Table 5, explains how he derived this estimate range for the skilled trades:

TABLE 6

Summary of Sobotka Cross-Section Study of Selected Building Trades in 32 Large Cities in 1939*

LINE NUMBER AND STATISTIC	OCCUPATION GROUP						
	Carpenters (1)	Masons (2)	Painters (3)	Plasterers (4)	Plumbers (5)	Composite (6)	Average (7)
10. Regression value of Y at largest X among 32 cities	182	188	157	174	226	168	. . .
11. Regression value of Y at smallest X among 32 cities	142	160	117	146	162	140	. . .
12. Ratio of line 10 to line 11, less unity	0.28	0.18	0.34	0.19	0.40	0.20	0.30
13. Regression value of Y at eighth-largest X among 32 cities	161	170	134	158	197	160	. . .
14. Regression value of Y at eighth-smallest X among 32 cities	146	163	123	149	175	144	. . .
15. Ratio of line 13 to line 14, less unity	0.10	0.04	0.09	0.06	0.13	0.11	0.09
16. Eighth-largest X among 32 cities	103	80	46	86	53	74	. . .
17. Eighth-smallest X among 32 cities	37	43	20	39	30	31	. . .

* Sources: Transcribed or computed from Sobotka's dissertation, pp. 43–44, 46, Tables 4 and 6; ll. 10–15 (except col. 7) appear in his "The Union Influence on Wages: The Construction Industry," p. 136, Table 2.

per percentage point of extent of unionism for skilled construction
workers and about 0.05 per cent per percentage point of extent of
unionism for common building labor.) That these estimates are subject
to large margins of error is indicated both by the discussion in preceding
paragraphs and by the relatively low correlation coefficients, shown on
line 9 of Table 5, between the adjusted earnings ratios and the extent of
unionism estimates.

Sobotka estimated the relative wage impact of unionism for other years
from time series data. Table 7 summarizes the most relevant of these
data for key years. The "average hourly earnings" series for skilled
construction workers is that of the *Engineering News-Record* and is
based on wage rate data collected from large contractors in large cities.
The extent to which this series includes wage rates of nonunion workers
is not known. However, since the degree of unionization of skilled
employees of large contractors in large cities was probably high throughout 1914–50, I presume that the construction series is essentially an
average of wage rates of unionized skilled workers.[35] In what follows, I
therefore assume that the movements of the series are not affected by
changing weights of union and nonunion wage rates.[36] The wage series for
manufacturing is Rees's average hourly earnings series for manufacturing.[37]

---

1. For each of the occupation groups he computed the regression value of the
adjusted earnings ratio, Y, for the city with the highest extent of unionism (l. 10) and
for the city with the lowest extent of unionism (l. 11). The ratios of the first regression
values to the second, less unity, are shown on l. 12. Sobotka felt, without explaining
why, that the figures on l. 12, multiplied by 100, were overestimates of the relative wage
effects that he sought to measure.

2. Therefore, he also computed similar regression values for the eighth-largest and
eighth-smallest estimates of extent of unionism and the ratios, less unity, of the first
regression values to the second. These computations are shown on ll. 13, 14, and 15
(ll. 16 and 17 show the eighth-largest and eighth-smallest estimates of extent of unionism
among the thirty-two cities). He stated his final estimates as ranges, with lower limits
given by l. 15 (multiplied by 100) and upper limits by l. 12 (multiplied by 100). For the
skilled trades composite (col. 6) the range is 11 to 20 per cent. Notice, however, that
the average range (col. 7), which he did not compute, is considerably wider: from 9 to
30 per cent.

[35] Except during the 1930's, the series follows closely the Bureau of Labor Statistics
series of average union wage rates for journeyman construction workers—see Sobotka,
p. 59. Col. 1 of Table 7 is from Sobotka's dissertation, p. 59, Table 8.

[36] Sobotka also presented and analyzed the *Engineering News-Record* series for
unskilled construction workers. I have omitted discussion of this series because I
suspect that the union-nonunion composition of the series may have changed substantially over time.

[37] Albert Rees, *New Measures of Wage-Earner Compensation in Manufacturing, 1914–*

TABLE 7

HOURLY WAGES FOR SKILLED CONSTRUCTION WORKERS AND FOR PRODUCTION
WORKERS IN MANUFACTURING, SELECTED YEARS, 1914–50

YEAR	AVERAGE HOURLY EARNINGS		
	Manufacturing Wage-Earners (1)	Skilled Construction Workers (2)	Ratio of Col. (2) to Col. (1) (3)
1914................	$0.220	$0.565	2.57
1919................	0.477	0.780	1.64
1923................	0.499	1.12	2.24
1929................	0.530	1.36	2.57
1931................	0.502	1.32	2.63
1935................	0.537	1.07	1.99
1939................	0.603	1.44	2.39
1944................	1.00	1.64	1.64
1945–48 average......	1.17	1.93	1.65
1950................	1.46	2.52	1.73

It would appear from Table 7, column 3, that the effect of building
trades unionization on the relative wages of unionized skilled construction
workers was about 7 to 8 per cent higher in 1914 and 1929 than in 1939.
Two factors, however, may account completely for this seeming difference in relative wage effect:

1. In 1914 and 1929 the extent of unionism of manufacturing wage-earners
was low—about one person out of six to eight—and differed little from that in
the labor force as a whole.[38] In 1939, on the other hand, close to one-half of
wage-earners in manufacturing were unionized, and the extent of unionism of
these workers was roughly thirty percentage points higher than that in the
whole labor force.[39] Thus unionism may have raised the relative wages of
manufacturing wage-earners by about 3 to 6 per cent in 1939 compared to 1914
and 1929.[40] Adjustment of the 1939 figure in column (3) for an effect of this
size would raise it to 2.46–2.53.

2. In 1939 the demand for construction labor relative to that for manufacturing labor, as judged by the ratio of employment in construction to employment in manufacturing and the similar ratio for national income originating,
was abnormally low. Adjustment for this relative demand factor would tend
to raise the 1939 figure in column (3) relative to the corresponding figures for
1914 and 1929.

1957 (New York: National Bureau of Economic Research, 1960), Occasional Paper 75,
Table 1. This series, of course, was not available to Sobotka at the time of his study
and he used the Bureau of Labor Statistics average hourly earnings series for manufacturing.

[38] Wolman, *op. cit.*, pp. 116–18 and 224–28.

[39] See chap. iv, n. 3, p. 138 and chap. vii, Table 72, p. 244; see also the source cited
in n. 22 above, p. 62.

[40] See pp. 190 ff.

In the light of these two adjustments, I judge that the impact of building unionism on the relative wages of unionized skilled building workers was about the same in 1914 and 1929 as in 1939.

During both world-war inflationary periods the skilled construction worker/manufacturing wage-earner wage differential narrowed by almost one-half in ratio terms. The magnitude of the narrowing is about the same as that which occurred during 1939 to 1945–48 between basic steel manufacturing and all manufacturing and between rubber tire manufacturing and all manufacturing.[41] Furthermore, I judge that in construction during both war inflations, as in basic steel and rubber tires during the World War II inflation, the fall in wages relative to all manufacturing, though mainly the result of other factors, was caused in part by a decline in the relative wage impact of unionism.

Such declines in the relative wage effects of unionism during inflationary periods are consistent with the view that collective bargaining tends to make the money wages of unionized workers less responsive than they otherwise would be to underlying demand and supply conditions for labor. The *rise* of the construction/manufacturing differential during the *deflation* from 1929 to 1931 also is consistent with this view.[42] By 1935, however, the skilled construction/manufacturing wage ratio was far below its level in 1929 and 1931. The extent of the decline in the ratio from 1929 to 1935 strongly suggests that in the latter year the effect of building trade unionism on the relative wages of unionized skilled workers was considerably less than in 1929.

III.6. RUSH V. GREENSLADE: BITUMINOUS COAL MINING, 1909–57[43]

The United Mine Workers union dates from 1890, but until 1899 its membership was a small fraction of employment in bituminous coal mining, and collective bargaining between the mine operators and the union did not begin until 1898. By 1902, nearly one-half of the employees in the industry were unionized, and by World War I the fraction may have been near 60 per cent. At the end of and immediately following the

---

[41] See pp. 56 and 62.

[42] In part, this rise in the apparent differential between construction and manufacturing, as well as the wartime declines in the differential, may be spurious, the result of comparing average wage *rates* in construction with average hourly *earnings* in manufacturing.

[43] Rush V. Greenslade, "The Economic Effects of Collective Bargaining in Bituminous Coal Mining" (unpublished Ph.D. dissertation, University of Chicago, 1952). Mr. Greenslade wrote his dissertation under a faculty committee of which I was a member.

war the extent of collective-bargaining coverage of bituminous coal miners increased to approximately 75 per cent.

The period 1923–28 was one of rapid decline in the union's collective-bargaining position in the industry, the immediate cause of which was the initial success in maintaining high union wage scales won in 1920 in the face of the money wage deflation that followed. Wages and coal prices fell drastically in nonunion mines, and the union was unable to prevent most of the union mines from becoming open shops. By 1929, only the mines in Illinois and Indiana remained unionized.

In 1934 the United Mine Workers, with the assistance of the National Industrial Recovery Act, succeeded in organizing almost all of the bituminous coal mining industry, and from that time to the present the extent of unionism in the industry has been close to 100 per cent. For the last twenty-five years the UMW has commonly been regarded as an exceptionally strong union, with relative wage effects well above the average for all unions. Mr. Greenslade's findings regarding the relative wage impact of the UMW tend to support this popular opinion.

Greenslade's findings came principally from an examination of the variation over time of average hourly compensation in bituminous coal mining and in manufacturing industries. Table 8 presents these time series, along with related data on days worked per year, total employment, and extent of unionism in bituminous coal mining.[44] Both the manufacturing and the coal average hourly compensation series include wage supplements. The key wage series in Table 8 is column (3), the ratio of average hourly compensation in bituminous coal mining to that in manufacturing. As Greenslade recognized, the movements of this relative wage series reflect not only the effects of unionism in coal mining but also (a) after 1934, the effects of unionism in manufacturing and (b) effects of factors other than unionism. The effects of unionism in manu-

---

[44] In constructing the table, I have extended the series to 1957 and have replaced some of the figures used by Greenslade with revised or new series that have become available since Greenslade completed his study. The sources of the series in Table 8 are:

Col. (1): 1890–1928, Greenslade's Table 8; 1929–57, Ethel B. Jones, "Hours of Work in the United States, 1900–1957" (unpublished Ph.D. dissertation, University of Chicago, 1961), Table 2.

Col. (2): 1890–1914, Albert Rees, *Real Wages in Manufacturing, 1890–1914* (Princeton: Princeton University Press, 1961), Table 10; 1915–57, Rees, source cited in n. 37 above.

Cols. (4) and (5): 1890–1944, Greenslade's Tables 1 and 7; 1945–57, U.S. Bureau of Mines, *Minerals Yearbook*, II, *Fuels*, 1960 issue, p. 53.

Col. (6): Greenslade's study, pp. 19–25.

TABLE 8

AVERAGE HOURLY COMPENSATION, EXTENT OF UNIONISM, DAYS WORKED
PER YEAR, AND EMPLOYMENT IN BITUMINOUS COAL MINING;
AVERAGE HOURLY COMPENSATION IN MANUFACTURING;
1890–1957

YEAR	AVERAGE HOURLY COMPENSATION			DAYS WORKED PER YEAR	MEN EMPLOYED (THOUSANDS)	EXTENT OF UNIONISM (PER CENT)
	Bituminous Coal (1)	Manufac- turing (2)	(1) ÷ (2) (3)	(4)	(5)	(6)
1890...	$0.180	$0.144	1.25	226	192	↑
1891...	0.169	0.144	1.17	223	206	
1892...	0.179	0.145	1.23	219	213	Less than 5
1893...	0.188	0.151	1.25	204	230	
1894...	0.171	0.139	1.23	171	245	
1895...	0.158	0.138	1.14	194	240	←—Less than 5
1896...	0.147	0.144	1.02	192	244	
1897...	0.138	0.140	0.99	196	248	
1898...	0.170	0.137	1.24	211	256	Increasing to about 50
1899...	0.185	0.146	1.27	234	271	
1900...	0.213	0.151	1.41	234	304	
1901...	0.237	0.158	1.50	225	340	
1902...	0.242	0.165	1.47	230	370	↑
1903...	0.265	0.170	1.56	225	416	
1904...	0.267	0.169	1.58	202	438	
1905...	0.270	0.172	1.57	211	461	
1906...	0.285	0.184	1.55	213	478	
1907...	0.278	0.191	1.46	234	513	About 50
1908...	0.281	0.184	1.53	193	516	
1909...	0.277	0.186	1.49	209	543	
1910...	0.286	0.198	1.44	217	556	
1911...	0.293	0.202	1.45	211	550	
1912...	0.309	0.207	1.49	223	549	↓
1913...	0.307	0.221	1.39	232	572	
1914...	0.316	0.220	1.44	195	584	
1915...	0.331	0.226	1.46	203	558	About 60
1916...	0.373	0.262	1.42	230	561	
1917...	0.479	0.316	1.52	243	603	
1918...	0.596	0.417	1.43	249	615	
1919...	0.697	0.477	1.46	195	622	
						About 70
1920...	0.936	0.553	1.69	220	640	About 75
1921...	0.918	0.488	1.88	149	664	
1922...	0.903	0.451	2.00	142	688	
1923...	0.920	0.499	1.84	179	705	
1924...	0.807	0.516	1.56	171	620	Declining to less than 25
1925...	0.723	0.513	1.41	195	588	
1926...	0.722	0.517	1.40	215	594	
1927...	0.692	0.522	1.33	191	594	
1928...	0.672	0.522	1.29	203	522	
1929...	0.655	0.534	1.23	219	503	
1930...	0.647	0.530	1.22	187	493	Less than 25
1931...	0.612	0.506	1.21	160	450	
1932...	0.507	0.446	1.14	146	406	

TABLE 8—*Continued*

YEAR	AVERAGE HOURLY COMPENSATION			DAYS WORKED PER YEAR	MEN EMPLOYED (THOUSANDS)	EXTENT OF UNIONISM (PER CENT)
	Bituminous Coal (1)	Manufacturing (2)	(1) ÷ (2) (3)	(4)	(5)	(6)
1933...	$0.471	$0.441	1.07	167	419	?
1934...	0.631	0.527	1.20	178	458	
1935...	0.702	0.542	1.30	179	462	
1936...	0.740	0.553	1.34	199	477	
1937...	0.823	0.633	1.30	193	492	
1938...	0.868	0.639	1.36	162	441	
1939...	0.834	0.638	1.31	178	422	
1940...	0.834	0.670	1.24	202	439	
1941...	0.943	0.737	1.28	216	457	
1942...	1.009	0.864	1.17	246	462	
1943...	1.095	0.975	1.12	264	416	More than 90
1944...	1.201	1.05	1.14	278	393	
1945...	1.282	1.06	1.21	261	383	
1946...	1.475	1.13	1.31	214	396	
1947...	1.811	1.30	1.39	234	419	
1948...	2.203	1.41	1.56	217	442	
1949...	2.287	1.46	1.57	157	434	
1950...	2.462	1.55	1.59	183	416	
1951...	2.725	1.73	1.58	203	373	
1952...	2.844	1.83	1.55	186	335	
1953...	3.142	1.94	1.62	191	293	
1954...	3.204	1.97	1.63	182	227	
1955...	3.366	2.05	1.64	210	225	
1956...	3.661	2.15	1.70	214	228	
1957...	3.925	2.27	1.73	203	229	

facturing after 1934, he pointed out, tend to make the series understate the relative wage impact of the United Mine Workers in coal mining in these years.

There were two periods covered by the table in which the relative wage series was probably little affected by unionism, namely, 1890–98 and 1929–33. In these periods the relative wage averaged about 1.20 to 1.25 during years in which days worked per year were above 200 and employment was not changing rapidly, but in poorer years the relative wage ranged down to nearly 1.00. Greenslade felt that during periods (such as 1899–1909) in which days worked per year averaged close to 220 or better *and* employment was increasing rapidly in coal mining, the relative wage in the absence of unionism might be somewhat above 1.20. With these relative wage figures as rough benchmarks, he estimated that the United Mine Workers had raised relative wages in bituminous coal mining "considerably" in the early 1920's and in 1948–51 and "somewhat" in the period 1934–40.

He did not attempt, however, to replace these adjectives with numbers. In Table 9, I have made rough numerical estimates of the UMW's relative wage impact from the data in Table 8, using Greenslade's method of establishing benchmark levels of relative wages in the absence of unionism. Column (1) of the table is from column (3) of Table 8. The benchmark level of the relative wage, column (2), is a *very crude* estimate of the level of the relative wage in the absence of unionism, both in coal mining and elsewhere. This estimate for a given year or period is based on the level of the actual relative wage in the periods 1890–98 and 1929–33 and the employment situation (days worked per year and men employed) in the given year. The estimate also makes a small allowance for effects of unionism in manufacturing in 1937–39 and 1948–57. The ratio, shown in column (4), of column (1) to column (2), minus unity, is a rough estimate of the amount, in ratio terms, by which unionism raised the average relative wage of bituminous coal miners.

TABLE 9

Estimation of the Relative Wage Effects of Unionism in
Bituminous Coal Mining, 1909–57

YEAR	RELATIVE WAGE		EXCESS EXTENT OF UNIONISM	RELATIVE WAGE EFFECT		
	Actual	Benchmark		$[(1) - (2)] \div (2)$	(See Text)	
	(1)	(2)	(3)	(4)	(5)	(6)
1909–13 average...	1.45	1.23	0.45	0.18	0.44	0.38–0.43
1914–18 average...	1.45	1.23	0.50	0.18	0.39	0.33–0.38
1919.............	1.46	1.21	0.60	0.21	0.37	0.31–0.36
1920.............	1.69	1.23	0.65	0.37	0.62	0.50–0.57
1921.............	1.88	1.10	0.65	0.71	1.3	1.0 –1.1
1922.............	2.00	1.10	0.65	0.82	1.5	1.2 –1.3
1924.............	1.56	1.15	0.60	0.36	0.67	0.57–0.62
1926.............	1.40	1.15	0.40	0.22	0.64	0.52–0.58
1929.............	1.23	1.15–1.23	?	0.00–0.07	...	...
1931.............	1.21	1.10–1.15	?	0.05–0.10	...	...
1933.............	1.07	1.00	?	0.07	...	...
1937–39 average...	1.32	1.05	0.80	0.26	0.33	0.27–0.32
1945.............	1.21	1.21	0.70	0.00	0.00	0.00
1948–52 average...	1.57	1.20	0.70	0.31	0.47	0.33–0.42
1953–55 average...	1.63	1.20	0.70	0.36	0.55	0.37–0.46
1956–57 average...	1.72	1.18	0.70	0.46	0.72	0.48–0.58

In the notation of chapter ii, the figures in column (4) are estimates for bituminous coal mining of the Variant A-I index less unity, $R - 1$. These estimates depend not only on the impact of unionism on the relative wages of union and nonunion coal miners but also on the difference between the extent of unionism in bituminous coal mining and the extent of unionism in the whole labor force [see equations (9) and (11') in chap. ii, pp. 28–29]. Furthermore, they are not comparable conceptually to the β- or B-type estimates of Variant A-III that I have set as the standard form in this study.

I have converted the figures in column (4) to B form according to the formula given in section ii.9 of chapter ii (p. 43):

$$converted\ A\text{-}I\ index\ =\ antilog\ of\ (\log R)/U,$$

where the figures in column (4) are $R - 1$, and U is the excess of the extent of unionism in bituminous coal mining over the extent of unionism in the labor force as a whole. The figures in column (3) are estimates of U based on Table 72 in chapter vii and column (6) of Table 8. The converted indexes, less unity, are shown in column (5).

Such converted indexes, however, tend to be biased estimates of the effect of unionism on the average wage of union labor relative to the average wage of nonunion labor in the covered segment of the labor force. I discuss this bias in chapter ii (p. 43). Fortunately, the amount of the bias may be estimated with the help of equation (30) from chapter ii (p. 43):

$$(\log R)/U \cong B(1 + \bar{p}/U) - \overline{pB}/U,$$

where $\bar{p}$ is the extent of unionism in the economy as a whole, B is the logarithm of the index of the effect of unionism on the average wage of union labor in the industry to the corresponding average wage of nonunion labor, and $\bar{B}$ is the logarithm of the similar index for the whole labor force. Equation (30) implies that

$$B \cong \frac{\log R + \overline{pB}}{U + \bar{p}}. \tag{30'}$$

I have used the degree of unionization figures in Table 72 of chapter vii as the estimates of $\bar{p}$. To obtain a lower-limit estimate of B, I set $\bar{B}$ equal to zero. The antilogarithms, less unity, of the resulting estimates of B are the lower ends of the estimate ranges given in column (6) of Table 9. In chapter v (pp. 188–93), I estimate that $\bar{B}$ probably was less than 0.25 throughout the last four decades, except possibly at the bottom of the depression in the 1930's. Therefore, in calculating the upper-limit estimate of B, I put $\bar{B}$ at 0.25.

The figures in columns (4), (5), and (6) indicate that, except possibly in 1929–33 and probably also during much of World War II, the relative wage impact of unionism in bituminous coal mining has been quite large. Indeed, only the failure of the United Mine Workers to maintain its collective-bargaining position in bituminous coal mining in the 1920's makes the figures for the years 1921 and 1922 credible, and, in spite of the rapid decline of coal mining employment in the last decade, I view with considerable disbelief the estimates of the relative wage effects in the 1950's.

Table 10 reproduces the relevant portion of a table (Greenslade, Table 11) in which Greenslade compared the average daily earnings of bituminous coal miners in four different regions of the United States. For the years covered by the table, the hours worked per day differed little among the regions. After 1933 all four regions were essentially completely unionized, and the differences in earnings among the regions, 1935–40, reflect factors other than unionism associated with the regions. In the period 1919–33, however, there were also differences in degree of unionization among the regions:

Illinois and Indiana were more or less fully unionized throughout 1919–33.

Pennsylvania and Ohio were partially unionized from 1919 to 1927, nonunion during 1928–33.

West Virginia and Kentucky were partially unionized from 1919 to 1924, nonunion during 1926–33.

Alabama, Virginia, and Tennessee were nonunion except in 1919–21.

TABLE 10

AVERAGE DAILY EARNINGS IN BITUMINOUS COAL MINING, BY REGION, 1919–40

YEAR	AVERAGE DAILY EARNINGS				(1) ÷ (2) MINUS UNITY	(1) ÷ (3) MINUS UNITY	(3) ÷ (4)	1.25 × (4)	(1) ÷ (8) MINUS UNITY
	Illinois and Indiana	Pennsylvania and Ohio	West Virginia and Kentucky	Alabama, Virginia, and Tennessee					
	(1)	(2)	(3)	(4)	(5)	(6)	(7)	(8)	(9)
1919.....	$6.41	$5.61	$5.49	$4.31	...	...	...	...	...
1921.....	8.57	7.17	7.18	5.28	...	...	...	...	...
1924.....	8.49	6.60	5.60	4.31	...	...	...	5.39	0.58
1926.....	8.11	5.85	5.10	4.04	...	0.59	1.26	5.05	0.61
1929.....	6.87	5.15	4.79	3.93	0.33	0.43	1.22	4.91	0.40
1931.....	6.98	4.77	4.80	3.77	0.46	0.45	1.27	4.71	0.48
1933.....	5.56	3.51	3.51	2.85	0.58	0.58	1.23	3.56	0.56
1935.....	5.27	4.97	4.87	3.77	...	...	1.29	...	...
1936.....	6.01	5.48	5.32	4.26	...	...	1.25	...	...
1939.....	5.64	5.73	5.67	4.64	...	...	1.22	...	...
1940.....	6.27	5.93	5.77	4.65	...	...	1.24	...	...

Thus the ratios (minus unity) of earnings in Illinois and Indiana to earnings in the other regions during periods in which the latter were nonunion, with allowance for "regional" wage differentials, are estimates of the amount by which the United Mine Workers raised the relative wages of *union* miners compared to what they would have been in the absence of unionism in the industry. The principal "regional" wage differential was that between the Alabama-Virginia-Tennessee region and the other three regions. Table 10 indicates that the regional differences among the other three regions were relatively small.

Column (5) is the excess, in ratio terms, of average daily earnings in Illinois and Indiana over average daily earnings in Pennsylvania and Ohio. Column (6) makes a similar comparison of Illinois-Indiana with West Virginia-Kentucky. In the period 1926–40 during which the Alabama-Virginia-Tennessee and the West Virginia-Kentucky regions were equally unionized (both nonunion or both union), there was a more or less constant regional difference in daily earnings of about 25 per cent between the two regions, as shown in column (7). In column (8) the earnings of the Alabama-Virginia-Tennessee region have been increased by 25 per cent to adjust for this differential. Column (9) is the ratio (minus unity) of earnings in Illinois and Indiana to these adjusted earnings in the Alabama-Virginia-Tennessee region.

The figures in columns (6) and (9) for 1924 and 1926 are about the same size as those for these years in column (6) of Table 9 and thus support the estimates of the relative wage impact of the United Mine Workers in Table 9. The 1926–33 figures in columns (5), (6), and (9) of Table 10 indicate that the impact of the United Mine Workers on relative wages of *union* miners declined considerably from 1926 to 1929, but then rose from 1929 to 1933.

III.7. JOHN E. MAHER: SEVEN MANUFACTURING INDUSTRIES, 1950[45]

The starting point of Professor Maher's study of "Union, Nonunion Wage Differentials" was an emphatic rejection of the method used by Ross, Goldner, Levinson, and Garbarino to estimate the influence of unionism on interindustrial wage differentials.[46] Comparisons of changes over time in the average hourly earnings of industries differing in degree of unionization, Maher argued, are likely to yield highly unreliable estimates of the real impact of unionism. Average hourly earnings differentials, he stated, reflect not only effects of unionism but also the effects of differences among industries in (a) methods of wage payments; (b) proportions of employees receiving overtime and other premium wage

[45] John E. Maher, "Union, Nonunion Wage Differentials," *American Economic Review*, XLVI, No. 3 (June, 1956), 336–52.

[46] The Ross-Goldner, Levinson, and Garbarino studies are reviewed in the first three sections of chap. iv.

rates; (c) the distributions of their working forces by region, size of city, and size of establishment in which employed; (d) the compositions of their working forces by skill, age, sex, etc.; and (e) the structure of their product and factor markets.

To control for these factors, Maher imposed on his study strong criteria of wage comparability:

1. The union and nonunion workers whose wages at a given date were to be compared should be of the same sex; of approximately the same work experience (learners and apprentices should be separated from more experienced workers); and employed in the same locality (standard metropolitan area), detailed industry, detailed occupation, in establishments (plants) of approximately the same size.

2. Average wage *rates* rather than average hourly earnings should be compared. (He thus excluded wage comparisons involving workers paid under incentive systems.)

Wage data in such detail were available to him in unpublished tabulations of the 1950 Bureau of Labor Statistics sample surveys of wages in selected industries, localities, and occupations. Maher could not have used these data to estimate "union, nonunion wage differentials," of course, had they not also been classified by unionization. The Bureau's unionization classification, however, was crude: a plant and all of the wage data pertaining to it were considered to be "union" if at least half the workers employed in the plant were covered by collective-bargaining agreements; otherwise the plant and its wage data were classified "nonunion." Since the Bureau's surveys covered office- as well as production-worker occupations, it is very likely that at least the office occupations in "union" plants were *not* covered by collective-bargaining agreements. On the other hand, some of the wage data for "nonunion" plants may have pertained to workers covered by collective-bargaining agreements, with craft unions representing only a minority of plant employees.[47]

Maher's criterion of wage comparability was so strong that he excluded entirely the data for several of the industries covered in the Bureau's 1950 surveys. Furthermore, within the seven industries included in his study, the wage comparisons, as shown in Table 11, excluded large fractions of the plants (and presumably, also, occupations) covered by the BLS surveys according to a nonrandom selection criterion. For five of the

[47] Furthermore, I strongly doubt that 50 per cent is a critical level of unionization of a plant in the sense that at all lower levels of unionization, unionism has *no* effects at all on plant wages, but as soon as the 50 per cent level is reached, *all* wages in the plant are more or less equally affected by unionism.

seven industries his wage comparisons in each case cover less than 5 per cent [col. (10) of Table 11] of the employees in plants surveyed by the BLS, and in none of the seven industries did he cover as many as one out of five of the employees in surveyed plants. Thus, given the nonrandomness of his coverage, his sample findings for each industry may contain serious bias as estimates for the industry as a whole.[48]

In the following description of Maher's analysis of his data, I mean by a "cell" a particular combination of industry, standard metropolitan area, plant size class, detailed occupation, sex, and worker experience class. Altogether, Maher's study covered 410 cells or wage comparisons. Table 12 shows the distribution of the cells by industry and for each industry the number, but not the names, of cities (standard metropolitan areas) and of white-collar and nonwhite-collar occupations covered.[49] The paper reports a few other bits of information on the distribution of the cells, but does not provide any clues regarding the identification of the nonwhite-collar occupations covered by the comparisons within industries. Thus I can only guess that the exclusion of incentive workers may have led to overrepresentation of time workers, such as maintenance craftsmen, whose extent of unionism may have differed less between "union" and "nonunion" plants than that of the excluded workers.

Within each cell, Maher calculated the unweighted within-plant mean wage rate of covered time workers for each plant represented in the cell and then, separately for union and nonunion *plants*, the unweighted mean of the within-plant mean wage rates. He then subtracted the cell mean for nonunion plants from the cell mean for union plants, obtaining a

[48] In this connection, the following comparisons, derived from Table 11, are relevant:

	AVERAGE NUMBER OF EMPLOYEES PER PLANT		
INDUSTRY	In Plants Surveyed by BLS (1)	In Plants Included by Maher (2)	Ratio of Col. (2) to Col. (1) (3)
Paints and varnishes..........	43	80	1.8
Wooden furniture............	126	177	1.4
Footwear....................	252	271	1.1
Cotton textiles..............	442	843	1.9
Hosiery.....................	171	240	1.4
Automotive parts............	389	238	0.6
Women's dresses.............	33	26	0.8

[49] Col. (1) of Table 12 is from Maher's Table II; cols. (2), (3), and (4) are from correspondence with Professor Maher. In some industries and standard metropolitan areas the wage comparisons covered fewer than the number of occupations indicated in Table 12.

TABLE 11

INDUSTRY, PLANT, AND EMPLOYEE COVERAGE OF MAHER STUDY*

INDUSTRY	NUMBER OF PLANTS				
	Covered by BLS Survey (1)	Maher Study			
		Total		Union (Number) (4)	Nonunion (Number) (5)
		Number (2)	Per Cent of Col. (1) (3)		
Paints and varnishes..	460	84	18	38	46
Wooden furniture[a]....	244	57	23	29	28
Footwear[b]..........	102	40	39	19	21
Cotton textiles.......	224	12	5	6	6
Hosiery[c]............	85	21	25	10	11
Automotive parts[d]....	26	8	31	4	4
Women's dresses.....	110	10	9	5	5
Total.............	1,251	232	19	111	121

INDUSTRY	NUMBER OF EMPLOYEES					
	Total in Plants Surveyed by BLS (6)	Maher Study				
		Total in Plants Included by Maher		Total Covered in Maher's Wage Comparisons		
		Number (7)	Per Cent of Col. (6) (8)	Number (9)	Per Cent of Col. (6) (10)	Per Cent of Col. (7) (11)
Paints and varnishes..	19,993	6,699	34	2,810	14	42
Wooden furniture[a]....	30,859	10,062	33	5,570	18	55
Footwear[b]..........	25,709	10,854	42	330	1	3
Cotton textiles.......	99,091	10,117	10	1,460	1	14
Hosiery[c]............	14,566	5,040	35	600	4	12
Automotive parts[d]....	10,123	1,904	19	270	3	14
Women's dresses.....	3,599	264	7	60	2	23
Total.............	203,940	44,940	22	11,100	5	25

* Source: Transcribed or computed from Maher, *op. cit.*, p. 339, Table I.
[a] Other than upholstered.
[b] Men's Goodyear welt and women's cement process.
[c] Full fashioned, men's seamless, and children's seamless.
[d] Engine and chassis.

single "union, nonunion wage differential" for the cell. Table 13 shows the unweighted mean of the cell differentials for each of the seven industries. (Table 13 is from Maher's Table III.) According to Maher, all of the means in Table 13, except that for wooden furniture, were *statistically* insignificant—that is, his sample data, viewed as drawn at random from their respective industries, do not rule out with great certainty the possibility that the true mean "union, nonunion wage differential" in six of the seven industries was zero. On the other hand, the statistical

TABLE 12

DISTRIBUTION OF MAHER'S WAGE COMPARISONS (CELLS) BY INDUSTRY AND
NUMBER OF CITIES AND OCCUPATIONS COVERED IN EACH INDUSTRY

INDUSTRY	NUMBER OF WAGE COMPARISONS (CELLS) (1)	NUMBER OF CITIES COVERED (2)	NUMBER OF OCCUPATIONS COVERED	
			Nonwhite Collar (3)	White Collar (4)
Paints and varnishes.....	172	11	11	4
Wooden furniture........	126	8	12	2
Footwear..............	39	5	4	2
Cotton textiles.........	24	2	12	2
Hosiery...............	20	3	5	3
Automotive parts........	23	1	16	0
Women's dresses........	6	1	5	0

insignificance does not imply that unionism truly had a negligible effect on the average relative wage of each of the industries except wooden furniture, or even that the best estimate of these effects was zero.

TABLE 13

MEAN DIFFERENTIAL BY INDUSTRY

Industry	Mean Differential (Cents per Hour)
Paints and varnishes..............	−0.67
Wooden furniture................	+7.57
Footwear......................	−3.72
Cotton textiles..................	+1.83
Hosiery........................	+4.90
Automotive parts................	+4.35
Women's dresses.................	+9.80

Three problems arise in using Maher's data to estimate the impact of unionization on the average relative wage of union workers in each of the seven industries included in his study.

1. It is likely that the relative wage effects of unionism varied considerably within each of the seven industries from one "cell" to another. Under these circumstances, *nonrandom* samples of the cells, such as Maher's, may contain substantial, though unknown, sample *bias*, particularly when the samples are small.

2. For estimating *relative* wage effects of unionism, the figures in Table 13 must be converted into percentage differentials by dividing each figure by the corresponding mean wage of the nonunion workers included in the calculation of the mean absolute differential. Maher's paper does not provide these nonunion mean wage figures. Furthermore, since his

samples were not drawn at random from each industry, it cannot be presumed that these mean wage figures are close to the corresponding means for each industry as a whole. However, to obtain at least rough estimates of the union/nonunion percentage differentials, I have divided each of the figures in Table 13 by the corresponding average hourly earnings in the industry in 1950.[50] Table 14 contains these estimates.

3. The mean percentage differential in wages between the "union" and "nonunion" *plants* in a particular industry may differ conceptually from the effect of unionism on the average wage of union labor in the industry relative to the average wage of the industry's nonunion labor because, as pointed out earlier, some of the workers in union *plants* (that

TABLE 14

ESTIMATES OF MEAN UNION/NONUNION WAGE
DIFFERENTIALS BY INDUSTRY

Industry	Differential (Per Cent)
Paints and varnishes	0
Wooden furniture	+6
Footwear	−3
Cotton textiles	+2
Hosiery	+4
Automotive parts	+2
Women's dresses	+7

is, plants in which at least half the workers were covered by collective-bargaining agreements) may not have been covered by collective-bargaining agreements. Thus it is likely that the white-collar workers (see Table 12) were nonunion in both union and nonunion plants. Similarly, some workers in nonunion plants may have been covered by collective-bargaining agreements. A crude allowance for the effect of this factor would raise the figures in Table 14 for wooden furniture by about one percentage point and that for hosiery by about two to three percentage points.[51]

---

[50] I computed the average hourly earnings figures from U.S. Bureau of the Census, *Annual Survey of Manufactures: 1949 and 1950* (Washington, 1952), Table 1.

[51] The assumptions underlying my calculation of the adjustment factors were:
1. All white-collar workers were nonunion.
2. Nonwhite-collar workers were unionized in union plants, but nonunion in nonunion plants.
3. The relative frequency of white-collar cells among all cells was approximately equal to the ratio of col. (4) to the sum of cols. (3) and (4) in Table 12.
4. White-collar wages were the same in both union and nonunion plants.
I did not apply the adjustment factor to the footwear industry.

In summary, Maher's study leads me to the following rough estimates of the effects of unionism on the union/nonunion relative wage in each of the seven manufacturing industries in 1950:

Paints and varnishes, footwear, cotton textiles, and automotive parts: about 0 per cent.
Wooden furniture, hosiery, and women's dresses: about 7 per cent.

III.8. Joseph L. Craycraft: Barbers, 1948 and 1954[52]

In an unpublished paper, Professor Craycraft estimated the effects of unionism in barbershops on the relative earnings of barbers from cross-section data covering twenty large cities in 1948 and 1954. The cities, those for which the Bureau of Labor Statistics published data on the price of haircuts, were:

Atlanta	Cleveland	Minneapolis	St. Louis
Baltimore	Detroit	New York	San Francisco
Boston	Houston	Philadelphia	Scranton
Chicago	Kansas City	Pittsburgh	Seattle
Cincinnati	Los Angeles	Portland	Washington, D.C.

For each of these areas Craycraft estimated the degree of organization, X, of barbers by dividing the membership (as of December, 1956) of the Journeyman Barbers, Hairdressers, Cosmetologists and Proprietors International Union of America in the area by the number of barbershop proprietors and employees for the workweek ending nearest November 15, 1954. The employment data in the denominators were obtained from the 1954 *Census of Business* and pertained to the standard metropolitan areas with the above names. These estimates of extent of unionism in barbershops, he recognized, were crude because (a) the union membership and employment data were for dates two years apart; (b) the Barbers Union has members employed outside barbershops, for example, in beauty shops; (c) not all *union* barbers are represented by the Barbers Union; and (d) the boundaries of the city areas for which the membership data were supplied may not have been the same as those of the *Census* standard metropolitan areas of the same name.

Craycraft calculated the average annual earnings, W, of barbershop employees for each of the twenty standard metropolitan areas in 1948 and 1954 from payroll and employment data in the 1948 and 1954 business censuses. He correlated the average wage, W, among cities with

[52] Joseph L. Craycraft, "A Cross-Section Analysis of the Effect of Unionism on the Relative Earnings of Barbers" (unpublished A.M. paper, University of Chicago, 1957). Mr. Craycraft wrote his paper under my supervision.

the degree of organization, X. The regression coefficients of W on X (each divided by the corresponding twenty-city mean of W) for the two dates were:

1948: 0.18 per cent per percentage point difference in extent of unionism.
1954: 0.27 per cent per percentage point difference in extent of unionism.

These numbers, Craycraft judged, contained not only the effects of barber unionization but also effects of other factors on the differences among the cities in barber earnings. To control, at least roughly, for these other factors, he divided the annual earnings of barbers, W, in each city area by the corresponding average annual earnings, W_s, of employees in selected service trades[53] for which payroll and employment data were reported in the 1948 and 1954 business censuses. The regression co-efficients (each divided by the twenty-city mean ratio of W to W_s) of the barber/service trade earnings ratios, $Y = W/W_s$, on degree of organization were:

1948: 0.02 per cent per percentage point difference in extent of unionism.
1954: 0.19 per cent per percentage point difference in extent of unionism.

Thus the expression of barbers' earnings as ratios to the earnings of workers in selected service trades eliminated the apparent wage differential effect of barber unionization in the 1948 data and reduced the estimated effect in the 1954 data by one-third.

In six of the twenty city areas, according to the 1950 *Census of Population*, there was an appreciable difference between the ratio of white male to total male persons employed as "barbers, beauticians, and manicurists" and the ratio of white males to total male persons employed as "service workers, except private household." Therefore, Craycraft also calculated the regressions of the barber/service earnings ratio, $Y = W/W_s$, on degree of organization, X, and the difference (estimated from the 1950 *Census of Population*) between the fraction of male barbers who were white and the corresponding fraction for male service workers. The partial regression coefficients (each divided by the corresponding twenty-city mean value of Y) of Y on X were:

1948: 0.01 per cent per percentage point difference in extent of unionism.
1954: 0.19 per cent per percentage point difference in extent of unionism.

[53] The selected service trades were:
  1948: personal services, business services, automobile repair services and garages, and miscellaneous repair services.
  1954: the industry groups covered in 1948 and, in addition, amusement and recreation services, motion pictures, and hotels, motels, tourist courts, and camps.

These coefficients, which are almost the same as those of the preceding paragraph, suggest that barber unionization had little or no effect on the relative wages of union barbers in 1948 and a positive effect of about 19 per cent in 1954.

These estimates, however, are subject to the same types of bias as those affecting the estimates for the building trades derived similarly from Sobotka's study (see pp. 65–70):

1. They may be biased downward by a positive correlation among cities between the extent of unionism of barbers and the effects of unionism on the relative wages of employees in the service trades base group. In the United States as a whole the extent of unionism of employees in the service trades group was low (see chap. vii, p. 250, Table 74). Undoubtedly, employees in these service industries were somewhat more extensively unionized in the twenty large cities included in Craycraft's study than in the United States as a whole. I doubt that the differences among the cities in degree of unionization of these employees, however, were large or much correlated with corresponding differences in unionization of barbers. Consequently, I judge that the amount of this downward bias was small.

2. As pointed out earlier, Craycraft's estimates, X, of the extent of unionism of barbers by city are crude. Errors in X probably tend to make the regression coefficients of Y on X too low.[54] The variance of X among the twenty cities was 545 per cent squared, equivalent to a standard deviation of X of 23.3 per cent. This variance is not so large that it suggests serious errors in estimating the X's.

3. Since within each of the twenty cities the services of nonunion barber shops are substitutes in demand for those of union shops, it is probably true that the effects of unionism on the wages of *union* barbers relative to the wages of nonunion barbers were positively correlated among the cities with the extent of unionism of barbers. Under these circumstances the regression coefficient estimates tend to exceed the average union/nonunion relative wage effect of unionism for barbers.[55]

The relative "wage" concept underlying Craycraft's estimates is that of relative *annual earnings*. Unfortunately, data by city on the hours of work of barbers are not available. However, it is more likely that barber unionism lowered the relative hours of work of union barbers than that it increased or had no effect on relative hours; hence I suspect that the effect of barber unionism on the relative annual earnings of union barbers was less than the corresponding effect on the relative wage per man-hour of labor service.

Three of the biases discussed in the preceding paragraphs were in the

[54] Turn to n. 30 above, p. 67. If the errors of measurement, $\epsilon = X - p$, were uncorrelated with p, then

$$\sigma_X^2 = \sigma_p^2 + \sigma_\epsilon^2.$$

[55] See chap. ii, pp. 31 ff.

downward direction; the fourth was an upward bias. I doubt that the combined effect of the four sources of bias was large, and I can only guess that the biases made Craycraft's estimates too low rather than too high.

Labor cost per haircut is a substantial fraction of the price of a haircut. Moreover, the establishment of uniform schedules of prices of barbershop services among union shops in given city areas is commonly an inseparable part of the setting of union wage scales for barbers. Thus there is reason to expect that barber unionization would have roughly the same percentage impact on haircut prices as on barber wages. Craycraft calculated the regression among the twenty city areas of the average price of haircuts, as reported by the Bureau of Labor Statistics for October–December, 1955, on degree of organization. The regression coefficient (divided by the twenty-city mean haircut price) of haircut price on degree of organization was 0.36 per cent per percentage point difference in extent of unionism. This result suggests that barber unionization may have had a considerably larger effect on haircut price differentials than on barber wage differentials among cities.

This estimate is probably biased upward substantially by the effects of factors other than unionism that are positively correlated among the cities with the extent of barber unionism. In this respect the estimate is more nearly comparable to Craycraft's first estimate, 0.27 per cent (in 1954), of the relative *wage* impact of barber unionism than to his more highly adjusted relative wage effect estimates.

Furthermore, as Craycraft pointed out, the regression coefficient of reported average haircut prices on degree of organization may contain an upward bias resulting from the BLS procedure in collecting haircut price data. Agents of the Bureau interviewed barber-union officers in each locality regarding the degree of unionization of barbershops in the locality. In city areas in which, according to the union officers, the degree of unionization was at least 75 per cent, the haircut price figures reported by the Bureau were the uniform price scales established for union shops.[56] In other localities the Bureau's reported haircut price averages

[56] The Bureau did not disclose the names of the cities for which the reported haircut price was the uniform price set for union shops. However, it is very likely that these were the cities for which the reported haircut price was a round figure—$1.50, $1.75, etc.—that remained unchanged for a period of months before changing in stepwise fashion to a new round figure. Fifteen of the twenty cities included by Craycraft in his study displayed such haircut price characteristics in the figures reported by the BLS. For eight of these fifteen cities his estimates of the degree of unionization of barbershop employees and proprietors were below 50 per cent, indicating either (a) that his estimates of degree of unionization were badly in error or (b) that the BLS agents were misled by their interviews with local union officers regarding the extent to which barbershops were unionized.

were based on sample surveys of both union and nonunion shops. Haircut prices were surely higher typically in union than in nonunion shops. Thus the BLS haircut price data used by Craycraft probably contained measurement errors that were positively correlated among the twenty city areas with the degree of organization of the areas. Such errors would tend to bias upward the regression coefficient of haircut prices on degree of organization.

Both casual observation and economic analysis suggest that differences in haircut prices between union and nonunion shops reflect, to a considerable extent, differences in services performed: customer waiting time is less and the haircut better in union shops. Given these service differences, it is quite possible that barber unionism and the associated fixing of minimum prices in union shops would have a larger impact on relative haircut prices than on relative wages of barbers.

III.9. ELTON RAYACK: MEN'S CLOTHING MANUFACTURING, 1919–57[57]

Unionization of wage-earners employed in the manufacture of men's, youths', and boys' suits, coats, and overcoats—in short, men's clothing— began in 1914 with the formation of the Amalgamated Clothing Workers of America (ACWA). By 1919 the ACWA had organized well over half, perhaps three-fourths, of the wage-earners in the industry. During the 1920's and until 1933, however, the extent of unionism in the industry declined and in 1933 may have been less than 50 per cent. With the coming of the New Deal the union quickly organized most of the industry; since 1935, nonunion employment in the industry has probably accounted for less than 10 per cent of total wage-earner employment in the industry.

Table 15 contains Professor Rayack's classification of the major producing centers by degree of unionization and his estimates for these cities of *adjusted* average hourly earnings of wage-earners for the period 1911–32. Rayack derived his estimates of average hourly earnings, before adjustment, from data collected periodically in the industry by the Bureau of Labor Statistics during 1911–32. The wage data gathered in each of the Bureau's surveys covered only a part of each of the years indicated in Table 15, and large employers were markedly overrepresented in the Bureau's samples. The figures in the table, therefore, may

[57] Elton Rayack, "The Effect of Unionism on Wages in the Men's Clothing Industry, 1911–1955," (unpublished Ph.D. dissertation, University of Chicago, 1957). Mr. Rayack wrote his dissertation under a faculty committee of which I was a member. For a condensed version of his study, see his "The Impact of Unionism on Wages in the Men's Clothing Industry, 1911–1956," *Labor Law Journal*, IX, No. 9 (September, 1958), 674–88.

contain substantial sampling errors and biases. Rayack adjusted these hourly earnings estimates essentially by dividing each figure by an estimate, based on data from the *Census of Manufactures*, for the same city and date of average annual earnings in all manufacturing industries. The purpose of the adjustment was to eliminate the effects of factors other than unionism on the differences among the cities in average hourly earnings in men's clothing.

To estimate the effect of the ACWA on relative average hourly earnings of union workers for the years 1919–26, Rayack compared the employment weighted mean adjusted average hourly earnings of five strongly unionized cities (New York, Chicago, Rochester, Boston, and

TABLE 15

Adjusted Average Hourly Earnings in Men's Clothing Manufacturing, Major Producing Centers, 1911–32*

(Cents per Hour)

Line Number	City	1911–13 Average	1919	1922	1924	1926	1928	1930	1932
1...	New York[a]	25.2 n	52.7 u	84.7 u	88.9 u	87.6 u	85.9 u	79.9 u	58.3 u
2...	Chicago	23.2 n	46.3 u	78.1 u	87.8 u	92.3 u	93.4 u	84.9 u	57.9 u
3...	Rochester	25.0 n	50.1 u	65.4 u	75.7 u	81.4 u	79.4 u	80.8 u	62.8 u
4...	Boston	...	57.6 u	67.4 u	79.9 u	85.6 p	83.0 p	82.7 p	55.8 p
5...	Cincinnati	24.5 n	40.1 n	70.4 n	78.6 n	83.0 p	87.0 u	81.8 u	55.9 u
6...	Baltimore	25.1 n	61.1 u	89.1 u	83.6 u	82.6 u	64.0 n	59.0 n	38.8 n
7...	Philadelphia	24.8 n	44.6 n	64.2 n	70.3 n	77.6 n	71.3 n	73.5 u	57.0 u
8...	Buffalo	...	37.4 n	...	...	67.3 n	58.8 n	64.4 n	40.2 n
9...	St. Louis	...	41.3 n	...	...	67.8 n	66.8 n	61.1 n	43.0 n
10...	Cleveland	...	39.4 n	...	...	66.2 n	64.8 n	60.5 n	46.6 n
11...	Union mean	...	51.0	78.5	85.3	87.3	...	...	...
12...	Nonunion mean	...	42.5	67.1	74.8	77.6	...	...	...
13...	Line 11 ÷ line 12	...	1.20	1.17	1.14	1.12	...	...	...
14...	Mean of "u" cities	...	51.7	79.8	85.7	87.6	87.4	80.7	58.4
15...	Mean of "n" cities	24.6	41.8	66.5	73.4	72.3	67.0	60.2	42.0
16...	Line 14 ÷ line 15	...	1.24	1.20	1.17	1.21	1.30	1.34	1.39

* Sources: Ll. 1–10 are from Rayack dissertation, pp. 18–26 and Tables 17 and 19; l. 11, employment weighted mean of figures for New York, Chicago, Rochester, Boston, and Baltimore given in Rayack dissertation, Tables 11 and 16; l. 12, employment weighted mean of figures for Cincinnati and Philadelphia given in Rayack dissertation, Tables 11 and 16 (1926 figure is for Philadelphia only); l. 14, employment weighted mean of figures for "u" cities; l. 15, employment weighted mean of figures for "n" cities.
Essentially the same data as are shown on ll. 1–13 are contained in Rayack's "The Impact of Unionism on Wages in the Men's Clothing Industry," pp. 680–82 and 684, Tables 5–7 and 9.
[a] The letter "u" denotes strongly unionized cities; "n," weakly unionized or nonunion cities; and "p" denotes partial unionization.

Baltimore) with the corresponding mean for one or two weakly unionized or nonunion cities (Cincinnati and Philadelphia in 1919–24, Philadelphia in 1926). Notice that in 1911–13, before the formation of the ACWA, there was very little dispersion among the cities in adjusted hourly earnings. The means for the union cities are on line 11, those for the nonunion cities on line 12, and the ratio of the first to the second on line 13. From the ratios on line 13, Rayack estimated that the effect of the ACWA on the average relative wage of union workers declined steadily from about 20 per cent in 1919 to about 12 per cent in 1926. Because of changes in unionization status among the cities, he did not make similar estimates for 1928–32.

In order to extend the estimates to 1932 and to make use of all of the data available in Table 15, I have made the calculations shown on lines 14 to 16. Line 14 is the employment weighted[58] mean adjusted average hourly earnings of all of the strongly unionized ("u") cities in each year, line 15 the corresponding mean for the weakly unionized and nonunion ("n") cities, and line 16 the ratio of line 14 to line 15. The ratios on line 16 indicate that the effect of the ACWA on relative wages of union workers in the industry may have been higher rather than lower, in 1928–32 than in the early 1920's. However, imperfections in the adjustment of average hourly earnings for factors other than unionism, sampling biases in the underlying BLS data, and differences from one date to another in the cities surveyed by the Bureau and in the unionization status of the cities make date-to-date comparisons of the figures on line 16 unreliable indicators of the "trend" in the relative wage effects of the ACWA.

Three of the cities in the table experienced a reversal of their unionization status during 1919–32. Baltimore, strongly unionized in the early 1920's with adjusted hourly earnings above the average for unionized cities, was nonunion in 1928–32 with adjusted hourly earnings below the average for the nonunion cities. Both Cincinnati and Philadelphia, weakly unionized in the early 1920's, became strongly unionized by 1930, and their relative wage position increased substantially from 1919–24 to 1930–32. These positively correlated changes in unionization and relative wage position thus support the ratios on line 16 as estimates of the effect of the ACWA on relative wages of union workers.

Given relative wage effects of the size of those estimated on lines 13 and 16, one would expect employment in union cities to drop relative to

[58] Rayack did not report the weights he used in computing the means on ll. 11 and 12 of Table 14 and, therefore, I have been unable to compute means on ll. 14 and 15 that use his weighting system. The weight I used for each city was the 1923–29 average of the four relative employment figures for the city given in Table 16. (For Buffalo the weight was 1 per cent of the total weight of the ten cities in Table 15.)

Comparison of the 1922 and 1924 figures on l. 13 with the corresponding figures on l. 16 indicates that my weighting system yielded slightly higher estimates of relative wage effects than Rayack's.

employment in nonunion cities. Table 16, which is from Rayack's study (pp. 18–26 and Table 20), shows that such declines in relative employment did occur.

TABLE 16

DISTRIBUTIONS OF WAGE-EARNER EMPLOYMENT IN MAJOR
PRODUCING CENTERS, MEN'S CLOTHING, 1923–29
(Per Cent)

City	1923	1925	1927	1929
New York.........	23.8 u	21.0 u	21.0 u	19.0 u
Chicago..........	18.1 u	15.0 u	13.3 u	11.8 u
Rochester........	6.9 u	7.1 u	7.8 u	7.1 u
Boston...........	3.0 u	2.7 u	2.9 p	2.6 p
Cincinnati........	3.8 n	4.7 n	4.8 p	3.9 u
Baltimore........	5.0 u	6.2 u	5.7 p	6.3 n
Philadelphia......	5.9 n	6.3 n	7.1 n	7.2 n
St. Louis.........	2.1 n	2.4 n	2.6 n	2.6 n
Cleveland........	2.9 n	3.2 n	3.1 n	3.8 n
Rest of U.S......	28.5 n	31.4 n	31.7 n	35.7 n

Rayack's estimates of the relative wage impact of the ACWA during 1932–55 rest largely on comparisons of the ratio of average hourly earnings in men's clothing to average hourly earnings in all manufacturing industries for given dates with the corresponding value of this ratio in the pre-union base period (1911–13). In the base period, average hourly earnings in the men's clothing industry were approximately the same as average hourly earnings in all manufacturing industries. It is instructive to compare the estimates yielded by these time series comparisons in 1919–32 with the cross-section estimates of Table 15.

Table 17 presents index numbers (1911–13 = 100) of average hourly earnings in the men's clothing industry [col. (1)], average hourly earnings in all manufacturing industries [col. (3)], and the ratio of the first to the second [col. (4)]. The average hourly earnings estimates for men's clothing in column (1) derive, for the most part, from the same BLS survey data that underlie Table 15. Because of quite substantial differences from survey to survey in coverage within and among cities, the figures in column (1) undoubtedly contain some sizable errors. The average hourly earnings series in column (3) is that of the Bureau for the years 1919–32, with a small adjustment to make the series conform in dating to column (1). The figure in column (3) for 1911–13 is based on BLS figures for 1909 and 1914 and Paul Douglas's annual estimates for all manufacturing ("payroll" industries) in the period 1909–14.

During 1911–32 the extent of unionism of wage-earners in manufacturing, on the average, probably differed little from the extent of

TABLE 17

AVERAGE HOURLY EARNINGS IN MEN'S CLOTHING MANUFACTURING AND IN ALL MANUFACTURING, 1911–32*

| YEAR | AVERAGE HOURLY EARNINGS (1911–13 = 100) | | | RATIO OF COL. 1 TO | | EXTENT OF UNIONISM | | RELATIVE WAGE EFFECT (SEE TEXT) | |
| | Men's Clothing | | Manufacturing (3) | Col. (3) (4) | Col. (2) (5) | In Men's Clothing (6) | Excess over Labor Force (7) | (8) | (9) |
	All (1)	Nonunion (2)							
1911–13.........	100	100	100	1.00	1.00	..	..	..	..
1919............	244	219	220	1.11	1.11	0.73	0.63	0.15–0.19	0.15
1922............	310	270	219	1.42	1.15	0.88	0.78	0.48–0.53	0.17
1924............	323	298	252	1.28	1.08	0.83	0.75	0.34–0.38	0.10
1926............	319	294	253	1.26	1.09	0.73	0.65	0.37–0.41	0.13
1928............	311	272	259	1.20	1.14	0.63	0.55	0.34–0.38	0.23
1930............	298	245	255	1.17	1.22	0.70	0.62	0.25–0.28	0.33
1932............	215	171	198	1.09	1.26	0.70	0.62	0.13–0.16	0.39

* Sources: Cols. (1) and (3) were computed from Rayack dissertation, Table 7 (the average hourly earnings data in the latter table are also contained in his "The Impact of Unionism on Wages in the Men's Clothing Industry, 1911–1956," p. 677, Table 2); col. (2) was computed from l. 15, Table 15 [1919 figure has been adjusted to make it comparable to 1919 figure in col. (1)]; col. (6) is estimated extent of unionism in cities covered by BLS surveys (see Bureau of Labor Statistics Bulletins 265, 329, 387, 435, 557, and 594), method of estimation described in n. 59 below; col. (7) is col. (6) minus estimates of extent of unionism in labor force as a whole given in chap. vii, Table 72, p. 244.

unionism in the labor force as a whole, so that it is reasonable to suppose that relative wages in manufacturing were affected inappreciably by unionism. Assume that in 1911–32 the average relative wage differential between the men's clothing industry and all manufacturing industries was inconsequentially affected by factors other than unionism in the men's clothing industry. Then the figures in column (4) are Variant A-I type indexes, R, of the effect of unionism on the average relative wage of union and nonunion workers taken together in men's clothing. The figures on line 16 of Table 15, however, estimate the effect of unionism on the average wage of union workers relative to the average wage of nonunion workers in men's clothing—that is, in the notation of chapter ii, they estimate (the antilogarithm of) B in men's clothing.

To make the figures in column (4) comparable to those on line 16 of Table 15, I have used the same conversion formula, equation (30′), that I applied in Table 9 for bituminous coal mining (see p. 78) with $\bar{B}$ set equal to zero and, alternatively, to 0.25. In column (6) I show admittedly crude estimates of the extent of unionism of the men's clothing wage-earners included in column (1).[59] Column (7) is the excess of column (6) over the estimates given in Table 72 of chapter vii of the extent of unionism in the whole labor force. The figures in column (8) are the antilogarithms, less unity, of the estimates of B (the effect of unionism on the average wage of union workers relative to the average wage of nonunion workers in men's clothing) resulting from the application of equation (30′) to the data in columns (4), (6), and (7). The estimates in column (8) are much higher than those on line 16 of Table 15 for the years 1922–26, much lower in 1932, and the trend in column (8) is the reverse of that on line 16, Table 15.

Column (2) of Table 17 is line 15 of Table 15 expressed as an index number series. Because of date-to-date differences in the cities included in the computation of line 15, this index is a rough estimate, at best, of the true index of average hourly earnings of nonunion workers in men's clothing. Column (5) is the ratio of column (1) to column (2). The figures in this column are Variant A-II type indexes, the given group comprising all wage-earners in the industry and the benchmark group the nonunion workers. In the notation of chapter ii, the logarithms of column (5) are

---

[59] The BLS bulletins containing the wage data underlying col. (1) show the number of men's clothing wage-earners covered in each of the Bureau's surveys by city. Using Rayack's classification of the cities by unionization status, I estimated the extent of unionism of the workers included in col. (1) as the ratio of the sum of the number of covered workers in strongly unionized cities and half the number in partially unionized cities to the total number of wage-earners covered in all of the cities surveyed.

$$p \log R_u + (1 - p) \log R_n - \log R_n = p \log (R_u/R_n) = pB.$$

Hence to convert column (5) to estimates of B, it is necessary to divide the logarithms of column (5) by column (6). The antilogarithms, less unity, of the resulting estimates of B are the figures in column (9) of Table 17. The series in column (9) is somewhat lower than the series in line 16 of Table 15, except in 1930 and 1932, but otherwise resembles the latter rather closely.

The differences between the estimates in column (8) and those in column (9) stem almost entirely from the differences between columns (2) and (3). Are the differences between the latter columns mainly the result of (a) effects of the ACWA on average hourly earnings of men's clothing wage-earners in weakly unionized and nonunion cities or (b) effects of factors other than unionism, including errors of measurement? The ACWA conceivably could have caused men's clothing wages in nonunion and weakly unionized cities to have been higher than they otherwise would have been, for (1) by raising wages, costs, and prices in union cities relative to nonunion and weakly unionized cities, the ACWA increased the relative demand for labor in men's clothing manufacture in the latter cities, and (2) some firms in the latter cities may have raised the relative wages of their employees with the thought of preventing or postponing their unionization. This explanation, however, fits the data in Table 17 poorly.[60]

I think it is much more likely that the differences between the two columns were the result of statistical and economic factors other than unionism. For example, a considerable part of the apparent decline in wages in men's clothing relative to manufacturing from 1922 to 1932 may be the result of greater coverage and reduced bias in the Bureau of Labor Statistics sample surveys of wages in men's clothing manufacture (Rayack, pp. 36–37). Furthermore, *Census of Manufactures* data cited by Rayack (his Table 2) show that value added by manufacture in the men's clothing industry relative to all manufacturing industries increased from 1919 to 1921 and then declined by about 40 per cent by 1929. These data indicate that the relative demand for labor in men's clothing decreased greatly during the 1920's.

Table 18 presents average hourly earnings indexes for the men's clothing industry and for all manufacturing industries for the period 1933–57. The index of average hourly earnings in men's clothing manufacture was computed from the series used by Rayack. However, for

---

[60] On this explanation, the 1919–32 figures in col. (2) of Table 17 should exceed the corresponding figures in col. (3), yet only four of the seven observations meet this test.

manufacturing [col. (2)] I have used Albert Rees's historical series for manufacturing in preference to the BLS series Rayack used. The esti-

TABLE 18

AVERAGE HOURLY EARNINGS IN MEN'S CLOTHING AND IN
MANUFACTURING, 1933–57*

| YEAR | AVERAGE HOURLY EARNINGS (1911–13 = 100) | | | EXCESS EXTENT OF UNIONISM | (SEE TEXT) |
	Men's Clothing (1)	Manufac- turing (2)	(1) ÷ (2) (3)	(4)	(5)
1933	233	208	1.12	?	?
1934	333	249	1.34	0.88	+0.36 to +0.39
1935	327	256	1.28	0.87	+0.30 to +0.33
1936	310	258	1.20	0.87	+0.21 to +0.24
1937	326	289	1.13	0.80	+0.14 to +0.18
1938	325	287	1.13	0.78	+0.14 to +0.19
1939	299	287	1.04	0.77	+0.04 to +0.09
1943	424	445	0.95	0.71	−0.05 to +0.01
1946–48 . . .	635	582	1.09	0.70	+0.09 to +0.17
1953	785	862	0.91	0.68	−0.09 to −0.03
1957	885	995	0.89	0.69	−0.12 to −0.05

* Sources: Col. (1) was computed from average hourly earnings figures in Rayack dissertation, Tables 7 and 10 (1957 average hourly earnings figure from Bureau of Labor Statistics, *Employment and Earnings*, 5, No. 11 [May, 1959], Table SC-1); col. (2) was computed from average hourly earnings figures in Rees, *Real Wages in Manufacturing, 1890–1914*, Table 10, and Rees, *New Measures of Wage-Earner Compensation in Manufacturing, 1914–1957*, Table 1; col. (4) equals 0.95 minus figures (divided by 100) in Table 72 of chap. vii.

mates in column (4) of the excess of extent of unionism in men's clothing over the extent of unionism in the whole labor force assume that throughout 1934–57 the extent of unionism in men's clothing was 95 per cent. For the labor force as a whole I have used the extent of unionism estimates given in chapter vii, Table 72.

The figures in column (5) are my computations rather than Rayack's. They are estimates, comparable to those in column (8) of Table 17, of the effect of unionism on wages of union workers relative to wages of nonunion workers in men's clothing manufacture which assume that (a) unionism had a negligible impact on relative wages in manufacturing as a whole and (b) the changes from the base date (1911–13) to given dates in the relative average hourly earnings differential between men's clothing and all manufacturing were mainly the result of unionization in the men's clothing industry. Rayack emphasized that these assumptions were, at best, rough approximations to the truth.

The apparently great effect of the ACWA on relative wages of union workers in men's clothing in 1934 and 1935 Rayack attributed in large part to the "powerful assistance" received by the ACWA from the labor provisions of the NIRA code in the men's clothing industry. He explained the 1935–39 decline in the apparent effect of the ACWA in terms of three factors: (a) the great growth of unionism in manufacturing industries, (b) the large decline in the relative demand for labor in the men's clothing industry, and (c) the demise of the NIRA codes. He did not attempt to estimate the combined effect of these factors.

If unionism in 1939 raised average relative wages in manufacturing by approximately 3 to 6 per cent,[61] then allowance for this factor would raise the 1939 figure in column (3) to about 1.07 to 1.10. From 1933 to 1939, value added by manufacture in men's clothing declined by about one-third relative to value added by manufacture in all manufacturing industries (Rayack, Tables 2 and 4). A decline of this size in the relative demand for labor in men's clothing might very well have caused average hourly earnings in men's clothing to fall by something like 5 per cent relative to average hourly earnings in manufacturing. Such an effect, combined with the effect of unionization in manufacturing industries, would raise the 1939 figure in column (3) to about 1.12 to 1.16 and the 1939 range in column (5) to about 0.13 to 0.23.

For the whole period 1940–55, Rayack estimated that the effect of the ACWA on relative wages in the men's clothing industry did not exceed 5 per cent. Indeed, despite the rather high level of average hourly earnings in men's clothing relative to average hourly earnings in manufacturing immediately following World War II, Rayack stated that the ACWA may have made relative wages in men's clothing lower than they would have been in the absence of unionization in the industry. In support of this position he cited newspaper and trade reports of labor shortages in the industry and of the payment of wages above those required in union contracts. The latter, of course, does not imply that unionism had a *negative* effect on relative wages in the industry. Moreover, evidence that labor shortages existed in the industry is too imprecise to demonstrate conclusively that the effects of unionization on relative wages of union workers on the average were negative rather than small and positive.[62]

If the effect of the ACWA on relative wages in men's clothing manufacturing was small—5 per cent or less—in 1946–48, then the data in

[61] See p. 72 and pp. 190 ff.

[62] In this connection, see the discussion on pp. 49–53 of the reports of labor shortages in basic steel manufacturing in 1945–47.

Although I have accepted Rayack's estimate that the impact of the ACWA on relative wages in men's clothing did not exceed 5 per cent after the early 1940's, I regard this estimate as highly tentative, particularly for the years 1946–48.

columns (3) and (5) of Table 18 are a formidable hurdle to a finding that the relative wage effect of the ACWA was positive in the 1950's. Rayack noted that four factors may have caused average hourly earnings in men's clothing to decline relative to average hourly earnings in all manufacturing industries after 1946–48:

1. "Fringe benefits" per hour in men's clothing manufacture rose relative to corresponding benefits on the average in all manufacturing.

2. The ratio of female to male wage-earners increased somewhat more in the men's clothing industry than in other manufacturing industries on the average.

3. In the middle and late 1950's, unionism may have raised average relative wages in manufacturing industries.

He estimated that allowance for these three factors would raise the ratio of average hourly earnings in men's clothing to average hourly earnings in all manufacturing by roughly 8 per cent, that is, the figures in column (3) for 1953 and 1957 would be increased by about 0.07.

4. The demand for labor in men's clothing manufacture relative to that in all manufacturing declined sharply after 1946–48. From 1947 to 1953 the ratio of value added by manufacture in men's clothing to value added by manufacture in all manufacturing industries fell by almost one-half (Rayack, Table 4). If this decline in relative demand reduced average hourly earnings in men's clothing relative to average hourly earnings in manufacturing by about 5 per cent, then the effect of the decline, combined with the effects of the other three factors, would make the figures for 1953 and 1957 in columns (3) and (5) of Table 18 positive, though small.

Finally, it should be added, the index in column (1) may contain significant measurement errors, for it rests on an estimate of average hourly earnings in 1911–13 derived from wage data obtained by the Bureau of Labor Statistics from non-probability samples of wages in selected cities, occupations, and establishments. Although Rayack attempted to correct for sampling bias in the base period average hourly earnings, the data from which the bias correction factor was estimated were for the 1920's. Thus it is quite conceivable that there may be an error as large, say, as 10 per cent in the base of the index in column (1).

III.10. STEPHEN SOBOTKA AND OTHERS: COMMERCIAL AIRLINE PILOTS, 1956[63]

Commercial airline pilots in the United States have been fully unionized by the Air Line Pilots Association since the early 1940's. In 1956 the average number of pilots employed on U.S. scheduled airlines was about

[63] Stephen Sobotka et al., "Analysis of Airline Pilot Earnings" (unpublished mimeographed MS, Transportation Center, Northwestern University, 1958).

12,000 and their mean annual earnings about \$12,000. The study discussed here, written by the staff of the Transportation Center, is an economic and statistical analysis of the earnings of these pilots and of the elements in their pay structure.

Although the study presents evidence suggesting that the Air Line Pilots Association may have raised the relative wages of airline pilots throughout much of the period 1933–56, the most detailed evidence is for 1956. For that year the authors estimated (or provided data from which estimates could easily be made):

Y_p, the present value at age twenty-five of expected future lifetime earnings of airline pilots as airline pilots (that is, excluding expected earnings of former pilots after their being "grounded" and transferring to alternative pursuits) under 1956 conditions;

Y_{gp}, the present value at age twenty-five of expected future lifetime earnings of former pilots (that is, the expected future earnings of grounded airline pilots in alternative pursuits) under 1956 conditions;

Y_e, the present value at age twenty-five of expected future lifetime earnings of chemical engineers, the nonunion benchmark group, both as chemical engineers and as former chemical engineers who transfer to other pursuits, under 1956 conditions; and

T_p, T_e, the accumulated value to age twenty-five of the net cost of training airline pilots and chemical engineers, respectively, under 1956 conditions.

Then to a first approximation, the percentage effect of the Air Line Pilots Association on the relative wage position of airline pilots relative to the absence of effective unionization of these pilots is[64]

$$100 \left[\frac{Y_p}{(Y_e - Y_{gp}) - (T_e - T_p)} - 1 \right].$$

[64] Let B be the effect, in per cent, of the Air Line Pilots Association on the relative wages of airline pilots. Then in the absence of unionization of the airline pilots, the present value at age twenty-five of expected net lifetime earnings of airline pilots (including their earnings as both pilots and former pilots in other pursuits, but net of their training costs) would be

$$Y_{gp} - T_p + \frac{100 Y_p}{100 + B}.$$

The corresponding net present value for chemical engineers is $(Y_e - T_e)$. If chemical engineers are a fully appropriate benchmark group, then in the absence of unionization of airline pilots the two present values would be equal:

$$Y_e - T_e = Y_{gp} - T_p + \frac{100 Y_p}{100 + B}. \tag{a}$$

The solution of this equation for B is the formula given in the text.

In their calculations of the present values of expected lifetime earnings of pilots and

The key figures are: $V_p = \$193,500$; $Y_e - Y_{gp} = \$160,200$; and $T_e - T_p = +\$3,600$ if Air Force trained or $-\$13,200$ if privately trained (single- and multi-engine craft, 1,178 flight training hours). If the Air Force training figure is applicable, the estimated percentage relative wage effect of

engineers, the authors made no adjustment for deaths occurring before age sixty-five. I have therefore recalculated the present values after adjusting expected earnings of pilots, former pilots, engineers, and former engineers for mortality experienced by U.S. white males in 1956 (U.S. National Office of Vital Statistics, *Vital Statistics of the United States, 1956* [Washington, 1958], I, xcii, Table BD). The mortality adjustment, not included in the estimates of B given in the text, changes the estimates of B by one percentage point or less.

Equation (a) and the computations in the text based on it disregard the personal income tax. If the tax were a constant fraction, k, of earnings, then (a) should be changed to

$$B = 100 \left[\frac{Y_p}{(Y_e - Y_{gp}) - \dfrac{T_e - T_p}{1 - k}} \right] - 100. \tag{b}$$

With a proportional tax equal to 15 per cent, the first estimate of B given in the text would be changed from a range of 12 to 24 per cent to a range of 12 to 25 per cent; the revised estimate range given later in the text would be changed from one of 24 to 30 per cent to a range of 21 to 34 per cent.

Equation (a) also neglects variations of the relative wage effects of the Air Line Pilots Association among pilots with different years of experience. In their study the authors present evidence (pp. 5, 90, and 126–32) suggesting that the relative wage effects tend to increase on the average as seniority increases. Let B_t be the average relative wage effect for pilots with t years of experience. Then (a) should be written

$$Y_e - T_e = Y_{gp} - T_p + 100\Sigma[y_{pt}/(1 + r)^t(100 + B_t)], \tag{a'}$$

where y_{pt} is the average annual earnings of pilots with t years of experience, r is the discount rate, and the sum extends over all years of experience. Comparison of equation (a) with equation (a') yields the result

$$100 + B = \frac{\Sigma y_{pt}/(1 + r)^t}{\Sigma y_{pt}/(1 + r)^t(100 + B_t)}. \tag{c}$$

That is, $(100 + B)$ is a weighted *harmonic* mean of the indexes $(100 + B_t)$ with weights equal to discounted average earnings by years of experience.

Let n_t be the number of pilots with t years of experience in 1956. Then the average relative wage effect index that I seek to estimate is the weighted *geometric* mean of the indexes $(100 + B_t)$ by years of experience, with weights $n_t y_{pt}$. Call this mean B'. If the B_t's are unequal, then the geometric mean of the $(100 + B_t)$, *with the same weights as in B*, is greater than B. In addition, the differences between the weights, $n_t y_{pt}$, in B' and the weights, $y_{pt}/(1 + r)^t$, in B are positively correlated with t (when r is equal to 0.1). Thus if B_t increases on the average as t increases, B' surely exceeds B.

Although the authors present the key statistics for estimating B, they did not carry through the calculations to numerical estimates by means of equation (a). Both the equation and the calculation of the estimate ranges for B given in the text are mine rather than theirs.

the Air Line Pilots Association for airline pilots is about 24 per cent; if the private training cost estimate is applicable, the effect is about 12 per cent.

The authors estimated the figures in the preceding paragraph (or the data from which I have derived them) as follows:

Y_p and Y_{gp}: From a survey (conducted by them) they obtained data on the average annual earnings of pilots in 1956 by single years of experience. The survey, which covered 81 per cent of all pilots employed in U.S. scheduled airlines, also provided data on the percent of pilots grounded in 1956 by years of experience. Because of the youth of the air transportation industry, no pilot in 1956 had more than twenty-nine years of experience in the occupation. The authors assumed, however, that the working life of an airline pilot as an airline pilot was thirty-five years. The typical airline pilot began his career at age twenty-five, terminated his piloting service at age sixty, and then spent five years in other pursuits. Accordingly, they stretched the distribution of earnings by years of experience from a twenty-nine-year to a thirty-five-year span. The resulting earnings series was then adjusted to take into account transfers out of the airline pilot occupation. The transfer out rates were estimated from the authors' survey data on pilot grounding experience in 1956. This adjusted series, capitalized at age twenty-five with a 4 per cent discount rate, was their estimate of Y_p.

All pilots who transferred out were assumed to earn in alternative pursuits the average earnings of male persons of the same age and education in the labor force as a whole. The authors' estimates of average earnings by age and education in the labor force as a whole were based chiefly on *Census of Population* data. The series of expected earnings of a pilot in alternative pursuits, capitalized at age twenty-five with a 4 per cent discount rate, was their estimate of Y_{gp}.

Y_e: Their basic earnings data for chemical engineers by years of experience were from a survey of 1956 earnings by the Engineers Joint Council. These data were adjusted for transfers out of chemical engineering and for earnings in alternative pursuits. The resulting series, capitalized at age twenty-five with a 4 per cent discount rate, was their estimate of Y_e. (They assumed that the working life of a chemical engineer began at age twenty-four and terminated at age sixty-five.)

In their estimates of Y_p, Y_{gp}, and Y_e, the authors made no adjustments for transfers out because of death, and the earnings figures were taken before income tax.

T_e, T_p: They assumed that the costs of training of chemical engineers and airline pilots were the same until age twenty, both groups by then having completed two years of college education. Thereafter the costs of training of the two groups diverge.

Chemical engineer: Completes two more years of college or university training, spends two years in military service as an officer, and enters chemical engineering at age twenty-four.

Airline pilot, Air Force trained: Spends five years in the Air Force, the first two as a cadet, the last three as an officer.

Airline pilot, privately trained, single-engine and multi-engine, 1,178 hours of flight time: Spends two years in military service as a draftee, then enters the labor force full-time for three years. During the three years of employment in the labor force his earnings are the same on the average as those of males of the same age and education. During these three years he also buys pilot training on week ends and evenings totaling 1,178 hours on single-engine and multi-engine craft.

All training costs were accumulated to age twenty-five at 4 per cent interest.

The principal source of uncertainty in the over-all estimate of the effects of the Pilots Union on pilots' wages is in the supply price of pilot training. If the Air Force was "graduating" pilots qualified for and desiring civilian employment as airline pilots in large enough numbers to satisfy the civilian demand for pilots with pilot wages at the level they would have in the absence of pilot unionization, then the appropriate training supply price is that for Air Force training. If this was not true in 1956, then the appropriate training cost is the higher private training cost. The authors of the study did not commit themselves on this question.

However, on the basis of their data, it appears to me that they overestimated the cost of pilot training, particularly that for private training, compared to the cost of training chemical engineers:

1. They assumed two years of college or university training for airline pilots, although their data show that new pilots hired in 1956 averaged 1.8 years of college schooling. On the other hand, the census data for 1950 indicate that chemical engineers averaged *more than* 4.0 years of schooling beyond high school.

2. In estimating the training cost of privately trained pilots (single- and multi-engine) they assumed 1,178 hours of flight experience, all purchased from private flying schools and spread over three years of week ends and evenings. New pilots hired by the airlines in 1956 averaged 1,178 hours of flying time. Spreading 1,178 hours of flight training time over three rather than fewer years increases the cost of training to the trainee by postponing the day he begins service as an airline pilot. It seems reasonable to assume that the 1,178 hours could be purchased within one year of elapsed time.

3. They assumed implicitly that the private rate of return on college-level training was 4 per cent. Gary S. Becker's estimates of the private rate of return on college-level training in 1940 and 1950 were more than twice as large.[65]

Therefore, I have calculated revised estimates of the relative wage effect of the Air Line Pilots Association on the relative wages of commercial airline pilots in 1956 as follows:

I have used a 10 per cent interest rate, rather than one of 4 per cent, in computing the present values at age twenty-five of pilot and engineer (and former pilot and former engineer) earnings and of pilot and engineer training costs.

I have assumed that 1,178 hours of flight training time, for the privately trained pilot, could be obtained in one year immediately preceding employment as a commercial airline pilot. (The privately trained pilot, I assume, would sacrifice about 800 hours of employment at $1.95 per hour during the year, in addition to bearing the direct cost of the flight training.)

The revised estimates of the relative wage effect of the Air Line Pilots Association are 24 per cent if private training costs are applicable and 30 per cent if Air Force training is applicable.

These estimates are not fully adjusted, however, for factors other than unionism. In particular:

1. The values of Y_p, Y_{gp}, Y_e, T_p, and T_e were calculated without adjustment for deaths occurring before age sixty-five. The authors omitted this adjustment on the ground that there was no evidence that the death rate for airline pilots was significantly higher than that for chemical engineers. However, the estimates of the relative wage effect of the Air Line Pilots Association are not independent of the death rate, even if it is the same for pilots, former pilots, engineers, and former engineers. For these data, an adjustment for mortality, using mortality rates for U.S. white males in 1956, would have changed the estimates by less than one percentage point.[66]

2. The values of Y_p, Y_{gp}, and Y_e were calculated before, rather than after, income tax. I judge that the income tax adjustment would change the preceding estimates by perhaps three or four percentage points.[67]

3. Data in the 1950 *Census of Population*[68] indicate that the average hours of work of airline pilots may have been lower than for chemical engineers. The mean hours per week for the census week of 1950 was about 10 per cent less for "airplane pilots and navigators" than for "chemical engineers." On the

[65] Gary S. Becker, "Underinvestment in College Education?" *American Economic Review*, L, No. 2 (May, 1960), 346–54.

[66] See n. 64 above.

[67] *Ibid.*

[68] U.S. Bureau of the Census, *United States Census of Population: 1950* (Washington, 1956), Special Report P-E No. 1B, *Occupational Characteristics*, Table 15.

other hand, this difference may have been offset or more than offset by the "layover" time and greater irregularity of the hours of work of airline pilots.

4. More important, *commercial airline* pilots are a select group among all those employed as airplane pilots. Their earnings, even in the absence of unionism, would have exceeded those of other pilots on the average. On the other hand, chemical engineers also are a select group, both among engineers and, more broadly, among professional and technical employees. It is not at all clear that the choice of chemical engineers as a benchmark group, therefore, has led to overestimation rather than underestimation of the effects of collective bargaining on the relative wage of airline pilots.

III.11. MELVIN LURIE: LOCAL TRANSIT, 1920–48[69]

Unionization in the local transit industry (street railways and buses) had become significant as early as 1903, but until the 1940's a quite substantial fraction of local transit firms were nonunion. By 1948, however, local transit firms in the great majority of cities had been unionized.

Professor Lurie's dissertation deals with the effects of unionism on the relative wages of local transit motormen (including bus drivers), an occupational group comprising over half the wage-earners employed by local transit firms. The occupation is a semiskilled one, is relatively homogeneous among firms, and until fairly recently the persons employed in the occupation were almost entirely white males whose average age differed little among cities.

Lurie's estimates of the effects of unionization on the relative wages of motormen were based on comparisons of wage *rates* for motormen in union and nonunion cities. Table 19 summarizes these estimates for selected years. The basic wage rate data underlying Table 19 were collected by the American Transit Association (ATA) from member firms employing a large majority of all transit employees in the United States. Each member firm reported its wage scale for motormen and whether its employees were union or nonunion. The reported wage scale was usually a length of service progression from a beginning rate to a top rate, with increases after specified increments of service.

Lurie's Estimate 1 (the numerical notation distinguishing among the types of estimates is mine) was made as follows:

1. He first excluded the minority of transit firms (a) whose unionization

---

[69] Melvin Lurie, "The Measurement of the Effect of Unionization on Wages in the Transit Industry" (unpublished Ph.D. dissertation, University of Chicago, 1958). Mr. Lurie wrote his dissertation under a faculty committee of which I was a member. The essential portions of his dissertation are contained in his "The Effect of Unionization on Wages in the Transit Industry," *Journal of Political Economy*, LXIX, No. 6 (December, 1961), 558–72.

TABLE 19

ESTIMATES OF THE EFFECT OF UNIONIZATION OF LOCAL TRANSIT
MOTORMEN ON THEIR RELATIVE WAGE RATES, 1920–48*

YEAR	RELATIVE WAGE EFFECT (PER CENT)				
	Estimate 1	Estimate 2	Estimate 3	Estimate 4	Estimate 5
1920.........	15.5	. . .	. . .	. . .	. . .
1923.........	13.9	. . .	. . .	. . .	. . .
1925.........	12.8	15.2	20.1	18.2	. . .
1929.........	15.9	19.1	17.0	14.9[a]–18.7	. . .
1933.........	17.9	22.7	24.2	21.9[a]	. . .
1934.........	20.2	. . .	. . .	. . .	16.9
1937.........	12.1	. . .	. . .	. . .	. . .
1938.........	. . .	. . .	. . .	2.5[a]–5.8	3.8
1948.........	. . .	. . .	. . .	9.4[a]	3.8

* Source: Lurie, "The Effect of Unionization on Wages in the Transit Industry," p. 561, Table 1.
[a] Wholesale trade deflator; see text.

status changed during 1920–37 and (b) which did not report to the ATA in every year in 1920–37.

2. The remaining firms were then classified by region (South and non-South), by population of city (less than 100,000; 100,000–400,000; over 400,000), and by unionization (union or nonunion). Within each region-city size class he computed the ratio of the employment weighted mean *top* wage rate of union firms to the corresponding mean for nonunion firms. (The *top* wage rate in each firm was the maximum wage rate in the length of service progression.) Finally, he computed the employment weighted mean for all region-city size classes of the class union-nonunion wage ratios.

Estimate 2 is exactly like Estimate 1 except that instead of using the *top* wage rate for motormen in each firm, he computed a weighted average of the length of service step rates from the beginning rate to the top rate. Each step rate was weighted less heavily, the greater the length of service required to achieve the rate. Estimate 2, therefore, is probably superior to Estimate 1.

Estimate 3 differs from Estimate 2 in that the former was computed from the wage rate data for all firms reporting to the ATA in a given year. Estimate 4 differs from Estimate 3 in the procedure used to control for wage differentials among cities of different size. In Estimate 4, Lurie adjusted for city size within region by dividing the average wage rate for motormen in each city by estimates of the average annual earnings of persons employed in wholesale trade (estimates in which the wholesale trade deflator was used are identified in the table) or, alternatively, in manufacturing industries. The Estimate 4 figure for 1948 is less reliable than the corresponding figures for the other years because in 1948 the number of nonunion firms reporting to the ATA was small.

The Estimate 5 figure for 1934 was obtained as follows. The mean *top* wage rate *index*, 1925–30 = 100, for the period 1934–41 was computed for (a) two cities that became unionized in 1933 and (b) twelve benchmark cities of the same region and city size class whose unionization status was unchanged during 1925–41. The ratio (minus unity) of the first index to the second, expressed in per cent, is the percentage gain in wages of the two cities relative to the benchmark cities from "before" unionization to "after" unionization. The figure for 1938 was calculated in a similar manner. It pertains to 21 cities that became unionized in 1936–37. The 1938 benchmark group included 86 cities, the "before" period was 1925–35 (excluding 1931–33), and the "after" period was 1938–41. The 1948 figure relates to 44 cities that became unionized between 1938 and 1948. The 1948 benchmark group covered 120 cities, the "before" date was 1938, and the "after" date was 1948. At each of the three dates the Estimate 5 figures refer to the relative wage effects of unionization in the cities most recently unionized. If, as seems likely, there was a positive correlation among the cities between the effects of unionism on the relative wages of motormen and the length of time the motormen had been unionized, the Estimate 5 figures will be biased downward relative to the other estimates in the table for corresponding dates.[70]

The figures in the table indicate that during the 1920's, unionization of transit motormen raised their relative wage *rate* position by 15 to 20 per cent and that this unionization effect increased to 20 to 25 per cent at the bottom of the Great Depression, then declined to 6 per cent or less in 1938. Both estimates for 1948 were below 10 per cent.

The estimates in Table 19 exclude all effects of unionization of transit motormen on their wages except effects on their wage *rates*; in particular, the estimates exclude effects of unionization on premium rates, payments for "time not worked," and wage supplements. From fragmentary data, chiefly data for the Chicago Transit Authority and data collected by the ATA, Lurie estimated that before 1939 the non-wage rate effects of unionization on the relative wages of motormen were negligible but that in 1948 these non-wage rate effects were equivalent to an effect of about 8 per cent on relative wage rates. Thus the estimated total (wage rate plus non-wage rate) effect of unionization on the relative wages of transit

---

[70] The statement in the text is based on the argument that the order in which motormen became unionized, city by city, was one in which unionization occurred first in the cities in which the conditions for achieving wage gains were most favorable.

motormen in 1948 was about 12 to 18 per cent, slightly lower than the effect estimated for the 1920's. The estimate for 1948, however, is much less reliable than the corresponding estimates for the 1920's. Lurie cited some evidence in the ATA data suggesting that the estimate for 1948 may have been biased upward relative to the estimates for earlier years by perhaps as much as five percentage points.

I have added Table 20 in order to make a rough and ready estimate of the change since 1948 in the relative wage impact of local transit unionization. Since the end of World War II, employment in local transit has declined rapidly. In 1958, transit employment was only about half as

TABLE 20

AVERAGE HOURLY COMPENSATION AND EMPLOYMENT IN LOCAL RAILWAYS
AND BUS LINES AND IN ALL INDUSTRIES, 1946–58*

YEAR	AVERAGE HOURLY COMPENSATION			EMPLOYMENT (1946 = 100)	
	Local Railways and Bus Lines (1)	All Civilian Wage and Salary Employees (2)	(2)/(1) (3)	Local Railways and Bus Lines (4)	All Wage and Salary Employees (5)
1946......	$1.12	$1.13	0.99	100	100
1947......	1.26	1.27	0.99	98	100
1948......	1.37	1.38	0.99	84	102
1949......	1.48	1.44	1.03	82	99
1950......	1.54	1.52	1.01	77	103
1951......	1.62	1.64	0.99	74	111
1952......	1.72	1.73	0.99	71	114
1953......	1.78	1.83	0.97	69	116
1954......	1.89	1.91	0.99	66	113
1955......	1.94	1.98	0.98	61	116
1956......	2.03	2.09	0.97	57	119
1957......	2.14	2.22	0.96	55	120
1958......	2.21	2.33	0.95	52	116

* Sources: Col. (1) is the product of (a) average hourly earnings of wage-earners and (b) the ratio of the total compensation to the total wages and salaries of wage and salary employees. The source of (a) is *Employment and Earnings*, V, No. 11 (May, 1959), Table SC-1, and the multilithed "employment, hours, and earnings" releases of the Bureau of Labor Statistics. The sources of (b) are the U.S. Department of Commerce, Office of Business Economics, *U.S. Income and Output* (Washington, 1958), Tables VI-1 and VI-2, and the *Survey of Current Business*, XXXIX, No. 7 (July, 1959), p. 32. For col. (2), see chap. vi, Table 57 [col. (3)], p. 207. Cols. (4) and (5) are index numbers of the number of full-time equivalent wage and salary employees computed from the Department of Commerce sources cited for (b) of col. (1); the relevant table in the sources is Table VI-13.

large absolutely as in 1946 and only four-ninths as large relative to employment in the whole economy.

Despite the large decline in relative employment, average hourly compensation of transit wage-earners fell only slightly relative to the average hourly compensation of all civilian wage and salary employees. Thus I doubt that the effect of local transit unionization on the relative wages of transit workers was appreciably less in 1958 than in 1948; indeed, the effect actually may have increased from 1948 to 1958.

III.12. Leonard A. Rapping:
Seamen in Ocean Transportation, 1939–57[71]

Except during 1916–22, the degree of unionization of unlicensed seamen employed on U.S. ships operating out of Atlantic and Gulf ports was quite low before 1935. In the decade 1935–45, however, unionization of these seamen increased rapidly, and by the end of World War II, almost all of the seamen were represented in collective bargaining by either the National Maritime Union or the Seafarers' International Union. Mr. Rapping's dissertation estimates the effects of these unions on the relative wages of East Coast seamen in the period 1939–57.

Columns (1), (2), and (3) of Table 21 compare the average daily earnings of East Coast seamen with the average hourly earnings of production workers in manufacturing industries during the period 1923–57.[72] The earnings series for seamen, estimated by Rapping, includes fringe benefit payments and a crude allowance for the value of shipboard subsistence (room and board). The earnings series for manufacturing is that calculated by Albert Rees and includes private fringe benefits but not employer contributions to public social insurance programs.

The relative earnings series in column (3) is not adjusted for changes in either the occupational, age, sex, race, etc., composition of the seamen and manufacturing labor forces or in the wage differentials associated with these factors. Fragmentary data on wages and employment by race and sex, cited by Rapping (his pp. 55–58), indicate that the race and sex factors were of negligible emportance in explaining the movements of the relative earnings series in column (3).

In 1957 the actual hours worked per day by seamen averaged about 8.5; in 1933, scheduled hours per day averaged about 8.9 (Rapping, p. 20). No other data on the hours of work of ocean seamen are available. These two bits of information suggest that the hours worked by seamen probably have changed very little. It is more likely that seamen's hours have fallen instead of rising and, therefore, that adjustment of column (3) for the changes in seamen's hours would increase the upward trend of the series.

[71] Leonard A. Rapping, "The Impact of Federal Subsidies and Maritime Unionism on the Relative Earnings of Seamen" (unpublished Ph.D. dissertation, University of Chicago, 1961). Mr. Rapping wrote his dissertation under a faculty committee of which I was a member.

[72] In estimating the impact of unionism on the relative wages of seamen, Mr. Rapping excluded the data for the years 1942–45. During these years the relative earnings of seamen were exceptionally high, to an extent difficult to estimate, because of wartime hazards in ocean shipping.

TABLE 21

EARNINGS AND EMPLOYMENT: SEAMEN AND PRODUCTION WORKERS
IN MANUFACTURING INDUSTRIES, 1923–41, 1946–57*

	EARNINGS			EMPLOYMENT (1935 = 100)		
YEAR	East Coast Seamen (Daily, Including Subsistence and Fringe Benefits) (1)	Manufacturing Production Workers (Hourly, Including Fringe Benefits) (2)	Ratio of Col. (1) to Col. (2) (1935 = 1) (3)	Seafaring Jobs (4)	Manufacturing Production Workers (5)	Ratio of Col. (4) to Col. (5) (6)
1923..	$ 3.25	$0.479	1.25	...	...	...
1924..	3.41	0.498	1.26	...	...	...
1925..	3.43	0.497	1.27	102	109	93
1926..	3.46	0.503	1.27	106	111	95
1927..	3.44	0.510	1.24	109	109	100
1928..	3.46	0.513	1.24	111	109	102
1929..	3.56	0.522	1.25	114	116	98
1930..	3.36	0.522	1.18	109	101	107
1931..	3.15	0.499	1.16	100	85	117
1932..	2.83	0.441	1.18	96	73	132
1933..	2.66	0.437	1.12	97	80	120
1934..	2.71	0.533	0.93	98	94	104
1935..	2.92	0.537	1.00	100	100	100
1936..	3.12	0.543	1.06	103	109	94
1937..	3.47	0.607	1.05	96	119	81
1938..	3.47	0.606	1.05	90	101	89
1939..	4.14	0.605	1.26	90	113	80
1940..	4.52	0.635	1.31	89	121	74
1941..	5.21	0.702	1.36	87	150	58
1946..	9.91	1.09	1.67	204	167	122
1947..	11.22	1.25	1.65	169	176	96
1948..	12.44	1.37	1.67	134	175	77
1949..	13.07	1.42	1.69	118	160	74
1950..	13.80	1.50	1.69	129	169	76
1951..	16.17	1.65	1.80	149	181	82
1952..	19.56	1.77	2.03	141	181	78
1953..	21.38	1.88	2.09	128	190	67
1954..	21.77	1.90	2.11	113	173	65
1955..	22.88	1.97	2.14	102	180	57
1956..	24.31	2.07	2.16	101	182	56
1957..	25.61	2.16	2.18	102	178	57

* Source: Rapping dissertation, Tables 1 and 3.

The seafaring employment series in column (4) of Table 21 is not strictly comparable in coverage to the earnings series in column (1). Column (4) covers West Coast as well as East Coast seamen, both officers and unlicensed personnel, but excludes civilian seamen employed by the Military Sea Transportation Service. Therefore, column (4) only roughly indexes the employment of all East Coast unlicensed seamen. The manufacturing employment series in column (5) is that of the U.S. Bureau of Labor Statistics.

The relative earnings of East Coast seamen rose by about 70 per cent from 1923–29 to 1953–57. This large relative wage increase cannot be explained by a correspondingly large increase in the relative demand for seaman labor, for in 1953–57 the relative employment of East Coast seamen was lower than in 1923–29 and was declining.[73] For this reason, Rapping explained the movements of the relative earnings series mainly in terms of relative supply factors, including unionism.

1. *Real income and the consumption aspects of employment.*—Conditions of work that are relatively discommodious, Rapping argued, are inferior commodities or discommodities: as real income per head rises, the relative demand schedules for them fall; that is, as real income per head rises, the relative supply prices of labor to occupations characterized by relatively discommodious working conditions will also tend to rise. The hazards of seafaring, the confinement of the seaman's leisure to the ship on which he is sailing, and the extended periods the seaman is away from home, Rapping felt, make seafaring a discommodious occupation relative to manufacturing occupations on the average.

In estimating the elasticity of the relative earnings of seamen with respect to real income, Rapping used Milton Friedman's series on expected (or permanent) real income per capita.

2. *The cutting off of the supply of alien seamen.*—In 1914, more than half the unlicensed seamen employed on U.S.-flag vessels were aliens. In 1938, the last year for which such data are available, the proportion was slightly less than 10 per cent. (Fragmentary data indicate that the proportion of aliens employed in the 1950's was almost the same as in 1938.) This large decline in the employment of alien seamen stemmed mainly from the legislative prohibitions during the 1930's against the employment of aliens on U.S. ships.

It is reasonable to expect that this cutting off of the alien labor supply to the U.S. maritime industry tended to raise the relative wages paid to unlicensed seamen on U.S.-flag ships. The amount of increase in the relative wages of unlicensed seamen resulting from the cutting off of the alien labor supply can be estimated, at least roughly, from comparisons of the average base wage of unlicensed seamen with that of officers (Rapping, pp. 27–28). (Beginning in 1866, U.S. citizenship has been required of all officers on U.S. vessels.) Between 1914 and 1938 the average base wage of unlicensed seamen rose by about one-ninth relative to the average base wage of officers.

It is not clear, however, that all of this one-ninth increase was caused

[73] Although col. (6) exaggerates the change in relative employment of East Coast seamen from 1923–29 to 1953–57, the change was surely a decline rather than an increase (see Rapping, p. 5).

by the restrictions on the employment of alien seamen. Thus, for example, the same forces which have caused wage differentials according to skill to decline secularly in the United States may also explain part of the decline in the wages of officers relative to unlicensed seamen.

3. Unionism.—From 1923 to about 1935 the extent of unionism was quite low, not only in the economy generally, but also among both seamen and production workers in manufacturing. Thus it is very likely that during this period, unionism had a negligible effect on the earnings of seamen relative to the earnings of manufacturing wage-earners and to the earnings of all labor in the economy. Accordingly, Rapping assigned values of zero to the unionism variable for the period 1923–35.

From 1935 to about 1946, unionism extended rapidly among both seamen and manufacturing wage-earners. In 1946 and later years, almost all unlicensed seamen and about two-thirds of manufacturing wage-earners were unionized. It is not clear from the available data when this difference of about thirty percentage points in extent of unionism emerged, although it is very doubtful that the difference was that large before 1939. In any case, unless the maritime unions were more effective than the unions in manufacturing in raising the relative wages of their members, a thirty-percentage-point difference in extent of unionism would account for only a small increase—less than 6 per cent, Rapping judged from earlier studies—in the wages of seamen relative to the wages of manufacturing wage-earners.

Rapping doubted that the maritime unions were appreciably more effective in raising the relative wages of their members during the period before 1950 than were the manufacturing unions. Beginning about 1950, however, economic circumstances, in his judgment, turned strongly in favor of the maritime unions. The key to the change was the federal operating wage differential subsidy program. For ship operators under the subsidy program, increases in labor cost resulting from higher wage rates are almost entirely covered by additional subsidy payments. Before 1950 the fraction of seamen employed on subsidized ship operations was quite low, but during the 1950's the fraction became substantial.

Thus in estimating the impact of unionism on the wages of seamen relative to the wages of manufacturing workers, Rapping used the following "dummy" variable as an approximation of the true unionism variable:

U_1: assigned values of zero for 1923–49 and unity thereafter.

He also experimented with two alternative unionism series:

U_2: assigned values of zero for 1923–46 and unity thereafter.
U_3: assigned values of zero for 1923–38 and unity thereafter.

The simplest of the econometric models Rapping used to estimate the numerical magnitude of the effect of unionism on the earnings of seamen relative to the earnings of manufacturing wage-earners was

$$\log W = a + b \log Y + cU + \lambda,$$

where W is relative earnings as given in column (3) of Table 21, Y is Friedman's expected real income per head series, U is one of the three "dummy" variables (U_1, U_2, U_3) used as proxies for the unionism variable, and λ is a random variable. This model assumes that the relative supply of seamen was infinitely elastic and that demand factors therefore played no part in explaining the variations in relative wages. Table 22 summarizes the results of fitting this model to the data.

The three different unionism series yield rather different estimates of the effect of unionism on the wages of seamen relative to the wages of production workers in manufacturing: U_1, about 18 per cent; U_2, about 8 per cent; and U_3, about 2 per cent. On the basis of "goodness of fit" and the independent evidence regarding the federal subsidy program, Rapping placed somewhat greater confidence in the estimate derived from the U_1 series than in the estimates from the other two series.

Rapping also fitted several equations which included relative demand variables along with the above relative supply variables. The addition of the demand variables contributed negligibly to the explanation of the variation in relative earnings. Furthermore, the unionism coefficients were about the same in the presence of the demand variables as in Table 22. The smallest coefficient in the presence of the demand variables was -0.021 and the largest was 0.20 (see Rapping, Table 7).

TABLE 22

SUMMARY OF MULTIPLE REGRESSIONS UNDERLYING RAPPING'S ESTIMATES*

REGRESSION NUMBER	R^2	REGRESSION COEFFICIENTS AND THEIR STANDARD ERRORS			
		b	c		
			U_1	U_2	U_3
1......	0.939	0.887 (0.081)	0.16 (0.039)	...	...
2......	0.903	0.969 (0.214)	...	0.074 (0.094)	...
3......	0.901	1.10 (0.142)	...	...	0.016 (0.060)

* Source: Rapping dissertation, Table 4. In fitting the model to the data, Rapping used logarithms to the base 10 for log W and log Y. In Table 22 I have converted his results—only the figures for the coefficient c and its standard error are affected—to those he would have obtained had he used the *natural* logarithms of W and Y.

R^2 is the square of the multiple correlation coefficient. The figures in parentheses are the standard errors of the regression coefficients.

These estimates of the value of the "unionism" coefficient do not take into account the effect of unionism on the average wage of manufacturing wage-earners relative to the average wage of all labor in the economy. On the basis of earlier studies of unionism in manufacturing industries, Rapping judged that this relative wage effect of unionism in manufacturing did not exceed approximately 5 per cent throughout 1939–57 and may have been close to zero at the end of and immediately following World War II. Accordingly, he estimated that the impact of unionism on the wages of East Coast unlicensed seamen relative to the average wage of all labor in the economy was approximately 5 to 23 per cent.

These figures, 1.05 and 1.23 in index form, are Variant A-I indexes. To convert them to B-form estimates, I have used equation (30′) (p. 78), with $\bar{p}$ set equal to 0.26, U to 0.65, and $\bar{B}$ to zero and, alternatively, to 0.25. The antilogarithms of the resulting estimates of B yield the range 1.06 to 1.35. Thus Rapping's data indicate that unionization of East Coast seamen raised their average relative wage by 6 to 35 per cent.

III.13. Friedman and Kuznets: Physicians, 1929–34[74]

Conventionally, we regard as unions—that is, as "trade" or "labor" unions—only voluntary associations which consider themselves to be unions and have as their chief purpose the improvement of the terms of employment of those they represent through concerted action in the labor market. There are many other organizations, not usually regarded by their members as unions, which engage in concerted actions that may affect the terms of employment of their members. The American Medical Association is an example.

Chapter iv of the Friedman-Kuznets study of the income of independent professional workers examines economic factors explaining income differences among the professions, especially the income differential between physicians and dentists. As a byproduct, Professors Friedman and Kuznets have estimated the effect on the physician/dentist income differential of limitations on entry into medical practice.[75]

[74] Milton Friedman and Simon Kuznets, *Income from Independent Professional Practice* (New York: National Bureau of Economic Research, 1945).

[75] Here and throughout this section the expression "limitations on entry into medical practice" and similar expressions should be construed narrowly as "restrictions of numbers entering medical training or practice." Thus the "effect on the physician/dentist income differential of limitations on entry into medical practice" estimated by Friedman and Kuznets is not the same conceptually as the "effect of organized medicine on the income of physicians relative to the income of dentists." In particular, neither Friedman and Kuznets nor I have estimated the size of the effect on the relative income of physicians of either (a) barriers to entry of enterprises into

From sample data collected by the U.S. Department of Commerce they calculated the mean net incomes of physicians and dentists in independent practice for the years 1929–34, as shown in columns (1) and (2) of Table 23 below. For the period as a whole, the mean net income of

TABLE 23

MEAN NET INCOME OF PHYSICIANS AND DENTISTS IN
INDEPENDENT PRACTICE, 1929–34*

YEAR	MEAN NET INCOME		RATIO OF COL. (1) TO COL. (2) (3)
	Physicians (1)	Dentists (2)	
1929...............	$5,573	$4,176	1.335
1930...............	4,965	3,920	1.267
1931...............	4,300	3,350	1.284
1932...............	3,235	2,473	1.308
1933...............	2,985	2,178	1.371
1934...............	3,431	2,387	1.437
1929–34 average.....	4,081	3,081	1.325

* Source: Friedman and Kuznets, *op. cit.*, p. 104.

independent physicians was about 32.5 per cent higher than that for independent dentists. Since the fraction of all practitioners who were salaried in 1929–34 was small and about the same in medicine as in dentistry, the average income differential between *all* physicians and *all* dentists, they judged, was nearly the same as that for those in independent practice.

Adjustment of the net income differential for differences between the professions in their distributions of workers by number of years in practice and by geographic location (region and size of community), they estimated, would *raise* the differential from 32.5 per cent to about 34 to 46 per cent.

What accounts for this large differential in the incomes of physicians and dentists who live in the same community and who have been in practice the same number of years? Medicine and dentistry, Friedman and Kuznets argued (pp. 123–24),

---

the medical training industry or (b) higher—that is, more restrictive—standards of medical training for new practitioners imposed by state legislation or privately by organized medicine. For this reason, the empirical findings of this section should not be interpreted as evidence that there is free entry of workers into medical practice and of firms into the medical training industry, or that organized medicine has had little or no effect on the relative wages of physicians.

are related professions requiring somewhat similar abilities and training. Many of the persons choosing one of the professions might be expected to have considered the other as an alternative. Moreover, since the preliminary training required for the two professions is virtually identical, the final choice between them can be postponed longer than between most other professions. If entry into the two professions were equally easy or difficult, one might expect an adjustment of the levels of return in them that would equalize their net attractiveness in the eyes of a considerable fraction of those in a position to choose between them. Any difference in income would then be explained by the type of adjustment discussed in the introduction to this chapter, i.e., the levels of return would be "equilibrium" levels, in the sense that they would be relative returns resulting from the free and moderately rational choice of profession by prospective entrants.

That the observed difference in incomes (34 to 46 per cent) was larger than the equilibrium difference was established by data on entry alone (pp. 124–25). In particular, for the period 1935–41 they estimated that more than four times as many persons applied annually for admission to U.S. medical schools as applied for admission to U.S. dental schools, although there were only about twice as many practicing physicians as dentists.

An excess of the observed income difference over the equlibrium difference—correspondingly, an excess of the ratio of applicants to medical schools to applicants to dental schools over the ratio of physicians to dentists—could have been caused, however, by rising demand for physicians relative to dentists, or by a falling excess of the costs of training physicians over the costs of training dentists, rather than by greater difficulty of entry into medicine than into dentistry. In the appendix to this chapter (sec. iii. 14), I present and analyze data on the income of physicians and dentists, the number of physicians and dentists, the freshman and total enrollment of medical and dental schools, and the number of graduates of these schools. Throughout the period from about 1929 to about 1946 the ratio of medical school freshmen to dental school freshmen exceeded the ratio of physicians to dentists and the latter ratio increased. Furthermore, except during 1936–41, the income differential between physicians and dentists widened substantially (1929–51). These data cannot be explained by relative supply factors—differences between medicine and dentistry in costs of training and in conditions of entry— under unchanging conditions of demand for physicians relative to demand for dentists. That is, the data indicate that during most of the period from 1929 to the end of World War II the demand for physicians was rising relative to the demand for dentists.

The income and entry data, however, do not rule out the possibility that "organized medicine" limited the number of those entering medicine during the 1930's. For the school year 1933–34, U.S. medical schools accepted 7,543 out of 12,128 applicants for admission. In each of the five following school years the number of applicants for admission to medical school was almost the same as in 1933–34 (for example, in 1938–39 the total number of applicants was 12,131), yet the number of applicants *accepted* dropped sharply to 6,223 in the school year 1938–39. This decline in the number of applicants accepted, which coincided with expressions of concern by leaders in the medical profession regarding the number and quality of persons admitted to medical schools (see Friedman and Kuznets, pp. 12–14, and 27), is affirmative evidence of restriction of numbers entering medicine.

Friedman and Kuznets estimated that roughly one-half—seventeen percentage points—of the observed difference in incomes of physicians and dentists living in the same community and in practice the same number of years was accounted for by the longer period of training (by about three years) of physicians than of dentists (for the details of the estimate, see Friedman and Kuznets, pp. 142–48). The most important element in the additional cost of training to physicians was the postponement of income for three years. At an interest rate of 4 per cent per annum, which was the interest rate they used, the postponement alone accounted for a 12.5 per cent difference in the incomes of physicians and dentists.

Although in 1929–34 the mean income of physicians exceeded that of dentists by 32.5 per cent, the dispersion of income among physicians was so much greater than that among dentists that the first quartile income of physicians was considerably below the first quartile income of dentists. The greater uncertainty of returns in medicine than in dentistry presented to prospective entrants by the larger variability of medical incomes, Friedman and Kuznets speculated, was an attraction rather than a deterrent to entry into medicine. That is, allowance for the difference between the professions in income variability, they judged, would make the equilibrium difference in their incomes *less than* 17 per cent.

Similarly, they were of the opinion that the less-regular and longer hours of work, less freedom from the demands of patients, greater physical and mental strain, and longer postponement of marriage and financial independence in medicine compared to dentistry were more than offset by the higher prestige of physicians, the greater opportunity in medicine to render service, the more scientific character of medical practice, and the smaller extent of routine or "uninteresting" work in medicine.

Thus in their estimation, differences between medicine and dentistry in amount of training, income variability, and nonpecuniary aspects of training and practice accounted for no more than about half the observed difference in income. The remaining part, about 15 to 25 per cent, they attributed primarily to greater difficulty of entry into medicine than into dentistry.[76] They emphasized that their estimates were highly tentative.

I think it is likely that Friedman and Kuznets overestimated the effect of greater difficulty of entry into medicine on the income of physicians relative to that of dentists. The most probable source of appreciable error in their estimate, I judge, is in the interest rate used to estimate the difference in income that would compensate physicians for the extra training in medicine. Gary S. Becker has estimated that the rate of return, computed for private costs and for private returns net of income taxes, earned by the average urban white male college graduate on his college education was about 12.5 per cent in 1940 and about 10 per cent in 1950.[77] Moreover, the comparisons of the income and education of professional and nonprofessional workers in 1935–36 made by Friedman and Kuznets (pp. 81–94 and 148–51) also suggest that the private rate of return earned then by professional workers on their extra years of training was considerably higher than 4 per cent, the rate of interest

---

[76] Friedman and Kuznets judged that the (roughly) half of the observed difference in income which they had *not* explained by the differences in training, income variability, and nonpecuniary factors was not attributable to greater scarcity of the innate abilities needed in medicine than of those needed in dentistry. They gave two reasons for doubting that conditions of relative supply of innate abilities to the two professions were a major factor in the income difference between medicine and dentistry. First, the type of ability needed in the two professions appeared to be much the same for both. Second, though medical schools presumably selected for admission those applicants that they judged were ablest, the percentages of new applicants—those applying for the first time—accepted for admission by medical schools in 1927, 1928, and 1929 were only slightly higher than the corresponding percentages among applicants that previously had been denied admission.

These data, however, are inconclusive evidence that medical schools in 1927–29 did not select for admission those they deemed the ablest. As Friedman and Kuznets pointed out, previously refused applicants may have obtained additional training before applying again, and repeat applicants, to a greater extent than new applicants, may apply to schools with high acceptance rates.

In this connection the following data are relevant. During the period July, 1951, to March, 1959, an examination required for the Ph.D. degree in economics at the University of Chicago was offered on sixteen semiannual occasions. Of the 225 papers written by candidates who had *not* previously written the examination, 47.6 per cent were graded "pass." Of the 61 papers written by candidates who had previously written the examination, 45.9 per cent were graded "pass."

[77] "Underinvestment in College Education?" pp. 346–54.

they used. Had they used an interest rate of 8 per cent, their estimate of the income difference compensating for the extra training in medicine would have been *at least* 26 per cent rather than 17 per cent. The corresponding figures for rates of interest of 10.0 and 12.5 per cent are 33 and 42 per cent, respectively.[78]

The preceding paragraph suggests that the excess of the observed over the equilibrium income difference between physicians and dentists in 1929–34 may have been substantially less than was estimated by Friedman and Kuznets.[79] Moreover, as I have already pointed out, there is a strong presumption that in 1929–34 the trend of relative demand favored medicine rather than dentistry. Thus part of the excess of the observed over the equilibrium income differential, in my judgment, should be attributed to this demand factor.

In Table 24, I show the Department of Commerce estimates of mean net annual income, 1948–51, of all (both salaried and nonsalaried) civilian physicians and dentists, excluding only interns, residents, and teachers. The average difference between the mean net income of all physicians and that of all dentists in Table 24 is 57.8 per cent. In this period a larger proportion of physicians than of dentists (a) lived in communities in which in both medicine and dentistry incomes were relatively high, (b) were in salaried employment rather than nonsalaried practice, (c) were in years in practice classes that earned relatively high incomes, (d) were

---

[78] These figures take into account only the postponement of the medical income stream for three years. They were calculated from the formula

$$[(1 + i)^3 - 1]100,$$

where i is the rate of interest in decimal form.

[79] Given Becker's findings, it is quite possible that the interest rate appropriate for calculating the income differential in 1929–34 which would compensate for three extra years of medical training was 10.0 to 12.5 per cent. But then the calculated compensating differential would be as large as the observed differential of 34 to 46 per cent, apparently contradicting the earlier inference, from the data on entry, that the observed income difference was larger than the equilibrium difference. However, this comparison does not take into account the net nonpecuniary advantages of medicine relative to dentistry. Friedman and Kuznets judged that the nonpecuniary aspects of training and practice favored medicine rather than dentistry. Adjustment for this factor would tend to raise the observed income difference. Furthermore, the comparison does not allow for the trends in the training and income of physicians and dentists. In the twenty to twenty-five years preceding 1929 there was a marked upward trend in the amount of formal training of physicians entering practice. Dentistry experienced somewhat similar changes in training of new entrants, but with a considerable lag behind the changes in medicine. Thus the income difference expected by those choosing between medicine and dentistry in 1929–34 may have exceeded the observed (measured) income difference.

TABLE 24

MEAN NET INCOME OF CIVILIAN PHYSICIANS AND DENTISTS,
1948–51*

Year	Physicians (1)	Dentists (2)	Physicians ÷ Dentists (3)
1948.......	$10,634	$6,912	1.538
1949.......	11,058	7,037	1.571
1950.......	11,538	7,293	1.582
1951.......	12,518	7,743	1.617

* Sources: *Survey of Current Business*, XXX, No. 1 (January, 1950), 8–16;
XXXI, No. 7 (July, 1951), 9–26; XXXII, No. 7 (July, 1952), 5–7.

white, (e) were female, and (f) worked a full work year. I estimate that after allowing for these differences between the two professions, the mean net income of all civilian physicians exceeded that of all civilian dentists by about 51 to 60 per cent.[80]

The preceding estimate of the difference between the mean net income of physicians and that of dentists makes no allowance for income taxes.

[80] The estimates for each of the statistical factors mentioned in the text are:

Community size (population)...................	+0.4 to +1.6 per cent
Region......................................	−0.1 to +0.4 per cent
Class of worker (salaried versus nonsalaried)....	−4.9 to −3.6 per cent
"Years in Practice".........................	+2.9 to +3.3 per cent
Race.......................................	+0.2 to +0.2 per cent
Sex..	−0.5 to 0.0 per cent
Weeks worked per year.......................	+0.8 per cent
Combined effect............................	−1.3 to +4.3 per cent

A positive sign indicates that the differences between the distribution of physicians and that of dentists according to the specified factor tended to create an excess of the mean income of physicians over the mean income of dentists; a negative sign has the opposite meaning.

The figure, +0.8, for weeks worked per year is an estimate of the average excess (in per cent) of the mean weeks worked in 1949 by physicians, classified by class of worker and sex, over the corresponding mean for dentists.

I have put "years in practice" in quotation marks in the above summary because the estimates for this factor were made from data on the distributions of the number and income of physicians and of dentists by *age*, rather than the corresponding distributions by years in practice. I assumed that physicians had five fewer years in practice than dentists of the same age. Had I assumed that physicians and dentists of the same age also had the same number of years in practice, the estimates for "years in practice" would have been +6.5 to +7.6 per cent.

All of the above estimates, except for weeks worked per year, were made by the technique of standardized averages used by Friedman and Kuznets to estimate the effect on the difference between the income of physicians and that of dentists of differences between physicians and dentists in their distributions by community size and region and years in practice (Friedman and Kuznets, *op. cit.*, pp. 122–23). Because some of the factors were intercorrelated, I made the estimates for each factor in the

On the basis of some rough calculations, I estimate that the corresponding difference in mean net income after federal personal income taxes was approximately 44 to 52 per cent.[81]

In 1948–51 the difference between the length of training of new physicians and that of new dentists was approximately four years.[82] I estimate

presence of ("holding constant") as many of the other factors as the underlying data permitted.

For the community size, region, class of worker, years in practice (age), and sex estimates, the underlying data on the number and income of physicians were the Department of Commerce survey data for the year 1949 (*Survey of Current Business* [July, 1951], 9–26); the underlying data for dentists were those of the Department of Commerce for the year 1948 (*Survey of Current Business* [January, 1950], 8–16). The data for the race and weeks worked per year estimates were from the 1950 census (*United States Census of Population: 1950*, Special Report P-E No. 1B, *Occupational Characteristics*).

[81] The Department of Commerce surveys (*Survey of Current Business* [January, 1950], 8–16, and [July, 1951], 9–26) provided a distribution of all civilian dentists by net income for 1948 and a similar distribution for physicians for 1949. I estimated the net income distributions for each of the professions in the other years of the period 1948–51 from (a) the mean income figures in Table 24 and (b) a Lorenz distribution of net income for each profession assumed to be the same in each year as in the year (1948 for dentists, 1949 for physicians) for which the size distribution was available.

To estimate the mean income tax in each year for each profession, I assumed that (a) the unknown distributions of practitioners by their "adjusted gross income" for income tax purposes were the same as the corresponding distributions of the practitioners by their net income as reported in or estimated from the Department of Commerce data and (b) the applicable income tax rate in each year in each adjusted gross income class was the average rate for income tax payers in the class as reported in the U.S. Internal Revenue Service's *Statistics of Income for 1953* (Part 1, pp. 54–55). The estimated mean income tax for the four years for dentists was 12 per cent of the mean net income (before tax) of dentists; the corresponding mean income tax for physicians was 17 per cent of their mean net income (before tax).

[82] Table 25 shows the number of internships and residencies filled during the period 1941 to 1958. In each of the last four years of the table, the ratio of the sum of internships and residencies held by U.S. doctors to the sum of the graduates in the preceding four years was approximately unity, indicating that in these years internship and residency training averaged about four years per graduate (more precisely, 3.85 years). However, not all of the internships and residencies held by U.S. doctors were held by the most recent medical school graduates. Thus 3.85 years overestimates for this period the average number of years of internship and residency training per doctor about to begin practice.

For 1948–52, residency data are not available for the school year 1948–49, and both the residency and internship data include some foreign physicians. If the proportion of internships and residencies held by foreign doctors in 1949–52 was the same as in 1954–58, the data in the table imply that in 1949–52, internship plus residency training averaged about 3.3 years per graduate of the preceding four years. This figure is subject to the same upward bias as the figure for 1954–58. On the other hand, the data in the

that at an interest rate of 10 per cent (that suggested by Becker's findings for 1950), the difference in mean annual net income after taxes just sufficient to compensate for 4.0 extra years of training in medicine would amount to about 46 per cent. The corresponding figures for 3.5 and 4.5 extra years of medical training are 40 and 54 per cent, respectively.[83]

TABLE 25

HOSPITAL INTERNSHIPS AND RESIDENCIES, 1941–58*

SCHOOL YEAR	INTERNSHIPS FILLED		RESIDENCIES FILLED		MEDICAL SCHOOL GRADUATES (5)
	Total (1)	By U.S. Doctors (2)	Total (3)	By U.S. Doctors (4)	
1941–42........	7,219	...	4,100	...	5,163
1942–43........	5,200	...	3,500	...	5,233
1943–44........	5,300	...	4,500	...	10,303
1944–45.	5,600	...	...	...	5,136
1945–46........	6,300	...	...	...	5,826
1946–47........	...	...	...	...	6,389
1947–48........	...	...	...	...	5,543
1948–49........	7,248	...	...	...	5,094
1949–50	7,030	...	17,490	...	5,553
1950–51........	6,821	...	14,595	...	6,135
1951–52........	7,866	...	15,851	...	6,080
1952–53........	7,645	...	16,867	...	6,668
1953–54........	8,275	...	18,617	...	6,881
1954–55........	9,066	7,305	20,494	17,219	6,977
1955–56........	9,603	7,744	21,425	17,251	6,845
1956–57........	9,893	7,905	23,012	18,259	6,796
1957–58........	10,198	8,119	24,976	19,433	6,861

* Sources: U.S. Public Health Service, *Health Manpower Source Book* (Washington, 1959), Publication No. 263, sec. 9, p. 25; U.S. Congress, House, *Medical School Inquiry* (staff report to the Committee on Interstate and Foreign Commerce; Washington, 1957), p. 259.

table suggest that the per cent of internships and residencies held by foreign physicians in 1949–52 was probably appreciably less than the corresponding per cent in 1954–58. Thus I estimate that in 1948–51 the average length of internship and residency training of physicians about to begin practice was roughly three and one-third years.

The average amount of college preprofessional training of medical school freshmen enrolled in the school years 1948–52, as shown in Table 26, was about 3.7 years. The average amount of the college predental training of all dental undergraduates enrolled in 1951–52 was 3.1 years. The length of professional undergraduate training in both medical and dental schools was four years.

Thus in 1948–51, premedical training exceeded predental training by about $\frac{2}{3}$ of a year on the average, undergraduate medical and dental training were of equal length, and *graduate* medical training averaged about $1\frac{10}{3}$ years, making a total excess of medical training over dental training of roughly 4 years.

[83] The percentage difference in annual income just sufficient to compensate for the extra years of training of physicians may be estimated from the equation given by Friedman and Kuznets (*op. cit.*, pp. 142–43):

$$R = 100(1 + i)^t \frac{1 + \dfrac{v + c}{V}}{1 - \dfrac{u}{y}(1 - p)} - 100,$$

where

R is the compensating difference in income in per cent;

These estimates of the difference in income compensating for the extra training in medicine are approximately the same size as the measured difference in income in 1948–51.

TABLE 26

PREPROFESSIONAL TRAINING OF MEDICAL SCHOOL FRESHMEN AND
DENTAL SCHOOL UNDERGRADUATES, 1948–52

SCHOOL YEAR	PER CENT OF MEDICAL SCHOOL FRESHMEN WITH SPECIFIED YEARS OF COLLEGE PREMEDICAL TRAINING[a]				MEAN YEARS OF PREMEDICAL TRAINING[b]
	2 Years (1)	3 Years (2)	4 or More Years (3)	All Years (4)	(5)
1948–49............	0.8	35.5	63.7	100.0	3.6
1949–50............	1.0	27.2	71.8	100.0	3.7
1950–51............	0.9	20.3	78.8	100.0	3.8
1951–52............	1.1	21.5	77.4	100.0	3.8
1948–52 average.....	1.0	26.1	72.9	100.0	3.7

	PER CENT OF DENTAL SCHOOL UNDERGRADUATES WITH SPECIFIED YEARS OF COLLEGE PREDENTAL TRAINING[c]				MEAN YEARS OF PREDENTAL TRAINING[b]
	2 Years	3 Years	4 or More Years	All Years	
1948–49............	48.9	20.8	30.4	100.0	2.8
1949–50............	43.4	24.1	32.5	100.0	2.9
1950–51............	38.1	25.1	36.7	100.0	3.0
1951–52............	31.0	26.2	42.8	100.0	3.1

[a] Source: American Medical Association, *Journal of the American Medical Association,* annual issues containing the report of the Council on Medical Education.
[b] In computing these means, the per cent of students with more than four years of college preprofessional training was assumed to be negligible.
[c] Computed from American Dental Association, *Dental Students' Register,* annual issues.

t is the number of years of extra training in medicine;

i is the interest rate at which future returns and costs are discounted;

u is the number of years by which working life in dentistry exceeds working life in medicine;

V is the present value of the returns in dentistry for all except the last u years of working life in dentistry;

v is the present value of the returns in dentistry for these last u years;

y is the length of a dentist's working life in years;

c is the present value of the extra direct costs (tuition, books, etc.) of medical training minus the present value of earnings during internship and residency, including earnings in kind; and

p is the ratio of average annual income in dentistry during last u years of working life to average annual income during first $(y - u)$ years.

To a first approximation, $u = t = 4$ in 1948–51 and y was of the order of magnitude of 45 to 50. The 1948 Department of Commerce data (*Survey of Current Business* [January, 1950], 8–16) indicate that the mean income of dentists aged sixty-five and over was slightly less than half that earned by younger dentists, suggesting that p was roughly 0.5. Under the 1948–51 conditions, c was surely negative (because of internship and residency earnings) and, I suspect, c was numerically larger than v at an interest rate of 10 per cent. However, $(v + c)$ must have been small numerically compared to V. Therefore, the compensating difference in income in 1948–51 was approximately $R = 100(1 + i)^t - 100$.

The preceding comparison indicates that in 1948–51 the equilibrium income differential may have been as large as the measured differential.[84] The conclusion is supported by the data presented in the appendix to this chapter (sec. iii. 14). In particular, both in 1947–48 and in 1955–56 (data on dental school applicants are not available for the intervening school years), the ratio of the number of applicants for admission to medical schools to the corresponding number for dental schools was lower, though in 1955–56 only slightly lower, than the ratio of physicians to dentists. Moreover, in both of these years the fraction of applicants accepted for admission was higher for medical schools than for dental schools.

Thus neither the data on training and income nor the data on entry indicate that at the rates of remuneration existing in 1948–51, medicine was more attractive than dentistry to prospective practitioners.[85]

III.14. Appendix

The aggregate of the physicians in practice may be regarded as a stock of durable goods producing medical services; similarly, the dentists in practice form a stock producing dental services. In what follows I assume that:

1. The ratio of the stock of physicians to the stock of dentists is approximated satisfactorily by the ratio of the physicians in practice to the dentists in practice; and that

2. The ratio of deaths and retirements per year among medical practitioners to those among dental practitioners depends negligibly on differences in income between the two practices and differs little from the ratio of physicians to dentists.

Under these conditions the ratio of the stock of physicians to the stock of dentists and the ratio of physicians to dentists will increase, decrease,

---

[84] For 1948–51, as for 1929–34, it is difficult to make an explicit numerical adjustment of the income data for trends in medical and dental income and for differences between medicine and dentistry in income variability and in nonpecuniary aspects of training and practice. In 1929–34 the coefficient of variation of annual net income in medicine was about 50 per cent greater than that in dentistry (Friedman and Kuznets, *op. cit.*, p. 108). In 1948–51, there was little difference between medicine and dentistry in income variability (*Survey of Current Business* [January, 1950], 11, and [July, 1951], 13), particularly if allowance is made for personal income taxes.

Data on hours of work in the 1950 census (*United States Census of Population: 1950*, Special Report P-E No. 1B, *Occupational Characteristics*) indicate that in 1950 the mean number of hours of work per week of physicians was approximately 57 to 59, about one-third larger than the mean, 43 to 44, for dentists. I know of no similar data on hours of work for the 1920's and 1930's.

[85] See n. 75 above.

or remain constant as the ratio of new entrants per year into medicine to new entrants per year into dentistry exceeds, falls short of, or is equal to the ratio of physicians to dentists.

Under given conditions of demand for the services of physicians and dentists, both the difference between the actual mean net income (after taxes) of physicians and that of dentists and the corresponding expected future difference in income, as prospective entrants see it, will tend to be greater, the smaller is the ratio of physicians to dentists. Given the nonpecuniary aspects of medical and dental training and practice and the distributions of tastes for these aspects among prospective entrants, the fraction of prospective entrants who will choose medicine over dentistry will tend to be larger, if there is free entry, the greater is the difference expected by prospective entrants between the mean income *after taxes and costs of training* in medicine and the corresponding mean income in dentistry. Under the demand conditions for the services of physicians and dentists and the supply conditions, including training costs, for new entrants prevailing at a given date, there is some expected income difference at which the ratio of those who would choose medicine to those who would choose dentistry would be the same as the ratio of physicians to dentists. This income difference is the *equilibrium* income difference, and the corresponding ratio of physicians to dentists is the *equilibrium* ratio of practitioners.

If at the given date the income difference expected by prospective entrants were the same as the equilibrium income difference, then the ratio of prospective entrants choosing medicine to those choosing dentistry would equal the existing ratio of physicians to dentists, and, under the given demand and supply conditions, there would be no tendency for the existing income difference or the existing ratio of physicians to dentists to change.

Free entry, of course, does not guarantee that at all times the actual and equilibrium income differences be equal and, therefore, that the existing ratio of physicians to dentists be equal to the equilibrium ratio. For example, if the demand for the services of physicians were continually to grow relative to the demand for the services of dentists, then with free entry and given conditions of supply of new entrants, the income difference expected by prospective entrants would persistently exceed the corresponding equilibrium income difference, the existing ratio of physicians to dentists would persistently be less than the corresponding equilibrium ratio, and the ratio of prospective entrants choosing medicine to those choosing dentistry would continually exceed the existing ratio of physicians to dentists. Thus an excess of the ratio of persons seeking to enter medicine to persons seeking to enter dentistry over the ratio of physicians to dentists is not necessarily evidence of greater limitations on entry into medicine than into dentistry.

Hence suppose that there are limitations on entry into medicine but not into dentistry and that the limitations are objective and well-known minimum standards of training of physicians which are higher than would otherwise be established by the demands of consumers of the services of physicians. Assume also that at the time the standards are imposed, the market for the services of physicians and dentists is in long-run equilibrium in the sense stated in the preceding paragraphs. The imposition of the standards has the immediate effect of raising the difference between the expected cost of medical training and the expected cost of dental training, as prospective entrants see it, and thus lowers the expected difference between the income after taxes and costs of training in medicine and that in dentistry. The ratio of prospective entrants into medicine to prospective entrants into dentistry, therefore, will decline below the existing ratio of physicians to dentists. Shortly, the ratio of medical school graduates to dental school graduates will also fall below the physicians/dentists ratio and the latter itself will decline. But as the ratio of physicians to dentists declines, the mean net income (before costs of training) of physicians will tend to rise relative to the corresponding mean income in dentistry. Hence the income difference expected by prospective entrants eventually will rise. The adjustment process will continue until the expected income difference has risen to the new equilibrium income difference in the presence of the minimum standards.

Notice that while the adjustment process is going on, the ratio of would-be physicians to would-be dentists is *lower* than the ratio of physicians to dentists. Once the adjustment to the new standards has been completed, there will be no tendency attributable to the imposition of the standards for the ratio of would-be physicians to would-be dentists to differ from the ratio of physicians to dentists.

Minimum standards of the above type do have the enduring effect of making the difference between the income *gross of costs of training* of physicians and that of dentists higher than it otherwise would be, but only by enough to compensate the physicians subject to the standards for the increment in training costs resulting from the imposition of the standards. Exemption of physicians already in practice from complying with the standards will tend to increase their income *net* of costs of training.

Suppose that, in contrast to the case just considered, the limitations on entry into medicine were to consist of concerted actions which restricted the number of entrants into medicine to a level lower than would otherwise prevail and that the criteria for selecting new entrants were very poorly known to the prospective entrants. To simplify the exposition, I assume that the restriction of numbers takes place at the point of entry into medical school, that premedical training is highly unspecialized to medicine, and that the selection procedure is a strictly random one. These restrictions will have the following effects: (a) a lower ratio of *accepted* applicants to medical schools to *accepted* applicants to dental schools; (b) subsequently, lower ratios of medical school graduates to dental school graduates and of medical practitioners to dental practitioners; and (c) higher observed and expected income differences (net of taxes and costs of training) between medicine and dentistry. Such limitations on entry could thus persistently hold the observed income difference above the equilibrium difference without leading to an increase in the ratio of physicians to dentists or an excess of the ratio of medical freshmen (or graduates) to dental school freshmen (or graduates) over the ratio of physicians to dentists.

The second type of limitation, moreover, tends to cause the ratio of persons seeking to enter medical schools to persons seeking to enter dental schools to be higher for a cohort of prospective entrants, relative to the corresponding ratios of medical school accepted applicants to dental school accepted applicants, medical school freshmen to dental school freshmen, and medical school graduates to dental school graduates, than would be true with free entry. However, a higher rate of attrition (through failure to be admitted to professional schooling or from lack of success at later points in the process of preparing for entry into practice) among would-be physicians than among would-be dentists is good evidence of greater restriction of numbers into medicine than into dentistry only if such a difference in attrition rates would not be observed under free entry.

The preprofessional training of physicians and dentists is not highly specialized. Medical and dental school faculties and physical facilities, on the other hand, are relatively highly specialized to the particular professional training. Moreover, both medical and dental schools are commonly affiliated with non-profit institutions, universities, which are unaccustomed to the use of tuition rates to ration admissions among applicants. Thus there is reason to expect that, under free entry, prospective entrants to professional training would be more responsive to changes in underlying demand conditions than would the schools that provide the training. Therefore, with free entry, the attrition rate in a given professional training in the short run would tend to be positively correlated over time with the number of applicants per year for admission to professional schools and the attrition rate would tend to be higher in the short run in the profession in which the demand for new practitioners was growing most rapidly. Of course, even in the absence of adjustments of the actual ratio of physicians to dentists to the corresponding equilibrium level of the ratio, there might be a persistent tendency for the attrition rate among would-be physicians to *differ* from that among would-be dentists. However, I have been unable to think of any very plausible reason why the rate for physicians should *exceed* that for dentists rather than the reverse.

Turn now to Tables 27, 28, 29, 30, and 31. The first two tables show the number of practitioners, professional schools, students, and graduates in medicine and dentistry. Table 29 contains the ratios of the figures in Table 27 to those in Table 28. Table 30 contains data on applicants to medical and dental schools. Table 31 shows the mean net income of nonsalaried physicians and nonsalaried dentists for the period 1929–51.

By 1895, most of the states had administrative organizations to examine and license physicians, but the premedical and medical training requirements were not high. The period of rapid increase in minimum training standards began in 1904 with the establishment of the American Medical Association's Council on Medical Education (on these and later developments in medicine and dentistry see Friedman and Kuznets, chap. i). Before 1905 the number of medical schools, their enrollment, and their graduates had been growing rapidly enough to maintain an approximately constant number of physicians per capita in the United States. Between the school year 1903–1904 and that of 1918–19, the number of medical schools fell by almost one-half, medical school enrollment and graduates declined by more than one-half, and physicians per capita fell by one-ninth. From 1918–19 to 1928–29 the number of medical schools fell by another 10 per cent. Medical school enrollment and graduates increased, however, but the decline in physicians per capita did not stop until 1929. In 1929 there were one-fifth fewer physicians per capita than in 1900. Unquestionably, the decline from 1904 to 1929 in physicians per capita stemmed in large part from the increased standards of training imposed in medicine.

The raising of training standards in dentistry came later and was less pronounced. Although the number of dental schools decreased by one-third from 1900 to 1930, there was no marked tendency for enrollment and graduates of dental schools to fall until the mid-1920's, and the number of dentists per capita increased by one-third from 1900 to 1929.

TABLE 27

PHYSICIANS, MEDICAL SCHOOLS, STUDENTS, AND GRADUATES, 1900–1959*

YEAR	NUMBER OF PHYSICIANS[a]	MEDICAL SCHOOLS				PHYSICIANS PER 100,000 POPULATION[a]
		Number[a]	Students		Graduates[b]	
			Total[b]	Freshmen[b]		
	(1)	(2)	(3)	(4)	(5)	(6)
1900........	119,749	160	25,171	...	5,214	157
1904........	128,950	160	28,142	...	5,747	157
1910........	135,000	131	21,526	...	4,440	146
1916........	145,241	95	14,012	3,582	3,518	142
1918........	147,812	90	13,630	4,283	2,670	141
1921........	145,404	83	14,466	4,825	3,186	134
1923........	145,966	80	16,960	5,162	3,120	130
1925........	147,010	80	18,200	5,492	3,974	127
1927........	149,521	80	19,662	6,009	4,035	126
1929........	152,503	76	20,878	6,277	4,446	125
1930........	154,600[c]	76	21,597	6,457	4,565	125[c]
1931........	156,406	76	21,982	6,456	4,735	126
1932........	...	76	22,135	6,260	4,936	...
1933........	...	77	22,466	6,426	4,895	...
1934........	161,359	77	22,799	6,457	5,035	128
1935........	...	77	22,888	6,356	5,101	...
1936........	165,163	77	22,564	6,605	5,183	129
1937........	...	77	22,095	5,910	5,377	...
1938........	169,628	77	21,587	5,791	5,194	131
1939........	...	77	21,302	5,764	5,089	...
1940........	175,163	77	21,271	5,794	5,097	133
1941........	...	77	21,379	5,837	5,275	...
1942........	180,496	77	22,031	6,218	5,163	134
1943........	...	76	22,631	6,425	5,223	...
1944........	...	77	48,195	13,209	10,303	...
1945........	...	77	24,028	6,523	5,136	...
1946........	...	77	23,216	6,060	5,826	...
1947........	...	77	23,900	6,564	6,389	...
1948........	...	77	22,739	6,487	5,543	...
1949........	201,277	78	23,670	6,688	5,094	135
1950........	203,400	79	25,103	7,042	5,553	134
1951........	205,500	79	26,186	7,177	6,135	133
1952........	207,900	79	27,076	7,436	6,080	132
1953........	210,900	79	27,688	7,542	6,668	132
1954........	214,200	80	28,227	7,525	6,881	132
1955........	218,061	81	28,583	7,645	6,977	132
1956........	...	83	28,748	7,742	6,845	...
1957........	226,625	85	29,130	8,014	6,796	132
1958........	230,600	85	29,473	8,030	6,861	132
1959........	...	85	29,614	8,128	6,895	...

* Sources: *Health Manpower Source Book*, sec. 9, pp. 9, 23; *Medical School Inquiry*, p. 211; U.S. Bureau of the Census, *Historical Statistics of the United States, Colonial Times to 1957* (Washington, 1960), p. 34; U.S. Bureau of the Census, *Statistical Abstract of the United States: 1960* (Washington, 1960), p. 73; *Journal of the American Medical Association*, annual issues containing the report of the Council on Medical Education.
   a Cols. (1) and (6): Physicians as of July 1 of the specified year, including those retired or not in practice for other reasons, but excluding graduates of the specified year.
   b Cols. (2), (3), (4), and (5): Medical schools, students, and graduates for the academic session ending in the specified year; includes University of Puerto Rico since 1954.
   c Estimated from corresponding figures for 1929 and 1931.

TABLE 28

Dentists, Dental Schools, Students, and Graduates, 1900–1959*

YEAR	NUMBER OF DENTISTS[a]	DENTAL SCHOOLS				DENTISTS PER 100,000 POPULATION
		Number[b]	Students		Graduates[b]	
			Total[b]	Freshmen[b]		
	(1)	(2)	(3)	(4)	(5)	(6)
1900........	29,665	57	...	...	2,091	39
1910........	39,997	54	...	...	1,646	43
1916........	44,800c	49	...	...	2,835	44c
1918........	48,000c	46	...	...	3,345	47c
1921........	57,000c	45	11,745	...	1,795	53c
1923........	...	45	...	...	3,271	...
1925........	64,481	43	11,863	...	2,590	56
1927........	66,400c	40	10,333	...	2,642	56c
1929........	70,200c	40	8,200	...	2,442	58c
1930........	73,108	38	7,813	...	1,561	59
1931........	...	38	8,129	1,929	1,842	...
1932........	...	38	8,031	1,913	1,840	...
1933........	...	39	7,508	1,637	1,986	...
1934........	...	39	7,160	1,876	1,864	...
1935........	...	39	7,175	2,013	1,840	...
1936........	...	39	7,306	2,175	1,736	...
1937........	...	39	7,397	2,131	1,739	...
1938........	...	39	7,184	1,821	1,704	...
1939........	...	39	7,331	2,074	1,794	...
1940........	81,686	39	7,407	2,183	1,757	62
1941........	...	39	7,720	2,305	1,568	...
1942........	...	39	8,355	2,476	1,784	...
1943........	...	39	8,847	2,702	1,926	...
1944........	...	39	9,014	2,562	2,470	...
1945........	...	39	8,590	2,496	3,212	...
1946........	...	39	7,274	1,201	2,666	...
1947........	80,765	40	8,287	2,974	2,225	56
1948........	...	40	8,996	3,055	1,755	...
1949........	85,330	41	10,132	3,102	1,574	57
1950........	86,876	41	11,460	3,119	2,565	57
1951........	...	42	11,891	3,226	2,830	...
1952........	88,920	42	12,169	3,260	2,975	57
1953........	90,815	42	12,370	3,244	2,945	57
1954........	92,851	43	12,516	3,274	3,084	57
1955........	94,510	43	12,601	3,329	3,081	57
1956........	96,227	43	12,730	3,445	3,038	57
1957........	97,610	45	13,004	3,561	3,050	57
1958........	98,540	47	13,279	3,600	3,083	57
1959........	...	47	13,509	3,607	...	...

* Sources: *Health Manpower Source Book*, sec. 9, pp. 48, 55; *Medical School Inquiry*, p. 421.
a Col. (1): Dentists (gainful workers) as of *Census* date 1900 and 1910. Dentists as of July 1 for other years; includes dentists not in practice or retired and excludes graduates of the specified year.
b Cols. (2), (3), (4), and (5): Dental schools, students, and graduates for academic session (July 1 to June 30) ending in the specified year; includes University of Puerto Rico since 1958.
c Rough estimates computed from figures for other years.

As a consequence, I believe, of the greater increase in standards of training in medicine than in dentistry, the ratio of physicians to dentists (Table 29) fell by almost one-half from 1900 to 1929, and it was not until

TABLE 29

RATIOS OF PHYSICIANS TO DENTISTS AND OF MEDICAL SCHOOLS, STUDENTS AND
GRADUATES TO DENTAL SCHOOLS, STUDENTS AND GRADUATES, 1900–1959*

YEAR	PHYSICIANS ÷ DENTISTS (1)	MEDICAL SCHOOLS ÷ DENTAL SCHOOLS			
		Number (2)	Students		Graduates (5)
			Total (3)	Freshmen (4)	
1900.........	4.04	2.81	...	...	2.49
1910.........	3.38	2.43	...	...	2.70
1916.........	3.24	1.94	...	...	1.24
1918.........	3.08	1.96	...	...	0.80
1921.........	2.55	1.84	1.23	...	1.77
1923.........	...	1.78	...	...	0.95
1925.........	2.28	1.86	1.53	...	1.53
1927.........	2.25	2.00	1.90	...	1.53
1929.........	2.17	1.90	2.55	...	1.82
1930.........	2.11	2.00	2.76	...	2.92
1931.........	...	2.00	2.70	3.35	2.57
1932.........	...	2.00	2.76	3.27	2.68
1933.........	...	1.97	2.99	3.93	2.46
1934.........	...	1.97	3.18	3.44	2.70
1935.........	...	1.97	3.19	3.16	2.77
1936.........	...	1.97	3.09	3.04	2.99
1937.........	...	1.97	2.99	2.77	3.09
1938.........	...	1.97	3.00	3.18	3.05
1939.........	...	1.97	2.91	2.78	2.84
1940.........	2.14	1.97	2.87	2.65	2.90
1941.........	...	1.97	2.77	2.53	3.36
1942.........	...	1.97	2.64	2.51	2.89
1943.........	...	1.95	2.56	2.38	2.71
1944.........	...	1.97	5.35	5.16	4.17
1945.........	...	1.97	2.80	2.61	1.60
1946.........	...	1.97	3.19	5.05	2.19
1947.........	...	1.92	2.88	2.21	2.87
1948.........	...	1.92	2.53	2.12	3.16
1949.........	2.36	1.90	2.34	2.16	3.24
1950.........	2.34	1.93	2.19	2.26	2.16
1951.........	...	1.88	2.20	2.22	2.17
1952.........	2.34	1.88	2.22	2.28	2.04
1953.........	2.32	1.88	2.24	2.32	2.26
1954.........	2.31	1.86	2.26	2.30	2.23
1955.........	2.31	1.88	2.27	2.30	2.26
1956.........	...	1.93	2.26	2.25	2.25
1957.........	2.32	1.89	2.24	2.25	2.23
1958.........	2.34	1.81	2.22	2.23	2.23
1959.........	...	1.81	2.19	2.25	...

* Computed from Tables 27 and 28.

1928–29 that the ratio of medical to dental school enrollment exceeded
the ratio of physicians to dentists. The possibility cannot be ruled out,
however, that the decline in the ratio of physicians to dentists resulted
in part from rising demand for the services of dentists relative to the
demand for the services of physicians. Widening the difference between

TABLE 30

APPLICANTS TO MEDICAL AND DENTAL SCHOOLS, 1926–60*

SCHOOL YEAR	NUMBER OF APPLICANTS TO MEDICAL SCHOOLS			NUMBER OF APPLICANTS TO DENTAL SCHOOLS		
	Total (1)	Accepted (2)	Per Cent Accepted (3)	Total (4)	Accepted (5)	Per Cent Accepted (6)
1926–27.....	10,006	6,420	64.2	...	...	...
1927–28.....	11,019	6,496	59.0	...	...	...
1928–29.....	12,420	6,974	56.2	...	...	...
1929–30.....	13,655	7,035	51.5	...	...	...
1930–31.....	...	...	...	...	...	...
1931–32.....	...	...	...	...	...	...
1932–33.....	12,280	7,357	59.9	...	...	...
1933–34.....	12,128	7,543	62.2	...	...	...
1934–35.....	12,779	7,419	58.1	...	...	...
1935–36.....	12,740	6,900	54.2	...	...	...
1936–37.....	12,192	6,465	53.0	...	...	...
1937–38.....	12,207	6,410	52.5	...	...	...
1938–39.....	12,131	6,223	51.3	...	...	...
1939–40.....	11,800	6,219	52.7	...	...	...
1940–41.....	11,854	6,328	53.4	...	...	...
1941–42.....	11,940	6,822	57.2	3,350	2,797	83.5
1942–43.....	14,043	6,835	48.7	...	...	...
1943–44.....	...	...	...	...	...	...
1944–45.....	...	...	...	...	...	...
1945–46.....	...	...	...	...	...	...
1946–47.....	...	...	...	...	...	...
1947–48.....	18,829	6,682[a]	35.5	10,293	2,899	28.2
1948–49.....	24,242	6,973	28.8	...	...	...
1949–50.....	24,434	7,253[a]	29.7	...	...	...
1950–51.....	22,279	7,254	32.6	...	...	...
1951–52.....	19,920	7,663	38.5	...	...	...
1952–53.....	16,763	7,778	46.4	...	...	...
1953–54.....	14,678	7,756	52.8	...	...	...
1954–55.....	14,538	7,878	54.2	...	...	...
1955–56.....	14,937	7,969	53.4	7,205	3,445	47.8
1956–57.....	15,917	8,263	51.9	7,376	3,561	48.3
1957–58.....	15,791	8,302	52.6	7,286	3,600	49.4
1958–59.....	15,170	8,366	55.1	6,469	3,607	55.8
1959–60.....	14,952	8,512	56.9	6,498	3,573	55.0

* Sources: Friedman and Kuznets, *op. cit.*, pp. 14, 24; *Health Manpower Source Book*, sec. 9, p. 22; Association of American Medical Colleges, *Datagrams*, October, 1960; and unpublished data of the American Dental Association.

a Rough estimates computed from figures for other years.

the training of physicians and the training of dentists would tend to raise the income difference (before costs of training) between physicians and dentists; growing demand for dentists relative to physicians, on the other hand, would tend to reduce the income difference. Unfortunately, income data for physicians and dentists extending back of 1929 are not available.

It would also be useful to have similar historical data on the number of applicants for admission to medical and dental schools. If, as I pointed

TABLE 31

MEAN NET INCOME OF NONSALARIED PHYSICIANS AND
NONSALARIED DENTISTS, 1929–1951*

YEAR	MEAN NET INCOME					
	In Current Dollars		Ratio of Col. (1) to Col. (2) (3)	In 1947–49 Dollars		Col. (4) minus Col. (5) (6)
	Nonsalaried Physicians (1)	Nonsalaried Dentists (2)		Nonsalaried Physicians (4)	Nonsalaried Dentists (5)	
1929........	5,224	4,267	1.224	7,127	5,821	1,306
1930........	4,870	4,020	1.211	6,821	5,630	1,191
1931........	4,178	3,422	1.221	6,428	5,265	1,163
1932........	3,178	2,479	1.282	5,442	4,245	1,197
1933........	2,948	2,188	1.347	5,331	3,957	1,374
1934........	3,382	2,391	1.414	5,913	4,180	1,733
1935........	3,695	2,485	1.487	6,295	4,233	2,062
1936........	4,204	2,726	1.542	7,089	4,597	2,492
1937........	4,285	2,883	1.486	6,979	4,695	2,284
1938........	4,093	2,870	1.426	6,788	4,760	2,028
1939........	4,229	3,096	1.366	7,120	5,212	1,908
1940........	4,441	3,314	1.340	7,414	5,533	1,881
1941........	5,047	3,782	1.334	8,024	6,013	2,011
1942........	6,735	4,625	1.456	9,663	6,636	3,027
1943........	8,310	5,715	1.465	11,311	7,723	3,588
1944........	9,802	6,649	1.474	13,035	8,842	4,193
1945........	10,975	6,922	1.586	14,272	9,001	5,271
1946........	10,202	6,381	1.599	12,233	7,651	4,582
1947........	10,726	6,610	1.623	11,231	6,921	4,310
1948........	11,327	7,039	1.609	11,018	6,847	4,171
1949........	11,744	7,146	1.643	11,536	7,020	4,516
1950........	12,324	7,436	1.657	11,988	7,233	4,755
1951........	13,432	7,820	1.718	12,101	7,045	5,056

* Sources: Cols. (1) and (2) are from *Survey of Current Business,* January, 1950, pp. 8–16, Table 2; July, 1951, pp. 9–26, Table 1; July, 1952, pp. 5–7. The cost of living index used to calculate cols. (4) and (5) from cols. (1) and (2) is the Bureau of Labor Statistics, "Consumer Price Index."

out earlier, the limitations on entry imposed in the period before 1930 consisted entirely of higher, objective minimum standards of training, one would expect to observe ratios of *accepted* applicants (or freshman enrolled) to total applicants which on the average were no lower in medicine than in dentistry. However, to the extent that the limitations restricted numbers (at the point of entry into professional school) without raising standards and costs of training in a way which was easily perceivable to prospective entrants, the limitations would tend to lower the ratio of accepted to total applicants in medicine below that in dentistry. However, there are no data on applicants to dental schools before 1941–42. In that year, dental schools accepted 83.5 per cent of their applicants (Table 30). This figure is much higher than any of the figures for medical schools in the period 1926–27 to 1941–42. However, the ratio of medical to dental school enrollment in 1941–42 was considerably higher than it was on the average in the 1920's. Furthermore, the income data in Table 31 indicate that the difference between the mean income (before taxes and costs of training) of physicians and that of dentists in each of the four or five years preceding 1941–42 was substantially higher than in 1929. Thus the data on applicants for 1941–42 may be a misleading basis for judging the differences between medical and dental schools in the per cent of applicants admitted during the period 1904–29.

From 1929 to 1949 the ratio of physicians to dentists increased by about one-ninth; from 1949 to the early 1950's the ratio apparently declined slightly and then became stable. With a small allowance for the imperfections in the data, the figures on medical and dental students and graduates are closely consistent with those for practitioners: the difference between the ratio of medical school freshmen to dental school freshmen and the ratio of physicians to dentists appears to have been positive from the late 1920's to 1945–46, slightly negative from 1946–47 to 1949–50, and close to zero thereafter; the difference between the ratio of medical to dental school graduates and the ratio of physicians to dentists was positive from 1930 to 1949, negative in the next three years, and then nearly zero.

Although data on applicants to medical schools are available beginning in 1926–27, there are few similar data for dental schools before 1955–56. (The American Dental Association has released data for the school years 1951–52, 1952–53, 1953–54, and 1954–55 which have been published in various places as data on "applicants to dental schools." These numbers, not shown in Table 30, refer, not to *all* applicants to U.S. dental schools, but only to those who in a given year took the Dental Aptitude Test and in the same year applied for admission to dental training.) In 1941–42, a year in which the ratio of physicians to dentists apparently was growing, the acceptance rate among applicants to dental schools was much higher than that among applicants to medical schools. In 1947–48, a year after the ratio of medical school freshmen to dental school freshmen had fallen below the ratio of physicians to dentists, the acceptance rate among dental school applicants was lower than the acceptance rate among medical school applicants. The acceptance rate in dental schools was slightly lower than in medical schools in the school years 1955–56 to 1957–58, but in 1958–60 the two acceptance rates differed but little.

The data on applicants to medical and dental schools viewed individually behave in most respects as expected, given low short-run elasticities of supply of training services: the per cent of applicants rejected, except in medical schools in the period 1934–35 to 1938–39, generally changed in the same direction as the number of applicants per year. However, the very sharp decline from 1934–35 to 1938–39 in the number and per cent of applicants accepted for admission to medical schools is a marked deviation from the expected pattern and incriminates organized medicine of a policy of restriction of numbers, at least during this period.

There is little evidence in the data on applicants for the years after World War II, however, to suggest that the difference between medicine and dentistry in difficulty of entry was greater than in the 1920's and 1930's or even that entry into medicine was more difficult than entry into dentistry. There were, it is true, fewer applicants per year accepted for admission to medical schools in the school years beginning in the four-year period 1947–50 than had been accepted in the three years beginning in the period 1932–34, yet the data suggest that in the postwar years the per cent of applicants accepted by medical schools was higher than that for dental schools.

The data in Tables 27–31 for 1929 and later years cannot be explained by relative supply factors—differences between medicine and dentistry in costs of training and in conditions of entry—under given conditions of demand for physicians relative to demand for dentists, for both the ratio of physicians to dentists and the ratio of the mean income (before costs of training) of physicians to that of dentists rose from 1929 to 1949. Under given conditions of relative demand, an increasing difference between medicine and dentistry in costs of training or in difficulty of entry would tend to increase the difference in income (before costs of training) between physicians and dentists, but would tend to reduce the ratio of physicians to dentists; a falling difference in costs of training or in difficulty of entry would have opposite effects. Thus these data indicate an upward trend in the demand for physicians relative to the demand for dentists from about 1929 to the end of World War II.

IV

Earlier Studies of Unions and Wage Differentials: The "Economy-wide" Studies

IV.1. The Ross–Goldner and the Ross Studies[1]

EACH OF THE STUDIES reviewed in chapter iii dealt with a small part of the labor force: those employed in a particular industry or occupation. In contrast, all of the studies discussed in this chapter cover relatively large segments of the economy.

Because Professors Ross and Goldner viewed their 1950 study as improving upon the 1948 study by Ross, I discuss the 1950 paper first.

For production workers in each of class I steam railroads, street railways and motor buses, electric light and power utilities, four mining industries employing a large fraction of production workers in the mining industry division, and forty-three manufacturing industries employing most of the production workers in that industry division, Ross and Goldner estimated for January–June, 1933, and the years 1938, 1942, and 1946: (a) average straight-time hourly earnings (ASTHE) and (b) extent of collective-bargaining coverage. For the base date, January–June, 1933, and each of the given dates, 1938, 1942, and 1946, they classified the industries according to their extent of collective-bargaining coverage as follows (the group notation is mine rather than the authors'):

Group A: more than 40 per cent unionized at base date.
Group 1: less than 40 per cent unionized at base date and given date.
Group 2: less than 40 per cent unionized at base date, 40 to 60 per cent unionized at given date.
Group 3: less than 40 per cent unionized at base date, 60 to 80 per cent unionized at given date.
Group 4: less than 40 per cent unionized at base date, 80 to 100 per cent unionized at given date.

For each of these five unionism groups they computed the mean increase (in cents per hour) in ASTHE from the base date to each of the given dates with the results shown in Table 32.

Assume for the moment that the differences among unionism groups in

[1] Arthur M. Ross, "The Influence of Unionism upon Earnings," *Quarterly Journal of Economics*, LXII, No. 2 (February, 1948), 263–86; Arthur M. Ross and William Goldner, "Forces Affecting the Interindustry Wage Structure," *Quarterly Journal of Economics*, LXIV, No. 2 (May, 1950), 254–81.

TABLE 32

MEAN INCREASE IN AVERAGE STRAIGHT-TIME HOURLY EARNINGS,
1933–38, 1933–42, AND 1933–46*

UNIONISM GROUP	MEAN INCREASE IN ASTHE FROM BASE DATE TO GIVEN DATE (Cents per Hour)		
	1933–38	1933–42	1933–46
A.........	11.9	18.8	48.2
1..........	19.2	31.1	57.1
2..........	19.1	34.0	56.3
3..........	27.8	37.6	64.1
4..........	36.4	53.1	68.3

* The means in Table 32, taken from Ross and Goldner's Table IV, are weighted arithmetic means with given date production-worker employment weights. The 1933–46 means are based on the data for 50 industries, those for 1933–42 on the data for 49 industries, and those for 1933–38 on the data for 48 industries.

wage changes from base date to given dates shown in Table 32 were, except for random factors, entirely the result of changes in unionism from base date to given dates. What does the table then imply with respect to the size of the relative wage effects of unionism in the period 1933–46?

Consider first Group A. This group (newspaper and periodical printing; book and job printing; furniture; manufacturing of marble, granite, slate, and other stone products; men's clothing manufacturing; and class I steam railroads), according to Ross and Goldner, was already about half-unionized in 1933. Therefore, it cannot be presumed that at the base date the effect of unionism on the average relative wage of this group was zero. However, the weighted mean ASTHE for this group at the base was the highest of the five groups (using the 1933–46 grouping). Thus Table 32 implies that for this group the relative wage effect of unionism declined substantially from 1933 to 1946. This result is not altogether surprising, for the effect of unionism on the average relative wage of this group may have been unusually high at the base date. Note that about three-fifths of the production workers in this group were employed in the class I railroad industry. Between 1929 and 1933 average hourly earnings of wage-earners in class I railroads rose about 20 per cent relative to average hourly earnings of wage-earners in all manufacturing industries.[2]

Now consider Groups 1–4. These four groups were more or less similarly situated with respect to unionism in the base date. In all of them the extent of unionism was low, probably differing little from extent of unionism in the labor force as a whole. Therefore, as a first approximation

[2] *Handbook of Labor Statistics* (1947 ed.), Bulletin No. 916, Table C-1.

it seems reasonable to assume that in 1933 the effects of unionism on the relative wages of these groups were negligible in size. But then under the above assumption that the figures in Table 32 reflect only random factors and the effects of unionism, the data in the table for these groups may be used to estimate the relative wage effects of unionism for these groups as of 1938, 1942, and 1946.

I have computed (from the data in Table 32 and in their Table I) for each given year (1938, 1942, and 1946) the regression of the mean increases in ASTHE from the base year to the given year on the midpoints of the extent of unionism classes in the given year. (The four observations in each regression, one for each unionism group, were weighted by production-worker employment in the given year.) For all three years the regression coefficient was approximately 0.2 cents per hour per percentage point difference in extent of unionism. This, in turn, implies that:[3]

[3] The figures in col. (1) of the table below are Albert Rees's estimates of average hourly earnings in manufacturing industries (see his *New Measures of Wage-Earner Compensation in Manufacturing, 1914–1957*, Table 1).

YEAR	AVERAGE HOURLY EARNINGS (Cents per Hour) (1)	REGRESSION COEFFICIENT	
		(Cents/Hour) (2)	(Per Cent) (3)
1938.........	60.3	0.20	0.33
1942.........	82.7	0.22	0.27
1946.........	108.	0.22	0.20

The regression coefficients computed from Table 32 are shown in col. (2). These coefficients, in cents per hour, have been converted to corresponding percentage coefficients by dividing 100 times col. (2) by col. (1).

Col. (1) of the table below shows the estimates of the extent of unionism in the labor force as a whole for 1938, 1942, and 1946 given in my Table 72 of chap. vii. The figures in col. (2) are estimates of the extent of unionism among wage-earners in manufacturing industries. They are based on the degree of unionization and wage-earner employment data in Ross and Goldner's Table I. Col. (3) is col. (2) minus col. (1). Col. (4) is the product of col. (3) and the regression coefficients in col. (2) of the table above. The figures in col. (4) are estimates of the effects of unionism on the wage differential in cents per hour between manufacturing wage-earners and all employees in the labor force. Comparison of the figures in col. (4) with those in col. (1) of the table above indicates that in all three years the effect of unionism on the relative wages of wage-earners in manufacturing industries was about 10 per cent.

YEAR	EXTENT OF UNIONISM		COL. (2) MINUS COL. (1) (Per Cent) (3)	COL. (3) TIMES REGRESSION COEFFICIENT (Cents/Hour) (4)
	Employed Labor Force (Per Cent) (1)	Wage-Earners in Manufacturing (Per Cent) (2)		
1938........	17	48	31	6.2
1942........	19	54	35	7.7
1946........	26	69	43	9.5

1. At money wage levels equal on the average to those in manufacturing, the estimated average *relative* wage effect of a *one* percentage point difference in extent of unionism among industries was about 0.33 per cent in 1938, 0.27 per cent in 1942, and 0.20 per cent in 1946; and

2. In all three years the effect of unionism on the average relative wage in manufacturing industries was about 10 per cent.

(The computations of relative wage effects of unionism given above in this paragraph, though based chiefly on the data in Ross and Goldner Tables I and IV, are mine, not theirs. At no point in their paper did they attempt to squeeze out of these data *any* numerical estimates of the impact of unionism on relative wage differentials among industries.)

The estimates of relative wage effects of unionism in the preceding paragraph assume, of course, that the effects of other factors on money wage differentials among industries in the period 1933–46 either were of negligible importance or were uncorrelated with the effects of unionism. The period from 1933 to 1946 was one of rapid inflation of the general level of money wages. The average straight-time hourly earnings of the fifty industries covered in their Table IV rose by almost 125 per cent from 1933 to 1946. Furthermore, the industries in unionism Groups 3 and 4 had average straight-time hourly earnings that were substantially higher than the corresponding averages for Groups 1 and 2. For example, in 1933 the averages by unionism groups (using the 1933–46 groups) were: Group 1, 26.1 cents per hour; Group 2, 40.5; Group 3, 47.0; and Group 4, 52.4. These data suggest that the effects of inflation on money wage differentials may have been large and positively correlated with the changes in extent of unionism and, therefore, that Table 32 may lead to overestimates of the effects of unionism during the period.

The Ross and Goldner choice of the money wage unit in their comparisons of wage changes among unionism groups was not a casual one. They devoted almost half their paper to presentation and discussion of evidence that led them to this choice. Briefly, their reasons were:

1. For each industry included in their study and for each of the periods 1933–38, 1938–42, 1942–46, and 1933–46 they computed the percentage increase in average earnings from the first to the last year in the period. These percentage increases were then classified according to the level of average earnings in the first year of the period (see their Table II). They observed that in all four periods the higher the average earnings in the first year of the period, the lower the average percentage *increase* in average earnings from the first to the last year of the period. From these data they concluded (p. 263) that "Table II makes it clear that percentage differentials were compressed continuously throughout the 1933–46 period."

2. They then computed a similar table (Table III) in which the percentage changes were replaced by the corresponding money wage changes. They observed that these absolute changes in wages had little correlation with the levels of wages in the first year of each period and concluded (p. 265) that "if absolute differentials have widened as the general level of earnings has advanced, during the period under consideration, the widening has been so small as to be insignificant."

It was this evidence of declining relative wage differentials, but apparently more or less constant money wage differentials, which led them to choose the money wage unit in their wage change comparisons.

The authors' conclusions (quoted above), however, do not follow from the data in their Tables II and III.[4] Although relative wage differentials did decline during the period 1933–46, *absolute differentials increased substantially.* From their Table I, I have computed three measures of absolute dispersion and three measures of relative dispersion for 1933 and 1946. The measures are shown in Table 33. The three measures of relative wage dispersion were substantially smaller in 1946 than in 1933.

---

[4] The error made by Ross and Goldner in interpreting their Tables II and III, commonly called the "regression fallacy," is one that has often been made in empirical studies of wage dispersion, yet is rarely discussed in statistical textbooks. The following is a formal treatment of the error. Denote by:

x and y:	wages at the base date and the given date, respectively;
σ_x and σ_y:	the standard deviations of wages at the base and given dates, respectively;
$d = y - x$:	the changes in wages from the base date to the given date;
$\Delta\sigma = \sigma_y - \sigma_x$:	the change in wage dispersion from the base date to the given date;
r:	the simple correlation coefficient between x and y;
b_{dx} and b_{dy}:	the simple regression coefficients of d on x and d on y, respectively.

It follows from the definitions of simple correlation and regression coefficients that

$$b_{dx} = \frac{\Delta\sigma}{\sigma_x} - \frac{\sigma_y}{\sigma_x}(1 - r) \qquad\text{(a)}$$

and

$$b_{dy} = \frac{\Delta\sigma}{\sigma_y} + \frac{\sigma_x}{\sigma_y}(1 - r). \qquad\text{(b)}$$

The usual form of the regression fallacy is that b_{dx} and $\Delta\sigma$ have the same sign. Equation (a) shows that unless $r = +1$, b_{dx} may be zero or even negative when $\Delta\sigma$ is positive. If b_{dx} is positive, however, $\Delta\sigma$ must also be positive. In general, b_{dx} is an underestimate of $\Delta\sigma/\sigma_x$. The regression fallacy much less often takes the form of assuming that b_{dy} and $\Delta\sigma$ have the same sign. Equation (b) shows that in general, b_{dy} is an *overestimate* of $\Delta\sigma/\sigma_y$.

TABLE 33

ABSOLUTE AND RELATIVE WAGE DISPERSION, 1933 AND 1946

MEASURE OF DISPERSION	AMOUNT OF DISPERSION		
	1933	1946	1946/1933
Standard deviation (cents per hour)...............	11.95	16.46	1.38
Mean deviation from mean (cents per hour)........	9.35	13.54	1.45
Interquartile range (cents per hour)...............	15.2	23.2	1.53
Standard deviation divided by mean (per cent).....	25.8	15.5	0.60
Mean deviation divided by mean (per cent)........	20.2	12.7	0.63
Interquartile range divided by median (per cent)....	33.5	22.6	0.67

However, absolute wage dispersion widened by 38 to 53 per cent, depending on which measure of dispersion is used.[5]

The data in Table 81 of chapter ix confirm both the narrowing of percentage wage dispersion and the widening of money wage dispersion among industries observed in Ross and Goldner's data for the period 1933–46. In Table 81, relative wage dispersion as measured by the standard deviation of relative wages declined by 30 per cent and the corresponding measure of money wage dispersion increased by 51 per cent. (The statistics in Table 81 are fixed weighted measures of dispersion of average *annual* full-time compensation of civilian wage and salary employees among all industries in the United States. The levels of these measures are therefore affected by dispersion among industries in full-time hours of work. However, *trends* in hours of work, by and large, have been so similar among industries that the trends in Table 81 probably reflect fairly closely the trends in interindustrial dispersion of average *hourly* wages.) On the other hand, Table 81 suggests that these changes in dispersion from 1933 to 1946 were atypical of the longer-run movements. There was little trend in relative wage dispersion and an enormous —more than 200 per cent—upward movement in money wage dispersion from the late 1920's to the late 1950's.

Table 81 also shows that during the period 1933–46, but not the longer

[5] Absolute money wage dispersion, as measured by the standard deviation of money wages among industries, increased in each of the three subperiods 1933–38, 1938–42, and 1942–46:

Year	Standard Deviation (1933 = 100)
1933.................	100
1938.................	119
1942.................	127
1946.................	138

period covered by the table, absolute *real* wage dispersion was more nearly constant than either relative or absolute money wage dispersion. This is also true of the Ross-Goldner data. Among the forty-four industries in their unionism Groups 1–4, absolute *real* wage dispersion in 1946 differed by less than 3 per cent from that in 1933. (The conversion of absolute money wage dispersion to absolute real wage dispersion was accomplished by dividing the first by the U.S. Bureau of Labor Statistics Consumer Price Index.) Had Ross and Goldner measured wage changes in absolute *real* units (1946 dollars) instead of absolute *money* units, they would have obtained the results shown in Table 34.

TABLE 34

MEAN INCREASE IN REAL STRAIGHT-TIME HOURLY
EARNINGS BY UNIONISM GROUP, 1933–46

Unionism Group	Weighted Mean Increase in Real ASTHE 1933–46 (1946 Cents)
1.	43.5
2.	35.8
3.	40.2
4.	41.7

The regression coefficient of the wage changes on the midpoints of the extent of unionism classes computed from Table 34 is only 0.048 cents per hour per percentage point difference in extent of unionism. This coefficient is only about one-fifth as large as that computed for 1933–46 from Table 32. It implies that the effect of unionism on the average relative wage in manufacturing industries in 1946 was about 2 per cent rather than 10 per cent and that the average relative wage effect of a one percentage point difference in extent of unionism among industries in 1946 was about 0.04 per cent rather than 0.2 per cent.

It is always possible to measure wages in such a way that their dispersion among industries is *exactly* the same at the base and given dates: express wages in units of their measure of dispersion. For example, had Ross and Goldner divided each 1933 wage observation by the standard deviation of wages in 1933 and each 1946 wage observation by the standard deviation of wages in 1946, then the standard deviation of wages so measured would have been unity in both years. Using this procedure on the data for Groups 1 to 4 yields almost exactly the same results as measuring wage changes in absolute real units.

Although it is clear that Ross and Goldner felt that in measuring wage changes in absolute money units they were in effect holding wage dispersion approximately constant, they did not regard this as sufficient to eliminate the effects of all factors other than unionism on the wage changes. In particular, they observed that employment changes, in per cent, from the base date to the given dates were positively correlated with the corresponding changes in absolute money wages and in degree of unionization, although they did not report the magnitude of these correlations. (For the period 1933–46 and the industries in Groups 1–4, the simple correlations of the employment changes with the changes in wages in both real and money units and with the changes in degree of unionization were quite low numerically.) They also noted a tendency for "degree of oligopoly" (degree of concentration of output among producing firms) to correlate positively with the wage changes and the changes in degree of unionization, although they did not present output concentration data. They did not attempt, however, to isolate the wage differential effects of unionism from those of employment change and degree of oligopoly (pp. 280–81):

From an analytical standpoint, the difficulty is that these three influences (unionization, employment change, and oligopolistic market structure) have been operative in substantially the same group of industries. Statistical means are not at hand to disentangle their separate effect or to establish which, if any, is the primary cause. Our own belief is that unionization is a source of wage advantage, which operates most effectively under facilitating environmental circumstances. When large numbers of workers are being added to the payrolls of an industry and when oligopoly profits are available to be tapped, facilitating circumstances are present. Under conditions which have recently prevailed in the United States, unionization has thus been a necessary but not sufficient condition for larger-than-average increases in earnings.

The 1948 paper by Professor Ross differs from the 1950 paper by Ross and Goldner in the following respects:[6]

1. The base date was January, 1933, and only one given date, January, 1945, was used.

2. Industries in which the degree of unionization of wage-earners in 1933 was at least 25 per cent were excluded. The 1948 study was confined to industries in which extent of unionism was low at the base date—there was no group of industries comparable to Group A in the Ross-Goldner study. In both papers, however, bituminous coal mining was classified as poorly organized in 1933, although Leo Wolman's data indicate that in 1933 bituminous coal mining was at least 50 per cent unionized.[7] (Exclusion of this industry from those covered

---

[6] In preparing my brief review, I was greatly helped by an unpublished note on Ross's study which Harold M. Levinson made available to me.

[7] Wolman estimated that the extent of trade union organization in coal mining was 64.9 per cent in 1932 and 61.5 per cent in 1933. (These figures are contained in Table VIII, p. 229, of his *Ebb and Flow in Trade Unionism.*) Greenslade's study of unionism in bituminous coal mining suggests, however, that in early 1933 less than 25 per cent

in Ross's paper would have reduced only slightly the relative wage effects of unionism observed in the study.) Ross also included furniture manufacturing, although the Ross-Goldner study classified the industry as at least 40 per cent unionized in 1933.

3. The industries included in the 1948 inquiry were classified into four unionism groups with the same degree of unionization class limits as Groups 1 to 4 in the Ross-Goldner paper. (I shall use the same notation for the Ross unionism groups as for the corresponding Ross-Goldner groups). However, in the 1948 paper the industries were classified according to the degree of unionization of wage-earners in 1945 rather than in 1946. Among the industries included in Groups 1 to 4 in both studies, the following five were classified differently by degree of unionization:

INDUSTRY	UNIONISM GROUP	
	Ross Study	Ross-Goldner Study
Chemicals, except rayon..............	1	2
Canning and preserving.............	2	3
Dyeing and finishing textiles.........	2	3
Rayon and allied products...........	3	4
Electrical machinery................	3	4

4. The industries included in Groups 1 to 4 in the two papers were not quite the same. Coverage comparison is somewhat difficult because of differences in industry titles. It appears that the following four industries, included in Ross's paper, were not included in Ross and Goldner Groups 1 to 4: furniture, knit goods, crude petroleum and natural gas, and non-alcoholic beverages. Their exclusion from the 1948 study would have affected the results only slightly. On the other hand, the following eight industries, included in the Ross-Goldner Groups 1 to 4, were not covered by Ross: cotton textiles; shoes, cut stock, and findings; electric light and power; clocks and watches; aluminum manufactures; leather; anthracite mining; and street railways and motor buses. Three of these were excluded because Ross estimated that their degree of organization in 1933 exceeded 25 per cent: leather; shoes, cut stock, and findings; and anthracite mining. Cotton textiles was excluded because its January 1933 average straight-time hourly earnings was less than twenty-five cents. The others presumably were excluded because comparable data were not available for both base and given dates. The exclusion of cotton textiles, in particular, was unfortunate. Had Ross included this industry, the apparent relative wage effects of unionism observed in his study would have been approximately halved.

5. The methods of analysis used in the two papers were not the same.

---

of employed bituminous coal miners may have been unionized (see Greenslade's dissertation, pp. 19–24). Thus it is not clear that Ross erred in including bituminous coal mining among the weakly unionized industries in early 1933.

In the 1948 paper, Ross argued (p. 270):

Now, it is almost universally true that as the general level of earnings through-out the economy advances over any considerable period, absolute differentials are widened and percentage differentials are narrowed. This means that (in the absence of any counter-acting influence) the high-paid industries enjoy a larger dollar increase and a smaller percentage increase than the low-paid industries, and *vice versa*.

Furthermore, since the industries that were highly unionized in 1945 also tended to be high paid, even in 1933, comparison of absolute wage changes among unionism groups would tend to overstate, percentage comparisons to understate the wage effects of unionism. To get around this difficulty, Ross compared the wage changes from the base date to the given date among unionism groups only within industry groups which had roughly the same base date wage. That is, in his comparisons of wage changes among unionism groups, Ross held base date wages approximately constant. Ross and Goldner did not follow this procedure, not because they felt that it was wrong, but because they assumed that absolute money wage dispersion was more or less constant and that, therefore, "such a round-about technique is unnecessary" (Ross and Goldner, p. 265).

Table 35 is essentially a reproduction of Ross's summary table (p. 273).

TABLE 35

MEAN PERCENTAGE INCREASE IN REAL HOURLY EARNINGS, 1933–45

AVERAGE STRAIGHT-TIME HOURLY EARNINGS JANUARY 1933 (Dollars)	UNIONISM GROUP			
	1	2	3	4
0.250–0.399............	63.2	69.8	72.2	. . .
0.400–0.499............	. . .	43.2	52.4	61.4
0.500–0.650............	28.9	. . .	34.0	50.6

As the table suggests, Ross computed for the industries in each wage class and unionism group the weighted (1945 production-worker employment weights) mean percentage increase in real average straight-time hourly earnings from January, 1933 to January, 1945. Although Ross pointed out that within each wage class the mean percentage increase in wages rose as degree of unionization rose, he did not attempt a numerical estimate of the average relative wage effect of unionism per percentage point change in degree of organization.

To make such an estimate, I converted the figures in Table 35 to ratios of 1945 to 1933 wages and then computed the regression of the logarithms of these ratios on the logarithms of the midpoints of the January 1933 wage classes and the midpoints of the degree of unionization class intervals for the unionism groups. (In computing the regression, each observation in Table 35 was weighted by the December, 1945, production-worker employment of the industries included in the observation.) The resulting partial regression coefficient of the wage ratios on extent of unionism was 0.23 per cent per percentage point difference in extent of unionism.

As pointed out earlier, had Ross not excluded cotton textiles, the above estimate of the relative wage impact of unionism would have been reduced by approximately one-half. Exclusion of bituminous coal mining would have lowered the estimate by about another 5 per cent. These two adjustments together lower the estimated relative wage effect to about 0.10 per cent per percentage point difference in extent of unionism among industries.

IV.2. THE 1951 LEVINSON STUDY[8]

Professor Levinson, using a technique similar to that of the Ross paper on data that were largely the same as those examined by Ross and by Ross and Goldner, came to the conclusion (p. 62) that "by 1946 and 1947, the correlation between unionism and earnings, if any can be said to have existed at all, was weaker than at any previous time." These three papers—by Ross, Ross and Goldner, and Levinson—are the most frequently cited studies of the impact of unions on wage differentials, and their failure to arrive at similar conclusions from apparently similar data and methods has puzzled many economists.

Levinson examined two rather distinct sets of data, of which only one ("Sample II," which I discuss first) is closely comparable to the data studied by Ross and by Ross and Goldner. The "Sample II" study differs from the Ross and Ross-Goldner studies in the following respects:

1. The base date was the *year* 1933, rather than January, 1933 (Ross), and January–June, 1933 (Ross-Goldner). The given dates were annual for each of the years 1934–47, rather than January, 1945 (Ross), and the years 1938, 1942, and 1946 (Ross-Goldner).

2. As in the Ross study, Levinson excluded industries that he estimated were at least 25 per cent unionized in 1933. Ross and Goldner excluded from unionism Groups 1 to 4 industries that they estimated were at least 40 per cent unionized in 1933. Despite the general similarity of criteria for excluding industries that were substantially unionized in 1933, there were some differences among the papers in the industries excluded. Levinson excluded, but Ross included, bituminous coal mining; on the other hand, Ross excluded and

[8] Harold M. Levinson, "Unionism, Wage Trends, and Income Distribution, 1914–1947," *Michigan Business Studies*, X, No. 1 (Ann Arbor: Bureau of Business Research, Graduate School of Business, University of Michigan, 1951), used by permission.

Levinson included leather tanning. The latter difference between Ross and Levinson is of no importance. As was pointed out earlier, the inclusion by Ross of bituminous coal mining may have raised the apparent average relative wage effect of unionism in his study by about 5 per cent.

There were more differences between Levinson and Ross and Goldner in industries excluded on the ground of substantial unionization in 1933. Levinson excluded bituminous and anthracite coal mining, street railways and motor buses, and shoes, cut stock, and findings, all of which were included by Ross and Goldner, while the latter excluded furniture, which was included by Levinson. These differences, however, explain very little of the differences between Levinson and Ross and Goldner in their findings.

3. There were several other differences in industry coverage in the three papers. The most important one, by all odds, was Ross's exclusion of the cotton textiles industry. I noted above that had Ross included this industry, the apparent wage effects of unionism observed in his study would have been halved. Aside from the differences noted under point 2 above, there was little difference in industry coverage for the period 1942–46 between Levinson and Ross and Goldner. In the earlier years, 1938–41, however, the coverage was somewhat broader in the latter study. Some rough computations I have made indicate that these differences in coverage had little effect on findings of the two studies.

4. Levinson's classification of industries at given dates by degree of unionization was the same as that of Ross and Goldner for 1938 and 1946, but differed from those of Ross and of Ross and Goldner at other given dates. For the given years 1942–45, Levinson classified by degree of unionization in *1946*, Ross for the given date January, 1945, by degree of unionization in 1945, and Ross and Goldner for the given year 1942 by degree of unionization in that year. According to the Bureau of Labor Statistics data used in all three papers, degree of unionization increased in quite a number of industries between 1942 and 1946. Levinson's unionization classification for the period 1942–45, therefore, tends to overestimate somewhat the *changes* in extent of unionism from base date to given dates and thus tends to underestimate the corresponding wage effects of unionism *per unit change in extent of unionism*. Similarly, for the periods 1934–38 and 1939–41, Levinson classified by degree of unionization in the terminal year of each period. In this respect his figures for 1938 are comparable to those of Ross and Goldner, but his figures for 1941, based on the estimates of degree of unionization in that year, may be more comparable than his 1942 figures to those of Ross and Goldner for 1942.

Furthermore, the class intervals of Levinson's degree of unionization classes for 1938 and 1941 are not the same as those of Ross and Goldner for 1938 and 1942 (the designation of the groups by Roman and Arabic numerals is mine):

Levinson (1938, 1941)	Ross and Goldner (1938, 1942)
Group I: Almost none	Group 1: 0 to 40 per cent
Group II: Moderate proportion	Group 2: 40 to 60 per cent
Group III: About half	Group 3: 60 to 80 per cent
Group IV: Large proportion	Group 4: 80 to 100 per cent

Comparison of the industries classified by Levinson in Groups I–IV with those classified by Ross and Goldner in Groups 1–4 suggests that the percentage class limits of Groups I to IV are roughly as follows: Group I, 0 to 20 per cent; Group II, 20 to 40 per cent; Group III, 40 to 60 per cent; and Group IV, 60 to 100 per cent.

Levinson classified the industries covered in his "Sample II" study into three base date (1933) wage classes, with class limits almost exactly the same as those of the Ross paper, and within wage classes into four unionism groups as indicated above. For each wage class and unionism group and for given years 1934–47, he computed the fixed weighted mean given year wage index, with 1933 = 100.[9] Table 36 reproduces the portions of his Tables 11, 12, and 13 which are most relevant to the comparisons with the works of Ross and of Ross and Goldner.

I have computed from the data in Table 36 the regressions, one for each year, of the logarithms of the wage indexes on the logarithms of the midpoints of the base date wage classes and the midpoints of the degree of unionization classes. (The observations in the regressions were unweighted.) The partial regression coefficients, in percentages, of the wage indexes on the change in degree of unionization are shown, together with similar coefficients computed from the Ross and Ross-Goldner data that I discussed earlier, in Table 37. The "unadjusted Ross-Goldner" figures are those computed from their Tables I and IV. The "adjusted" figure

---

[9] This procedure differs from that of Ross in one respect: Ross calculated the weighted mean of the ratios of given date wages, y, to base date wages, x. Levinson calculated the ratio of the weighted mean of given date wages to the weighted mean of base date wages. These two statistics differ only in the weighting system used. Ross calculated

$$\frac{\Sigma f\left(\frac{y}{x}\right)}{\Sigma f},$$

where f denotes his weighting system. Levinson calculated

$$\frac{\Sigma Fy}{\Sigma Fx} = \frac{\Sigma Fx\left(\frac{y}{x}\right)}{\Sigma Fx},$$

where F denotes his weighting system. Levinson would obtain precisely the same results as Ross if

$$\frac{f}{\Sigma f} - \frac{Fx}{\Sigma Fx}$$

were uncorrelated with y/x.

for 1946 I have not computed similar figures for 1938 and 1942—was computed from these data after converting the money wage changes from 1933 to 1946 to real wage changes. Notice that the adjusted figure is almost the same as that computed from Levinson's data for 1946.

TABLE 36

WEIGHTED AVERAGE STRAIGHT-TIME HOURLY EARNINGS (1933 = 100)

YEAR	BASE DATE WAGE CLASS AND UNIONISM GROUP											
	\$0.250–\$0.399				\$0.400–\$0.499				\$0.500–\$0.659			
	I	II	III	IV	I	II	III	IV	I	II	III	IV
1938.....	128	140	135	...	134	137	128	146	129	...	145	145
1941.....	...	160	151	...	...	146	150	161	...	143	153	158
	1	2	3	4	1	2	3	4	1	2	3	4
1944.....	207	219	209	...	193	177	193	190	165	180	184	192
1945.....	225	228	221	...	200	184	200	198	172	187	190	198
1946.....	272	257	254	...	225	210	229	227	195	212	214	220

Thus the difference between the Levinson and Ross-Goldner findings may stem largely from the failure of the latter to observe and allow for the substantial increase in money wage dispersion in the period 1933–46. Similarly the "adjusted Ross" estimate for January, 1945, is close to the

TABLE 37

ESTIMATES OF THE PERCENTAGE EFFECT OF UNIONISM ON RELATIVE WAGES AMONG INDUSTRIES PER PERCENTAGE POINT DIFFERENCE IN EXTENT OF UNIONISM, DERIVED FROM THE LEVINSON, ROSS, AND ROSS-GOLDNER STUDIES, 1938, 1941, 1942, 1944–46
(Per Cent)

STUDY	DATE						
	1938	1941	1942	1944	January 1945	1945	1946
Levinson......................	0.16	0.17	...	0.09	...	0.07	0.05
Ross and Goldner (unadjusted)...	0.33	...	0.27	...	...	...	0.20
Ross and Goldner (adjusted).....	...	...	...	...	...	...	0.04
Ross (unadjusted)...............	...	...	...	...	0.23	...	...
Ross (adjusted).................	...	...	...	...	about 0.10	...	...

estimates calculated from the Levinson "Sample II" data for 1944 and 1945.

I turn now to Levinson's "Sample I" data, which extend back to 1914. Table 38 summarizes the industry and occupational coverage of these data by base date (1914) wage class and unionism group for the period

1914–33.[10] The wage data for all of the industry-occupations preceded by the letter *a* are the Bureau of Labor Statistics weighted averages of *minimum wage rates for union workers specified in union contracts*. For all of the other industry-occupations, the wage data are *average hourly earnings* derived from Bureau of Labor Statistics and National Industrial Conference Board data.

For each wage class and unionism group, Levinson calculated the given year mean wage index (1914 = 100). I have computed from his Table 5 the ratio of the index for the group "unionized throughout" to the index for the group "substantially nonunionized throughout." These ratios, for selected given years, are shown in Table 39.

Since it cannot be presumed that there were no effects of unionism on the relative wages of the union wage-earners in 1914, the figures in Table 39 at best measure the *changes* in these effects from 1914 to given years. When the table is interpreted in this way, the figures suggest that on the average the impact of unionism on relative wages of union workers fell substantially during World War I, rose to a level about 20 per cent above that in 1914 during the deflation of 1920–21, increased slightly between 1922 and 1929, and then rose sharply again in the deep deflation following

[10] Tables 38 and 39 exclude four industries studied by Levinson in which the degree of unionization changed substantially during the period 1914–33: bituminous coal mining (the wage data are for the states of Ohio, Indiana, and Illinois), full-fashioned hosiery manufacturing, men's clothing manufacturing, and the railroad shopcrafts. The table below shows for key years the index number (1914 = 100) of the ratio of the average wage in each of these industries to the average wage in nonunion industries in the

YEAR	INDUSTRY			
	Bituminous Coal Mining	Men's Clothing	Full-fashioned Hosiery	Railroad Shopcrafts
1914.........	100	100	100	100
1920.........	83	111	...	110
1922.........	147	142	114	119
1928.........	95	123	147	105
1929.........	91	...	...	109
1932.........	...	98	91	116
1933.........	...	...	...	119

same 1914 wage class. Bituminous coal mining was quite extensively unionized before World War I, but following 1921 the degree of unionization of the mines dropped steadily until 1933. Men's clothing and full-fashioned hosiery became unionized during and immediately following the war; in both industries the extent of unionism was lower in 1932 than in the 1920's. The railroad shopcrafts also became unionized during the war, but the loss of a major strike in 1922 weakened their position in later years of the 1920's.

TABLE 38

Wage-Earner Coverage of Levinson's "Sample I" Data by 1914
Wage Class and Unionism Group, 1914–33

Unionized Throughout	Nonunionized Throughout
Wage Class I: $0.400 to $0.599	
[a] Printing trades, newspaper and book and job [a] Building trades: journeymen [a] Granite and stone Railroad train and engine service [a] Metal trades [a] Millwork	Steel: highly skilled Meat packing: highly skilled Sawmills: highly skilled
Wage Class II: $0.300 to $0.399	
[a] Bakers [a] Longshoremen [a] Bookbinders	Automobiles: Skilled and semiskilled Steel: skilled and semiskilled Gas: skilled and semiskilled Paint and varnish: skilled and semiskilled Electric power: skilled and semiskilled Electric mfg.: skilled and semiskilled
Wage Class III: $0.200 to $0.299	
Anthracite mining [a] Teamsters [a] Building trades: helpers and laborers [a] Street railways	Foundry and machine shop products Paper and pulp: skilled and semiskilled Rubber manufacturing Agricultural equipment Furniture: skilled and semiskilled Chemicals Paper products: skilled and semiskilled Leather tanning: skilled and semiskilled Meat packing: skilled and semiskilled
Wage Class IV: $0.100 to $0.199	
[a] Printing: bindery women Railroads: unskilled Woolen goods	Sawmills Silk and rayon manufacturing Cotton goods manufacturing

[a] Bureau of Labor Statistics weighted averages of minimum wage rates for union workers specified in union contracts; see text.

1929 to a level averaging roughly 40 per cent above the 1914 level. In other words, Table 39 suggests that during the period 1914–33, unionism produced great rigidity in the money wages of union workers to increases —and particularly to decreases in the general level of money wages—so that the *relative* wage effects of unionism for union workers tended to vary contracyclically to the general money wage level. In this connection, notice also that the Levinson "Sample II" data (see Table 37) indicate that money wages of union workers may have been somewhat rigid

TABLE 39

RATIO OF MEAN WAGE OF UNION WAGE-EARNERS TO MEAN WAGE OF
NONUNION WAGE-EARNERS BY 1914 WAGE CLASS (1914 = 100)

YEAR	1914 WAGE CLASS			
	$0.100 to $0.199 (IV)	$0.200 to $0.299 (III)	$0.300 to $0.399 (II)	$0.400 to $0.599 (I)
1914.........	100	100	100	100
1920.........	78	103	100	81
1922.........	118	128	118	117
1929.........	121	127	116	127
1931.........	135	133	119	145
1933.........	137	134	123	177

against the increases in the general level of money wages which followed 1941.

I suspect, however, that Table 39 exaggerates the rigidity of money wages of union workers. The numerators of the ratios in the table are averages mainly of union contract minimum wage rates; the denominators are averages of hourly earnings figures. Union contract minimum wage rates, partly because they are minima and partly because contract minima are not always observed, tend to be more rigid against changes in demand and supply conditions than the corresponding wage rates actually paid. Averages of wage *rates*, in turn, tend to have less cyclical variability than corresponding averages of hourly *earnings*.

The industry coverage in Levinson's "Sample I" for the given years 1933–47 is considerably thinner than for the earlier years. Lack of data forced him to discard his Wage Class I and to combine Wage Classes II and III (though dropping longshoremen and gas: skilled and semiskilled) and the six industries in his Wage Class IV are divided among five unionism groups. The following summary deals only with the data for his Wage Classes II and III combined.

The industries in this combined wage class were divided into four unionism groups as follows (the designation of the groups by a letter and numbers is mine and is comparable to the notation used for the Ross-Goldner unionism groups):

Group A: unionized throughout.
Group 2: 40 to 60 per cent unionized in 1946, substantially nonunion in 1933.
Group 3: 60 to 80 per cent unionized in 1946, substantially nonunion in 1933.
Group 4: 80 to 100 per cent unionized in 1946, substantially nonunion in 1933.

For each group, Levinson calculated the index, with 1914 = 100, of the fixed weighted mean given year wages (1933–47). Table 40 shows these indexes for selected years, plus the same indexes with 1933 as the base year (that is, with 1933 = 100).

TABLE 40

INDEXES OF MEAN WAGES BY UNIONISM GROUP FOR LEVINSON'S
WAGE CLASSES II AND III, 1914–46

	UNIONISM GROUP							
	2		3		4		A	
YEAR	1914 = 100	1933 = 100	1914 = 100	1933 = 100	1914 = 100	1933 = 100	1914 = 100	1933 = 100
1914..........	100	47	100	55	100	52	100	41
1933..........	215	100	182	100	194	100	243	100
1938..........	293	136	261	143	297	153	297	122
1942..........	351	163	326	179	362	187	345	142
1946..........	453	211	424	233	441	227	434	179

Levinson's "Sample I" data for Groups 2, 3, and 4 in Table 40 permit a rough check on the sensitivity of estimates of unionism's relative wage impact to the choice of base date. The indexes with 1933 = 100 suggest relative wage effects of unionism in 1938 and 1942 that are considerably larger than those for 1938 and 1941 estimated from Levinson's "Sample II" data, while the indexes with 1914 as base indicate much smaller effects. However, the suggestion in these data that the use of 1933 as base date may lead to large exaggeration of unionism's relative wage effects in the late 1930's and early 1940's is not firmly grounded. For estimating these effects, it may be quite misleading to classify industries by their extent of unionism in *1946*. Therefore, I have reclassified the industries in Table 40 by their degree of unionization in *1942*, using information from the Levinson and Ross-Goldner studies.[11]

[11] The degree of unionization data are ambiguous with respect to the classification of "foundry and machine shop products." Although I have classified this industry in Group 3 in Table 41, the data suggest that it might have been just as reasonable to classify it in Group 4. Had I classified foundry and machine products in Group 4 rather than Group 3, the wage indexes for Groups 3 and 4 in Table 41 would have been:

	BASE PERIOD AND UNIONISM GROUP					
YEAR	1914 = 100		1920–29 average = 100		1933 = 100	
	Group 3	Group 4	Group 3	Group 4	Group 3	Group 4
1914............	100	100	44	45	52	51
1920–29.........	228	220	100	100	119	113
1933............	192	195	84	88	100	100
1942............	347	358	152	163	181	184

If the above indexes were substituted for those in Table 41, the apparent relative wage effects of unionism in 1942 would be a bit smaller when 1914 or 1920–29 is used as the base, but would be the same with 1933 as base.

Group 2, less than 40 per cent unionized in 1942:
   Paper and pulp, skilled and semiskilled;
   Electric power, skilled and semiskilled;
   Paint and varnish, skilled and semiskilled;
   Paper products, skilled and semiskilled; and
   Chemicals.
Group 3, 40 to 60 per cent unionized in 1942:
   Agricultural equipment;
   Foundry and machine shop products;
   Leather tanning, skilled and semiskilled;
   Meat packing, skilled and semiskilled; and
   Furniture, skilled and semiskilled.
Group 4, more than 60 per cent unionized in 1942:
   Automobiles, skilled and semiskilled;
   Steel, skilled and semiskilled;
   Electrical manufacturing, skilled and semiskilled; and
   Rubber manufacturing.

At the same time, in order to reduce the importance of transitory factors in the base period, I have made the years 1920–29 a base period.

Table 41 presents unweighted indexes of mean wages by unionism group for each of the years 1914, 1920–29 average, 1933 and 1942 on each of three bases: 1914, 1920–29 average, and 1933. The table indicates that the classification of industries by extent of unionism in *1946*, in Table 40, may indeed have been misleading in judging relative wage

TABLE 41

INDEXES OF MEAN WAGES BY UNIONISM GROUP WITHIN LEVINSON'S
WAGE CLASSES II AND III, 1914–42

YEAR	BASE PERIOD AND UNIONISM GROUP											
	1914 = 100				1920–29 average = 100				1933 = 100			
	A	2	3	4	A	2	3	4	A	2	3	4
1914.....	100	100	100	100	39	44	45	45	40	47	53	51
1920–29..	259	225	224	222	100	100	100	100	105	106	118	112
1933.....	247	213	190	198	95	95	85	89	100	100	100	100
1942.....	341	337	344	365	131	150	153	164	138	158	181	184

effects of unionism in years earlier than 1946, for such effects now appear not only when 1933 is the base but also with 1914 or 1920–29 as base. Notice that the size of the effects is almost completely independent of the choice between 1914 and 1920–29 as base. On the other hand, the effects appear to be considerably larger with a 1933 base than with either of the other two base periods.

In summary, on the basis of the data in the Ross, Ross-Goldner, and Levinson studies, I would estimate that the average relative wage effect of unionism per percentage point difference among industries in extent of unionism was roughly 0.15 to 0.20 per cent in the late 1930's and early 1940's, no more than half this size in 1944–45, and 0.05 or less in 1946–47. The average effect may have been somewhat larger during the 1920's and early 1930's than it was later. Furthermore, these figures, together with other data in the Levinson and Ross-Goldner studies, indicate a tendency for the relative wages of union workers to rise during periods of rapid deflation and to fall during periods of rapid inflation.

IV.3. THE GARBARINO STUDY OF MANUFACTURING INDUSTRIES[12]

Professor Garbarino's paper examined empirically the relationship of the changes in wages from 1923 to 1940 among thirty-four manufacturing industries to the extent of unionism of these industries at the beginning of 1942, their degree of concentration of output among firms in 1935, and their changes in output per man-hour from 1923 to 1940. His basic data were:

Y (this and the symbols which follow are mine rather than Garbarino's), the index (1923 = 100) of average hourly earnings in 1940;

Z, the index (1923 = 100) of output per man-hour in 1940 (Y and Z were obtained from a Bureau of Labor Statistics study of productivity and unit labor cost);[13]

p, a BLS classification of industries according to extent of collective-bargaining coverage at the beginning of 1942;[14] and

C, the National Resources Committee estimates for 1935 of the per cent of output produced by the four largest firms in each industry.

(Near the end of his study, Garbarino also looked into the relation among industries between the wage index, Y, and changes in employment from 1923 to 1940, but he gave this employment variable only a minor role in explaining variations in the wage index among industries.)

Garbarino observed that although the wage index, Y, was positively correlated among industries with the productivity index, degree of concentration, and extent of unionism, the correlation with extent of unionism was small (in statistical language: "not significantly different from

---

[12] Joseph W. Garbarino, "A Theory of Interindustry Wage Structure Variation," *Quarterly Journal of Economics*, LXIV, No. 2 (May, 1950), 282–305.

[13] U.S. Bureau of Labor Statistics, *Productivity and Unit Labor Cost in Selected Manufacturing Industries, 1919–1940* (Washington, 1942).

[14] Florence Peterson, "Extent of Collective Bargaining Coverage at Beginning of 1942," *Monthly Labor Review*, LIV, No. 5 (May, 1942), 1066–70.

zero"). The rank correlation between the wage index and the productivity index was 0.60; that between the wage index and degree of concentration, 0.67 (Garbarino, pp. 298–99). Although he gave the productivity index, Z, the leading position in explaining the variation among industries in the wage index, Y, he did not attempt to estimate numerically the extent to which the variation in each of the three explaining variables, Z, C, and p, contributed to the variation in the wage index, Y.

I have therefore made some additional computations with his data (Tables II and III), but with the following modifications:

1. The BLS estimates of extent of unionism used by Garbarino classified manufacturing industries into four groups:
   Group   I: almost entirely under written agreements;
   Group II: large proportion under written agreements;
   Group III: about half under written agreements; and
   Group IV: moderate proportion under written agreements.
This language is ambiguous, but I judge from later BLS estimates that the class limits and "midpoints" of these groups were, roughly:
   Group   I: 80 to 100 per cent, midpoint 90 per cent.
   Group II: 60 to 79 per cent, midpoint 70 per cent.
   Group III: 40 to 59 per cent, midpoint 50 per cent.
   Group IV: under 40 per cent, midpoint 20 per cent.
I assigned to each industry the midpoint of its extent of unionism group.

2. The relevant measure of extent of unionism, however, is not the extent of unionism at the beginning of 1942, but the *change in extent of unionism from 1923 to 1940*. In the main, the industries included in Garbarino's study had low and probably similar degrees of unionization in 1923. Furthermore, it is likely that the classification of industries by average extent of unionism in 1940 was not substantially different from that at the beginning of 1942. Thus the differences among industries in extent of unionism at the beginning of 1942 approximate the corresponding differences in the *changes* in extent of unionism from 1923 to 1940. However, Wolman's data[15] suggest that two industries included by Garbarino, "news and periodicals" in Group II and "boots and shoes" in Group III, were moderately unionized in 1923. Therefore, I classified the first of these in Group III and the second in Group IV.

3. In my reworking of Garbarino's data I *weighted* the data for each industry by the average number of wage-earners employed in the industry in 1929.[16] (Garbarino's calculations gave each of the industries equal weight.) The dispersion of 1929 wage-earner employment among the "industries" in-

---

[15] *Ebb and Flow in Trade Unionism*, Table VII.

[16] The source of the weights was U.S. Works Progress Administration, National Research Project on Reemployment Opportunities and Recent Changes in Industrial Techniques, *Production, Employment, and Productivity in 59 Manufacturing Industries, 1919–1936*, Report No. S-1, Part 1, May 1939, Table VIII.

cluded in Garbarino's study was quite extensive; the weights ranged from about 14,000 to almost 450,000. Furthermore, there were marked correlations between the weights and some of the variables. Thus my computations yielded results which in some instances were quite different from Garbarino's.

4. I excluded two industries, "glass" and "coke," which Garbarino had not classified by extent of unionism. (Garbarino also excluded these two industries in his computations dealing with extent of unionism.)

The weighted simple correlations among the wage index, Y, the productivity index, Z, changes in extent of unionism, p, and degree of concentration, C, were (r_{yz} is the simple correlation coefficient between Y and Z, etc.): $r_{yz} = 0.27$; $r_{yp} = 0.62$; $r_{yc} = 0.70$; $r_{zp} = 0.01$; $r_{zc} = 0.24$; and $r_{pc} = 0.76$. I have also computed the multiple regression of the wage index on changes in extent of unionism, the productivity index, and degree of concentration. The partial regression coefficient for extent of unionism, expressed as a ratio to the weighted mean wage index, was 0.15 per cent per percentage point difference among industries in extent of unionism. This figure is almost the same as the corresponding figures for 1938 and 1941 computed from Levinson's "Sample II" data (see Table 37).

None of the industries, except possibly "news and periodicals" and "boots and shoes," included in Garbarino's study was appreciably unionized at any time in the period 1923–29. Therefore, the changes in wage differentials among the industries which occurred in the period 1923–29 should have been negligibly influenced by unionism. Let Y' denote the wage index for 1929 (1923 = 100) and Z' the corresponding productivity index. (The source of Y' and Z' was the same as that for Y and Z.)[17] It seems reasonable to suppose that the degree of concentration of the covered industries in the 1920's did not differ substantially from that observed in 1935. That is, I assume that C approximates the degree of concentration in the 1920's.

If the relationship between the wage index, Y, the productivity index, Z, degree of concentration, C, and changes in extent of unionism, p, observed in the multiple regression of Y on Z, C, and p were a stable one, then it should have approximately the same coefficients (for Z and C) as the similar regression fitted to the data for 1923–29 (the regression of Y' on Z' and C'), but omitting changes in extent of unionism in 1923–29 because they were generally small.

The multiple regression fitted to the 1923–40 data had the following coefficients:

[17] See n. 13 above.

$$\frac{1}{M_y} b_{yp \cdot zc} = 0.15 \text{ per cent per percentage point change in extent}$$
$$\text{of unionism;}$$

$$\frac{M_z}{M_y} b_{yz \cdot pc} = 0.072 \text{ per cent per 1.0 per cent change in man-hour}$$
$$\text{productivity;}$$

and

$$\frac{1}{M_y} b_{yc \cdot pz} = 0.25 \text{ per cent per percentage point of degree of}$$
$$\text{concentration;}$$

where M is the weighted mean of the variable indicated in the subscript; $b_{yp \cdot zc}$ is the partial regression coefficient of Y on p in the presence of Z and C; and the other b's are similarly defined. The coefficients of the regression fitted to the 1923–29 data were:

$$\frac{M_{z'}}{M_{y'}} b_{y'z' \cdot c} = 0.31 \text{ per cent per 1.0 per cent change in man-hour}$$
$$\text{productivity;}$$

and

$$\frac{1}{M_{y'}} b_{y'c \cdot z'} = -0.036 \text{ per cent per percentage point of degree of}$$
$$\text{concentration.}$$

The differences between these coefficients for 1923–29 and those for 1923–40 cast doubt on the usefulness of the relationship observed in the 1923–40 data.

I also calculated the regression of the wage changes, Y', from 1923 to 1929 on the productivity changes, Z', from 1923 to 1929 and the changes in extent of unionism, p, from 1923 to 1940 in order to see whether an *apparent* effect of unionism would show up, even though the *true* effect of unionism on wage differentials among industries included in the Garbarino study during 1923–29 surely must have been small. The resulting coefficients were:

$$\frac{1}{M_{y'}} b_{y'p \cdot z'} = 0.049 \ (0.32) \text{ per cent per percentage point change}$$
$$\text{in extent of unionism from 1923 to 1940;}$$

and

$$\frac{M_{z'}}{M_{y'}} b_{y'z' \cdot p} = 0.22 \ (0.11) \text{ per cent per 1.0 per cent change in}$$
$$\text{man-hour productivity.}$$

The numbers in parentheses are the corresponding figures derived from the regression fitted to the 1923–40 data, but omitting the degree of concentration variable.

Notice that the coefficient for the changes in extent of unionism from

1923 to 1940 was much lower in the regression fitted to the 1923–29 data than in the regressions fitted to the 1923–40 data. This lends some support to the view that the effects of unionism on wage differentials appearing in the latter regressions may not be spurious. Nevertheless, the instability between the 1923–29 and 1923–40 regressions in the coefficients for the productivity and concentration variables raises doubts that the presence of these variables in the correlation of wage changes with changes in extent of unionism constitutes effective control over the factors other than unionism affecting changes in wage differentials.

The instability of the coefficients is not surprising. Consider first the relation between wage changes and degree of concentration. The degree of concentration figures used by Garbarino were estimates of the absolute levels of concentration by industry in 1935 rather than estimates of the changes in these levels from 1923 to 1940. Furthermore, it is likely that in other years during 1923–40 the differences among industries in concentration were highly correlated with the corresponding differences in 1935 and that the *changes* in concentration during 1923–40 were *poorly* correlated with the *levels* of concentration in 1935. Therefore, it is more plausible to interpret the concentration figures as indicators of differences among industries in their absolute levels of concentration in 1923–40 than as indicators of the corresponding differences in the *changes* from 1923 to 1940 in concentration.

Some economists have argued that firms enjoying monopoly profits tend to share their gains with their employees through higher wages. This argument, however, implies a positive correlation among industries between degree of monopoly, or oligopoly, at a given date and average wages at that date (or between *changes* in average wages and *changes* in degree of monopoly) rather than a positive correlation between wage *changes* and degree of monopoly. Indeed, the notion that firms in highly concentrated industries initially paying wages as high as those paid in less-concentrated industries would not only continue thereafter to enjoy monopoly gains enabling them to grant, year after year, significantly higher wage *increases* than those in less concentrated industries but would also grant such increases is, intuitively, not very plausible. In any case, the *negative* correlation between wage changes from 1923 to 1929 and degree of concentration makes this interpretation of the positive correlation between wage changes from 1923 to 1940 and degree of concentration highly dubious. Furthermore, there was a marked negative correlation between percentage changes in average hourly earnings from *1940 to 1947* and degree of concentration among the industries included in Garbarino's study.[18]

The preceding comments do not imply that the positive correlation between wage changes from 1923 to 1940 and degree of concentration observed by Garbarino was spurious, but, rather, that the correlation should not be interpreted as signifying that greater concentration alone is sufficient to produce greater wage changes. Two lines of argument have been advanced for including degree of concentration coupled with another variable or variables among the factors explaining wage changes.

The first states that the effect of *unionism* on the relative wages of an industry will tend to be greater, the greater the degree of concentration in the industry. (I interpret the concluding remarks of the Ross-Goldner paper in this vein.)

Turn to equation (9) of chapter ii:

$$\log R = p \log R_u + (1 - p) \log R_n.$$

The preceding view of unionism avers that for a given extent of unionism, p in an industry, the effect, R_u, of unionism on the average relative wage of the union labor in the industry will tend to be greater, the greater the degree of concentration of output in the industry. Thus this line of argument suggests that the mathematical product of degree of concentration and extent of unionism be included among the variables explaining wages.

On this reasoning, the numerically small coefficient for degree of concentration in the 1923–29 regression of wage changes on degree of concentration may be interpreted as reflecting the inconsequential changes in extent of unionism among industries in the period 1923–29, and the much larger coefficient for degree of concentration in the 1923–40 regression as resulting from an important impact of unionism on changes in wages from 1923 to 1940.

The second argument states that the short-run response of money wages to changes in underlying demand and supply conditions tends to be smaller, the greater the degree of concentration. On this line of reasoning, the small coefficient for degree of concentration in the 1923–29

[18] The source of the average hourly earnings figures from which I calculated the percentage changes was the *Handbook of Labor Statistics* (1947 ed.), Bulletin No. 916, Table C-1. The degree of concentration figures were those in Garbarino's paper. The rank correlation between degree of concentration and percentage change in average hourly earnings was −0.56.

The industries included in the calculation of the rank correlation are those that Garbarino classified by degree of unionization.

The calculated rank correlation may contain some error arising from imperfect matching of the BLS industry headings against those in Garbarino's paper. However, I doubt that the error is appreciable.

regression reflects the stability of monetary conditions during 1923–29, the large coefficient for 1923–40 the greater downward rigidity of money wages in industries of high concentration than in industries of low concentration under the depression conditions that followed 1929.

As a crude test of these arguments, I have calculated from Garbarino's data the multiple regression of Y on p, C, and the product, pC, of p and C.[19] The partial regression coefficients, all divided by the mean, M_y, of Y were:

$$\frac{1}{M_y} b_{yp \cdot c, \, (pc)} = 0.36 \text{ per cent per percentage point of degree of unionization;}$$

$$\frac{1}{M_y} b_{y(pc) \cdot p, \, c} = -0.68 \text{ per cent per percentage point squared of } pC;$$

$$\frac{1}{M_y} b_{yc \cdot p, \, (pc)} = 0.65 \text{ per cent per percentage point of degree of concentration.}$$

These results are consistent with the second argument but not the first. Indeed, the negative sign of the regression coefficient for the product variable, pC, suggests that the effect of unionism on the average relative wage of an industry, given the extent of unionism of the industry, is lower, the higher the degree of concentration in the industry. I obtained somewhat similar results for manufacturing industries in 1947–58, using the Bowen-Levinson data discussed later in this chapter (see pp. 177 ff.).

In this multiple regression, the estimated value, $\hat{\beta}$, of the Variant A-III coefficient, β, depends upon the average degree of concentration as follows:

$$\hat{\beta} = (b_{yp \cdot c, \, (pc)} + M_c b_{y(pc) \cdot p, \, c})/M_y = 0.36 - (0.305)(0.682) =$$
0.15 per cent per percentage point of degree of unionization.

This estimate is the same as that obtained from the regression of Y on p, C, and Z.

I turn now to the interpretation of output per man-hour as a wage-determining variable. The demand function for labor in an industry may be formulated in such a way that the quantity of labor demanded depends upon the output per man-hour in the industry, as the following simple example illustrates. Assume that the aggregate production function in the industry is linear and homogeneous and has a constant elasticity of substitution:

[19] I omitted the productivity variable, Z, since it was weakly correlated with both p and C. Its inclusion, therefore, would not have affected the partial regression coefficients for p, C, and pC appreciably.

$$Q = (aE^{-b} + AK^{-b})^{-1/b}, \tag{a}$$

where Q is the industry's output, E the industry's labor input, K the industry's capital input, a and A are positive parameters determined by "technological" conditions, and $1/(1 + b)$ is the elasticity of substitution, which I denote by σ. In long-run competitive equilibrium, the demand price of labor, or wage rate, w, is equal to the value of the marginal physical product of labor:

$$w = Pa[E^{-1}(aE^{-b} + AK^{-b})^{-1/b}]^{1+b} = Pa(Q/E)^{1/\sigma} = Paz^{1/\sigma}, \tag{b}$$

where $z = Q/E$ is output per man-hour and P is the price of the product of the industry.

Let the total revenue function for the output of the industry be

$$V = cP^{1-\eta}, \tag{c}$$

where η is the elasticity of demand for the output of the industry and c is a set of variables which cause the demand schedule to shift over time. Since $E = Q/z$ and $Q = cP^{-\eta}$,

$$E = cP^{-\eta}z^{-1}. \tag{d}$$

Multiply equation (b) by equation (d), obtaining

$$wE = acP^{1-\eta}z^{(1-\sigma)/\sigma} = aVz^{(1-\sigma)/\sigma}. \tag{e}$$

This is one way of writing the demand function for labor so that it includes z.

Assume that the supply function of labor to the industry in the absence of unionism is

$$E = dw^s, \tag{f}$$

where s is the elasticity of supply and d is the set of variables tending to shift the supply schedule. Now combine equations (e) and (f) and solve for w. The solution, in logarithmic form, is

$$\log w = \frac{1}{1+s} [\log a - \log d + \log V + \frac{1-\sigma}{\sigma} \log z]. \tag{g}$$

This is the long-run wage-determining equation apart from effects of unionism.

Denote by the symbol Δ the excess of the value in 1940 (or 1929) over the value in 1923 of the indicated variable, and assume that s and σ were the same at both dates. Then it follows from equation (g) that

$$\Delta \log w = \frac{1}{1+s} [\Delta \log a - \Delta \log d + \Delta \log V + \frac{1-\sigma}{\sigma} \Delta \log z]. \tag{h}$$

Assume that s and σ were distributed among industries independently of the other variables on the right-hand side of equation (h). Then the regression coefficient b_{YZ} of $\Delta \log w$ on $\Delta \log z$ in the absence of controls for the variables $\Delta \log a$, $\Delta \log d$, and $\Delta \log V$ is

$$b_{YZ} = M_{1/(1+s)}[b_{aZ} - b_{dZ} + b_{VZ} + M_{(1-\sigma)/\sigma}], \qquad (i)$$

where $M_{1/(1+s)}$ and $M_{(1-\sigma)/\sigma}$ are the means of $1/(1+s)$ and $(1-\sigma)/\sigma$, respectively, and b_{aZ}, b_{dZ}, and b_{VZ} are the simple regression coefficients of $\Delta \log a$, $\Delta \log d$, and $\Delta \log V$ on $\Delta \log z$. Since some or all of the regression coefficients on the right-hand side of equation (i) will vary from one pair of dates to another, the numerical size and sign of the regression coefficient b_{YZ} will tend to be unstable.

IV.4. THE GOLDNER STUDY[20]

William Goldner's estimation of the impact of unionism on wage differentials was a part of a larger study of factors affecting wage differentials among workers of different skill levels. The paper reviewed here is a progress report on this broader study.

Professor Goldner's basic wage data were derived from Bureau of Labor Statistics sample surveys of occupational wages conducted in thirty-nine standard metropolitan areas, including most of the largest ones, in the period September, 1951 to May, 1952. The survey of establishments in each area covered all industry divisions (except agriculture, mining, contract construction, government, and railroads) and a standard list of occupations[21] which included the following:

1. Skilled, maintenance: carpenters; electricians; machinists; maintenance men, general utility; mechanics, automotive; mechanics; and painters.
2. Semiskilled, warehousing and shipping: order fillers; packers; shipping and receiving clerks; stock handlers and truckers, hand; truck drivers, medium; and truckers, power (fork lift).
3. Unskilled, custodial: guards; janitors, porters, and cleaners (men); janitors, porters, and cleaners (women); and watchmen.

For each standard metropolitan area, the surveys yielded the following data used by Goldner in his study:

1. Average hourly earnings (excluding premium pay for overtime and night work), in cents per hour, for (a) all of the above occupations taken together, W; (b) the seven "skilled" occupations taken together, S; and (c) the four "un-

---

[20] William Goldner, "Labor Market Factors and Skill Differentials in Wage Rates," Industrial Relations Research Association, *Proceedings of the Tenth Annual Meeting* (1958), pp. 207–16.
[21] Professor Goldner supplied the list of occupations to me.

skilled" occupations taken together, U. The averages were standardized for occupation by using fixed occupational weights, the same for all cities.

2. Z_1, the per cent of workers employed in establishments in which the majority of workers were covered by collective-bargaining agreements.[22]

Goldner supplemented these data with the following data computed from the 1950 *Census of Population:*

3. Z_2, the (logarithm of) population of the area.

4. Z_3, the per cent of workers in the area employed in durable goods manu-facturing.

5. Z_4, the ratio of per capita rural income to per capita urban income in the metropolitan region.

From these data Goldner computed multiple regressions of each of W, S, and U on Z_1, Z_2, Z_3, and Z_4, with the following results:

(a) $W_{\text{computed}} = \text{constant} + 0.54\, Z_1 + 1.00\, Z_2 + 0.28\, Z_3 + 0.21\, Z_4;$

(b) $S_{\text{computed}} = \text{constant} + 0.46\, Z_1 + 1.16\, Z_2 + 0.04\, Z_3 + 0.00\, Z_4;$ and

(c) $U_{\text{computed}} = \text{constant} + 0.47\, Z_1 + 0.72\, Z_2 + 0.40\, Z_3 + 0.30\, Z_4.$

The unweighted mean of W for the thirty-nine areas was 135.4 cents per hour; S, 180.8 cents per hour; and U, 109.7 cents per hour. Thus these regressions estimate that the average *relative* wage effect of unionism per percentage point difference in extent of unionism was approximately:

0.40 ($= 0.54/1.354$) per cent for all covered occupations together;

0.25 ($= 0.46/1.808$) per cent for the skilled occupations; and

0.43 ($= 0.47/1.097$) per cent for the unskilled occupations.[23]

[22] The per cent of workers employed in establishments in which the majority of workers are covered by collective-bargaining agreements may differ significantly from the per cent of workers covered by collective-bargaining agreements. On this matter, see the discussion of the BLS figures in Table 79 in the appendix to chap. vii (sec. vii. 5). Furthermore, the 1951–52 occupational wage surveys used a cutoff sampling technique that excluded all establishments employing a small number of employees. Since small establishments less frequently are unionized than large establishments, the cutoff sampling procedure will tend to produce an upward bias in estimates of extent of collective-bargaining coverage.

[23] I obtained almost exactly the same estimates by regressing the natural logarithms of W, S, and U, respectively, on $Z_1/100$, Z_2, Z_3, and the natural logarithm of Z_4. The partial regression coefficients of log W, log S, and log U on $Z_1/100$ are themselves the estimates of the average relative wage impact of unionism in per cent per percentage point difference in extent of unionism. These coefficients were: 0.40 (0.08) for all covered occupations together; 0.27 (0.07) for the skilled occupations; and 0.43 (0.10) for the unskilled occupations. The figures in parentheses are the standard errors of the regression coefficients. The multiple correlation coefficients for these logarithmic regressions were almost the same as those for the corresponding arithmetic regressions computed by Goldner.

(The preceding three numbers were computed by me rather than by Goldner.) The last two numbers suggest that unionism tends to narrow relative wage differentials by skill.

I think it is likely, however, that Goldner's procedure has attributed to unionism effects on wage differentials among cities and among occupations which were the result of other factors. Although the wage data he used were standardized for differences among the areas in the distribution of their working forces among the included occupations, I judge that they were not standardized for a number of other differences among the areas in the composition of their working forces. There were, for example, some substantial differences among the areas in the average years of schooling of their adult populations. Perhaps most important of all, there were large differences among the areas in the per cent of nonwhite employees in their working forces, and these may have been associated with substantial differences among the areas in wage differentials between white and nonwhite workers. Eight of the thirty-nine areas had unusually high proportions, compared to the other thirty-one areas, of nonwhite workers in their labor forces (Atlanta, Birmingham, Houston, Jacksonville, Memphis, New Orleans, Norfolk-Portsmouth, and Richmond). Moreover, these areas were probably those in which the white/nonwhite wage differential was greatest. Furthermore, the average value of Z_1 in these eight areas was considerably below the average of Z_1 in the other thirty-one areas. Thus I think it is likely that failure to take into account the white/nonwhite differences among the areas may have led to overestimation of the wage differential effects of unionism.

The amount of overestimation on this score, however, is likely to be much greater for the unskilled and semiskilled occupations than for the skilled occupations because the ratio of nonwhite to white workers employed in skilled occupations is generally much less than the corresponding ratios for unskilled and semiskilled work. This observation is consistent with the wage differentials by skill shown in Goldner's data. The *smallest* percentage differential between skilled and unskilled workers among the eight southern areas listed above was larger than the *largest* percentage differential among the other thirty-one areas. Furthermore, among these thirty-one areas, the simple regression coefficient of the ratio, S/U, of skilled wages to unskilled wages on the extent of unionism, Z_1, was zero to two decimal places.

The discussion in the preceding two paragraphs has not taken account of the inclusion in Goldner's regressions of the variables Z_3 (per cent of workers employed in durable goods manufacturing) and Z_4 (ratio of per capita rural income to per capita urban income). Both of these variables are positively correlated with "region," that is, both are higher, on the average, in the non-South than in the South. Thus it is possible that these variables may have caught most of the wage effects of white/nonwhite differences among the areas.

To check on this possibility, I examined the residuals from Goldner's regression for the unskilled occupations. The residuals had a noticeable South/non-South pattern, averaging lower in the South than in the non-South. Furthermore, the residuals tended to be higher on the average in the areas in which population had been growing, relatively, most rapidly. I therefore fitted to Goldner's data (together with census data on population) the multiple regressions of log S on $Z_1/100$, Z_2, $Z_3/100$, log Z_4, Z_5 (or Z_5'), and Z_6 and of log U on the same variables. (The regressions were linear in these variables.) The variable Z_5 is a "dummy" variable serving as a proxy for a more precise "white/nonwhite" variable. For all of the nonsouthern areas, Z_5 is zero; for the eight southern areas listed earlier, Z_5 is unity. The variable Z_5', used as an alternative to Z_5, differs from Z_5 only in treating two additional cities (Louisville and Oklahoma City) as southern rather than nonsouthern. Z_6 is the logarithm of the ratio of 1950 population to 1940 population of the metropolitan area.[24] The regressions are summarized below in Table 42. I have also included in Table 42 similar regressions which exclude both Z_5 (or Z_5') and Z_6.

The inclusion of the "white/nonwhite" (or "regional") variable, Z_5 or Z_5', as expected, had scarcely any effect on the regressions for the skilled occupations. On the other hand, the addition of this variable to the regression for the unskilled occupations substantially increased the multiple correlation coefficient, lowered the regression coefficient for the variable Z_4 to approximately zero, and greatly reduced the regression coefficient for the extent of unionism variable, Z_1.

The partial regression coefficients for $Z_1/100$ in Table 42 are estimates of the Variant A-III coefficient, β, for skilled and unskilled workers, respectively. These coefficients should, in principle, be weighted (see chap. ii, sec. ii.6). In calculating the regressions in Table 42, however, the observations for each city received equal weight, although the cities varied rather widely in the number of employees covered in the BLS surveys. Furthermore, inspection of the scatter diagram relating the observations on log U to those on Z_1 suggested that the weighted multiple regressions for the unskilled occupations would differ somewhat from the corresponding unweighted regressions in Table 42.

Therefore, I also computed the weighted regression of log U on $Z_1/100$,

[24] These ratios were taken from Table 10 of the *Statistical Abstract of the United States: 1960.*

TABLE 42

SUMMARY OF MULTIPLE REGRESSIONS FITTED TO GOLDNER DATA*

DEPENDENT VARIABLE	R^2	REGRESSION COEFFICIENTS AND THEIR STANDARD ERRORS						
		$Z_1/100$	Z_2	$Z_3/100$	$\log Z_4$	Z_5	Z'_5	Z_6
$\log S$	0.72	0.232	0.027	0.126	−0.014	−0.034	. . .	0.193
		(0.066)	(0.010)	(0.106)	(0.036)	(0.027)		(0.061)
$\log S$	0.72	0.207	0.027	0.125	−0.044	. . .	−0.054	0.204
		(0.071)	(0.010)	(0.105)	(0.047)		(0.037)	(0.062)
$\log S$	0.63	0.260	0.025	0.017	−0.008	−0.012	. . .	. . .
		(0.074)	(0.011)	(0.113)	(0.040)	(0.030)		
$\log S$	0.63	0.257	0.025	0.016	−0.013	. . .	−0.013	. . .
		(0.080)	(0.011)	(0.114)	(0.053)		(0.039)	
$\log S$	0.63	0.270	0.025	0.022	0.001	. . .	. . .	. . .
		(0.069)	(0.011)	(0.111)	(0.033)			
$\log U$	0.89	0.265	0.033	0.404	0.065	−0.191	. . .	0.155
		(0.081)	(0.012)	(0.131)	(0.044)	(0.034)		(0.075)
$\log U$	0.87	0.199	0.033	0.405	−0.028	. . .	−0.228	0.175
		(0.098)	(0.014)	(0.144)	(0.065)		(0.050)	(0.085)
$\log U$	0.88	0.287	0.031	0.316	0.070	−0.173	. . .	. . .
		(0.084)	(0.013)	(0.130)	(0.046)	(0.034)		
$\log U$	0.85	0.242	0.031	0.312	−0.001	. . .	−0.192	. . .
		(0.100)	(0.014)	(0.143)	(0.067)		(0.050)	
$\log U$	0.79	0.433	0.027	0.392	0.197	. . .	. . .	. . .
		(0.104)	(0.017)	(0.169)	(0.050)			

* R^2 is the square of the multiple correlation coefficient. The figures in parentheses are the standard errors of the regression coefficients above them.

Z_2, $Z_3/100$, $\log Z_4$, Z_5, and Z_6, weighting the observations for each city by the number of unskilled workers covered by the BLS survey for the city, with the following results:

REGRESSION COEFFICIENTS AND THEIR STANDARD ERRORS

R^2	$Z_1/100$	Z_2	$Z_3/100$	$\log Z_4$	Z_5	Z_6
0.87	0.143	0.045	0.412	0.027	−0.244	0.273
	(0.059)	(0.007)	(0.071)	(0.033)	(0.029)	(0.051)

Notice that the regression coefficient for the extent of unionism variable, Z_1, in the weighted regression is only about half as large as the corresponding coefficient in Table 42. The antilogarithm, less unity, of 0.143 is 0.15. Thus the weighted regression indicates that unionism raised the average wage of unionized unskilled workers by about 15 per cent relative to the average wage of nonunion unskilled workers.

A similar scatter diagram relating $\log S$ to Z_1 suggested that weighted regressions for the group of skilled occupations would not differ much from the unweighted regressions. As a closer check, I computed both the weighted and the unweighted regressions of log S on $Z_1/100$ and Z_2. In the weighted regressions for the skilled occupational group, the weight for each city was the number of skilled workers covered by the BLS survey for the city. The regression coefficients were:

	$Z_1/100$	Z_2
Weighted regression..............	0.240	0.028
Unweighted regression...........	0.277	0.025

These coefficients, together with those in Table 42, indicate that the value of β for the skilled group was about 0.18—that is, unionism raised the average wage of unionized skilled workers by about 20 per cent relative to the average wage of nonunion skilled workers.

Even these figures, however, may be biased upward as estimates of β by errors in Z_1 as an estimate of the degree of unionization of each of the individual occupational groups. First, there is some evidence that the reported figures for Z_1 were rounded: eighteen of the thirty-nine figures were multiples of 5 per cent. Dispersion of rounded figures tends to be less than the dispersion of the unrounded figures. Second, Z_1 in each city is the per cent of all workers in the city employed in establishments in which the majority of workers were covered by collective-bargaining agreements. Thus Z_1 is not the same conceptually as the average extent of unionism of all workers in the city. The direction of the bias resulting from this conceptual difference between extent of unionism and Z_1 is not clear. Third, Z_1 does not purport to measure the extent of unionism in the individual occupational groups. Indeed, it is a sort of average degree of unionization of all occupations taken together, and its dispersion among cities will therefore tend to be less than the average dispersion of degree of unionization *within* occupations or occupational groups. Underestimation of the dispersion of extent of unionism in the occupational groups tends, in turn, to cause overestimation of the regression coefficients for the extent of unionism variable.

IV.5. THE TULLOCK STUDY[25]

The basic wage data used by Professor Tullock were the Depaitment of Commerce time series on average annual earnings per full-time employee by industry. These series extend back to 1929 and cover all wage and salary employees in the economy. For each of the approximately

[25] Gordon Tullock, *The Sources of Union Gains* (Research Monograph 2, Thomas Jefferson Center for Studies in Political Economy, University of Virginia; Charlottesville, 1959). Tullock's examination of the relative wage impact of unionism comprises chap. ii of his monograph.

seventy industry groups into which the Department of Commerce divides the economy in its national income statistics. Tullock computed the relative wage—the ratio of average annual earnings in the industry group to average annual earnings in all industries. From these data he calculated the five-year average relative wage in the base period, 1929–33, and in three given periods, 1938–40, 1948–52, and 1953–57. These, in turn, he converted to index numbers, with 1929–33 = 100.[26] He also computed relative wage index numbers for 1953–55, with 1929–31 = 100.

Tullock classified the industry groups by their estimated degree of unionization in the base period and given periods as follows:

Category I, substantially nonunion in 1929–33, completely unionized (80 to 100 per cent) in 1948–52 and later: water transportation; metal mining; rubber products; automobiles and automobile equipment; bituminous and other soft-coal mining; highway freight transportation and warehousing; and metals, metal products, and miscellaneous manufactures.

Category II, substantially nonunion in 1929–33, significantly (40 to 80 per cent), but not completely, unionized in 1948–52 and later: textile mill products; tobacco manufactures; electrical machinery; machinery, except electrical; chemicals and allied products; utilities (electric and gas); highway passenger transportation, n.e.c.; paper and allied products; products of petroleum and coal; lumber and furniture products; stone, clay, and glass products; leather and leather products; food and kindred products; and telephone, telegraph, and related services.

Category III, unionized in both 1929–33 and 1948–52 and later: contract construction; railroads; anthracite mining; printing, publishing, and allied industries; apparel and other finished fabric products; and local railways and bus lines.

Category IV, substantially nonunion in both 1929–33 and 1948–52 and later: all other industries.[27]

---

[26] He did not express the relative wage figures for 1953–57 as index numbers, and he made no explicit use of these figures beyond the observation (p. 12) that "from inspection it is clear that no serious changes in my conclusion would be required if this average were substituted for the 48–52 average."

[27] "Farms," "agricultural services, forestry, and fisheries," and "transportation equipment, except automobiles" were excluded from all categories, the first two on the ground that farmers "have had the benefit of a superior labor union called the United States Government" and the third because its industry composition had changed greatly from the base to the given period.

I presume that the federal programs that Tullock had in mind as benefiting farmers were the price-support programs for a number of farm products. These could have raised the relative wages of *hired* agricultural labor (only wage and salary employees are included in the Department of Commerce wage series, so that farm proprietors would have been excluded) only by (a) fixing a minimum wage higher than would otherwise be paid, or (b) raising the skill or other qualifications for farm employment, or

For each of Categories I and II and for Categories III and IV together, he computed the unweighted mean or median of the 1948–52 relative wage indexes, 1929–33 = 100, as follows: Category I, 125; Category II, 100; Categories III and IV, 86 (median). I have calculated from his Table II the unweighted means of the 1948–52 indexes (1929–33 = 100) for Categories III and IV. I have also calculated from the data in his Tables II and V-1 the unweighted mean indexes by unionism category for the other given periods. These means are given in Table 43.

TABLE 43

UNWEIGHTED MEAN RELATIVE WAGE INDEXES BY UNIONISM CATEGORY

Unionism Category	1938–40 (1929–33 = 100)	1948–52 (1929–33 = 100)	1953–55 (1929–31 = 100)	1953–57 (1929–33 = 100)
I.....	118	125	130	133
II.....	103	100	101	101
III.....	97	93	88	92
IV.....	96	84	85	83

If the figures in Table 43 are interpreted as indicating the magnitudes on the average of relative wage changes from the base to the given periods which are attributable to unionism, they imply that the average relative wage effects of unionism were large. I assume from Tullock's definitions of his unionism categories that he would have estimated roughly the following changes from 1929–33 (or 1929–31) to 1948–52 and later years in the average extent of unionism in each of his unionism categories: Category I, about eighty percentage points; Category II, about fifty percentage points; Category III, (?); Category IV, about ten percentage points. These changes in extent of unionism for Categories I, II, and IV, together with the corresponding average changes in relative wages in Table 43, imply an average relative wage effect of unionism per percentage point difference in extent of unionism of about 0.5 per cent in 1948–52 and about 0.6 per cent in 1953–57. (In making these estimates, I weighted each unionism category by its average full-time equivalent employment over the period 1929–57.)

I have several reservations, however, about these estimates derived from Tullock's data:

(c) reducing the relative supply of agricultural labor at given relative wages, or (d) raising the relative demand for farm labor at given relative wages. I fail to see how the price-support program did any of (a), (b), and (c), and if the rise in relative wages was caused by (d), farm employment should have increased rather than decreased from 1929 to 1952. I am puzzled, therefore, by Tullock's exclusion of farms and agricultural services, forestry, and fisheries.

1. His classification of industries by degree of unionization, as he emphasized, was crude. In my judgment, the classification contains some significant errors:

(a) *In 1929–33:* Both bituminous coal mining and highway freight transportation and warehousing were substantially unionized in this period (see Table 76 in chap. vii). These industries probably should have been classified in Category III rather than Category I; since both industries had unusually large increases in wages from 1929–33 to 1948–52 and 1953–57, this would lower the average increase for Category I and raise the average increase for Category III.

(b) *In 1948–52 and later:* The data in Table 76 of chapter vii indicate that if rubber products and metals, metal products, and miscellaneous manufactures are considered "completely unionized" and thus in Category I, then products of petroleum and coal; highway passenger transportation, n.e.c.; services allied to transportation; and telephone, telegraph, and related services should also be classified in Category I. With these changes and those in (a), the mean wage index for 1948–52 is 111 rather than 125. The same extent of unionism data also indicate that radio broadcasting and television, air transportation (common carriers), and pipeline transportation belong in Category II rather than Category IV. These revisions, together with those indicated above, change the mean wage index for Category II in 1948–52 to 96 but do not change the mean index for Category IV.

2. For my purposes the *unweighted* mean is inappropriate for averaging wage indexes among industries whose wage indexes and employment differ as much as those in Tullock's study. For example, the weighted (Department of Commerce estimates of full-time equivalent employment in 1950 used as weights) mean index for Tullock's Category I in 1948–52 was 114; the unweighted mean was 125.

3. In my opinion, Tullock erred in excluding farms and agricultural services, forestry, and fisheries from his Category IV.[28] Had he included both, the weighted mean index for this category would have been significantly higher.

4. The Department of Commerce average annual full-time earnings series used by Tullock do not include wage supplements. However, the same publications which contain these series also contain comparable data on wage supplements, so that it would have been simple to compute average annual full-time compensation, including the supplements. Inclusion of the supplements would have raised slightly the relative wage indexes of the more highly unionized industries.

5. A significant part of the rise from 1929–33 to 1948–52 and later in the *annual* earnings of the more highly unionized industries relative to the annual earnings of the less highly unionized industries was caused by a corresponding rise in the annual hours of work of the first group of industries relative to the annual hours of work of the second group. I doubt very much that this rise in relative hours of work was an effect of unionism.

6. Changes in the relative demand for labor in the industries in which extent

[28] See n. 27 above.

of unionism increased most after 1929–33 account for part, I believe, of the increases from 1929–33 to 1948–52 and later in the average relative wage of these industries. For example, the fraction of the national income originating in the industries in Tullock's unionism Category I was 58 per cent larger in 1948–52 than in 1929–33. Thus despite the increase in their average relative wage, relative employment[29] in these industries increased by about 16 per cent from 1929–33 to 1948–52. Furthermore, for unionism Category I, the base period was one of rapidly declining relative employment and relative output, while in 1948–52, relative employment and relative output were increasing.[30]

The Department of Commerce wage data used by Tullock have the virtue of covering all wage and salary employees in the economy. In chapter vi, I make extensive use of these data to estimate the average relative wage effect of unionism per percentage point difference in extent of unionism. The chapter vi estimates, which take into account the preceding comments, are much less than half as large as those I derived above from Table 43.

IV.6. THE BOWEN STUDY AND THE LEVINSON STUDY FOR THE JOINT ECONOMIC COMMITTEE[31]

Neither of these recent studies deals primarily either with unionism or with relative wages, and neither contains numerical estimates of the impact of unionism on relative wages. However, both studies include empirical analyses of factors, including unionism, affecting relative wage differentials among manufacturing industries in the period since 1946.

Professor Bowen's analysis of the changes in wage differentials in the manufacturing sector is presented in chapter v of his monograph. He divided the period January, 1947–June, 1959, into six subperiods as follows:

I.1. Jan., 1947–Jan., 1949		(R) I.4. Dec., 1953–May, 1955	
(R) I.2. Jan., 1949–Oct., 1950		I.5. May, 1955–Sept., 1957	
I.3. Oct., 1950–Dec., 1953		(R) I.6. Sept., 1957–June, 1959.	

[29] As measured by the ratio of the number of full-time equivalent employees in these industries to the corresponding number for the economy as a whole.

[30] This and the preceding statements regarding the relative employment and the relative output (relative national income originating) of unionism Category I are based on the Department of Commerce employment and national income data by industry.

[31] William G. Bowen, *Wage Behavior in the Postwar Period* (Industrial Relations Section, Princeton University, 1960); Harold M. Levinson, *Postwar Movements of Prices and Wages in Manufacturing Industries* (Study Paper No. 21, prepared in connection with the "Study of Employment, Growth, and Price Levels," Joint Economic Committee, 86th Cong., 2d sess.; Washington, 1960).

The even numbered or "recession" (R) periods are those in which the unemployment rate was above 4.3 per cent in each month. In the odd-numbered periods the unemployment rate generally was below 4.3 per cent. The (R) periods, in turn, he divided into "contraction" and "recovery" periods as follows:

II.1. Jan., 1949–Nov., 1949	II.4. Sept., 1954–May, 1955
II.2. Nov., 1949–Oct., 1950	II.5. Sept., 1957–Aug., 1958
II.3. Dec., 1953–Sept., 1954	II.6. Aug., 1958–June, 1959.

(The odd-numbered periods are those in which the unemployment rate generally was rising, the even-numbered periods those of declining unemployment.)

For each of these periods and for each of the two-digit manufacturing industry groups, Bowen computed, from Bureau of Labor Statistics data, the percentage change (at an annual rate), w, in average hourly earnings. He analyzed the variation among manufacturing industries in the relative wage changes, w, in each period in terms of four factors:

e, the percentage change in production-worker employment (at an annual rate); computed from Bureau of Labor Statistics seasonally adjusted data.

p, the average annual rate of return on stockholders' equity (after taxes); from data of the Federal Trade Commission and the Securities and Exchange Commission.

c, the degree of concentration in 1954; computed from a report of the U.S. Senate Subcommittee on Antitrust and Monopoly. In each two-digit industry group the degree of concentration was a shipment weighted average of concentration ratios in the four-digit industries comprising the two-digit industry group. The concentration ratio in each four-digit industry was the percent of total shipments made by the four largest firms in the industry.

s, Bureau of Labor Statistics estimates of the per cent of workers who in 1958 were employed in establishments in which a majority of workers were covered by collective-bargaining agreements.[32]

His reasons, in brief, for choosing these four explanatory variables were (pp. 56–57):

e: "To serve as a very crude index of differential trends in the demand for labor."

p: "Because of the numerous theoretical and empirical studies that have suggested that high-profit firms are more likely to be liberal with wage increases than low-profit firms."

[32] The per cent of workers *employed* in establishments in which the majority of workers are covered by collective-bargaining agreements may differ substantially from the per cent of workers *covered* by collective-bargaining agreements. On this matter, see the discussion of the BLS figures in Table 79 in the appendix to chap. vii (sec. vii. 5).

c and *s*: "The effect of both unions and industrial concentration on wages has been hotly debated for quite some time, and there are certainly *a priori* reasons for thinking that the existence of 'market power' in both labor and product markets is likely to lead to a greater downward rigidity of wages in times of depression and to a more rapid rate of wage increase in prosperous times."

For each of the subperiods in 1947–59, Bowen calculated the multiple and partial correlations among the two-digit manufacturing industries[33] between the wage changes, *w*, and the explanatory variables, *e*, *p*, *c*, and *s*. Table 44, which was drawn from his Tables E-1 and E-2, summarizes his results.

TABLE 44

Multiple and Partial Correlations among Manufacturing Industries between Wage Changes and Selected Variables, by Period, 1947–59

PERIOD	MULTIPLE CORRELATION COEFFICIENT	PARTIAL CORRELATIONS BETWEEN WAGE CHANGES, *w*, AND			
		Employment Changes *e*	Average Profits *p*	Degree of Concentration *c*	Degree of Unionization *s*
Jan. 47–Jan. 49	0.84	+0.82	+0.68	+0.68	−0.23
(R) Jan. 49–Oct. 50.	0.55	+0.06	+0.38	−0.18	−0.40
Jan. 49–Nov. 49.	0.24	−0.16	+0.15	+0.05	−0.19
Nov. 49–Oct. 50.	0.91	+0.87	−0.13	−0.55	−0.74
Oct. 50–Dec. 53.	0.82	−0.03	+0.38	+0.25	+0.56
(R) Dec. 53–May 55	0.72	−0.23	+0.00	+0.56	+0.18
Dec. 53–Sept. 54	0.59	+0.12	+0.37	−0.55	+0.36
Sept. 54–May 55	0.75	−0.14	−0.21	+0.64	−0.08
May 55–Sept. 57	0.94	+0.90	+0.09	−0.84	+0.62
(R) Sept. 57–June 59	0.73	+0.08	+0.01	+0.41	−0.19
Sept. 57–Aug. 58	0.75	+0.15	−0.08	+0.72	−0.16
Aug. 58–June 59	0.58	−0.21	−0.12	+0.45	−0.08

The view that in both prosperity and depression the wage changes in an industry tend to be algebraically larger, the more highly unionized and the more highly concentrated is the industry, implies positive partial correlations among industries between wage changes and both the degree of concentration and the degree of unionization variables. The negative correlations between these variables in some of the subperiods of 1947–59 thus tend to contradict this view.[34]

[33] The industry group "ordnance and accessories" was excluded from these calculations because data on degree of concentration and average rate of return on stockholders' equity were not available for this group. Thus his correlations covered nineteen separate two-digit industry group headings.

[34] See also my discussion of concentration and wage changes in the review of Garbarino's study earlier in this chapter (pp. 159–61).

There is a good deal of evidence in the studies reviewed in earlier pages (see the summary in chap. v, pp. 190–91) that on the average the relative wage effects of unions began to decline well before the end of World War II. Bowen's results suggest that the decline may have continued until about 1951, and was followed by a period of generally increasing relative wage effects which lasted until about 1957. (Notice, however, that there was little correlation between the wage changes and degree of unionization in the period September, 1954–May, 1955.) The *amount* of increase in relative wage effects of unionism, in per cent per percentage point difference in degree of unionization, cannot be deduced, however, from the partial correlation coefficients in Table 44.

Professor Levinson's analysis of the postwar changes in wage differentials among the two-digit manufacturing industries, in section 2 of his study, differs from Bowen's in the following respects:

1. Levinson analyzed the year-to-year changes (and the changes for the two subperiods 1947–53 and 1953–58) rather than the changes during subperiods marked off according to the level of unemployment.

2. His concentration measure was not the same as Bowen's. In each two-digit industry group, the numerator of the concentration measure was the total value of the shipments in all four-digit industries in which the shipments of the eight largest firms comprised at least 50 per cent of total shipments. The denominator was the total shipments in the two-digit industry group.

3. He correlated the wage changes, not only with employment changes, degree of concentration, and average rates of return on stockholders' equity *after* taxes, but also with percentage changes in output, percentage changes in output per production-worker man-hour, and average rates of return on stockholders' equity *before* taxes (both current and lagged).[35]

4. At the time Levinson completed his study, the Bureau of Labor Statistics estimates of degree of unionization by manufacturing industry group in 1958, used by Bowen, were not available. Levinson based his estimates of the degree of unionization of each of the two-digit industry groups on much less satisfactory BLS data for 1946.

Table 45 compares Levinson's degree of unionization estimates with the BLS estimates for 1958 used by Bowen and with the percentage changes in straight-time average hourly earnings from 1947–53 and from 1953–58. I have added at the bottom of the table the weighted means of the earnings changes of the industries grouped by degree of unionization. The weight for each industry is its 1950 average production-worker employment.

[35] Levinson calculated both cross-section correlations among the two-digit industries and time series correlations within the two-digit industries among the years 1947–58.

TABLE 45

DEGREE OF UNIONIZATION AND CHANGES IN AVERAGE STRAIGHT-TIME
HOURLY EARNINGS, MANUFACTURING INDUSTRIES, 1947–58*

INDUSTRY	DEGREE OF UNIONIZATION		PER CENT CHANGE IN AVERAGE STRAIGHT-TIME HOURLY EARNINGS	
	Levinson's Estimates (Per Cent) (1)	1958 BLS Estimates (Per Cent) (2)	1947–53 (3)	1953–58 (4)
Primary metals...............	75–100	88.6	47.4	31.2
Printing....................	75–100	65.3	45.0	18.1
Machinery, except electrical....	75–100	67.9	43.8	24.6
Transportation equipment......	75–100	86.8	40.1	24.1
Electrical machinery..........	75–100	72.8	38.2	24.1
Rubber products.............	75–100	80.6	37.5	23.0
Apparel....................	75–100	59.7	18.0	13.7
Petroleum and coal products....	50–75	89.5	47.6	24.3
Paper products..............	50–75	75.5	45.5	26.3
Instruments.................	50–75	51.5	44.9	24.6
Stone, clay, and glass products..	50–75	77.9	44.3	22.9
Fabricated metal products......	50–75	70.6	43.9	24.9
Chemicals...................	25–50	65.4	49.2	26.7
Food and kindred products.....	25–50	68.1	46.0	25.2
Lumber and wood products.....	25–50	43.8	44.0	15.9
Furniture...................	25–50	49.6	41.9	16.1
Tobacco manufactures........	25–50	62.6	38.6	28.7
Leather and leather products....	25–50	49.3	31.1	14.9
Textile mill products..........	0–25	30.1	31.4	9.7

Degree of Unionization (Per Cent)	Weighted Mean Changes (Per Cent)	
75–100, Levinson estimates.........................	38	23
50– 75, Levinson estimates.........................	45	25
25– 50, Levinson estimates.........................	44	21
0– 25, Levinson estimates.........................	31	10
75–100, 1958 BLS estimates.........................	44	26
50– 75, 1958 BLS estimates.........................	40	23
25– 50, 1958 BLS estimates.........................	36	13

* Sources: Cols. (1), (3), and (4) are from Levinson, *Postwar Movements of Prices and Wages in Manufacturing Industries*, Table 5. Col. (2) is from Bowen, *op. cit.*, Table D-2.

Levinson concluded from the data in columns (1), (3), and (4) that
(p. 6) "there does not appear to be any general relationship between
union strength and wage changes." In the period 1947–53, as the means
at the bottom of the table suggest, the correlation between wage changes
and Levinson's estimates of degree of unionization was close to zero. In
the period 1953–58, however, the corresponding correlation was positive.
Furthermore, in both periods the wage changes correlate more highly
with the BLS unionization estimates for 1958 than with Levinson's
estimates.

Since the computations reported by Bowen and Levinson do not lead directly to estimates of the amount of change during the postwar period in the average relative wage effect of unionism per percentage point difference in extent of unionism, I have made some additional computations on their data in order to derive such estimates. Table 46 contains the data underlying these computations.

TABLE 46

WAGE AND RELATED DATA, MANUFACTURING INDUSTRIES, 1947–58*

Industry	Average Hourly Earnings in 1958 (1947–49 = 100) w (1)	Production-Worker Employment in 1958 (1947–49 = 100) e (2)	After Tax Profit Rate 1947–58 Average (Per Cent) $100p$ (3)	Degree of Concentration in 1954 (Per Cent) $100c$ (4)	Degree of Unionization in 1958 (Per Cent) $100s$ (5)
Food	167.3	87.5	9.84	34	68.1
Tobacco...........	168.8	75.7	10.88	76	62.6
Textiles	133.5	69.6	6.97	25	30.1
Apparel...........	130.3	98.6	5.56	14	59.7
Lumber...........	155.6	75.4	11.30	10	43.8
Furniture..........	151.6	100.7	11.96	17	49.6
Paper.............	167.5	109.6	12.16	23	75.5
Printing...........	152.4	113.4	13.24	17	65.3
Chemicals..........	172.5	100.4	13.09	43	65.4
Petroleum..........	164.8	84.4	13.25	35	89.5
Rubber............	161.9	91.4	11.71	55	80.6
Leather............	142.3	87.9	6.92	27	49.3
Stone, clay, glass....	164.4	96.0	13.47	41	77.9
Primary metals......	176.8	86.5	11.25	49	88.6
Fabricated metals....	164.8	102.1	11.85	28	70.6
Machinery, except electrical.........	164.2	91.4	11.92	31	67.9
Electrical machinery	158.3	117.1	13.13	53	72.8
Transportation equipment........	162.1	109.9	14.72	48	86.8
Instruments.........	166.4	105.8	11.84	43	51.5

* Sources: Cols. (1), (2), and (3) were transcribed or computed from Levinson, *Postwar Movements of Prices and Wages in Manufacturing Industries*, Tables A-2 to A-21. Cols. (4) and (5) were transcribed from Bowen, *op. cit.*, Tables D-1 and D-2.

I have fitted the following pair of multiple regression equations to the data in Table 46 (the symbols are identified in the column headings of the table):

$$\log w = a + b_e \log e + b_p p + b_c c + b_s s \qquad (a)$$

and

$$\log w = a + b_e \log e + b_p p + b_c c + b_s s + b_{cs} cs. \qquad (b)$$

The first equation assumes that the relative wage effects of unionism per unit extent of unionism were not correlated among industries with degree of concentration. It has often been argued, however, that the relative wage effect of unionism in an industry, given the extent of its unionization, will tend to be greater, the greater the degree of concentration of the industry. This line of reasoning, as I pointed out in the review of Garbarino's study earlier in this chapter (see pp. 160–61), suggests that the mathematical product, cs, of degree of concentration and degree of unionization be included among the variables explaining wage differentials among industries, as in the second equation above. On this hypothesis, the expected sign of the coefficient b_{cs} is positive.

Table 47 contains the results of fitting equations (a) and (b) to the data in Table 46. Note that the sign of the coefficient b_{cs} is negative rather than positive.

TABLE 47

MULTIPLE REGRESSIONS FITTED TO THE DATA IN TABLE 46*

EQUATION	R	R²	REGRESSION COEFFICIENTS AND THEIR STANDARD ERRORS				
			log e	p	c	s	cs
(a)	0.83	0.69	−0.11	2.06	0.12	0.12	...
			(0.10)	(0.67)	(0.09)	(0.10)	...
(b)	0.87	0.75	−0.18	2.21	0.84	0.52	−1.16
			(0.10)	(0.64)	(0.44)	(0.26)	(0.69)

* R is the multiple correlation coefficient. The figures in parentheses are the standard errors of the regression coefficients above them.

Although the estimates derived from earlier studies (see the summary in Table 49, chap. v) suggest that the average relative wage effect of unionism per unit extent of unionism may have been small in 1947–49, it is unsafe to assume that the average effect was zero. For this reason, the coefficients of the degree of unionism variable, s, estimate the *change* from 1947–49 to 1958 in the average relative wage effect of unionism, rather than the level of this effect in 1958. In the first equation, the estimate of the change is the coefficient b_s, which is equal to 0.12. In the second equation, the estimate of the change is $b_s + b_{cs}M_c = 0.52 - (1.16)(0.35) = 0.11$, where $M_c = 0.35$ is the mean value of c among the industries.

As a partial check on the preceding figures, I have also computed, using the data in Table 48, estimates of the change in the average relative wage effect of unionism per unit extent of unionism from 1948 to 1953 and from 1948 to 1957. These data cover all wage and salary employees in the economy, and the average annual compensation figures include wage supplements as well as wages and salaries. The appendix to this chapter (sec. iv. 7) gives the sources of the data in the table.

TABLE 48

AVERAGE ANNUAL COMPENSATION PER FULL-TIME EQUIVALENT EMPLOYEE,
NATIONAL INCOME, AND EXTENT OF UNIONISM, BY INDUSTRY*

LINE NUMBER AND INDUSTRY GROUP	AVERAGE ANNUAL COMPENSATION (1948 = 1)		NATIONAL INCOME ORIGINATING (1948 = 1)		EXTENT OF UNIONISM, 1953 (Per Cent) 100s
	1953 w_1	1957 w_2	1953 m_1	1957 m_2	
1. Farms..........................	1.113	1.134	0.784	0.721	1.3
2. Agricultural services, forestry, fisheries.....................	1.263	1.488	1.367	1.762	24.3
3. Metal mining...................	1.487	1.704	1.285	1.432	70.1
4. Anthracite mining...............	1.070	1.401	0.589	0.484	79.6
5. Bituminous mining..............	1.334	1.682	0.711	0.753	87.9
6. Crude petroleum, natural gas......	1.301	1.547	1.195	1.602	14.0
7. Non-metallic mining, quarrying....	1.381	1.652	1.426	1.761	32.1
8. Contract construction............	1.357	1.592	1.502	1.907	72.1
9. Food and kindred products.......	1.303	1.565	1.213	1.365	48.0
10. Tobacco manufactures............	1.332	1.777	1.658	1.969	54.9
11. Textile mill products.............	1.187	1.328	0.854	0.799	27.2
12. Apparel and other fabric products..	1.146	1.313	1.158	1.246	53.3
13. Lumber and wood products.......	1.322	1.540	1.096	1.046	39.7
14. Furniture and fixtures............	1.292	1.491	1.342	1.585	40.7
15. Paper and allied products........	1.330	1.601	1.422	1.733	59.8
16. Printing and publishing.........	1.270	1.480	1.361	1.725	40.8
17. Chemicals and allied products.....	1.370	1.710	1.472	1.915	40.8
18. Petroleum and coal products.......	1.422	1.740	1.082	1.184	59.8
19. Rubber products................	1.384	1.683	1.617	1.835	59.8
20. Leather and leather products......	1.226	1.415	1.083	1.189	44.2
21. Stone, clay, and glass products.....	1.385	1.678	1.477	1.831	61.2
22. Primary metal industries..........	1.444	1.786	1.587	1.878	71.0
23. Fabricated metals, including ordnance.....................	1.367	1.639	1.699	1.846	53.2
24. Instruments....................	1.409	1.709	1.921	2.395	33.8
25. Miscellaneous manufacturing......	1.277	1.520	1.323	1.488	41.2
26. Machinery, except electrical.......	1.393	1.632	1.571	1.809	47.4
27. Electrical machinery..............	1.331	1.603	1.924	2.318	48.1
28. Transportation equipment, except automobiles....................	1.329	1.608	3.057	4.027	51.9
29. Automobiles and equipment.......	1.549	1.863	1.896	1.901	80.3
30. Wholesale trade.................	1.268	1.536	1.273	1.643	4.2
31. Retail trade and automobile services	1.200	1.381	1.167	1.372	14.1
32. Banking........................	1.274	1.490	1.755	2.349	0.2
33. Security and commodity brokers, etc...........................	1.247	1.512	1.827	3.268	3.7
34. Finance, n.e.c...................	1.188	1.404	2.398	3.187	0.0
35. Insurance carriers...............	1.278	1.503	1.597	1.726	0.0
36. Insurance agents................	1.233	1.476	1.667	2.197	11.4
37. Real estate.....................	1.180	1.439	1.490	1.863	15.4
38. Railroads.......................	1.229	1.535	1.083	1.053	94.7
39. Local and highway passenger transportation.................	1.212	1.367	1.054	1.051	71.1
40. Highway freight and warehousing...	1.352	1.589	1.668	2.137	78.2
41. Water transportation.............	1.510	1.687	1.238	1.357	75.9
42. Air transportation...............	1.386	1.647	2.163	3.160	51.4
43. Pipeline transportation...........	1.307	1.512	1.521	1.609	50.0
44. Allied transport services..........	1.376	1.678	1.397	1.763	60.8

TABLE 48—*Continued*

LINE NUMBER AND INDUSTRY GROUP	AVERAGE ANNUAL COMPENSATION (1948 = 1)		NATIONAL INCOME ORIGINATING (1948 = 1)		EXTENT OF UNIONISM, 1953 (Per Cent) 100s
	1953 w_1	1957 w_2	1953 n_1	1957 n_2	
45. Telephone and telegraph..........	1.329	1.618	1.689	2.342	68.5
46. Radio and television..............	1.337	1.577	1.881	2.901	51.6
47. Utilities: electric and gas..........	1.392	1.697	1.732	2.199	41.1
48. Local utilities....................	1.308	1.646	1.588	2.079	0.0
49. Hotels, lodging places.............	1.194	1.353	1.170	1.367	27.5
50. Personal services.................	1.225	1.449	1.200	1.466	28.7
51. Private households...............	1.209	1.377	1.640	2.312	0.0
52. Commercial and trade schools and employment agencies...........	1.136	1.277	1.195	1.759	0.0
53. Business services, n.e.c...........	1.297	1.532	1.609	2.522	0.0
54. Miscellaneous repair services.......	1.270	1.450	1.255	1.689	0.0
55. Motion pictures..................	1.124	1.401	0.913	0.936	21.7
56. Amusement and recreation........	1.289	1.622	1.239	1.595	28.9
57. Medical and health services........	1.245	1.384	1.450	2.000	0.0
58. Legal services....................	1.335	1.744	1.359	1.782	0.0
59. Engineering and professional services......................	1.360	1.650	1.853	3.040	1.8
60. Educational services, n.e.c........	1.315	1.509	1.424	2.044	0.0
61. Nonprofit membership organizations	1.322	1.541	1.512	2.040	0.0
62. Federal general government........	1.303	1.593	1.668	1.932	15.4
63. Federal government enterprises....	1.343	1.574	1.455	1.739	79.2
64. State, local general government....	1.312	1.616	1.558	2.299	6.9
65. State, local government enterprises	1.280	1.470	1.756	2.093	29.8

* Sources: See the appendix to chap. iv (sec. iv. 7).

I have fitted the following multiple regressions to the data in Table 48:

$$\log w_1 = a_1 + b_1 s + c_1 \log n_1$$

and

$$\log w_2 = a_2 + b_2 s + c_2 \log n_2.$$

Below are the resulting regression coefficients and their standard errors (in parentheses).

b_1: 0.12	c_1: 0.14	b_2: 0.18	c_2: 0.13
(0.025)	(0.026)	(0.033)	(0.024)

(The multiple correlation coefficient for the first equation was 0.66; that for the second equation was 0.65.)

The coefficient b_1 indicates that between 1948 and 1953 the average relative wage effect of unionism increased by about 0.12 per cent per percentage point difference in extent of unionism. Similarly, the coefficient b_2 indicates an increase of about 0.18 per cent per percentage point difference in extent of unionism between 1948 and 1957. Both of these figures are overestimates, in my judgment, for the following reasons:

1. In the period following 1948, "full time" hours of work per man per year apparently fell less rapidly on the average in the industries in which extent of unionism was relatively high than in other industries. According to Table 56 in chapter vi, between 1948 and 1957, hours of work per man per year in the mining, construction, manufacturing, transportation, and public utilities industries (the Group *a* industries in the table) increased by 1.8 per cent relative to hours of work in other industries (the Group *b* industries). In this period, the extent of unionism of Group *a* industries exceeded that of Group *b* industries by about forty-five to fifty percentage points (see Table 51 in chap. vi). Hence the rise in hours worked in Group *a* industries relative to Group *b* industries was approximately 0.04 per cent per percentage point difference in extent of unionism.

2. In the same period, the proportion of Group *a* employees who were male, white, and in the relatively more skilled occupations increased relative to the corresponding proportion among Group *b* employees. Data in the appendix to chapter vi (sec. vi. 4, pp. 229 ff.) suggest that this change in the composition of the labor force in Group *a* relative to that in Group *b* would account for an increase of about 3.5 per cent in the average compensation of Group *a* employees relative to that of Group *b*. Such an increase amounts to about 0.07 per cent per percentage point difference in the extent of unionism of the two groups.

These data suggest that something like one-half of the relative wage changes attributed to unionism in the above regressions may be the result of inadequate adjustment of the wage data for hours of work and labor force composition differences among industries. For this reason, I would put the change from 1948 to 1957 in the effect of unionism on the average wage of all union labor relative to the average wage of all nonunion labor at closer to ten than to twenty percentage points.

IV.7. Appendix: Sources of the Data in Table 48

The first four columns of Table 48 were computed from U.S. Department of Commerce (Office of Business Economics) data by industry group in the following tables:

1948 and 1953, from *U.S. Income and Output:*
   Table I.10, national income originating;
   Table VI.1, compensation of employees;
   Table VI.2, wages and salaries; and
   Table VI.13, number of full-time equivalent employees.
1957, from *Survey of Current Business* (July, 1959), pp. 13–36, tables with the same numbers as those for 1948–53.

Average annual compensation per full-time equivalent employee is the ratio of "compensation of employees" to "number of full-time equivalent employees."

In Table 48, the data for the industry group "federal general government" exclude military employees. Although the source Tables VI.2 and VI.13 have separate entries for the civilian and the military employees of the federal government, in source Tables I.10 and VI.1 these two groups are combined. Hence to estimate the compensation of civilian employees (equal to national income for this group) in the federal general government, I assumed that the total compensation of federal general government employees was divided between the civilian and the military employees in the same ratio as their wage and salaries.

The extent of unionism figures in the last column of Table 48 were estimated as follows:

Lines 9–27: The denominators are the Department of Commerce estimates for 1958 of the number of full-time equivalent employees given in the *Survey of Current Business* source cited above. The numerators are U.S. Bureau of Labor Statistics estimates for 1958 of the number of workers employed in establishments in which the majority of workers were covered by collective-bargaining agreements. The source of these BLS figures is H. M. Douty, "Collective Bargaining Coverage in Factory Employment, 1958," *Monthly Labor Review*, No. 4 (April, 1960), 347, Table 1.

Other lines: The denominators are the Department of Commerce estimates for 1953 of the number of full-time equivalent employees given in Table VI.13 of *U.S. Income and Output*. The numerators, estimates of the number of employees covered by collective-bargaining agreements in 1953, are the same as those which underlie the extent of unionism estimates given in Table 76, chapter vii. See the appendix to chapter vii (sec. vii. 5, pp. 271 ff.) for derivation of these numerators.

V

The Impact of Unionism on the Average Wage of All
Union Labor Relative to the Average Wage
of All Nonunion Labor

V.1. Introduction

TABLE 49 assembles the estimates of the relative wage effects of unionism that I have drawn from the studies reviewed in chapters iii and iv.[1] The table contains three types of information on the relative wage effects of unionism:

1. Numerical estimates, in decimal points, of the effects of unionism at specified dates on the average wage of the covered union labor relative to the corresponding average wage of nonunion labor. In the notation of chapter ii, the numbers are estimates of the union/nonunion relative wage effect:

$$G_{R_u}/G_{R_n} - 1 = (\text{antilog of } B) - 1,$$

where G_{R_u} and G_{R_n} are the indexes (with a base of unity) of the effects of unionism on the average relative wage of union labor and of nonunion labor, respectively, and B is the natural logarithm of G_{R_u}/G_{R_n}. Thus the first entry, 0.05, in the table is an estimate that in 1939 the average wage of union building construction common labor was 5 per cent higher relative to the average wage of nonunion building construction common labor than it would have been in the absence of unionism.

2. Numerical estimates, in decimal form, of the *change* from a base date to a given date in the union/nonunion relative wage effect, that is,

$$\text{antilog } (B_g/B_b) - 1,$$

where B_g and B_b are the logarithms of the union/nonunion relative wage effects at the given date and base date, respectively.

3. Directions of change in the union/nonunion relative wage effect between two dates.

In interpreting Table 49, it is important to recognize that there is some statistical dependence among the estimates from the separate studies.

---

[1] Although Table 49 identifies each estimate by the author or authors of the study from which I drew the estimate, relatively few of the figures in the table are simply transcriptions of summary numbers presented in the studies themselves. On this point, see the introductory section of chapter iii and the reviews of the individual studies.

TABLE 49

ESTIMATES OF THE RELATIVE WAGE EFFECTS OF UNIONISM
DERIVED FROM EARLIER STUDIES
(In Decimal Points)

AUTHOR[a]	COVERAGE	ESTIMATED EFFECT	
		Date	Amount
Sobotka, iii.5	Building construction, common labor	1939	0.05
Sobotka, iii.5	Building construction, skilled craftsmen	1914	About equal to that in 1939
		1919	Less than in 1914
		1923	Greater than in 1919
		1929	About equal to that in 1939
		1931	Greater than in 1929
		1935	Less than in 1929
		1939	0.25
		1944–48	Less than in 1939
		1950	Greater than in 1945–48
Greenslade, iii.6	Bituminous coal miners	1909–13	0.38–0.43
		1914–18	0.33–0.38
		1919	0.31–0.36
		1920	0.50–0.57
		1921	1.0–1.1
		1922	1.2–1.3
		1924	0.57–0.62
		1926	0.52–0.61
		1929	0.33–0.43
		1931	0.45–0.48
		1933	0.56–0.58
		1937–39	0.27–0.32
		1945	0.00
		1948–52	0.33–0.42
		1953–55	0.37–0.46
		1956–57	0.48–0.58
Rayack, iii.9	Production workers in the manufacturing of men's and boys' suits and coats	1919	0.24
		1922	0.20
		1924	0.17
		1926	0.21
		1928	0.30
		1930	0.34
		1932	0.39
		1939	0.13–0.23
		1946–57	Approximately zero
Lurie, iii.11	Motormen in the local transit industry	1920–23	About equal to that in 1925
		1925	0.15–0.20
		1929	0.15–0.19
		1933	0.22–0.24
		1937	0.12
		1939	0.03–0.06
		1948	0.07–0.18
		1958	About equal to that in 1948
Levinson, iv.2	Wage-earners in selected mining, construction, manufacturing, transportation and public utility industries	1920	Less than in 1914
		1922	Greater than in 1914
		1929	Greater than in 1922
		1931	Greater than in 1929
		1933	Greater than in 1931

TABLE 49— *Continued*

Author[a]	Coverage	Estimated Effect	
		Date	Amount
Levinson, iv.2	Wage-earners in selected mining and manufacturing industries	1938 1941 1944 1945 1946	0.16 0.17 0.09 0.07 0.05
Rees, iii.2	Production workers in basic steel manufacturing	1939 1945–48	Greater than in 1945–48 Approximately zero
Scherer, iii.3	Employees of year-round hotels	1939 1948	0.00 0.06–0.10
Sobel, iii.4	Production workers in rubber tire manufacturing	1936–38 1945–48	0.10–0.18 Less than 0.10
Maher, iii.7	Employees in the manufacturing of paints and varnishes, footwear, cotton textiles, and automotive parts	1950	0.00
Maher, iii.7	Employees in the manufacturing of wooden furniture, hosiery, and women's dresses	1950	0.07
Craycraft, iii.8	Barbers in large cities	1948 1954	0.01 0.19
Sobotka and others, iii.10	Commercial airline pilots	1956	0.21–0.34
Rapping, iii.12	Seamen in East Coast ocean shipping	1950's	0.06–0.35
Friedman, Kuznets, iii.13	Nonsalaried physicians	1929–34	Substantially less than 0.25
Lewis, iii.13	Civilian physicians	1948–51	0.00
Ross, iv.1	Wage-earners in selected mining and manufacturing industries	January 1945	About 0.10
Ross and Goldner, iv.1	Wage-earners in mining, manufacturing, transportation, and public utility industries	1933 1938–42 1946	Greater than in 1938–42 Greater than in 1946 0.04
Garbarino, iv.3	Wage-earners in selected manufacturing industries	1940	0.15
Goldner, iv.4	Unskilled workers in selected occupations	1951–52	Less than 0.15

TABLE 49—*Continued*

AUTHOR[a]	COVERAGE	ESTIMATED EFFECT	
		Date	Amount
Goldner, iv.4	Skilled workers in selected occupations	1951–52	Less than 0.20
Tullock, iv.5	All wage and salary employees	1948–52 1953–57	Much less than 0.25 Much less than 0.30
Bowen, Levinson, iv.6	Production workers in manufacturing industries	1958	Exceeds effect in 1947–49 by 0.11–0.12
Lewis, iv.6	All wage and salary employees	1957	Exceeds effect in 1948 by about 0.10

[a] Numerals denote the chapter and section in this book containing a review of the study.

The dependence among the figures for the mid-1940's derived from the Levinson (discussed above, sec. iv.2), Ross (iv.1), and Ross and Goldner (iv.1) papers is almost perfect. There is also some dependence between the 1938 and 1941 Levinson (iv.2) estimates and the 1940 Garbarino (iv.3) estimate, and between the Tullock (iv.5) and the Lewis (iv.6) estimates. Moreover, the studies with broad coverage overlap in varying degree the other studies in the table.

The main task of this chapter is to estimate from the data in Table 49 the size of the impact of unionism on the economy-wide average wage of union labor relative to the economy-wide average wage of nonunion labor during the last forty years. The index of this economy-wide union/nonunion relative wage effect is

$$\text{antilog } \bar{B} = \bar{R}_{u/n} = \bar{R}_u/\bar{R}_n,$$

where $\bar{R}_u$ and $\bar{R}_n$ are the economy-wide indexes of the impact of unionism on the average relative wages of union labor and nonunion labor, respectively.

V.2. Bias in the Estimates

Although I show most of the numbers in Table 49 to two decimal places, many of the individual estimates undoubtedly contain large errors, stemming mainly, I judge, from incomplete control over factors other than unionism in the estimation procedures. Some of the differences between studies (or groups of labor) in the tabulated estimates no doubt consist more largely of errors of estimation than of real differences in relative wage effects of unionism. In some other instances the errors may hide real differences in effects that are not suggested by the table. Thus the errors of estimation impede the discovery of the factors causing dispersion in the relative wage effects among groups of labor, and the errors probably lead to overestimation of the amount of the dispersion (see chap. viii, pp. 279–80).

This chapter deals chiefly, however, with the *average* union/nonunion relative wage effect in the economy, rather than with dispersion in relative wage effects among groups of labor. The figures in Table 49, even though they contain substantial errors, will not lead to bias in the estimate of this average if (a) the errors do not tend more or less consistently to be in one direction and (b) the industries and occupations covered in the table are not a biased sample from the whole population of industries and occupations. The data in the table, I fear, are defective on both of these scores.

First, it appears to be true of studies of the relative wage impact of unionism that the estimates of the relative wage effects typically tend to diminish in size as they become more refined, especially as the factors other than unionism affecting wages are more completely controlled. For example, the introduction of two new variables and weighting of the observations in the Goldner regressions (see chap. iv, sec. iv. 4) reduced the relative wage effect estimate for the group of unskilled occupations by about 75 per cent. Other examples may be found in the reviews of the Scherer, Craycraft, Rapping, Friedman and Kuznets, Ross-Goldner, Ross, Tullock, and Lewis (chap. iv, sec. iv. 6) studies and in chapter vi. There are also counterexamples (see the reviews of the Rayack, Lurie, and Sobotka [airline pilots] studies), but they are less numerous and less striking. This suggests that refinement of the estimation procedures underlying the figures in Table 49 would tend to reduce the figures on the average.

Second, I suspect that the estimates derived from the Levinson (iv.2), Garbarino (iv.3), and Bowen and Levinson (iv.6) data by the Variant A-III or B-III procedure contain the conceptual upward bias (as estimates of union/nonunion relative wage effects, B's) that I discuss in section ii.7 of chapter ii (see especially pp. 39 ff.).

Third, I judge from my experience as an onlooker and, sometimes, adviser in several of the studies covered by the table that the industries and occupations selected for study consisted disproportionately of those in which the relative wage effects of unionism were believed to be exceptionally large. These beliefs, of course, may have been wrong, but if they were right, the sample of estimates in Table 49 has an upward bias on this account.

V.3. THE AVERAGE UNION/NONUNION
RELATIVE WAGE EFFECT IN THE ECONOMY

The range of the individual estimates of union/nonunion relative wage effects in Table 49 is very large: from zero to over 100 per cent. The figures for bituminous coal mining span the entire range. The estimates for this industry indicate that in 1921–22, immediately after the 1920–21 deflation, the relative wages of coal miners in unionized mines may have been more than twice as large as they would have been in the absence of unionization in coal mining. In contrast, it appears that near the end of World War II the relative wage position of unionized miners was *no* higher than in the absence of their unionization. Neither of these two extremes lasted very long. By the mid-1920's the estimated relative wage effect for coal miners, although large, was only about half that in 1921–22. Similarly, after 1945 the relative wage effect rose to a level in 1956–57 about the same as that in 1924–26.

An effect of the order of magnitude of 50 per cent or larger truly deserves to be called "very large." The data for bituminous coal mining thus tend to confirm the popular impression that the United Mine Workers has been exceptionally effective in raising the relative wage position of the unionized coal miners.

However, closer inspection of Table 49 reveals that the high figures for bituminous coal mining are really extreme. None of the other studies yielded estimates of the impact of unionism on wages of union workers relative to wages of nonunion workers as high as 40 per cent, and for only three of the other studies are there numerical estimates (or midpoints of estimate ranges) above 25 per cent:

Sobotka (iii.5): During at least part of 1930–34, the relative wage effect for skilled building craftsmen may have exceeded 25 per cent slightly.

Rayack (iii.9): Estimates for men's and boys' suits and coats manufacturing in the period 1928–32 ranged from 30 to 39 per cent.

Sobotka and others (iii.10): The estimate range for 1956 for commercial airline pilots is 21 to 34 per cent.

Moreover, the estimates for men's and boys' suits and coats manufacturing for the period 1947–57 were approximately zero.

Thus I strongly doubt that the effect of unionism on the average wage of all union workers relative to the average wage of all nonunion workers exceeded 25 per cent at any time since 1920 except, possibly, in 1921–22 and from about 1930 to about 1935. My doubts are reinforced by the following considerations:

1. The weighted average (with roughly estimated 1957 employment weights) of the following numerical estimates (or midpoints of estimate ranges) drawn from the "industry" studies reviewed in chapter iii was approximately 0.18, that is, about 18 per cent:

0.25, skilled building craftsmen in 1939 (Sobotka, iii.5);

0.05, common building labor in 1939 (Sobotka, iii.5);

0.53, bituminous coal miners in 1956–57 (Greenslade, iii.6);

0.18, production workers in men's clothing manufacturing in 1939 (Rayack, iii. 9);

0.12, motormen in local transit in 1958 (Lurie, iii.11);

0.08, hotel employees in 1948 (Scherer, iii.3);

0.00, employees in paints and varnishes, footwear, cotton textiles, and auto parts manufacturing in 1950 (Maher, iii.7);

0.07, employees in wooden furniture, hosiery, and women's dresses manufacturing in 1950 (Maher, iii.7);

0.19, large-city barbers in 1954 (Craycraft, iii.8);

0.27, commercial airline pilots in 1956 (Sobotka and others, iii.10);

0.20, seamen in the 1950's (Rapping, iii.12);

0.14, production workers in rubber tire manufacturing in 1936–38 (Sobel, iii.4).

The estimate from each study included in this average, if Table 49 presented more than one estimate for the period after 1935, was the highest figure shown for this period. Furthermore, if only one estimate was available after 1935 and that figure was for any date in the period 1945–49, the estimate was excluded from the average. (The reason for this exclusion is that Table 49 shows that the period 1945–49 was one in which the relative wage impact of unionism was unusually low.) Thus the zero estimates for basic steel manufacturing and for physicians were not included in the average.

2. The estimates from the global studies reviewed in chapter iv were:

Levinson (iv.2): 0.17 (in 1941), the highest of the numerical estimates drawn from this study;

Garbarino (iv.3): 0.15 (in 1940); and

Goldner (iv.4): 0.15 for unskilled workers and 0.20 for skilled workers (in 1951–52).

(The figures from the Ross and Ross-Goldner studies were lower, but they pertained to the period 1945–46.) In addition, I estimated from the Bowen (iv.6) and Levinson (iv.6) data and independently from other data (Lewis, iv.6) that the impact of unionism on the average wage of union workers relative to the average wage of nonunion workers was 10 to 12 per cent higher in 1957–58 than in 1947–49. I also have estimated (see the discussion below) that in 1945–49 this average relative wage effect of unionism did not exceed 5 per cent. These figures indicate that in 1957–58 the average effect was about 10 to 17 per cent.

3. The results yielded by my statistical study of "wage rigidity" effects of unionism in the next chapter (see pp. 219 ff.) indicate that the union/nonunion

relative wage effect probably was not greater than 20 per cent at any date in the period 1938–58.

There is a high degree of uniformity in the data summarized in the preceding paragraph that the average effect of unionism on the wages of union workers relative to the wages of nonunion workers in the United States since the late 1930's has not been larger than 20 per cent. Therefore, I put the upper-limit estimate of the average union/nonunion relative wage effect, $100(\overline{R}_{u/n} - 1)$, at 20 per cent for the period from about 1938 to date. Indeed, if my judgment that the estimates in Table 49 tend to be biased upward (see the preceding section) is correct, 20 per cent is an overestimate of the top value of $100(\overline{R}_{u/n} - 1)$ in this period.

I noted parenthetically in the next-to-last paragraph that the relative wage impact of unionism in the period beginning about 1945 and ending about 1949 was apparently at an unusually low level. Nine of the studies provide estimates for this period as follows:

Basic steel manufacturing: 0.00 in 1945–48 (Rees, iii.2);
Large-city hotels: 0.06–0.10 in 1948 (Scherer, iii.3);
Rubber tire manufacturing: less than 0.10 in 1945–48 (Sobel, iii.4);
Bituminous coal mining: 0.00 in 1945 (Greenslade, iii.6);
Large-city barbers: 0.01 in 1948 (Craycraft, iii.8);
Men's and boys' suits and coats manufacturing: 0.00 in 1946–48 (Rayack, iii.9);
Motormen in local transit: 0.07–0.18 in 1948 (Lurie, iii.11);
Physicians: 0.00 in 1948–51 (Lewis, iii.13);
Economy wide: about 0.10 in January 1945 (Ross, iv.1), 0.07 in 1945 (Levinson, iv.2), and 0.04–0.05 in 1946 (Ross and Goldner, iv.1, and Levinson, iv.2).

In addition, the data in the Sobotka (iii.5) study show a sharp fall from 1939 to 1945–48 in the relative wage position of skilled construction workers in large cities and the results of the "wage rigidity" study reported in chapter vi indicate that the relative wage impact of unionism in 1945–49 was probably close to zero. Hence I estimate that in 1945–49, unionism had little effect—5 per cent or less—on the union/nonunion relative wage. There is much less evidence for the period at the end of and just following World War I, but what there is suggests that in this period, too, the relative wage impact of unionism was unusually low.

Except for the years in and near to these war and postwar inflationary periods, however, the estimates (or midpoints of estimate ranges) of the effects of unionism on wages of union workers relative to wages of nonunion workers are 10 per cent or larger, with two exceptions:

Motormen in local transit (Lurie, iii.11): 3 to 6 per cent in 1938; and

Wage-earners in men's and boys' suits and coats manufacturing (Rayack, iii.9): 0 per cent, 1946–57.

It appears, then, that "normally"—that is, apart from periods of unusually rapid inflation—the effect of unionism on the average wage of all union workers relative to the average wage of all nonunion workers was at least 10 per cent.

All of the studies (Sobotka, iii.5; Greenslade, iii.6; Rayack, iii.9; Lurie, iii.11, and Levinson, iv.2) spanning the 1920's and 1930's show that the union/nonunion relative wage effect was greater in the early 1930's than in the late 1920's and late 1930's. (The Ross-Goldner data go back only to 1933, but they also suggest a decline in the union/nonunion effect after 1933.) This finding is supported by the results of the wage rigidity study in chapter vi. The chapter vi estimates suggest that the union/nonunion relative wage effect may have been close to 20 per cent in 1923–29, increased to a peak well above 25 per cent in about 1932, and then declined to less than 20 per cent before 1940.

V.4. WAGE RIGIDITY AND THE RELATIVE WAGE IMPACT OF UNIONISM

As the preceding paragraphs indicate, there is substantial agreement in the evidence provided by earlier studies that the impact of unionism on the union/nonunion relative wage has varied rather widely over time and in a systematic manner. In particular, the relative wage effect estimates appear to be negatively correlated with the rate of inflation (and, perhaps, positively correlated with the unemployment rate). The observation that unionism has affected relative wages least when the rate of inflation was exceptionally high and most during times of rapid deflation, of course, is not new. Rees, Friedman, Morton,[2] and other economists have attributed the phenomenon to rigidities or lags in the adjustment of money wages of union labor introduced by collective bargaining: the collective-bargaining contract commonly running for a

[2] Milton Friedman, "Some Comments on the Significance of Labor Unions for Economic Policy," in David McCord Wright (ed.), *The Impact of the Union* (New York: Harcourt Brace & Co., 1951), pp. 226–31 (see also his "Discussion," in Industrial Relations Research Association, *Proceedings of the Eleventh Annual Meeting*, 1958, pp. 212–16); Albert Rees, "Postwar Wage Determination in the Basic Steel Industry," *American Economic Review*, XLI, No. 3 (June, 1951), 395–99; and W. A. Morton, "Trade Unionism, Full Employment and Inflation," *American Economic Review*, XL, No. 1 (March, 1950), p. 18.

year or more, the reluctance of unions to accept wage cuts during periods of deflation lest the deflation not continue, and the similar reluctance of employers of union labor to agree to unusually large wage increases during periods of unexpectedly rapid inflation.

Chapter vi is a quantitative study, covering the period 1920–58, of the behavior of the average wage of employees in the

mining, construction, manufacturing, transportation, and communications and public utilities industries (which I call the Group *a* industries)

relative to the average wage of employees in the

agricultural; trade; finance, insurance, and real estate; service; and government (except military and work relief) industries (the Group *b* industries).

The Group *a* industries on the average employed about 85 per cent of the union members in the economy during 1920–58, although they employed a bit less than one-half of all wage and salary employees. Hence if unionism has tended to raise the relative wage position of union workers, it should also have tended to raise the average wage of Group *a* employees relative to the average wage of Group *b* employees—the *a/b* relative wage—the more so, the greater the excess of the extent of unionism in Group *a* over that in Group *b*. Furthermore, if wages in Group *a* were more rigid than wages in Group *b* to unexpected changes in underlying demand and supply conditions, especially the general price and wage levels, the *a/b* relative wage should have been negatively correlated with the expected rate of inflation (or with the excess of the actual over the expected general price or wage level). In particular, if the wage rigidity stemmed in considerable part from collective bargaining, the *a/b* relative wage should have been negatively correlated with the arithmetic product of the expected rate of inflation and the excess of the extent of unionism in Group *a* over that in Group *b*.

In chapter vi, I have computed multiple regressions (using annual time series for the period 1920–58) of the average wage (average hourly compensation) of wage and salary employees in Group *a* relative to the corresponding wage for Group *b* on the excess extent of unionism of Group *a* over Group *b*, the arithmetic product of this excess extent of unionism and the expected rate of inflation of the general price level (or general money wage level), and other relative wage variables (the ratio of the national income produced in Group *a* to that produced in Group *b*, the expected rate of inflation by itself, the extent of employment of the labor force, and others). The results in general accord with the propositions of the preceding paragraph and thus support the "wage rigidity" finding from the data of the earlier studies.

The findings in chapter vi and those drawn from earlier studies point to a significant increase in the relative wage impact of unionism as the rate of inflation fell from 1945–48 to 1957–58. Nevertheless, the rate of inflation in 1957–58 apparently was still large enough, according to the chapter vi estimates, to hold the impact of unionism on the union/nonunion relative wage to a level of about 15 per cent. Because I suspect that the biases in the figures from which I have derived this estimate tend toward overestimation of the union/nonunion relative wage effect, I put the magnitude of this effect in the late 1950's at 10 to 15 per cent.

V.5. Summary of Estimates of the Impact of Unionism on the Average Relative Wage of Union Workers and the Average Relative Wage of Nonunion Workers

Column (2) of Table 50 summarizes my estimates of the effect of unionism on the average wage of all union labor relative to the average wage of all nonunion labor at key dates in the last forty years. Since the effect of unionism on the average *relative* wage of all labor in the economy is always zero and since this average is the weighted geometric mean of the average relative wage of union labor and the average relative wage of nonunion labor, the relative weight for union labor being the average extent of unionism, $\bar{p}$, in the economy as a whole, it follows that

$$\log \bar{R}_u = (1 - \bar{p}) \log \bar{R}_{u/n} \text{ and } \log \bar{R}_n = -\bar{p} \log \bar{R}_{u/n},$$

where $\bar{R}_{u/n}$ is the index of the effect of unionism on the average wage of all labor relative to the average wage of all nonunion labor and $\bar{R}_u$ and $\bar{R}_n$ are the indexes of the effects of unionism on the average wage of union labor and nonunion labor relative to the average wage of all labor.

TABLE 50

SUMMARY OF ESTIMATES OF AVERAGE RELATIVE WAGE EFFECTS
OF UNIONISM IN SELECTED PERIODS
(Per Cent)

PERIOD	AVERAGE EXTENT OF UNIONISM IN THE ECONOMY $100\bar{p}$ (1)	AVERAGE RELATIVE WAGE EFFECT OF UNIONISM		
		Union Labor Relative to Nonunion Labor $100(\bar{R}_{u/n} - 1)$ (2)	Union Labor Relative to All Labor $100(\bar{R}_u - 1)$ (3)	Nonunion Labor Relative to All Labor $100(\bar{R}_n - 1)$ (4)
1923–29.........	7 to 8	15 to 20	14 to 18	−1
1931–33.........	7 to 8	>25	>23	<−1
1939–41.........	18 to 20	10 to 20	8 to 16	−4 to −2
1945–49.........	24 to 27	0 to 5	0 to 4	−1 to 0
1957–58.........	27	10 to 15	7 to 11	−4 to −3

The figures in column (2) are $100(\overline{R}_{u/n} - 1)$. Column (1) shows the estimates of the extent of unionism, $100\overline{p}$, in the economy as a whole (these estimates are from Table 72 in chap. vii). The estimates of the effect of unionism on the average *relative* wage of all union labor, $100(\overline{R}_u - 1)$, computed from columns (1) and (2) by means of the above formula, are shown in column (3). The corresponding figures for nonunion labor are in column (4).

In the period 1931–33, unionism may have raised the average relative wage position of union labor by more than 23 per cent and lowered that of nonunion labor by more than 1 per cent. In the inflation at the end of and just following World War II, unionism had little effect on the relative wages of union and nonunion labor. More recently, unionism, I estimate, has raised the average relative wage of union labor by about 7 to 11 per cent and reduced the average relative wage of nonunion labor by approximately 3 or 4 per cent.

VI

Wage Rigidity and the Relative Wage
Effects of Unionism

VI.1. Introduction

T HE EMPIRICAL WORK of this chapter has two chief purposes: (a) to supplement the information in preceding chapters regarding the average relative wage effects of unionism and, especially, (b) to examine further the apparent relation between wage rigidity and the relative wage effects of unionism suggested by earlier studies of unionism and relative wages.

The starting point of the empirical analysis is equation (11′) of chapter ii:

$$\log R = \overline{B}U + L$$
$$= \overline{B}(p - \overline{p}) + p(\log R_u - \log \overline{R}_u) + (1 - p)(\log R_n - \log \overline{R}_n),$$

where

R is the index of the effect of unionism on the average relative wage of an industry group at a particular date;

R_u and R_n are the corresponding indexes for the union and nonunion labor respectively in the group;

$\overline{R}_u$ and $\overline{R}_n$ are the all-industry averages of the R_u and R_n;

$\overline{B}$ is the logarithm of the index, $\overline{R}_u/\overline{R}_n$, of the effect of unionism on the average wage of all union labor in the economy relative to the corresponding average wage of all nonunion labor;

U is the excess of the extent of unionism, p, in the industry group over the extent of unionism, $\overline{p}$, in the economy as a whole; and

L is the weighted average of the deviations of $\log R_u$ and $\log R_n$ from their respective all-industry means, $\log \overline{R}_u$ and $\log \overline{R}_n$.

In this chapter, as in chapter v, my interest centers on the economy-wide average effect of unionism, as measured by $\overline{B}$, rather than on the dispersion of the relative wage effects of unionism among industries and other groups of labor. Accordingly, I have divided the economy into two large industry groups as follows:

Group a: all industries in the mining, contract construction, manufacturing, transportation, and communications and public utility industry divisions.

Group b: all other industries.[1]

[1] I have excluded, however, the following industry groups (the headings are those of

195

In the main, the industries in Group a are those in which, especially in the last twenty-five years, the extent of unionism was above the average for the whole economy.[2]

For industry groups as large as these, it is likely that the "residual" $L = p(\log R_u - \log \bar{R}_u) + (1 - p)(\log R_n - \log \bar{R}_n)$ was negligible in size compared to $\bar{B}(p - \bar{p})$. Throughout the period studied in this chapter (1919–58), more than 80 per cent of the union labor in the economy was employed in Group a. Therefore, it is improbable that R_u for Group a differed significantly from $\bar{R}_u$. For Group b, on the other hand, p apparently has never been as high as 0.10 (see Table 51 below). Thus for Group b the quantity $p(\log R_u - \log \bar{R}_u)$ was surely small, even if $R_u/\bar{R}_u$ was significantly different from unity. The extent of *nonunionism*, $1 - p$, was not negligible for either group, but I doubt that there was much dispersion between the two groups in the effects, R_n, of unionism on the relative wages of nonunion labor (in this connection, see the discussion in chap. ii, p. 23). I assume, therefore, that

$$\log R = \bar{B}(p - \bar{p}) \tag{31}$$

is a good approximation of equation (11').

The index R is the ratio, v/v_o, of the average relative wage in an industry group in the presence of unionism to the corresponding average in the absence of unionism. Therefore, equation (31) can be written:

$$\log v = \log v_o + \bar{B}(p - \bar{p}). \tag{32}$$

Write equation (32) for each of Groups a and b:

$$\left.\begin{aligned}\log v_a = \log v_{a,o} + \bar{B}(p_a - \bar{p}) \\ \log v_b = \log v_{b,o} + \bar{B}(p_b - \bar{p}).\end{aligned}\right\} \tag{32'}$$

Subtract the second equation from the first, obtaining

$$\log (v_a/v_b) = \log (v_{a,o}/v_{b,o}) + \bar{B}(p_a - p_b). \tag{33}$$

Since $v_a/v_b = w_a/w_b$ and $v_{a,o}/v_{b,o} = w_{a,o}/w_{b,o}$, where the w's are the average *absolute* wage counterparts of the v's, equation (33) can also be written in the form

$$\log (w_a/w_b) = \log (w_{a,o}/w_{b,o}) + \bar{B}(p_a - p_b). \tag{34}$$

---

the U.S. Department of Commerce): federal general government, military; federal general government, work relief; state and local general government, work relief; rest of the world.

The industry classification scheme underlying the division of the economy into the two groups, a and b, is that used by the U.S. Department of Commerce, Office of Business Economics, in their "national income" reports; see their *National Income*, 1954 edition, a supplement to the *Survey of Current Business*, Washington: 1954, p. 66.

[2] See the data in chap. vii, especially Table 76, and the data in Table 48 of chap. iv.

In order to simplify the notation in this chapter, I denote w_a/w_b by W, $w_{a,o}/w_{b,o}$ by W_o, and $p_a - p_b$ by P. In these symbols, equation (34) is

$$\log W = \log W_o + \bar{B}P. \tag{35}$$

Equation (35) divides the factors determining the actual a/b relative wage, W, into the factors other than unionism contained in W_o and the unionism factors $\bar{B}$ and P.

The factors, excluding unionism, that cause W_o to vary over time are those that cause the *relative* quantity of labor demanded by Group a or the *relative* quantity of labor supplied to Group a to change at given values of the relative wage W_o. Call these factors S. Indeed, if, in the absence of unionism, wages in the two groups would have been continually equal to their equilibrium values (that is, if there would have been no wage "rigidity" in the absence of unionism) or if wages in the two groups would have been out of equilibrium in the same ratio, then W_o would depend only on S. On the other hand, if, in the absence of unionism, wages in the two groups would have been unequally rigid to changes in *absolute* labor supply and demand conditions (especially the rate of unemployment and the general price level) common to both groups, then W_o also depends on these absolute conditions. Denote these absolute wage factors by T and express W_o as a function of S and T:

$$W_o = f(S, T). \tag{36}$$

If unionism is a wage rigidity factor, $\bar{B}$ also depends on the factors T. In addition, it is likely that the factors which caused the extent of unionism, $\bar{p}$, in the economy as a whole to vary may have caused the union/nonunion relative wage effect of unionism, $\bar{B}$, to change over time. These factors, which include such things as federal and state collective-bargaining legislation and the interpretation of existing law by law enforcement officers and the courts, are, in general, not measurable. Therefore, I have used $\bar{p}$ as a proxy for these factors. The hypothesis I test in this chapter is that $\bar{B}$ tended to be higher, the greater the *change* $\Delta_t \bar{p} = \bar{p}_t - \bar{p}_{t-1}$ in the extent of unionism in the labor force as a whole. There was little evidence, either in chapter v or in the empirical results of this chapter, of the upward trend in $\bar{B}$ that one would expect if $\bar{B}$ increased as $\bar{p}$ rose. Thus express $\bar{B}$ as a function of T, and $\Delta \bar{p}$:

$$\bar{B} = \bar{B}(T, \Delta\bar{p}). \tag{37}$$

Substitute equations (36) and (37) into equation (35):

$$\log W = \log f(S, T) + \bar{B}(T, \Delta\bar{p})P. \tag{38}$$

I estimate the unionism coefficient $\bar{B} = \bar{B}(T, \Delta\bar{p})$ in this chapter by fitting several explicit formulations of equation (38) to annual time series data, 1920–58, on W, P, $\Delta \bar{p}$, and variables entering S and T. The simplest formulations, presented in section vi.2, ignore the wage rigidity factors, T. In section vi.3, I experiment with several versions of equation (38) that include the rate of inflation of the general price level or the general money wage level and the rate of unemployment among the variables explaining W. The estimates of the unionism coefficient yielded by these experiments are consistent in their average level and in their variations over time with those derived, in chapter v, from earlier studies of unionism and wage differentials. In particular, the estimates support the notion that much of the variability in the unionism coefficient was caused by variations in the rate of inflation. The coefficient estimates were highest when the rate of inflation, currently and in the recent past, was least, and were lowest in the reverse situation.

VI.2. Estimates of the Unionism Coefficient That Ignore Wage Rigidity
A. The Extent of Unionism and Wage Data

In chapter ii, I defined the extent of unionism of an industry group as the ratio of the total employee compensation of union workers to the total employee compensation of all workers employed in the industry group. Unfortunately, employee compensation data rarely are available separately for union and nonunion workers. Furthermore, there are no time series data, by industry, on the number of workers covered by collective-bargaining agreements. I was therefore compelled to use extent of union membership as a proxy for extent of unionism.[3] The extent of union membership in an industry is the ratio of the number of union members to the total number of wage and salary workers (on a full-time equivalent basis) employed in the industry group.

The time series in Table 51 are estimates of the extent of union membership in Groups a and b and in the two groups together. The numerators of the "unadjusted" figures in columns (1), (2), and (3) are estimates (based chiefly on data collected from unions by Leo Wolman and Leo Troy) of the number of union members employed in Group a, Group b, and all industries, respectively. The corresponding denominators are estimates of the number of wage and salary workers (on a full-time equivalent basis) employed in Group a, Group b, and all industries.

Although unionism has been located disproportionately in industries whose employment was most sensitive to business cycle fluctuations, the

---

[3] See the appendix to chap. vii (sec. vii. 5), pp. 258 ff., for discussion of the differences between extent of unionism and extent of union membership.

EXTENT OF UNION MEMBERSHIP AMONG WAGE AND SALARY WORKERS, GROUPS a AND b AND ALL INDUSTRIES, 1919–58*

Year	Unadjusted Estimates (Per Cent) Group a (1)	Group b (2)	All-Industry Averages Variable Weights (3)	Fixed Weights (4)	Adjusted Estimates — α = 0.7 Group a (5)	Group b (6)	All Industries Variable Weights (7)	Fixed Weights (8)	Adjusted Estimates — α = 0.5 Group a (9)	Group b (10)	All Industries Variable Weights (11)	Fixed Weights (12)
1919	22.1	2.3	12.6	11.5								
1920	26.4	2.5	14.8	13.7	28.5	2.6	15.9	11.7	31.3	2.7	14.6	16.1
1921	30.7	2.8	15.9	15.8	29.7	2.8	15.5	14.7	28.4	3.0	17.5	14.9
1922	23.5	2.6	12.7	12.4	21.4	2.6	11.7	15.4	18.6	2.6	14.9	10.1
1923	18.4	2.4	10.5	9.9	17.4	2.3	10.0	11.4	16.1	2.3	10.3	8.8
1924	18.8	2.4	10.4	10.1	18.5	2.4	10.3	9.4	18.2	2.4	9.3	9.8
1925	18.3	2.4	10.2	9.8	18.2	2.4	10.1	10.0	18.1	2.5	10.1	9.8
1926	17.5	2.4	9.8	9.5	17.4	2.5	9.8	9.8	17.4	2.5	9.8	9.5
1927	18.1	2.4	9.9	9.8	18.2	2.4	9.9	9.5	18.2	2.7	10.0	9.9
1928	17.7	2.6	9.7	9.6	17.4	2.6	9.6	9.6	17.1	2.7	9.5	9.4
1929	16.5	2.6	9.1	9.1	16.3	2.8	9.1	9.0	16.0	2.9	9.0	9.0
1930	17.6	2.8	9.5	9.7	17.3	3.0	9.4	9.6	17.0	3.0	9.3	9.5
1931	20.2	3.0	10.4	11.0	20.0	3.3	10.3	11.0	19.9	3.3	10.3	10.9
1932	22.1	3.3	11.0	12.1	21.3	3.2	10.7	11.7	20.3	3.2	10.0	11.2
1933	20.7	3.2	11.0	12.1	20.2	3.4	10.3	11.2	19.6	3.5	14.0	10.9
1934	23.0	3.3	10.6	11.4	25.1	3.6	12.8	13.5	27.8	3.7	12.5	14.9
1935	22.8	3.4	11.8	12.5	23.2	3.8	12.2	12.8	23.7	4.0	13.4	13.1
1936	23.1	3.6	11.9	12.7	24.0	5.2	12.8	13.2	25.2	5.9	20.9	14.0
1937	30.3	4.7	12.3	16.7	34.1	5.5	18.3	18.7	39.2	5.8	18.8	21.4
1938	35.4	5.3	16.2	19.4	35.8	6.0	18.4	19.7	36.3	6.3	20.1	20.1
1939	35.3	5.7	18.1	19.6	36.4	6.1	19.3	20.2	37.8	6.4	21.7	21.0
1940	36.7	5.9	18.7	20.3	38.4	6.0	20.5	21.2	40.7	6.2	24.5	22.4
1941	37.7	5.9	19.7	20.8	40.6	6.3	22.6	22.2	44.5	6.1	26.2	24.2
1942	39.6	6.0	21.1	21.7	42.4	7.1	24.3	23.0	46.1	6.4	28.3	24.8
1943	42.7	6.1	22.9	23.3	45.3	7.9	26.5	24.5	48.7	7.4	29.5	26.2
1944	47.1	6.8	25.1	25.7	48.4	9.0	28.4	26.4	50.2	8.3	28.7	27.4
1945	50.4	7.6	27.6	27.6	50.0	9.2	28.7	27.6	49.6	9.7	30.5	27.6
1946	51.6	8.4	28.7	28.6	52.2	9.1	29.7	29.2	53.1	9.6	32.7	30.0
1947	53.0	8.9	29.1	29.5	54.8	9.0	31.3	30.5	57.1	9.2	31.3	31.9
1948	53.6	8.9	30.3	29.8	54.2	9.2	30.8	30.2	55.0	9.1	30.6	30.6
1949	55.2	9.0	30.5	30.6	54.2	9.2	30.0	29.4	53.0	9.3	29.5	29.6
1950	52.5	9.1	30.5	29.4	52.4	9.2	29.6	30.5	52.3	9.4	29.6	29.4
1951	53.0	9.0	29.6	29.6	54.8	9.2	31.1	30.3	57.2	9.3	32.3	31.8
1952	53.7	9.1	30.1	30.0	54.3	9.3	30.8	30.3	55.1	9.3	31.2	30.7
1953	55.4	9.1	30.4	30.8	56.9	9.6	32.2	31.5	58.8	9.4	33.2	32.5
1954	56.4	9.3	31.5	31.3	55.3	9.6	30.8	30.8	53.8	9.8	30.2	30.2
1955	55.2	9.4	31.3	30.8	55.4	9.6	31.0	31.0	55.7	9.8	31.3	31.3
1956	54.5	9.4	30.8	30.5	54.8	9.6	30.6	30.7	55.2	9.7	30.9	31.0
1957	55.7	9.5	30.3	31.1	56.1	9.6	30.8	31.3	56.6	9.7	31.1	31.6
1958	57.6	9.5	30.5	32.0	56.5	9.6	30.1	31.6	55.1	9.7	29.5	30.9

* See the appendix to chap. vi (sec. vi.4) for sources and methods of constructing these series.

cyclical variations, in per cent, of *reported* union membership in the economy as a whole and in Group *a* characteristically have been smaller than the corresponding variations in the employment of wage and salary workers. Thus the series in columns (1), (3), and (4) display a marked tendency to rise during cyclical declines in employment and to fall during cyclical inclines in employment. This contracyclical variability of the extent of union membership figures is, in my opinion, largely spurious—the result of a tendency by unions to report their "normal" membership rather than their actual employed membership.[4]

Let m^* be the normal (that is, the reported union membership) and m the actual employed membership in an industry group. I assume that normal and actual membership figures are related in approximately the following manner:

$$m_t^* - m_{t-1}^* = \alpha(m_t - m_{t-1}^*), \tag{39}$$

where $0 < \alpha < 1$ and t denotes the date. The solution of this equation for m_t is

$$m_t = m_t^*/\alpha - m_{t-1}^*(1 - \alpha)/\alpha. \tag{40}$$

Let N_t be the number of full-time equivalent employees in the industry group. The unadjusted extent of union membership figures in columns (1), (2), and (3) of Table 51 were obtained by dividing reported membership, m_t^*, by N_t, the adjusted figures in columns (5), (6), (7), (9), (10), and (11) by dividing m_t by N_t. For columns (5), (6), and (7) the adjustment coefficient, α is 0.7; for columns (9), (10), and (11) the adjustment coefficient is 0.5.

Denote by $p_t^* = m_t^*/N_t$ the unadjusted and by $p_t = m_t/N_t$ the adjusted extent of union membership figures. Then equation (40) implies that for Groups *a* and *b*,

$$\left.\begin{aligned} p_{a_t} &= \frac{1}{\alpha}\left[p_{a_t}^* - (1 - \alpha)\frac{m_{a_{t-1}}^*}{N_{a_t}} \right] \\ p_{b_t} &= \frac{1}{\alpha}\left[p_{b_t}^* - (1 - \alpha)\frac{m_{b_{t-1}}^*}{N_{b_t}} \right]. \end{aligned}\right\} \tag{41}$$

Subtract the second equation from the first and write P_t for $p_{a_t} - p_{b_t}$, P_t^* for $p_{a_t}^* - p_{b_t}^*$, and π_t for $m_{a_{t-1}}^*/N_{a_t} - m_{b_{t-1}}^*/N_{b_t}$, obtaining

$$P_t = P_t^*/\alpha - (1 - \alpha)\pi_t/\alpha. \tag{42}$$

Substitute the right-hand side of equation (42) for the extent of unionism variable P in the relative wage–determining equation (38) and assume that the unionism coefficient is a constant $\bar{B}$:

[4] This is discussed in more detail in the appendix to chap. vii (sec. vii. 5), p. 263.

$$\log W = \log f(S, T) + \frac{\overline{B}}{\alpha} [P^* - (1 - \alpha)\pi].\qquad(38')$$

Let b_{P^*} and b_π be the partial regression coefficients of $\log W$ on P^* and π in the presence of variables entering $\log f(S, T)$; b_{P^*} is an estimate of $\overline{B}/\alpha$ and $-b_\pi$ an estimate of $(1 - \alpha)\overline{B}/\alpha$. Thus the estimated values of α and $\overline{B}$ are

$$\left.\begin{array}{l}\text{estimate of } \alpha = 1 + b_\pi/b_{P^*} \\ \text{estimate of } \overline{B} = b_{P^*} + b_\pi.\end{array}\right\}\qquad(43)$$

The results of fitting several versions of equation (38′) to data in this section and the next suggested that α was at least 0.5 (see p. 221).

Table 52, columns (1), (2), and (3), contains the series on the auxiliary variable, m^*_{t-1}/N_t, used in calculating the adjusted extent of union membership figures in Table 51 from the unadjusted figures in the same table. Column (4) of Table 52 is the series for the variable π.

The all-industry series in columns (4), (8), and (12) of Table 51 are fixed weighted arithmetic means of the corresponding series for Groups *a* and *b*.

Table 53 shows three different estimates of the excess of the extent of union membership in Group *a* over that in Group *b*:

P^* = column (1) minus column (2) of Table 51;
P_1 = column (5) minus column (6) of Table 51; and
P_2 = column (9) minus column (10) of Table 51.

(The seeming discrepancies between Tables 51, 52, and 53 are the result of rounding.)

Table 54 shows the absolute average annual full-time compensation of wage and salary workers in Groups *a* and *b* and in all industries and the average annual full-time compensation of wage and salary workers in Group *a* relative to that in Group *b*. Average annual full-time compensation in an industry is the ratio of the total employee compensation to the total number of full-time equivalent employees in the industry. Employee compensation is the sum of wages and salaries and "supplements to wages and salaries." In the underlying data by industry, the wage and salary estimates are annual totals which include commissions, tips, bonuses, and payments in kind as well as what is commonly regarded as money wages and salaries. The "supplements to wages and salaries" include employer contributions for social insurance; employer contributions to private pension, health, and welfare funds; compensation for injuries; and a few other much less important items of labor income.

The number of full-time equivalent employees measures man-years of

TABLE 52

AUXILIARY VARIABLE USED IN CALCULATING ADJUSTED ESTIMATES IN TABLE 51*
(Per Cent)

Year	Group *a* (1)	Group *b* (2)	All Industries Variable Weights (3)	(1) − (2) (π) (4)
1919........	. . .	. . .	10.6	. . .
1920........	21.5	2.2	12.1	19.4
1921........	33.0	2.6	16.9	30.4
1922........	28.3	2.7	15.1	25.6
1923........	20.6	2.5	11.7	18.1
1924........	19.3	2.3	10.6	17.0
1925........	18.4	2.4	10.2	16.1
1926........	17.6	2.3	9.8	15.2
1927........	18.0	2.4	9.8	15.6
1928........	18.3	2.4	9.9	15.9
1929........	16.9	2.5	9.3	14.4
1930........	18.1	2.7	9.7	15.4
1931........	20.4	2.9	10.5	17.5
1932........	24.0	3.2	11.7	20.8
1933........	21.7	3.3	11.0	18.4
1934........	18.3	3.0	9.6	15.2
1935........	21.9	3.2	11.4	18.8
1936........	20.9	3.2	11.1	17.7
1937........	21.4	3.5	11.6	17.9
1938........	34.4	4.8	17.4	29.7
1939........	32.8	5.2	17.3	27.6
1940........	32.7	5.5	17.6	27.2
1941........	30.9	5.6	17.7	25.2
1942........	33.1	5.8	19.5	27.3
1943........	36.8	5.9	21.9	30.9
1944........	44.0	6.3	25.8	37.7
1945........	51.1	6.8	28.7	44.3
1946........	50.0	7.1	27.6	43.0
1947........	48.9	8.2	27.9	40.7
1948........	52.1	8.7	29.6	43.5
1949........	57.3	8.9	31.4	48.4
1950........	52.6	8.8	29.5	43.8
1951........	48.8	8.7	27.9	40.1
1952........	52.3	8.9	29.7	43.4
1953........	52.0	9.0	29.8	43.0
1954........	58.9	9.1	32.4	49.8
1955........	54.6	9.0	30.3	45.6
1956........	53.8	9.0	29.8	44.7
1957........	54.8	9.2	30.1	45.6
1958........	60.0	9.4	31.5	50.7

* See text for method of constructing these series.

full-time employment of wage and salary workers and its equivalent in work performed by part-time workers. Full-time employment is the number of hours of work which is customary at a particular time and place.

The series in columns (1), (2), and (3) are weighted arithmetic means of the average annual full-time compensation figures for the underlying

TABLE 53

EXCESS OF EXTENT OF UNION MEMBERSHIP IN GROUP *a* OVER EXTENT
OF UNION MEMBERSHIP IN GROUP *b**
(Per Cent)

Year	P^*	P_1	P_2
1920.	24.0	25.9	28.6
1921.	27.9	26.9	25.4
1922.	20.8	18.8	16.1
1923.	16.0	15.1	13.9
1924.	16.4	16.1	15.8
1925.	15.9	15.8	15.6
1926.	15.1	15.0	14.9
1927.	15.7	15.7	15.7
1928.	15.1	14.8	14.4
1929.	13.9	13.7	13.3
1930.	14.8	14.5	14.1
1931.	17.2	17.0	16.9
1932.	18.9	18.0	17.0
1933.	17.4	17.0	16.5
1934.	19.8	21.7	24.3
1935.	19.4	19.6	20.0
1936.	19.5	20.2	21.2
1937.	25.6	28.9	33.3
1938.	30.1	30.3	30.5
1939.	29.6	30.4	31.5
1940.	30.8	32.3	34.4
1941.	31.8	34.5	38.3
1942.	33.6	36.4	40.0
1943.	36.6	39.0	42.2
1944.	40.2	41.3	42.8
1945.	42.8	42.1	41.3
1946.	43.2	43.2	43.4
1947.	44.1	45.6	47.5
1948.	44.6	45.1	45.8
1949.	46.2	45.2	43.9
1950.	43.4	43.2	43.0
1951.	43.9	45.6	47.8
1952.	44.6	45.1	45.8
1953.	46.3	47.7	49.5
1954.	47.1	46.0	44.4
1955.	45.8	45.8	45.9
1956.	45.0	45.2	45.4
1957.	46.2	46.5	46.9
1958.	48.0	46.9	45.4

* See text for explanation of this table.

industry headings, with industry weights that are the same in all years. The series in column (4) is the variable weighted arithmetic mean obtained by dividing total employee compensation in all industries by the corresponding total number of full-time equivalent employees.

The average annual compensation of Group *a* employees relative to that of Group *b* employees is shown in column (5) of Table 54. I have used fixed rather than variable weights by industry in computing these

TABLE 54

AVERAGE ANNUAL FULL-TIME COMPENSATION, GROUPS *a* AND *b*
AND ALL INDUSTRIES, 1919–58*

| YEAR | AVERAGE ANNUAL FULL-TIME COMPENSATION (Dollars) | | | | GROUP *a* DIVIDED BY GROUP *b* (1)/(2) (5) |
| | Group *a* Fixed Weights (1) | Group *b* Fixed Weights (2) | All Industries | | |
			Fixed Weights (3)	Variable Weights (4)	
1919.........	1,364	1,099	1,223	1,172	1.241
1920.........	1,636	1,203	1,406	1,361	1.360
1921.........	1,452	1,208	1,322	1,238	1.202
1922.........	1,387	1,248	1,313	1,227	1.111
1923.........	1,516	1,289	1,395	1,320	1.176
1924.........	1,533	1,304	1,411	1,332	1.176
1925.........	1,549	1,343	1,439	1,357	1.153
1926.........	1,568	1,376	1,466	1,382	1.140
1927.........	1,587	1,375	1,474	1,390	1.154
1928.........	1,606	1,394	1,493	1,408	1.152
1929.........	1,607	1,413	1,504	1,424	1.137
1930.........	1,547	1,387	1,462	1,388	1.115
1931.........	1,423	1,335	1,376	1,296	1.066
1932.........	1,208	1,207	1,208	1,140	1.001
1933.........	1,155	1,109	1,130	1,067	1.041
1934.........	1,217	1,133	1,172	1,113	1.074
1935.........	1,290	1,176	1,229	1,168	1.097
1936.........	1,385	1,216	1,295	1,231	1.139
1937.........	1,502	1,272	1,380	1,322	1.181
1938.........	1,466	1,282	1,368	1,308	1.144
1939.........	1,534	1,295	1,407	1,347	1.185
1940.........	1,589	1,310	1,441	1,388	1.213
1941.........	1,788	1,373	1,567	1,542	1.302
1942.........	2,107	1,494	1,781	1,812	1.410
1943.........	2,381	1,684	2,010	2,110	1.414
1944.........	2,560	1,852	2,183	2,290	1.382
1945.........	2,632	1,993	2,292	2,362	1.321
1946.........	2,719	2,191	2,438	2,472	1.241
1947.........	3,009	2,385	2,677	2,709	1.262
1948.........	3,277	2,537	2,883	2,916	1.292
1949.........	3,352	2,626	2,966	2,992	1.276
1950.........	3,583	2,735	3,131	3,169	1.310
1951.........	3,916	2,891	3,371	3,442	1.355
1952.........	4,137	3,034	3,550	3,646	1.364
1953.........	4,356	3,162	3,721	3,835	1.378
1954.........	4,463	3,273	3,830	3,934	1.364
1955.........	4,705	3,411	4,016	4,124	1.379
1956.........	4,975	3,560	4,222	4,337	1.397
1957.........	5,214	3,720	4,419	4,544	1.402
1958.........	5,415	3,889	4,604	4,693	1.392

* See the appendix to chap. vi (sec. vi.4) for sources and methods of constructing these series.

relative wage figures in order to eliminate, to the extent permitted by the underlying industry data, the effects on relative wages of a changing distribution of employees among industries.

There are substantial positive correlations between the relative wage series in column (5) of Table 54 and the excess extent of unionism estimates in Table 53. Table 55 summarizes the simple regressions of the natural logarithms of the a/b relative wage series on P^*, P_1, and P_2 from Table 53 (the period covered by the regressions is 1920–58).

TABLE 55

Simple Regressions of the Logarithm of Average Annual Full-Time
Compensation, Group a Relative to Group b, on the Difference
between the Extent of Unionism of Group a and That of Group b*

Independent Variable	R^2	Regression Coefficient	Standard Error of Coefficient	Antilog of Coefficient
$P^*/100$..........	0.68	0.65	0.07	1.91
$P_1/100$..........	0.71	0.65	0.07	1.92
$P_2/100$..........	0.72	0.64	0.06	1.89

* R^2 is the square of the correlation coefficient.

In considerable part, these regression coefficients are registering the effects of changes in full-time hours of work that are positively correlated with the changes in the relative wage and the extent of unionism series. Table 56 shows the absolute annual full-time hours of work of wage and salary workers in Groups a and b and in all industries and the average annual full-time hours of work of wage and salary workers in Group a relative to the corresponding average for Group b. Average annual full-time hours of work in an industry is the ratio of total man-hours worked to the total number of full-time equivalent employees. The fixed weights used in constructing Table 56 are the same as those used in Table 54.

The figures in Table 56 derive mainly from man-hour and employment estimates made by Professor John Kendrick. Both in quantity and quality, the historical information on man-hours available to compilers of hours and wages data is much inferior to that on wages and salaries and number of employees, and it is quite likely that the series in Table 56 contain some important errors.

The series in Table 57 are estimates of absolute and relative average *hourly* compensation obtained by dividing the series in Table 54 by the corresponding series in Table 56.[5]

[5] Although, in keeping with the column headings of Tables 54 and 56, I have labeled four of the series in Table 57 as having fixed weights, none of the series in Table 57 is a fixed weighted arithmetic mean of underlying *hourly* compensation figures by industry.

Let w_a denote the series in col. (1) of Table 54, h_a the series in col. (1) of Table 56. Then the series in col. (1) of Table 57 is

$$\frac{w_a}{h_a} = \frac{\Sigma f_i w_i}{\Sigma f_i h_i} = \frac{\Sigma f_i h_i (w_i/h_i)}{\Sigma f_i h_i},$$

TABLE 56

AVERAGE FULL-TIME HOURS WORKED PER YEAR, GROUPS *a* AND *b*
AND ALL INDUSTRIES, 1919–58*

| YEAR | AVERAGE HOURS WORKED PER YEAR | | | | GROUP *a* DIVIDED BY GROUP *b* (1)/(2) |
| | Group *a* Fixed Weights (1) | Group *b* Fixed Weights (2) | All Industries | | |
			Fixed Weights (3)	Variable Weights (4)	(5)
1919.........	2,407	2,598	2,509	2,515	0.926
1920.........	2,491	2,595	2,546	2,564	0.960
1921.........	2,355	2,559	2,463	2,463	0.920
1922.........	2,461	2,565	2,517	2,522	0.959
1923.........	2,506	2,567	2,538	2,556	0.976
1924.........	2,419	2,563	2,496	2,509	0.944
1925.........	2,464	2,562	2,516	2,532	0.962
1926.........	2,465	2,557	2,514	2,534	0.964
1927.........	2,440	2,545	2,496	2,514	0.959
1928.........	2,445	2,542	2,496	2,517	0.962
1929.........	2,455	2,527	2,494	2,516	0.972
1930.........	2,271	2,483	2,384	2,406	0.915
1931.........	2,118	2,445	2,292	2,317	0.866
1932.........	2,001	2,373	2,199	2,227	0.843
1933.........	1,977	2,364	2,183	2,208	0.836
1934.........	1,841	2,224	2,045	2,067	0.828
1935.........	1,919	2,243	2,091	2,108	0.856
1936.........	2,033	2,299	2,174	2,186	0.884
1937.........	2,008	2,316	2,172	2,185	0.867
1938.........	1,884	2,275	2,092	2,113	0.828
1939.........	1,979	2,283	2,141	2,154	0.867
1940.........	1,995	2,286	2,150	2,159	0.873
1941.........	2,103	2,286	2,200	2,196	0.920
1942.........	2,199	2,310	2,258	2,242	0.952
1943.........	2,300	2,343	2,323	2,312	0.982
1944.........	2,323	2,345	2,335	2,327	0.991
1945.........	2,247	2,288	2,269	2,261	0.982
1946.........	2,109	2,192	2,153	2,151	0.962
1947.........	2,098	2,130	2,115	2,116	0.985
1948.........	2,084	2,104	2,094	2,097	0.990
1949.........	2,031	2,096	2,066	2,068	0.969
1950.........	2,045	2,067	2,057	2,062	0.989
1951.........	2,058	2,053	2,055	2,060	1.002
1952.........	2,054	2,050	2,052	2,058	1.002
1953.........	2,037	2,038	2,038	2,047	1.000
1954.........	2,000	2,015	2,008	2,021	0.993
1955.........	2,033	2,025	2,029	2,037	1.004
1956.........	2,024	2,013	2,018	2,024	1.005
1957.........	2,003	1,987	1,994	2,003	1.008
1958.........	1,974	1,973	1,973	1,982	1.001

* See the appendix to chap. vi (sec. vi.4) for sources and methods of constructing these series.

TABLE 57

AVERAGE HOURLY COMPENSATION, GROUPS *a* AND *b* AND
ALL INDUSTRIES, 1919–58*

YEAR	AVERAGE HOURLY COMPENSATION (Dollars)				GROUP *a* DIVIDED BY GROUP *b* (1)/(2) (5)
	Group *a* Fixed Weights (1)	Group *b* Fixed Weights (2)	All Industries		
			Fixed Weights (3)	Variable Weights (4)	
1919.	0.567	0.423	0.487	0.466	1.340
1920.	0.657	0.464	0.552	0.531	1.416
1921.	0.617	0.472	0.537	0.503	1.307
1922.	0.564	0.487	0.522	0.487	1.158
1923.	0.605	0.502	0.550	0.516	1.205
1924.	0.634	0.509	0.565	0.531	1.246
1925.	0.629	0.524	0.572	0.536	1.200
1926.	0.636	0.538	0.583	0.545	1.182
1927.	0.650	0.540	0.591	0.553	1.204
1928.	0.657	0.548	0.598	0.559	1.199
1929.	0.655	0.559	0.603	0.566	1.172
1930.	0.681	0.559	0.613	0.577	1.218
1931.	0.672	0.546	0.600	0.559	1.231
1932.	0.604	0.509	0.549	0.512	1.187
1933.	0.584	0.469	0.518	0.483	1.245
1934.	0.661	0.509	0.573	0.538	1.299
1935.	0.672	0.524	0.588	0.554	1.282
1936.	0.681	0.529	0.596	0.563	1.287
1937.	0.748	0.549	0.635	0.605	1.362
1938.	0.778	0.564	0.654	0.619	1.379
1939.	0.775	0.567	0.657	0.625	1.367
1940.	0.796	0.573	0.670	0.643	1.389
1941.	0.850	0.601	0.712	0.702	1.414
1942.	0.958	0.647	0.789	0.808	1.481
1943.	1.035	0.719	0.865	0.913	1.439
1944.	1.102	0.790	0.935	0.984	1.395
1945.	1.171	0.871	1.010	1.045	1.344
1946.	1.289	1.000	1.132	1.149	1.289
1947.	1.434	1.120	1.266	1.280	1.280
1948.	1.572	1.206	1.377	1.391	1.303
1949.	1.650	1.253	1.436	1.447	1.317
1950.	1.752	1.323	1.522	1.537	1.324
1951.	1.903	1.408	1.640	1.671	1.352
1952.	2.014	1.480	1.730	1.772	1.361
1953.	2.138	1.552	1.826	1.873	1.378
1954.	2.232	1.624	1.907	1.947	1.374
1955.	2.314	1.684	1.979	2.025	1.374
1956.	2.458	1.769	2.092	2.143	1.389
1957.	2.603	1.872	2.216	2.269	1.390
1958.	2.743	1.971	2.334	2.368	1.392

* See text for explanation of this table.

TABLE 58

SIMPLE REGRESSIONS OF THE LOGARITHM OF AVERAGE HOURLY COMPENSATION,
GROUP *a* RELATIVE TO GROUP *b*, ON THE DIFFERENCE BETWEEN
THE EXTENT OF UNIONISM OF THE TWO GROUPS*

Independent Variable	R^2	Regression Coefficient	Standard Error of Coefficient	Antilog of Coefficient
$P^*/100$..........	0.48	0.36	0.06	1.44
$P_1/100$..........	0.55	0.38	0.06	1.46
$P_2/100$..........	0.62	0.39	0.05	1.48

* R^2 is the square of the correlation coefficient.

Table 58 summarizes the simple regressions of the natural logarithm of the relative hourly compensation series in column (5) of Table 57 on the excess extent of unionism series in Table 53. (The period covered by the regressions is 1920–58.) Notice that both the regression and the correlation coefficients in Table 58 are substantially lower than those in Table 55.

I also calculated the regression of log W on P^* and π:

squared correlation coefficient, 0.73.
regression coefficients (standard errors in parentheses)
  for $P^*/100$; 1.49 (0.20);
  for $\pi/100$, -1.16 (0.20).

The implied value of the adjustment coefficient, α, is 0.22 = (1.49 − 1.16)/1.49—see equation (43)—and the implied value of the regression coefficient of log W on $P = (P^* - 0.78\pi)/0.22$ is 0.33 = 1.49 − 1.16.

B. A Simple Demand-Supply Model

Turn to equation (35):

$$\log W = \log W_o + \overline{B}P.$$

Let W denote the a/b relative average hourly compensation series in column (5) of Table 57. The counterpart, W_o, of W in the absence of unionism is a relative average hourly compensation series which differs from that for W in only one respect: the wages at which W_o is calculated are those which would have prevailed in the absence of unionism. In

---

where the sums extend over all industries in Group a, w_i is the average annual full-time compensation of the ith industry in Group a, h_i is the average annual full-time hours worked in this industry, w_i/h_i is the industry's average *hourly* compensation, and f_i is the fixed weight of the industry in the computation of w_a and h_a. Although f_i does not vary over time, h_i does. Therefore, the weight, $f_i h_i$, attached to the industry's average *hourly* compensation in w_a/h_a is not constant.

particular, the labor composition figures underlying W_o are the same as those for W, and both series contain the same measurement errors. Even if $\bar{B}$ were constant over time, the regression coefficients in Table 58 would err as estimates of $\bar{B}$ if log W_o and P were substantially correlated.

The factors, other than "wage rigidity" factors, entering W_o fall into two categories.

1. Statistical factors.—It is a major weakness of the wage series in Table 57 that they are not adjusted for changes in labor force composition, except partially for shifts in employment among industries. Unfortunately, annual data, 1919–58, on the distribution of man-hours worked by detailed industry, occupation, sex, color, etc., are not available. Incomplete data for recent years (see the appendix to this chapter [sec. vi.4], pp. 229 ff.) suggest that a considerable part of the increase in relative average hourly compensation which has taken place since 1946 in the more heavily unionized Group a industries was the result of changes in the distribution of employment by occupation, color, and sex. Although these data are insufficient to establish that failure to adjust the relative wage series for these statistical factors has led to overestimation of the average relative wage effect of unionism, there is considerable likelihood of such bias in the estimates made in this chapter.

2. Demand and supply factors.—Let E_d be the ratio of the "normal" or "long-run" relative quantity of labor demanded by Group a to that demanded by Group b, E_s the corresponding relative quantity of labor supplied, and Q the ratio of the value of output of Group a to that of Group b. I have approximated the long-run relative demand function at date t by

$$\log E_{dt} = c_o + c_q \log Q_t - c_w \log W_t \qquad (44)$$

and the long-run relative supply function by

$$\log E_{st} = C_o + C_w \log W_t - (c_w + C_w)\bar{B}P_t, \qquad (45)$$

where $\bar{B}$, c_o, c_q, c_w, C_o, and C_w are positive constants, c_w being the long-run elasticity of relative demand and C_w the long-run elasticity of relative supply.[6] If there were no lags in the adjustment of actual relative employment, E_t, to changes in demand and supply conditions, then $E_{dt} = E_{st} = E_t$, and

$$\log W_t = a_o + a_q \log Q_t + \bar{B}P_t, \qquad (46)$$

where $a_o = (c_o - C_o)/(c_w + C_w)$ and $a_q = c_q/(c_w + C_w)$.

[6] If the elasticity of demand for the output of Group a relative to that for Group b were unity and if aggregate production function for Group a were the same as that for Group b (except for a scale factor) and both were Cobb-Douglas functions, then c_q and c_w would equal unity.

In the short run, however, I assume that there is a simple distributed lag in relative quantity demanded,

$$\log E_t = \delta \log E_{dt} + (1 - \delta) \log E_{t-1}, \tag{47}$$

and also a similar lag on the supply side,

$$\log E_t = \gamma \log E_{st} + (1 - \gamma) \log E_{t-1}, \tag{48}$$

where δ and γ are constant adjustment coefficients. The solution of equations (44), (45), (47), and (48) for $\log W_t$ is

$$\log W_t = b_o + b_q \log Q_t + b_e \log E_{t-1} + b_P \bar{B} P_t, \tag{49}$$

where $b_o = (\delta c_o - \gamma C_o)/(\delta c_w + \gamma C_w)$, $b_e = (\gamma - \delta)/(\delta c_w + \gamma C_w)$, $b_P = 1 + c_w b_e$, and $b_q = \delta c_q/(\delta c_w + \gamma C_w)$.

Notice that the coefficient of the extent of unionism variable, P, in equation (49) is not the long-run unionism coefficient, $\bar{B}$, but $(1 + c_w b_e)\bar{B}$. This poses a problem in the estimation of $\bar{B}$. The coefficients b_e and $b_P \bar{B} = (1 + c_w b_e)\bar{B}$ can be estimated by fitting equation (49) to data on W, Q, E, and P. However, this procedure does not yield an estimate of the elasticity of demand c_w. Hence turn to equations (44) and (47). The solution of these equations for $\log E_t$ is

$$\log E_t = \delta c_o + \delta c_q \log Q_t - \delta c_w \log W_t + (1 - \delta) \log E_{t-1}. \tag{50}$$

I have estimated c_w by fitting this equation to the data on W, E, and Q.[7]

I have used national income as the measure of value of output and aggregate man-hours worked by wage and salary workers as the measure of the quantity of labor services. Columns (1) and (2) of Table 59 are indexes (with 1929 = 1) of the national income originating in Groups a and b. Column (3), the ratio of column (1) to column (2), is the estimate of the relative value of output, Q. The series in columns (4) and (5) are indexes (1929 = 1) of total man-hours worked by wage and salary workers in Groups a and b. Column (6) is the index of relative employment, E_t.

---

[7] Let $\hat{\delta}$ be the estimate of δ and $\hat{\delta c}_w$ the estimate of δc_w yielded by fitting equation (50) to the data. Then the estimate $\hat{c}_w$ of c_w is $\hat{\delta c}_w/\hat{\delta}$.

In the same manner, δc_q can be estimated. Let this estimate be $\hat{\delta c}_q$. Let $\hat{b}_q$ and $\hat{b}_e$ be the estimates of b_q and b_e obtained by fitting equation (49) to the data. Then an estimate $\hat{\gamma}$ of γ is

$$\hat{\gamma} = \hat{b}_e \hat{\delta c}_q/\hat{b}_q + \hat{\delta},$$

and an estimate of the long-run elasticity of relative supply, C_w, is

$$\hat{C}_w = (\hat{\delta c}_q/\hat{b}_q - \hat{\delta c}_w)/\hat{\gamma}.$$

TABLE 59

NATIONAL INCOME AND TOTAL MAN-HOURS WORKED, GROUPS *a* AND *b*,
1919–58 (1929 = 1)*

YEAR	NATIONAL INCOME			TOTAL MANHOURS WORKED		
	Group *a* (1)	Group *b* (2)	(1)/(2) (3)	Group *a* (4)	Group *b* (5)	(4)/(5) (6)
1919.......	0.763	0.802	0.950	0.948	0.741	1.280
1920.......	0.947	0.829	1.142	0.995	0.737	1.352
1921.......	0.665	0.716	0.929	0.778	0.752	1.036
1922.......	0.674	0.730	0.923	0.868	0.809	1.074
1923.......	0.855	0.818	1.046	0.993	0.854	1.162
1924.......	0.822	0.848	0.968	0.917	0.854	1.074
1925.......	0.883	0.895	0.986	0.953	0.889	1.072
1926.......	0.947	0.939	1.008	0.979	0.933	1.049
1927.......	0.905	0.959	0.944	0.962	0.948	1.015
1928.......	0.923	0.966	0.955	0.956	0.972	0.983
1929.......	1.000	1.000	1.000	1.000	1.000	1.000
1930.......	0.844	0.874	0.965	0.843	0.949	0.889
1931.......	0.606	0.732	0.828	0.677	0.879	0.771
1932.......	0.387	0.553	0.701	0.539	0.778	0.692
1933.......	0.376	0.503	0.748	0.542	0.758	0.715
1934.......	0.503	0.570	0.882	0.570	0.765	0.745
1935.......	0.584	0.672	0.869	0.622	0.800	0.777
1936.......	0.710	0.719	0.987	0.716	0.870	0.822
1937.......	0.823	0.822	1.002	0.762	0.921	0.828
1938.......	0.678	0.798	0.849	0.629	0.887	0.709
1939.......	0.788	0.825	0.954	0.712	0.913	0.780
1940.......	0.936	0.894	1.047	0.774	0.955	0.811
1941.......	1.320	1.053	1.253	0.967	0.999	0.968
1942.......	1.790	1.292	1.385	1.152	1.035	1.113
1943.......	2.177	1.509	1.442	1.303	1.059	1.231
1944.......	2.214	1.606	1.379	1.281	1.040	1.231
1945.......	1.981	1.701	1.165	1.142	1.023	1.116
1946.......	1.959	1.993	0.983	1.076	1.056	1.019
1947.......	2.361	2.123	1.112	1.128	1.060	1.064
1948.......	2.717	2.369	1.146	1.138	1.081	1.053
1949.......	2.578	2.347	1.098	1.037	1.080	0.960
1950.......	2.999	2.502	1.198	1.093	1.100	0.994
1951.......	3.527	2.781	1.268	1.179	1.133	1.040
1952.......	3.635	2.924	1.243	1.192	1.155	1.032
1953.......	3.891	3.007	1.294	1.226	1.169	1.048
1954.......	3.684	3.089	1.193	1.131	1.159	0.976
1955.......	4.159	3.304	1.259	1.186	1.200	0.988
1956.......	4.417	3.522	1.254	1.210	1.233	0.981
1957.......	4.556	3.727	1.222	1.189	1.243	0.957
1958.......	4.286	3.923	1.093	1.088	1.245	0.874

* See the appendix to chap. vi (sec. vi.4) for sources and methods of constructing these series.

The first four multiple regressions in Table 60 are the result of fitting equations (46) and (49) to the time series data on W [Table 57, col. (5)], E [Table 59, col. (6)], Q [(Table 59, col. (3)], and the extent of unionism variables P^*, P_1, P_2, and π (Tables 52 and 53). All of the regressions cover the period 1920–58. The dependent variable in the regressions is the natural logarithm of W, and $\log Q$ and $\log E_{t-1}$ are also natural logarithms.

TABLE 60

Multiple Regression Estimates of the Unionism Coefficient Based on Equations (46) and (49)

Regression Number (1)	R^2 (2)[a]	Regression Coefficients and Their Standard Errors[b]				Extent of Unionism Series (7)	Estimate of $\bar{B}$ (8)
		$\log Q$ (3)	$\log E_{t-1}$ (4)	$P/100$ (5)	$P\Delta\bar{p}/100$ (6)		
1.....	0.59	0.12 (0.06)	...	0.268 (0.079)	...	P_1	0.268
2.....	0.64	0.08 (0.06)	...	0.315 (0.075)	...	P_2	0.315
3.....	0.74	0.03 (0.05)	...	0.308 (0.065)	...	$\dfrac{P^* - 0.78\pi}{0.22}$	0.308
4.....	0.74	0.07 (0.07)	−0.04 (0.05)	0.290 (0.068)	...	$\dfrac{P^* - 0.77\pi}{0.23}$	0.309
5.....	0.74	0.18 (0.05)	−0.12 (0.04)	0.204 (0.066)	0.046 (0.015)	P_1	0.275

[a] R^2 is the square of the multiple correlation coefficient.
[b] The standard errors are shown in parentheses below the regression coefficients.

The model underlying the first three regressions is equation (46). In these regressions the estimate of the unionism coefficient $\bar{B}$ in column (8) is the same as the regression coefficient for the extent of unionism variable, $P/100$, in column (5). The three regression coefficients for $P/100$ are approximately equal to each other and are 7 to 30 per cent lower than the corresponding coefficients in Table 58 and in the associated text. [In fitting regression No. 3, the extent of unionism variable was a linear function of P^* and π; the adjustment coefficient ($\alpha = 0.22$) and the unionism coefficient in this regression were estimated from the regression coefficients for P^* and π by equation (43).]

Equation (49) is the model for regression No. 4. For this regression the estimate of the unionism coefficient in column (8) is different from the regression coefficient for $P/100$ in column (5). Let $\hat{b}_P\hat{B}$ denote the coefficient in column (5), $\hat{b}_e$ the coefficient in column (4), and $\hat{c}_w$ an estimate of the long-run elasticity of relative demand. Then the estimate, $\hat{B}$, of $\bar{B}$, as pointed out above, is

$$\hat{B} = \hat{b}_P\hat{B}/(1 + \hat{c}_w\hat{b}_e).$$

I estimated c_w by fitting the demand equation (50) to the data for the period 1920–58:

$$\log E_t = \text{constant} + 0.571 \quad \log Q_t - 0.637 \quad \log W_t + 0.572 \quad \log E_{t-1};$$
$$\qquad\qquad\qquad (0.0955) \qquad\qquad (0.2176) \qquad\qquad (0.0708)$$
$$R^2 = 0.884.$$

The figures in parentheses are the standard errors of the regression coefficients above them, and R^2 is the squared multiple correlation coefficient. This regression leads to the following estimates of the coefficients of equation (50):[8] $\hat{\delta} = 0.428$; $\hat{c}_q = 1.33$; and $\hat{\,}_w = 1.49$. Hence for regression No. 4, the estimated value of $(1 + c_w b_e)$ is $1 - (1.49)(0.04) = 0.94$, and the estimate of $\bar{B}$ is $0.290/0.94 = 0.309$.

The model for regression No. 5 is equation (49), except that $\bar{B}$ is assumed to depend upon the change, $\Delta_t \bar{p} = \bar{p}_t - \bar{p}_{t-1}$, in the extent of unionism in the economy as a whole:

$$\bar{B} = \bar{B}_o + \bar{B}_1 \Delta_t \bar{p}, \tag{51}$$

where $\bar{B}_o$ and $\bar{B}_1$ are constants. The hypothesis underlying equation (51) is that the same factors which tend to cause the extent of unionism in the economy as a whole to *increase* also tend to make the relative wage impact of unionism *high*. Thus I would expect the estimate of $\bar{B}_1$ to be positive, as it is in regression No. 5.

The estimate of the unionism coefficient for regression No. 5 is calculated at the mean value of $\Delta \bar{p}$ over the period 1920–58. The extent of unionism series from which $\Delta \bar{p}$ was computed is that in column (8) of Table 51, with $\Delta \bar{p}$ being measured in percentage points.

VI.3. VARIABILITY OF THE UNIONISM COEFFICIENT IN THE PRESENCE OF WAGE RIGIDITY

The regressions in Table 60 fail to explain at least one-fourth of the measured variance in the a/b relative wage, log W, during 1920–58. The unexplained variance is, no doubt, in part the result of errors of measurement in the relative wage series and incomplete adjustment of the series for changes in labor force composition (by industry, sex, race, occupation, etc.) of Group a relative to that of Group b (see the discussion on pp. 228 ff.). However, I suspect that neglect of wage rigidity factors and other errors in the specification of the relative wage-determining equations (46) and (49) account for the major portion of the unexplained variance.

The concept of wage rigidity is based on the distinction between an actual wage at a particular date and the corresponding equilibrium wage: the wage which would exist at the date if there were complete adjustment of wages to the supply and demand conditions prevailing at the date. Wages are "rigid" if their changes are in the right direction but too small to make actual wages equal to their equilibrium counterparts.

[8] These estimates, together with the figures in Table 60, imply very high estimates of the long-run elasticity of relative supply, C_w. [In this connection, see equations (46) and (49) and the preceding note.] The lowest estimate of C_w, that yielded by regression No. 1, is 11.3.

Let w_a^* be the average equilibrium money wage for Group a at a particular date; $y_a = w_a/w_a^*$ is the index of absolute wage disequilibrium for Group a. The counterparts of w_a^* and y_a for Group b are w_b^* and $y_b = w_b/w_b^*$. Similarly, $W^* = w_a^*/w_b^*$ is the equilibrium value of the a/b relative wage, and $Y = y_a/y_b = W/W^*$ is the index of *relative* wage disequilibrium. These definitions imply that

$$\log W_t = \log W_t^* + \log Y_t = \log W_t^* + \log y_{a_t} - \log y_{b_t}. \quad (52)$$

Equations (46) and (49), which are the models for the regressions in Table 60, are essentially equilibrium relative wage–determining equations. That is, the dependent variable on the left-hand side of the equations is $\log W^*$ rather than $\log W$. Although the independent variables in the Table 60 regressions are undoubtedly correlated with Y, this "disequilibrium" variable probably accounts for a substantial fraction of the residual variance in the regressions. Furthermore, if unionism was a wage rigidity factor, the resulting variability of the unionism coefficient, $\bar{B}$, over the period 1920–58 cannot be estimated except in the presence of Y.

Even in the absence of unionism there is some cost to employers in constantly changing wages in response to short-run changes in supply and demand conditions. The wage effects of the changes in market conditions must be discovered, employees must be informed of the wage changes, and revisions must be made in the employer's wage records. These and other costs remain in the presence of unionism. In addition, the freedom of unionized employers to change wages is restricted by collective-bargaining agreements. The negotiation of a new collective-bargaining agreement involves at the very least the cost of the time and effort of the negotiators and of the uncertainty regarding the outcome of the agreement. Moreover, there is some risk that differences between the parties may produce a costly testing of their relative strength in a work stoppage. Thus even if the language of collective-bargaining agreements commonly permitted the agreements to be opened at the choice of either party, the expectation by both of sizable negotiation costs would tend to make the agreements usually run for a period of a year or more, rather than only a few weeks, between openings.

The presence of an agreement running, say, for a term of twelve months, by transforming what would otherwise have been more continuous movements of wages into changes taking place in jumps a year apart, in itself would tend to produce some rigidity or lag in adjustment of wages to market conditions. On the other hand, since within many industries the collective-bargaining agreements expire at different times during the year and since some agreements specify within-year wage changes, the amount of rigidity produced in industry group wage averages by annual collective-bargaining negotiations would be appreciable only when large, unexpected changes in market conditions for union labor occurred.

However, the same expected costs which produce somewhat discontinuous wage changes in collective-bargaining agreements may also affect the amount of the wage changes in the short run. When a union has demonstrated to employers that it intends to stay in business and has the muscles to make the negotiation of *future* wage *reductions* costly to employers, the union thereby makes the expected cost to employers of a *currently* negotiated wage *increase* larger than it would be if they were confident that shortly the union would be ineffectual. Therefore, upward adjustments of wages under collective bargaining in response to changes in underlying demand conditions for labor will tend to be based on forecasts of these conditions having a longer time horizon than in the absence of unionism. By similar reasoning, in which the roles of the two parties are interchanged, the same is true of downward wage adjustments. Thus short-run or transitory changes in labor market conditions explain a smaller part, and long-run or permanent changes a larger part, of wage variations under unionism than in its absence.

The preceding argument may be put somewhat differently. A forecast of market conditions may be thought of as consisting partly of a forecast of the normal or permanent or long-run component and partly of a short-run or transitory deviation from this permanent component. In general, short-period forecasts of the permanent component will tend to be more accurate than similar forecasts of the transitory component; that is, forecasters will tend to differ less in their predictions of the permanent component than in their predictions of the deviations from it. The costs to both unions and employers of negotiating collective-bargaining agreements will be less, the less the differences in their forecasts. There is, therefore, an incentive to each party to give less weight to his forecast of the transitory component than he would give were his opposite an ineffectual adversary.

Reduced regard, in wage determination, to transitory variations in labor supply and demand variables will produce significant wage rigidity (or wage disequilibrium) only if for some of the variables the transitory variations are large and the elasticity of equilibrium wages, w^*, with respect to these variables is not small. Both the general price level and the rate of employment of the labor force satisfy these conditions. Unionism, by reducing the responsiveness of money wages of union labor to transitory changes in these variables, causes $\bar{B}$ to rise when the transitory changes are negative and to fall when the transitory changes are positive. Thus the wage rigidity hypothesis predicts that $\bar{B}$ tends to vary contracyclically. That is, $\bar{B}$ contains a transitory component opposite in sign to the transitory component in the general price level and the rate of employment of the labor force.

Let x be the actual value at a particular date of the general price level, x' the corresponding predicted value, and x^* the permanent component. The forecast error, $\log (x/x')$, I postulate, is proportional to the deviation, $\log x - \log x^*$, of the actual price level from its permanent component:

$$\log (x/x') = \rho \log (x/x^*) = \rho \log X, \qquad (53)$$

where $X = x/x^*$. The proportionality factor, ρ, is an indicator of absolute wage rigidity with respect to x; its value is zero if there is no wage rigidity.

If unionism causes wage rigidity, then ρ will tend to be greater, the greater is the extent of unionism, p, is an industry group. Assume, for simplicity, that ρ is a linear function of p;

$$\rho = k_o + k_1 p, \qquad (54)$$

where k_o and k_1 are positive constants. The indicator of wage rigidity in the absence of unionism, k_o, may differ between Groups a and b, but k_1, I assume, is the same for both groups. Substitute the right-hand side of equation (54) for ρ in equation (53):

$$\log (x/x') = (k_o + k_1 p) \log X. \qquad (53')$$

I apply the same reasoning to the rate of employment of the labor force. Let $z, z', z^*, Z, K_o,$ and K_1 be the counterparts for the rate of employment of $x, x', x^*, X, k_o,$ and k_1, respectively, for the price level. Then the counterpart of equation (53') for the rate of employment is

$$\log (z/z') = (K_o + K_1 p) \log Z. \qquad (53'')$$

I assume, finally, that the absolute relative wage disequilibrium, $\log y = \log (w/w^*)$ in each industry group is a linear function of the forecast errors,

$$\log y = r(k_o + k_1 p) \log X + s(K_o + K_1 p) \log Z, \qquad (55)$$

where r and s are constants the same for both groups. Since increases in x and z tend to increase the equilibrium wage, w^*, the signs of both r and s, on the wage rigidity hypothesis, are negative.

Write equation (55) for each of Groups a and b and subtract the equation for Group b from that for Group a. The result is

$$\log Y = r(k_{o_a} - k_{o_b}) \log X + rk_1 P \cdot \log X$$
$$+ s(K_{o_a} - K_{o_b}) \log Z + sK_1 P \cdot \log Z. \tag{56}$$

Turn now to equation (52). The specification of $\log W^*$ is the right-hand side of equation (49), with the wrinkle added by equation (51); that for $\log Y$ is the right-hand side of equation (56). Hence substitute from these equations into equation (52), obtaining the relative wage-determining equation underlying the estimates of the unionism coefficient in this section:

$$\log W_t = b_o + b_q \log Q_t + b_e \log E_{t-1} + b_x \log X + b_z \log Z$$
$$+ (b_P \bar{B}_o + b_P \bar{B}_1 \Delta_t \bar{p} + b_{Px} \log X_t + b_{Pz} \log Z_t) P_t, \tag{57}$$

where $b_x = r(k_{o_a} - k_{o_b})$, $b_z = s(K_{o_a} - K_{o_b})$, $b_{Px} = rk_1$, and $b_{Pz} = sK_1$. On the wage rigidity hypothesis, both b_{Px} and b_{Pz} are expected to be negative.

The permanent components, x^* and z^*, in X and Z remain to be specified. For the rate of employment variable, Z, I simply assumed that z^* was a constant, making $\log Z$ equal to $\log z$, except for a constant. Furthermore, if $\tilde{z}$ is the rate of *unemployment*, $\log z$ is approximately equal to $-\tilde{z}$. I therefore approximated $\log Z$ by $-\tilde{z}$. [Note that substitution of $\tilde{z}$ for $-\log Z$ in equation (57) changes the signs of b_z and b_{Pz}; in particular, the sign of b_{Pz} is expected to be positive when z is used as a substitute for $-\log Z$.]

For the general price level, however, I assumed that the permanent component, x^*, was related to the actual price level, x, in the following manner:

$$x_t^* / x_{t-1}^* = (x_t / x_{t-1}^*)^g, \tag{58}$$

where g is a constant between zero and unity. The solution of equation (58) for x^* is

$$\log x_t^* = g \sum_{i=0}^{\infty} (1 - g)^i \log x_{t-i}. \tag{59}$$

That is, x^* is a weighted average of current and past actual price levels, with weights that decline exponentially from the current date, t, to earlier dates. In the jargon of economics, a series constructed in this manner is an "expected" series; I shall refer to x/x^*, therefore, as the ratio of the actual to the "expected" price level.[9]

The unemployment rate figures in column (1) of Table 61 for the years 1920–57 are from *Historical Statistics of the United States, Colonial Times*

---

[9] It follows from equation (58) that $\log X = \log (x_t / x_t^*) = \dfrac{1-g}{g} \log (x_t^* / x_{t-1}^*)$. Therefore, the series for X is an "expected" *rate of inflation* series.

TABLE 61

UNEMPLOYMENT AND INFLATION VARIABLES, 1920–58

Year	Unemployment Rate (Per Cent) $100\bar{z}$ (1)	Actual/Expected Price Level X_1 (2)	Actual/Expected Wage Level X_2 (3)
1920.........	4.0	1.193	1.114
1921.........	11.9	1.010	1.016
1922.........	7.6	0.970	0.970
1923.........	3.2	0.993	0.989
1924.........	5.5	0.985	0.986
1925.........	4.0	1.002	0.976
1926.........	1.9	1.004	0.975
1927.........	4.1	0.984	0.972
1928.........	4.4	0.993	0.970
1929.........	3.2	0.994	0.966
1930.........	8.7	0.966	0.969
1931.........	15.9	0.895	0.952
1932.........	23.6	0.850	0.912
1933.........	24.9	0.886	0.907
1934.........	21.7	0.962	0.979
1935.........	20.1	0.967	0.980
1936.........	16.9	1.006	0.974
1937.........	14.3	1.013	0.996
1938.........	19.0	1.005	0.990
1939.........	17.2	0.999	0.975
1940.........	14.6	1.007	0.975
1941.........	9.9	1.058	0.995
1942.........	4.7	1.124	1.026
1943.........	1.9	1.140	1.027
1944.........	1.2	1.110	1.027
1945.........	1.9	1.091	1.027
1946.........	3.9	1.106	1.052
1947.........	3.6	1.146	1.060
1948.........	3.4	1.124	1.050
1949.........	5.5	1.083	1.023
1950.........	5.0	1.059	1.018
1951.........	3.0	1.088	1.026
1952.........	2.7	1.068	1.016
1953.........	2.5	1.053	1.012
1954.........	5.0	1.036	1.005
1955.........	4.0	1.028	0.998
1956.........	3.8	1.036	1.004
1957.........	4.0	1.045	1.008
1958.........	6.5	1.042	1.007

to 1957, Series D 47; the 1958 figure is from the *Statistical Abstract of the United States: 1960*, Table No. 263.[10] Column (2) shows the ratio of the actual to the expected price level. This series is based on indexes of the actual and the expected price level computed by Milton Friedman.

[10] I have lowered the 1957 and 1958 unemployment rate figures slightly from those shown in the source tables in order to make them more comparable to the unemployment figures for earlier years.

TABLE 62

SUMMARY OF MULTIPLE REGRESSIONS BASED ON EQUATION (57)

LINE NUMBER	STATISTIC[a]	REGRESSION NUMBER							
		1	2	3	4	5	6	7	8
1	R^2	0.865	0.874	0.925	0.925	0.912	0.911	0.891	0.901
	ESTIMATES OF $\bar{B}$								
2	1920–58 average	0.13	0.12	0.20	0.22	0.19	0.20	0.16	0.17
3	1945–49 average	⋯	⋯	0.03	0.03	0.04	0.05	0.02	0.00
4	1955–58 average	⋯	⋯	0.14	0.15	0.13	0.15	0.15	0.15
	REGRESSION COEFFICIENTS, STANDARD ERRORS[b]								
5	$\log Q$	0.33	0.36	0.35	0.34	0.35	0.34	0.28	0.29
6		(0.069)	(0.069)	(0.054)	(0.058)	(0.059)	(0.066)	(0.056)	(0.056)
7	$\log E_{t-1}$	⋯	⋯	0.094	0.074	0.12	0.10	⋯	⋯
8				(0.041)	(0.047)	(0.046)	(0.056)		
9	$\tilde{z}$	0.34	0.35	0.29	0.58	0.33	0.67	0.77	0.69
10		(0.062)	(0.058)	(0.11)	(0.22)	(0.11)	(0.23)	(0.28)	(0.24)
11	$\log X$	0.30	0.52	0.56	1.05	0.50	0.90	0.84	1.51
12		(0.13)	(0.18)	(0.30)	(0.55)	(0.33)	(0.64)	(0.32)	(0.54)
13	$P/100$	0.133	0.117	0.166	0.125	0.160	0.126	0.228	0.163
14		(0.059)	(0.058)	(0.091)	(0.074)	(0.094)	(0.080)	(0.094)	(0.075)
15	$P\Delta\bar{p}/100$	⋯	⋯	0.021	0.022	0.002	0.001	⋯	⋯
16				(0.010)	(0.010)	(0.006)	(0.006)		
17	$P\tilde{z}/100$	⋯	⋯	1.07	1.10	1.02	1.07	−0.16	0.032
18				(1.09)	(1.06)	(1.13)	(1.15)	(1.10)	(0.9)
19	$P\cdot\log X/100$	⋯	⋯	−1.61	−3.21	−1.24	−2.37	−1.94	−3.74
20				(0.94)	(1.84)	(0.99)	(2.03)	(0.99)	(1.84)
21	X series used	X_1	X_2	X_1	X_2	X_1	X_2	X_1	X_2
22	P series used, adjustment	$P^*{}_\pi$	$P^*{}_\pi$	P_1	P_1	P_2	P_2	P_2	P_2
23	coefficient (α)	0.55	0.51	0.7	0.7	0.5	0.5	0.5	0.5

[a] R^2 is the square of the multiple correlation coefficient.
[b] Standard errors are in parentheses on even-numbered lines.

Column (3) is the ratio of the actual to the expected all-industry money wage level. The actual wage level series underlying column (3) is that in column (3) of Table 57. The corresponding expected series was derived from the actual series by means of equation (58), with an "expectations" coefficient, g, equal to 0.5.[11] I use the series in column (3) as an alternative to that in column (2).

Table 62 summarizes the results of fitting equation (57) to the time series data on relative wages ($\log W$), relative value of output ($\log Q$), lagged relative employment ($\log E_{t-1}$), the unemployment rate ($\tilde{z}$), the inflation variables ($\log X_1$ and $\log X_2$), excess extent of unionism (P), and the changes ($\Delta \bar{p}$) in the average extent of unionism in the economy. In all of the regressions, $\log W$ is the dependent variable and the period covered is 1920–58. Table 63 identifies the variables used in the regressions.

TABLE 63

Identification of Variables in Table 62

Symbol	Identification
Q......	National income originating in Group a divided by national income originating in Group b, col. (3) of Table 59.
E_t.....	Total man-hours worked in Group a divided by total man-hours worked in Group b, col. (6) of Table 59.
$\tilde{z}$......	Unemployment rate in the labor force, expressed as a decimal, col. (1) of Table 61.
X_1.....	Ratio of actual to expected price level, col. (2) of Table 61.
X_2.....	Ratio of actual to expected money wage level, col. (3) of Table 61.
P^*.....	Unadjusted extent of union membership, excess of Group a over Group b, in percentage points, col. (1) of Table 53.
P_1......	Adjusted extent of union membership (with adjustment coefficient of 0.7), excess of Group a over Group b, in percentage points, col. (2) of Table 53.
P_2.....	Adjusted extent of union membership (with adjustment coefficient of 0.5), excess of Group a over Group b, in percentage points, col. (3) of Table 53.
π......	An auxiliary variable used in conjunction with P^* to estimate the adjustment coefficient α, in percentage points, col. (4) of Table 52.
$\Delta \bar{p}$.....	$\Delta_t \bar{p} = \bar{p}_t - \bar{p}_{t-1}$, where $\bar{p}$ is the all-industry average extent of union membership in per cent; in regressions 3 and 4 the series used for $\bar{p}$ is col. (8) of Table 51; in regressions 5 and 6 the series for $\bar{p}$ is col. (11) of Table 51.
W.....	Average hourly compensation in Group a divided by average hourly compensation in Group b, col. (5) of Table 57.

The model for regressions 1 and 2 is an abbreviated version of equation (57) which omits lagged relative employment, $\log E_{t-1}$, and all of the cross-product terms, $P\Delta \bar{p}$, $P\tilde{z}$, and $P \cdot \log X$. I calculated these re-

[11] An expectations coefficient, g, of approximately 0.5 maximizes the multiple correlation coefficient in multiple regressions based on equation (57) in which the ratio of the actual to the expected wage level is used as the estimate of X. The expected wage level series incorporates an adjustment for the upward trend in the actual wage level series.

gressions, in which the extent of unionism variable is a linear combination of P^* and π, chiefly to estimate the coefficient α for adjusting the extent of union membership figures. The resulting estimates of α (0.55 and 0.51) are given on line 23. The much lower estimates (0.22 and 0.23) yielded by regressions 3 and 4 in Table 60 were apparently caused by the omission of the unemployment and inflation variables in these regressions. Accordingly, in fitting the complete wage rigidity model, equation (57), I used two alternative excess extent of unionism series, one (P_2) with the adjustment coefficient of 0.5 suggested by regressions 1 and 2, and the second (P_1) with a higher coefficient, 0.7. That the multiple correlation coefficients were higher for the regressions using P_1 than for the corresponding regressions using P_2 indicates that the adjustment coefficient probably was greater than 0.5.

Regressions 3, 4, 5, and 6 include all of the variables in equation (57). Unfortunately, lagged relative employment, $\log E_{t-1}$, was substantially correlated with all of the terms involving the unemployment rate, $\bar{z}$, and the inflation variable, $\log X$. Regressions 7 and 8 exclude lagged relative employment and the cross-product of P and $\Delta \bar{p}$. (I omitted $P \Delta \bar{p}$ because its regression coefficient in regressions 3, 4, 5, and 6 was small [see line 15] and because it contributed little to explaining the variance of $\log W$.) The omission of $\log E_{t-1}$ in general increased the statistical significance of the remaining variables with one important exception: the regression coefficient for the joint unionism-unemployment variable, $P\bar{z}$, became negligible in size.

The regression coefficients (on line 19) for the joint unionism-inflation variables, $P \cdot \log X_1$ and $P \cdot \log X_2$, are negative and large numerically in all of the regressions, especially those omitting $\log E_{t-1}$. These coefficients imply that the unionism coefficient, $\bar{B}$, varied rather widely over the period 1920–58 and in the opposite direction to the "expected" rate of inflation, X.[12] Thus these data support the notion that unionism tended to make the money wages of union labor rigid against movements of the general price level and the general money wage level.

The evidence is less strong that the unionism coefficient, $\bar{B}$, varied appreciably in response to changes in the rate of unemployment. Five of the six regression coefficients for the unionism-unemployment variable on line 17 are positive, to be sure, and in regressions 3, 4, 5, and 6 the coefficients are large. However, only one of the regression coefficients is larger than its standard error, and in regressions 7 and 8 the coefficients are insignificant in both statistical and economic terms.[13]

[12] See n. 9 above.

[13] That variations in the rate of unemployment, at given values of the inflation

The small, positive regression coefficients for the variable $P\Delta\bar{p}$ on line 15 weakly support the hypothesis that the relative wage impact of unionism was greater, other factors being the same, during periods, such as 1935–40, when the extent of unionism in the economy as a whole was increasing fairly rapidly than in periods, such as the last decade, of little growth in extent of unionism. However, these coefficients and the data in Table 51 indicate that this factor accounts for only a small amount of variability in the unionism coefficient $\bar{B}$ in the last four decades.

Turn now to lines 2, 3, and 4 of Table 62, which show estimates of the average value of $\bar{B}$ calculated from the regression data for 1920–58, 1945–49, and 1955–58. Despite the differences in their details, regressions 3–8 yielded very similar estimates of $\bar{B}$: 0.16 to 0.22 for 1920–58, approximately zero in 1945–49, and 0.13 to 0.15 for 1955–58.[14] Table 64 shows estimates of $\bar{B}$ by five-year periods, 1920–58, calculated from the re-

TABLE 64

ESTIMATES OF THE UNION/NONUNION RELATIVE WAGE EFFECT
OF UNIONISM ($\bar{B}$), 1920–58
(In Natural Logs)

Period	$\bar{B}$	Period	$\bar{B}$
1920–24.........	0.16	1940–44.........	0.06
1925–29.........	0.23	1945–49.........	0.02
1930–34.........	0.38	1950–54.........	0.11
1935–39.........	0.20	1955–58.........	0.15

gression data for regression 7. Broadly speaking, these estimates in Tables 62 and 64 tend to confirm those derived in chapter v from the results of earlier studies, both in level and in the movements over time.[15]

---

variable (log X), may have produced little variability in the unionism coefficient $\bar{B}$ is not altogether surprising. On the one hand, wage rigidity produced by collective bargaining tends to make the unionism coefficient higher, the greater the rate of unemployment. On the other hand, unemployment among union members, I suspect, tends to reduce the capacities of unions to maintain their relative wage gains.

[14] The regression data suggest that the union/nonunion relative wage effect of unionism reached its lowest point (in the last twenty-five years) in 1947, increased until about 1955, and then declined slightly to 1957 or 1958.

[15] The estimates in Table 64 and those on lines 2, 3, and 4 of Table 62 are subject to substantial margins of statistical error. For example, the standard error of the estimate of $\bar{B}$ for 1930–34 in Table 64 is 0.122, that for the 1945–49 estimate is 0.077, and that for 1955–58 is 0.050. Furthermore, as I have emphasized, all of these estimates of the unionism coefficient, I suspect, are biased upward by quite incomplete adjustment of the relative wage series in col. (5) of Table 57 for changes in the labor force composition of Group a relative to that of Group b.

VI.4. APPENDIX: SOURCES AND METHODS OF CONSTRUCTING
THE BASIC TIME SERIES DATA IN CHAPTER VI

Table 51: Extent of Union Membership among Wage and Salary Workers, Groups a and b and All Industries, 1919–58.—The series in Table 51 are estimates of the percentage of wage and salary workers employed in Group *a*, Group *b*, and in the two groups together who were members of labor unions. The numerators of the percentages in columns (1), (2), and (3) are unadjusted estimates of the total number of union members employed in Group *a*, Group *b*, and in all industries, respectively. They were obtained as described below.

1. Total members, including Canadian, of U.S. unions.
   1919–34: Leo Wolman, *Ebb and Flow in Trade Unionism*, Table I.
   1935–57: Leo Wolman and Leo Troy, unpublished mimeographed tables, revised as of August 1959.
   1958: extrapolation of Wolman-Troy series with the help of data in U.S. Bureau of Labor Statistics, "Union Membership as a Proportion of Labor Force," a multilithed table released by the BLS in February 1960.

2. Total Canadian members of U.S. unions.
   1930, 1935, 1940, 1947, 1953, 1957: the unpublished Wolman-Troy estimates.
   All other years: interpolated and extrapolated with the help of data in various issues of Department of Labor of Canada, annual report on *Labor Organization in Canada*.

3. Total members, excluding Canadian, of U.S. unions, the numerators of the percentages in column (3) of Table 51.
   Item 1 less item 2.

4. Total members, including Canadian, employed in Group *b* industries.
   1919–34: Wolman, *op. cit.*, Table I, total of the membership figures for "public service, theaters and music, trade, hotels and restaurants, and domestic and personal service" industry groups plus the membership of four small unions.
   1935–57: unpublished Wolman-Troy estimates of the membership of all unions except three listed by them as having members in the "services, public service, and agriculture, forestry, and fisheries" industries.
   1958: extrapolation of the Wolman-Troy series with the help of the union membership figures in U.S. Bureau of Labor Statistics, *Directory of National and International Labor Unions in the United States, 1959*, Bulletin 1267.

5. Total members, excluding Canadian, in Group *b* industries, the numerators of the percentages in column (2) of Table 51.
   1930, 1935, 1940, 1947, 1953, 1957: unpublished Wolman-Troy estimates of the total number of members, excluding Canadian, in the "services, public service, and agriculture, forestry, and fisheries" industries.
   All other years: interpolated and extrapolated from above figures with the help of item 4.

6. Total members, excluding Canadian, in Group *a* industries, the numerators of column (1) of Table 51.

Item 3 less item 5.

The denominators of the percentages in columns (1), (2), and (3) are estimates of the number of full-time equivalent employees in Group *a*, Group *b*, and the two groups together. See the discussion of Table 54 for the sources and methods of constructing these employment estimates.

See pp. 200–201 for the method used to construct the adjusted extent of union membership estimates in columns (5), (6), (7), (9), (10), and (11) from the unadjusted series in Table 51 and the series for the "auxiliary" variable in Table 52.

The fixed weight for Group *a* in computing columns (4), (8), and (12) is 0.468; that for Group *b* is 0.532 = 1 − 0.468. (The average number of full-time equivalent employees in Group *a* over the period 1929–57 was 46.8 per cent of the corresponding average for Groups *a* and *b* together.)

Table 54: Average Annual Full-Time Compensation, Groups a and b and All Industries, 1919–58.—The average annual full-time compensation estimates in Table 54 for the years 1929–58 are based largely on data reported in the following publications of the U.S. Department of Commerce, Office of Business Economics:

National Income (1954 ed.), a supplement to the *Survey of Current Business* (1954), Tables 14, 15, 25, and 27, for 1929–45 estimates.

U.S. Income and Output, a supplement to the *Survey of Current Business* (1958), Tables VI-1, VI-2, VI-13, and VI-15, for 1946–56 estimates.

Survey of Current Business, 39, No. 7 (July, 1959), Tables VI-1, VI-2, VI-13, VI-15, pp. 3–43, for 1957–58 estimates.

These Department of Commerce reports provide annual data, 1929–58, on (1) wages and salaries, (2) employee compensation, (3) number of full-time equivalent employees, and (4) average annual full-time earnings for each of the approximately seventy industry groups into which the Department of Commerce divides the economy in tabulating national income and its components by industry of origin. These series cover only wage and salary workers.

The wage and salary estimates for each industry group are annual totals that include commissions, tips, bonuses, and payments in kind as well as what is commonly regarded as money wages and salaries. The estimates for the years since 1939 for industries covered by public social insurance programs are considered by the Department of Commerce to be extremely reliable; the wage and salary estimates for other industries and for the years 1929–38 are based on diverse sources and are considered to be less reliable. In particular, I suspect that the wage and salary figures for the agricultural sector and for private households may contain substantial errors.

The total employee compensation in each industry group is the sum of wages and salaries and "supplements to wages and salaries." The latter includes employer contributions for social insurance; employer contributions to private pension, health, and welfare funds; compensation for injuries; and a few other much less important items of labor income. The estimates by industry of compensation for injuries and of the employer contributions for social insurance, which comprised the bulk of wage supplements until about a decade ago, presumably are quite accurate. I have some reservations, discussed later (pp. 233 ff.), about the industry totals of employer contributions for private pension, health, and welfare funds. However, I have not attempted to produce better estimates.

The number of full-time equivalent wage and salary workers measures man-years of full-time employment of wage and salary earners and its equivalent in work performed by part-time workers. Full-time employment is defined in terms of the number of hours which is customary at a particular time and place. The sources of the basic data underlying these Department of Commerce employment estimates are in general the same as those for the wage and salary estimates.

For each of the industry groups the Department of Commerce has computed and published (in tables carrying the title "Average Annual Earnings per Full-Time Employee") the ratio of annual total wages and salaries to the annual average number of full-time equivalent wage and salary workers. For the purposes of this study, however, the ratio of annual total employee compensation to annual average full-time equivalent employment—average annual full-time compensation—is superior as a measure of the average wage to average annual full-time earnings, since the first, but not the second, includes wage supplements as well as wages and salaries. The distinction between wages and salaries and wage supplements is mainly one of traditional nomenclature. From the point of view of both employee and employer in both union and nonunion establishments, a dollar of wage supplements is approximately a perfect substitute for a dollar of wages and salaries. Therefore, I have used average annual full-time compensation in preference to average annual full-time earnings.

I computed "average annual full-time compensation" from the Department of Commerce data in the following manner: (a) for each industry heading I subtracted annual total wages and salaries from annual total employee compensation to obtain annual total wage supplements; (b) I then divided wage supplements by the corresponding average number of full-time equivalent employees; (c) this ratio was then added to the corresponding Department of Commerce figure for average annual full-time earnings. This procedure could not be followed for two groups of industries: (1) federal general government, which includes civilian, except work relief; military; and work relief; and (2) state and local general government, which includes public education; nonschool, except work relief; and work relief. The Department of Commerce publishes wage and salary figures for the six detailed industry headings, but publishes employee compensation figures only for the "general government" headings. I allocated the implied wage supplements for the "general government" headings among the three industries within each heading as follows: (a) zero wage supplements for the "work relief" categories and (b) wage supplements to the remaining categories in proportion to their wages and salaries.

There is evidence in the behavior of the resulting wage supplement series for these government industries that this crude estimating procedure has led to overestimation of wage supplements for the industry "federal-general government, civilian, except work relief" in years in which the military payroll was very high.

The industry classification scheme followed by the Department of Commerce is approximately the "two-digit" breakdown of the 1942 edition of the *Standard Industrial Classification Manual* (U.S. Bureau of the Budget), except that for manufacturing industries for the years 1948–58, the 1945 edition is used. For the following manufacturing industry headings (titles are from the 1942 edition of the *Manual*) the differences between the industry definitions of the 1942 and the 1945 editions of the *Manual* were substantial enough to make the Department of Commerce series for these industries for the years 1929–47 not "strictly comparable" to those for 1948–58:

> Lumber and timber basic products;
> Chemicals and allied products;
> Iron and steel and their products, including ordnance;
> Nonferrous metals and their products;
> Machinery, except electrical;
> Furniture and finished lumber products;
> Products of petroleum and coal;
> Miscellaneous manufacturing; and
> Electrical machinery.

These industries employ about one-half of manufacturing wage and salary workers, approximately one-seventh of all wage and salary workers, and union membership in these industries comprises about one-fourth of union membership in all industries. The loss of time series comparability at 1948 in the Department of Commerce data for these industries, therefore, is quite unfortunate. To restore the broken continuity of these series (on employee compensation and full-time equivalent employment) I have estimated new series for 1948–58, following the industry definitions of the 1942 *Manual*.

Almost all of the important changes in industry definitions between the 1942 and 1945 editions of the *Manual* were at the three-digit level. In making estimates of wages and salaries and full-time equivalent employment at the three-digit level I was able to use essentially the same estimating procedures and the same basic data—chiefly U.S. Bureau of Employment Security data (*Employment and Wages*, a special issue of the *Statistical Supplement* to the *Labor Market and Employment Security*) —as those used by the Department of Commerce. Where estimates of wages and salaries and employment for four-digit industries had to be made, I was forced to use data from sources other than those used by the Department of Commerce; mainly the *U.S. Census of Manufactures* (1947, 1954), the *Annual Survey of Manufactures* (1949 and 1950, 1951, 1952, 1953, 1955, 1956, 1957) and the Bureau of Labor Statistics series on employment and average weekly earnings by industry.

Some checks with the Department of Commerce estimates, particularly in 1948, indicate that my estimates of wages and salaries and full-time equivalent employment are close to what the Department of Commerce would have estimated if they had used the industry definitions of the 1942 *Manual* throughout. The estimates of wage supplements were somewhat cruder, since for them I had only the Department of Commerce data with which to work.

The figures in columns (1), (2), and (3) of Table 54 are fixed weighted arithmetic means of the average annual full-time compensation figures estimated for the underlying Department of Commerce detailed industry headings. For each industry heading the fixed weight is the average relative employment of the industry over the period 1929–57. The industry's average relative employment was obtained by summing over this period the industry's annual full-time equivalent employment estimates and dividing by the corresponding sum for all industries. In the all-industry averages in column (3), Group *a* has a weight of 0.468 and Group *b* a weight of 0.532.

The variable weighted all-industry average in column (4) of Table 54 is the ratio of the estimated total employee compensation for all Group *a* and Group *b* industries to the corresponding estimated total number of full-time equivalent employees.

The average annual full-time compensation figures for 1919–28 are extrapolations of those for later years and are based on Simon Kuznets' wage and salary, employee compensation, and full-time equivalent employment estimates. Kuznets' figures for detailed industry headings are given in his *National Income and Its Composition, 1919–1938* (New York: National Bureau of Economic Research, 1941).

The industry definitions he used were not quite the same as those used by the Department of Commerce, making it necessary for me to recombine his detailed data to match the Department of Commerce industry definitions. Furthermore, for twelve of the sixty-six industry groups in the Department of Commerce tabulations, Kuznets' tables provide employee compensation or employment estimates in less detail by industry. In addition, Kuznets used somewhat different sources of data and methods of estimation from those used by the Department of Commerce, so that in the overlapping years, 1929–38, the two sets of estimates are not the same.

These problems were dealt with in the following manner:

After recombining Kuznets' most detailed data to match Commerce definitions, the resulting series were expressed as index numbers with 1929 = 1. These index numbers were then multiplied by the corresponding estimates by the Department of Commerce for 1929. In this manner it was possible to extend back to 1919 the series on employee compensation and employment for fifty-four of the sixty-six Commerce industry groups, though in less detail— under forty-five instead of fifty-four industry group headings.

Essentially the same procedure was followed in extending to 1919 weighted means or totals for various groupings of the Commerce industry headings: weighted means were first computed for the group of Kuznets' industries most closely matching the group of Commerce industries, these means were converted to index numbers with 1929 = 1, and the index numbers multiplied by the corresponding Commerce figure for 1929.

Unquestionably the resulting estimates for 1919–29 are not really strictly comparable in accuracy to those yielded by the Commerce data for 1929–58.

As I have pointed out, it is an important weakness of the relative compensation figures in Tables 54 and 57 that they are not adjusted for changes in relative labor force composition, except partially for shifts in employment among industries. The annual data, 1919–58, required for such adjustment, unfortunately, are not available.

However, the Bureau of the Census *Current Population Reports* provide information for selected years since World War II on the income and number of wage and salary workers classified by major industry division and within each division by sex, occupation, color, and age. To these data can be added those of the 1940 and 1950 population censuses. In Tables 65, 67, and 68, I have attempted to estimate the order of magnitude of the relative wage effects of differences among major industry divisions in labor force composition by sex, color, and occupation.

Consider first Table 65, which estimates relative wage differences among major industries attributable to differences in the proportions of males in their working forces. From various issues of Series P-50 of the *Current Population Reports: Labor Force* it was possible to estimate the fraction of wage and salary workers who were male in each of the major industry divisions listed in the table for the years 1948, 1950, and 1956–58. Similar data in the 1940 and 1950 population censuses enabled me to make estimates of the proportion of males among employed persons (gainful workers in 1930) in each industry division in 1930, 1940, and 1950. From these estimates, I computed fixed weighted means (with the same weights as those in Tables 54 and 57) of the fraction male in all industries and in Groups *a* and *b*.

TABLE 65

INDEXES OF RELATIVE DIFFERENCES AMONG MAJOR INDUSTRIES IN DISTRIBUTION OF EMPLOYEES BY SEX, SELECTED YEARS, 1930–58

Industry Group	1958[a] (1)	1957[a] (2)	1956[a] (3)	1950[a] (4)	1948[a] (5)	1950[b] (6)	1950[c] (7)	1940[c] (8)	1930[d] (9)
Group *a*................	1.037	1.037	1.037	1.034	1.032	1.033	1.028	1.029	1.025
Mining, forestry, fisheries.............	1.090	1.091	1.095	1.094	1.094	1.092	1.085	1.080	1.074
Construction..........	1.098	1.098	1.098	1.098	1.097	1.091	1.085	1.079	1.073
Manufacturing........	1.021	1.022	1.022	1.015	1.014	1.017	1.012	1.013	1.011
Transportation, communication, public utilities........	1.049	1.048	1.049	1.055	1.048	1.048	1.043	1.049	1.039
Group *b*................	0.967	0.967	0.967	0.970	0.972	0.971	0.975	0.974	0.977
Agriculture...........	1.058	1.054	1.051	1.060	1.065	1.070	1.066	1.065	1.049
Wholesale and retail trade...............	0.979	0.979	0.980	0.980	0.975	0.979	0.984	0.997	1.002
Finance, insurance, real estate..............	0.933	0.939	0.948	0.953	0.953	0.955	0.961	0.984	0.985
Services[e]...............	0.909	0.909	0.910	0.914	0.923	0.916	0.926	0.912	0.909
Public administration...	1.018	1.019	1.017	1.019	1.014	1.015	1.008	1.013	1.039

[a] Based on estimates of the proportion of males among employed wage and salary workers. Basic data from various issues of Series P-50 of the *Current Population Reports: Labor Force*.

[b] Based on estimates of the proportion of males among employed wage and salary workers. Basic data from *U.S. Census of Population: 1950*, Special Report P-E, No. 1D, Table 4.

[c] Based on estimates of the proportion of males among employed persons. Basic data from the *U.S. Census of Population: 1950*, Vol. II, *Characteristics of the Population*, Part 1, U.S. Summary, Tables 56 and 130.

[d] Based on estimates of the proportion of males among gainful workers. Basic data from the *Sixteenth Census of the United States: 1940, Population, Comparative Occupation Statistics for the United States, 1870 to 1940*, Table 7.

[e] Including finance, insurance, and real estate.

Let M be the fraction male and $F = 1 - M$ the fraction female in an industry division, or Group a or b, and $\overline{M}$ and $\overline{F}$ the corresponding fractions for all industries. Then the indexes in Table 65 are

$$\text{index} = \frac{(M + 0.7F)/1.7}{(\overline{M} + 0.7\overline{F})/1.7} = \frac{1 - 0.3F}{1 - 0.3\overline{F}}.$$

That is, each index is the ratio of a weighted mean of M and F to the corresponding all-industries weighted mean of $\overline{M}$ and $\overline{F}$, with M and $\overline{M}$ having weights of unity and F and $\overline{F}$ weights of 0.7. There is another way of looking at the indexes. Abstract from all factors producing wage differentials except the sex factor and assume that the price of female labor is 70 per cent of that for male labor. Then the indexes in Table 65 are the resulting relative wages in each of the industry divisions and groups. Industries with relatively low proportions of employees who are female will have high (above unity) relative wages, and those with relatively high proportions of females will have low relative wages. The table shows that (a) a sex differential as large as 30 per cent would produce considerable dispersion in relative wages among industries and (b) on the average, the more highly unionized Group a industries have employed relatively fewer females.

We do not know precisely what the true sex differential in wages was for any of the years covered by Table 65. In 1949 the median wage and salary income of all female wage and salary workers in the experienced civilian labor force who worked at least fifty weeks in 1949 was only 64.2 per cent of the corresponding median for males (*U.S. Census of Population: 1950*, Special Report P-E No. 1B, *Occupational Characteristics*, Table 23). This figure surely exaggerates the true differential. Henry Sanborn has found that when account is taken of the differences between the sexes in their distribution by occupation, age and years of experience, education, color, hours worked per year, and size of city in which employed, the resulting average differential in 1949 was well below 30 per cent ("Income Differences between Men and Women in the United States" [unpublished Ph.D. dissertation, University of Chicago, 1960]). If the true differential were 15 per cent rather than 30 per cent, the deviations from unity of the relative wage indexes in Table 65 would have been about half as large.

Table 65 indicates that whether a 15 per cent or a 30 per cent constant sex differential is used, changing differences among the major industries in proportions of females employed would have caused numerically small changes in the wages of Group a relative to wages of Group b. In particular, for the period 1948–58 this factor would account for no more than a

1 per cent rise in Group *a* wages relative to Group *b* wages. Such a "small" increase in wages, however, cannot be considered to be negligible in explaining the total change in relative wages which occurred during this period. According to Table 57, average hourly compensation in Group *a* industries rose by less than 7 per cent relative to average hourly compensation in Group *b* industries. Thus changes in the proportions of females employed in the various industries from 1948 to 1958 may account for something like 5 to 15 per cent of the change in average wages in Group *a* relative to average wages in Group *b* between 1948 and 1958.

In Table 65 the sex differential is constant, the proportion male variable. Has the sex differential itself changed? Sanborn's study of the 1940 and 1950 *Census* data indicate that there was little change in the sex differential between 1939 and 1949. The data in Table 66, though much too crude for precise estimation of changes in the sex differential from 1950 to 1957, suggest a slight widening—by a percentage point or two—of the differential. This apparent widening, however, may be the result of slightly greater reductions in hours of work per year in the industries employing women in disproportionate numbers.

TABLE 66

RATIO OF FEMALE TO MALE MEDIAN WAGE AND SALARY INCOME:
PERSONS IN THE EXPERIENCED CIVILIAN LABOR FORCE,
BY MAJOR OCCUPATION GROUP, 1950–57*

Major Occupation in Survey Week	1957 (1)	1955 (2)	1953 (3)	1951 (4)	1950 (5)
Professional, technical, and kindred workers...........	0.60	0.59	0.61	0.61	0.58
Managers, officials, proprietors, except farm...............	0.53	0.60	0.50	0.65	0.50
Clerical and kindred workers..	0.66	0.67	0.64	0.64	0.69
Sales workers................	0.31	0.27	0.31	0.33	0.36
Craftsmen, foremen, and kindred workers...........	a	a	a	a	a
Operatives and kindred workers..................	0.53	0.57	0.56	0.57	0.59
Private household workers....	a	a	a	a	a
Other service workers........	0.43	0.41	0.44	0.41	0.39
Laborers, except farm and mine	a	a	a	a	a

* Source: Computed from data in various issues of *Current Population Reports: Consumer Income*, Series P-60.
a Median income for males or females not reported in source.

In Table 67, I show indexes, analogous to those in Table 65, measuring relative differences among the major industry divisions and between Groups *a* and *b* in proportions of nonwhite persons in their working forces. The constant wage differential by color used in Table 67 is 40 per cent.

This differential is only slightly smaller than the crude differential, shown in the 1950 census, between the median wage and salary income of nonwhite, male wage and salary workers and that of white, male workers. In any case it is apparent from the table that during the last two decades the fractions of nonwhite persons employed in the working forces of Groups *a* and *b* were so nearly the same that the changes in the fraction or in the wage differential by color would have produced negligible changes in the wages of Group *a* relative to the wages of Group *b*.

TABLE 67

INDEXES OF RELATIVE DIFFERENCES AMONG MAJOR INDUSTRIES IN DISTRIBUTIONS
OF EMPLOYEES BY COLOR, SELECTED YEARS, 1940–55

Industry Group	1955[a] (1)	1954[a] (2)	1951[a] (3)	1950[b] (4)	1948[a] (5)	1940[b] (6)
Group *a*....................	1.009	1.009	1.009	1.008	1.008	1.011
Mining, forestry, and fisheries..	1.018	1.013	0.979	1.014	0.962	1.002
Construction...............	1.005	1.004	1.006	1.003	1.008	1.004
Manufacturing..............	1.010	1.010	1.011	1.009	1.012	1.014
Transportation, communication, and other public utilities	1.005	1.004	1.009	1.006	1.007	1.007
Group *b*......................	0.992	0.992	0.992	0.992	0.993	0.990
Agriculture..................	0.978	0.979	0.979	0.972	0.973	0.958
Wholesale and retail trade.....	1.011	1.011	1.015	1.012	1.016	1.014
Services[c]....................	0.976	0.977	0.972	0.975	0.972	0.966
Public administration.........	1.001	1.000	1.007	1.007	1.010	1.020

[a] Based on estimates of the proportion of nonwhite persons among employed persons. Basic data from various issues of Series P-50 of the *Current Population Reports: Labor Force.*
[b] Based on estimates of the proportion of nonwhite persons among employed persons. Basic data for 1940 from *Sixteenth Census of the United States: 1940, Population: The Labor Force, Industrial Characteristics,* Table 1; 1950 data from *U.S. Census of Population: 1950,* Special Report P-E No. 1D, Table 2.
[c] Including finance, insurance, and real estate.

Table 68 treats in a parallel fashion the differences among major industry divisions and between Groups *a* and *b* in the distribution of their employees by occupation. The occupational classification and the assumed constant relative occupational wage differentials underlying Table 68 are those for full-time wage and salary workers in 1949 given in Table 69. Except for agriculture, the differences among the major industry divisions in their occupational distributions were small. Nevertheless, between 1950 and 1958 the changes in occupational composition were sufficiently different to raise wages in Group *a* by about 2.3 per cent relative to wages in Group *b*.

Table 69 suggests that between 1939 and 1949, relative occupational wage differentials may have narrowed quite substantially, but between 1949 and 1957 only slightly, if at all. These changes in differentials, however, would have had little effect on the average wage of Group *a* relative

TABLE 68

INDEXES OF RELATIVE DIFFERENCES AMONG MAJOR INDUSTRIES IN DISTRIBUTIONS
OF EMPLOYEES BY OCCUPATION, 1940, 1950, AND 1958

Industry Group	1958[a]	1950[b]	1940[b]
Group *a*	1.020	1.008	1.010
Construction	1.046	1.046	1.046
Manufacturing	1.018	1.003	1.005
Transportation, communication, and other public utilities	1.017	1.006	1.012
Group *b*	0.983	0.994	0.992
Agriculture	0.591	0.631	0.638
Wholesale and retail trade	1.069	1.075	1.111
Services[c]	0.998	1.016	0.973
All other industries	1.028	1.022	1.026

[a] Based on distribution of employed persons by major occupation and major industry given in *Current Population Reports: Labor Force*, Series P-50, No. 89, Table 17.
[b] Based on distribution of employed persons by occupation and industry; 1940 from *Sixteenth Census of the United States: 1940, Population: The Labor Force, Occupational Characteristics*, Table V; 1950 from *U.S. Census of Population: 1950*, Special Report P-E No. 1D, Table 6, and Special Report P-E No. 1C, Table 1.
[c] Including finance, insurance, and real estate.

to the average wage of Group *b* because their occupational distributions were so very similar.

In summary, the data in Tables 65 to 69 indicate that some, perhaps, of the decline in Group *a*'s relative wage during World War II and about half the subsequent increase may be accounted for by corresponding changes in the relative "quality" of Group *a*'s working force.

Another part of the apparent increase in the relative average annual full-time compensation of Group *a* employees since World War II may stem from errors in the underlying data on wage supplements, especially the estimates of "employer contributions to private pension and related plans."

There are three components in the "employer contributions to private pension and related plans":

1. Contributions to *pension* plans;
2. Contributions to *health and welfare* funds; and
3. Contributions for *group insurance*.

In general these employer contributions were important only after World War II. For this period the Department of Commerce estimates of pension contributions are based almost entirely on comprehensive tabulations by the U.S. Internal Revenue Service, and the estimates for this component presumably are quite accurate. However, I doubt that the corresponding estimates for contributions to health and welfare funds and for group insurance are equally accurate. For a few of the largest health and welfare funds (Amalgamated Clothing Workers, International Ladies Garment Workers Union, United Mine Workers, and American

TABLE 69

MEDIAN WAGE AND SALARY INCOME, MALES IN THE EXPERIENCED
CIVILIAN LABOR FORCE, SELECTED YEARS, 1939–57

MAJOR OCCUPATION IN SURVEY WEEK	ALL MALE WORKERS[a]					
	1957	1955	1953	1951	1950	1939
Professional, technical and kindred workers.	$5,601	$5,055	$4,816	$4,071	$3,874	$1,809
Farmers and farm managers.	469	461	493	482	711	373
Managers, officials, proprietors, except farm.	5,872	5,290	5,071	4,143	4,171	2,136
Clerical and kindred workers.	4,252	3,870	3,766	3,366	3,002	1,421
Sales workers.	4,379	4,315	3,716	3,539	3,148	1,277
Craftsmen, foremen, and kindred workers.	4,777	4,356	4,156	3,601	3,405	1,309
Operatives and kindred workers. .	3,984	3,586	3,415	3,064	2,736	1,007
Private household workers.	c	c	c	c	c	429
Other service workers.	2,894	2,778	2,806	2,426	2,299	833
Farm laborers and foremen.	940	971	817	982	986	309
Laborers, except farm and mine. .	2,763	2,387	2,406	2,170	1,850	673

	MALE YEAR-ROUND FULL-TIME WORKERS			
	All[a]			Wage and Salary Workers[b]
	1957	1955	1939	1949
Professional, technical, and kindred workers.	$5,990	$5,382	$2,100	$4,030
Farmers and farm managers.	454	414	430	2,361
Managers, officials, proprietors, except farm.	6,110	5,584	2,254	4,327
Clerical and kindred workers.	4,564	4,162	1,564	3,136
Sales workers.	5,143	4,937	1,451	3,270
Craftsmen, foremen and kindred workers.	5,216	4,712	1,562	3,378
Operatives and kindred workers. .	4,397	4,046	1,268	2,924
Private household workers.	c	c	549	1,471
Other service workers.	3,605	3,565	1,019	2,425
Farm laborers and foremen.	1,518	c	365	1,228
Laborers except farm and mine. . .	3,710	3,105	991	2,366

[a] Various issues of Series P-60 *Current Population Reports: Consumer Income.*
[b] *U.S. Census of Population: 1950*, Special Report P-E No. 1B, Table 23.
[c] Median not computed because of small number in sample survey.

Telephone and Telegraph Company), the Department of Commerce assembled contributions data. For the other health and welfare plans, they multiplied the number of employees covered by a plan (as reported by the Bureau of Labor Statistics and other sources) by average earnings of employees in the industry to obtain estimated wages of covered workers. These were then multiplied by estimated contribution rates (modal rates given in the BLS and other sources) to obtain the estimated amount of employer contributions. They estimated employer contributions for group insurance by industry, except in a few industries for which detailed data were available, by allocating their estimate of the all-industry total (excluding the few industries) according to the relative distribution among industries of employer contributions to *pension* plans.

Table 70 shows the ratio of the Department of Commerce estimates of employee compensation to the corresponding estimates of wages and salaries by industry in 1929, 1946, and 1958. Wage supplements did not become significant compared to wages and salaries until the late 1930's, and even in 1946 wage supplements exceeded 5 per cent of wages and salaries in only fourteen of the sixty-six industries listed in the table. In 1958, however, wage supplements exceeded 10 per cent of wages and salaries in thirteen industries and were a 5 per cent or greater fraction of wages and salaries in over two-thirds of the industries. Notice, moreover, that there was an appreciable tendency for wage supplements to increase most as a fraction of wages and salaries after 1929 in the Group *a* industries.

Unfortunately, there are a very few data from which one can appraise the Department of Commerce wage supplement figures. Recently the Bureau of the Census published data on "selected supplementary employee costs" in manufacturing industries in 1957 (*Supplementary Employee Costs, Costs of Maintenance and Repair, Insurance, Rent, Taxes, and Depreciation and Book Value of Depreciable Assets by Industry: 1957*, Special Report MC 58(1)-D11-1 of the *Census of Manufactures*, December, 1960). These data were obtained from a probability sample covering about fifty thousand manufacturing establishments. Although the "selected supplementary employee costs" is not quite as inclusive a category as the Department of Commerce wage supplements, the differences between the two concepts are, I judge, insignificant. Table 71 compares the Department of Commerce estimates of wage supplements (as a per cent of their estimates of wages and salaries) with the Bureau of the Census estimates of selected supplementary employee costs (as a per cent of their estimates of total payroll). For manufacturing as a whole and for two-thirds of the component industry groups, the differences between the two sets of figures are less than two percentage points. However, the dispersion of the census figures is less than that of the Commerce figures, and there is a positive correlation among industries between the excess of the Commerce figures over the census figures and

TABLE 70

RATIO OF TOTAL EMPLOYEE COMPENSATION TO TOTAL WAGES AND
SALARIES, BY INDUSTRY, 1929, 1946, AND 1958*

Industry	1929	1946	1958
All industries[a]	1.013	1.041	1.067
Agriculture, forestry and fisheries	1.003	1.005	1.020
Farms	1.003	1.004	1.019
Agricultural services, forestry, and fisheries	1.009	1.017	1.031
Mining	1.016	1.043	1.138
Metal mining	1.020	1.043	1.095
Anthracite mining	1.015	1.046	1.184
Bituminous and other soft-coal mining	1.015	1.043	1.199
Crude petroleum and natural gas	1.016	1.045	1.066
Non-metallic mining and quarrying	1.016	1.033	1.053
Contract construction	1.023	1.047	1.057
Manufacturing	1.009	1.046	1.086
Food and kindred products	1.013	1.048	1.071
Tobacco manufactures	1.007	1.065	1.147
Textile mill products	1.005	1.038	1.064
Apparel and other finished fabric products	1.004	1.044	1.079
Lumber and timber basic products[b]	1.007	1.040	1.050
Furniture and finished lumber products[b]	1.010	1.037	1.058
Paper and allied products	1.012	1.043	1.081
Printing, publishing, and allied industries	1.006	1.036	1.055
Chemicals and allied products[b]	1.011	1.063	1.112
Products of petroleum and coal[b]	1.051	1.179	1.328
Rubber products	1.007	1.039	1.093
Leather and leather products	1.006	1.033	1.056
Stone, clay, and glass products	1.015	1.046	1.084
Iron and steel and their products, including ordnance[b]	1.014	1.045	1.101
Nonferrous metals and their products[b]	1.006	1.044	1.101
Miscellaneous manufacturing[b]	1.007	1.040	1.064
Machinery, except electrical[b]	1.009	1.039	1.081
Electrical machinery[b]	1.010	1.062	1.095
Transportation equipment, except automobiles	1.008	1.048	1.073
Automobiles and automobile equipment	1.003	1.033	1.150
Wholesale and retail trade	1.006	1.032	1.044
Wholesale trade	1.005	1.031	1.043
Retail trade and automobile services	1.006	1.033	1.045
Finance, insurance, and real estate	1.026	1.052	1.093
Banking	1.034	1.096	1.170
Security and commodity brokers, dealers and exchanges	1.005	1.032	1.046
Finance, n.e.c.	1.062	1.040	1.098
Insurance carriers	1.011	1.028	1.056
Insurance agents and combination offices	1.013	1.029	1.047
Real estate	1.035	1.055	1.089
Transportation	1.020	1.059	1.083
Railroads	1.024	1.077	1.102
Local railways and bus lines	1.000	1.031	1.044
Highway passenger transportation, n.e.c.	1.035	1.051	1.078

TABLE 70—*Continued*

Industry	1929	1946	1958
Highway freight transportation and warehousing........	1.018	1.036	1.047
Water transportation.............................	1.009	1.026	1.096
Air transportation (common carriers)................	ᶜ	1.060	1.111
Pipeline transportation...........................	1.000	1.057	1.063
Services allied to transportation.....................	1.012	1.037	1.038
Communications and public utilities..................	1.020	1.087	1.127
Telephone, telegraph, and related services............	1.022	1.092	1.132
Radio broadcasting and television..................	ᶜ	1.028	1.022
Utilities, electric and gas..........................	1.016	1.088	1.131
Local utilities and public services, n.e.c..............	1.032	1.022	1.082
Services..	1.004	1.018	1.030
Hotels and other lodging places....................	1.005	1.033	1.047
Personal services................................	1.004	1.027	1.038
Private households...............................	1.001	1.001	1.009
Commercial and trade schools and employment agencies	1.030	1.095	1.022
Business services, n.e.c...........................	1.006	1.037	1.054
Miscellaneous repair services and hand trades.........	1.009	1.041	1.051
Motion pictures.................................	1.006	1.034	1.040
Amusement and recreation, except motion pictures......	1.003	1.028	1.035
Medical and other health services	1.003	1.008	1.025
Legal services...................................	1.000	1.017	1.028
Engineering and other professional services, n.e.c........	1.000	1.022	1.046
Educational services, n.e.c........................	1.007	1.025	1.052
Non-profit membership organizations, n.e.c............	1.007	1.029	1.048
Government and government enterprisesᵃ..............	1.035	1.065	1.082
Federal general government, civilianᵈ................	1.067	1.131	1.081
Federal government enterprises.....................	1.021	1.041	1.075
Public educationᵉ................................	1.026	1.045	1.085
State and local general government, non-schoolᵉ........	1.026	1.045	1.085
State and local government enterprises...............	1.006	1.012	1.043
Group *a* industries.................................	1.013	1.050	1.088
Group *b* industries.................................	1.013	1.034	1.050

* Except for the "all industries" and major industry division headings, these ratios were computed directly from Department of Commerce data on total employee compensation and total wages and salaries. The ratios for the "all industries" and major industry headings (with the exception of contract construction) are fixed weighted means of the ratios for the detailed industries listed under each major industry heading. The fixed weight for each industry was the simple mean of its full-time equivalent employment figures, one for each year, over the period 1929–57.

ᵃ Excludes military and work relief employees.

ᵇ 1958 ratio not strictly comparable to those for 1929 and 1946 because of changes in industry definition.

ᶜ Omitted because of likelihood of large (percentage) rounding error in employee compensation and wage and salary data.

ᵈ Total compensation for "federal general government" less wages and salaries for "federal work relief" divided by total wages and salaries for "federal general government" after subtracting total wages and salaries of "federal work relief."

ᵉ Total compensation for "state and local general government" less total wages and salaries for "state and local work relief" divided by total wages and salaries for "state and local general government" after subtracting total wages and salaries for "state and local work relief."

the corresponding changes in extent of unionism from 1929 to 1953 as estimated in Table 76 of chapter vii.

TABLE 71

WAGE SUPPLEMENTS AS A PER CENT OF WAGES AND SALARIES
IN MANUFACTURING INDUSTRIES, 1957

Industry	Department of Commerce (1)	Chamber of Commerce (2)	Census of Manufactures (3)
Food and kindred products.............	6.9	} 9.2	7.3
Tobacco manufactures.................	14.3		10.3
Textile mill products..................	6.3	} 7.8	6.1
Apparel and other finished fabric products	7.8		5.7
Lumber and wood products, except furniture..........................	5.0	} 7.5	5.6
Furniture and fixtures................	5.7		6.3
Paper and allied products.............	7.9		7.4
Printing, publishing and allied industries..	5.3	7.8	5.4
Chemicals and allied products..........	10.9	8.9	9.2
Products of petroleum and coal.........	31.5	12.8	12.8
Rubber products.....................	9.1	} 9.8	9.3
Leather and leather products...........	5.6		6.4
Stone, clay, and glass products.........	8.3	9.3	7.4
Primary metal industries..............	12.2	9.3	9.8
Fabricated metal products, including ordnance.........................	7.3	9.3	7.8[a]
Instruments........................	9.1	} 7.8	7.6
Miscellaneous manufacturing..........	6.4		6.9[b]
Machinery, except electrical...........	7.8	9.0	7.9
Electrical machinery..................	9.2	8.0	8.2
Transportation equipment, except automobiles......................	7.1	} 9.8	7.6
Automobiles and automobile equipment...	14.6		10.9
All manufacturing....................	8.9	9.0	7.8

[a] Excluding ordnance.
[b] Including ordnance.

Table 71 also shows similar figures which I have computed from data of the Chamber of Commerce of the United States for 1957 (*Fringe Benefits 1957* [Washington, 1958]). The Chamber of Commerce figures in Table 71 are ratios, expressed in per cent, of the sum of their estimates of "legally required payments" and "pensions and other agreed-upon payments" to the sum of their estimates of "payroll," "payments for time not worked," payments for "paid rest periods, lunch periods, etc.," and "other items." The Chamber of Commerce figures derive from a non-probability sample covering 656 manufacturing companies and are presumably less reliable than the census figures. Nevertheless, they also have smaller dispersion than the Department of Commerce figures.

Table 56: Average Full-Time Hours Worked per Year, Groups a and b and All Industries, 1919–58.—The sources of the data underlying Table 56 are:

Manufacturing.

1919–56: unpublished estimates of average hours worked per week per production worker made by Miss Ethel B. Jones; see her "Hours of Work in the United States, 1900–1957," Table 1. I multiplied Miss Jones's estimates of hours worked per week by 52 to convert them to an annual basis.

1957: the ratio of total man-hours worked by production workers in manufacturing to the annual average employment of production workers, computed from U.S. Bureau of the Census, *Annual Survey of Manufactures: 1957.*

1958: extrapolation of 1957 figure, using U.S. Bureau of Labor Statistics figures on average weekly hours of production workers in manufacturing in 1957 and 1958.

Other industries.

1919–57: unpublished worksheets supplied by John Kendrick from his study of productivity trends (*Productivity Trends in the United States* [Princeton, 1961], a publication of the National Bureau of Economic Research). These supplied annual estimates of (a) aggregate man-hours worked by wage and salary workers and (b) average full-time equivalent employment of wage and salary workers in each of the following industry divisions: farming; mining; contract construction; communications and public utilities; transportation; agricultural services, forestry, and fisheries; wholesale and retail trade; finance, insurance, and real estate; domestic service; other services; government enterprises; and general government, civilian. For each of these industry divisions I computed the ratio of (a) to (b). (In making this computation for "general government, civilian," I first excluded work relief employees, using Department of Commerce estimates of full-time equivalent employment of these workers and Professor Kendrick's figure on their average hours worked per year per employee.)

1958: extrapolations of the Kendrick series on average hours worked per year per full-time equivalent employee with the help of the Bureau of Labor Statistics series on average weekly hours (*Employment and Earnings*, V, No. 11 [May, 1959], Table SC-1), and the Bureau of the Census tabulations of hours worked by wage and salary workers as reported in the *Monthly Report on the Labor Force.*

The averages in columns (1), (2), and (3) of Table 56 are fixed weighted arithmetic means of the average annual full-time hours figures estimated for the separate industry divisions from the Jones and Kendrick data. The fixed weight for each industry division in Table 56 is the same as that for the same industry division in Table 54. Notice that the industry detail underlying Table 56 is much less than that underlying Table 54.

The variable weighted all-industry average annual full-time hours worked in column (4) of Table 56 is the ratio of the total annual man-hours worked by wage and salary workers in Groups *a* and *b* to the corresponding total number of full-time equivalent employees. For the years 1919–57, the full-time equivalent employment estimates are Kendrick's. (However, I excluded work relief employees from his figures for "general government, civilian," using the Department of Commerce estimates of the number of full-time equivalent work relief employees.) The 1958 full-time equivalent employment estimate is an extrapolation of the series for 1919–57 based on the Department of Commerce full-time equivalent employment figures.

The total man-hours worked per year figures, numerators of column (4), were obtained as follows:

Group a.

Manufacturing: the product of (a) average annual full-time hours per wage and salary worker estimated for this industry division and (b) the number of full-time equivalent employees in this industry division. For 1919–57, I used Kendrick's estimates of full-time equivalent employment. I estimated the 1958 employment figure by extrapolating Kendrick's series with the help of the Department of Commerce full-time equivalent employment data for manufacturing.

Other industries: the sum of Kendrick's aggregate man-hours figures for the mining, contract construction, transportation, and communications and public utilities industry divisions in 1919–57. In 1958, I used for each of these industry divisions the product of (a) average annual full-time hours estimated for the industry division and (b) the number of full-time equivalent employees in the division. I estimated (b) in the same manner as for manufacturing.

Group b.

1919–57: the sum of Kendrick's aggregate man-hours figures for farming; agricultural services, forestry, and fisheries; wholesale and retail trade; finance, insurance, and real estate; domestic service; other services; government enterprises; and general government, civilian (after excluding the aggregate man-hours worked by work relief employees).

1958: estimated in the same manner as for Group *a.*

All industries.

the sum of Group *a* and Group *b.*

The aggregate man-hours figures for Group *a* and Group *b* are shown as index numbers in columns (4) and (5) of Table 59.

Table 59: National Income and Total Man-hours Worked, Groups a and b, 1919–58.—For the construction of the total man-hours worked indexes in columns (4) and (5) of Table 59, see the preceding paragraph.

The Department of Commerce national income reports (in Table I-10) provide annual estimates of national income by industry, 1929–58, for each of approximately seventy industry headings matching those for their employment and employee compensation series, except that for the federal and state and local "general government" headings the reports do not give separate figures for the "work relief" and "military" headings. In order to exclude the national income originating in the latter industries (equal to employee compensation in these industries) from the totals for Group *b*, I estimated employee compensation in these industries by the method described in the discussion of Table 54 (see p. 226).

For the years 1919–28 the national income estimates in Table 59 are extrapolations of the series for 1929–58, using Simon Kuznets' estimates of net income originating (adjusted) by industry (*op. cit.*, Tables 43, 59, Q3, C3, M2, P2, A1, T3, F1, S2, and G2). The extrapolations were made as follows:

Group a: Kuznets' series for each of the mining, construction, manufacturing, and transportation and other public utility industry divisions were expressed as index numbers, with 1929 = 1, then multiplied by the corresponding Department of Commerce estimates of national income in 1929. The sum of the resulting figures for these industry divisions in each year was the estimate of national income originating in Group *a* in that year.

Group b: The same procedure was followed for the agriculture, trade, finance, services, and government industry divisions, except that for the government sector, Kuznets' estimates of wages and salaries (excluding military wages and salaries) were used. The sum of the estimates for Groups *a* and *b* was very close to Kuznets' estimate of aggregate national income.

VII

Dispersion in the Extent of Unionism among Industries in the United States

VII.1. INTRODUCTION

In CHAPTERS v and vi, I estimated the *average* effect of unionism on the wages of union labor relative to the wages of nonunion labor in the economy as a whole. In this chapter and the next, my chief concern is with the *dispersion* in the relative wage effects of unionism among groups of labor, especially among industries.

The effects of unionism on the average relative wages of different groups of labor will tend to vary among the groups because the groups are unequally unionized and because among equally unionized groups the relative wage effects are not all the same. If the effects, R_u, of unionism on the relative wages of union labor and the corresponding effects, R_n, for nonunion labor did not vary from one group to another, then in every group R_u would be equal to $\bar{R}_u$ and R_n would be equal to $\bar{R}_n$, where $\bar{R}_u$ and $\bar{R}_n$ are the economy-wide averages of the R_u and R_n, respectively. Furthermore, in that event,

$$\log R = \bar{B}(p - \bar{p}),$$

where R is the relative wage effect index for the group (that is, for the union and nonunion labor in the group taken together), p is the extent of unionism of the group, $\bar{p}$ is the economy-wide average extent of unionism, and $\bar{B}$ is the logarithm of the index, $\bar{R}_u/\bar{R}_n$, of the effect of unionism on the average wage of union labor relative to the average wage of nonunion labor in the economy as a whole. In this case, the percentage (logarithmic) differences among groups in the relative wage effects of unionism would be strictly proportional to the corresponding differences in their extent of unionism.

Conversely, if the extent of unionism, p, in every group were the same and, therefore, equal to $\bar{p}$, then in every group

$$\begin{aligned}\log R &= \bar{p}B + \log R_n \\ &= \bar{p}(\log R_u - \log \bar{R}_u) + (1 - \bar{p})(\log R_n - \log \bar{R}_n).\end{aligned} \qquad (60)$$

That is, the differences among groups in the relative wage effects of unionism, R, would depend only on inter-group differences in the indexes R_u and R_n.

More generally, the inter-group differences in the relative wage effect indexes, R, depend both on the corresponding differences in extent of unionism and on the differences in the R_u and R_n, as shown by equation (11'),

$$\log R = \bar{B}(p - \bar{p}) + L$$
$$= \bar{B}(p - \bar{p}) + p(\log R_u - \log \bar{R}_u) + (1 - p)(\log R_n - \log \bar{R}_n).$$

It follows from equation (11') that if the "residual" effects, L, were uncorrelated among groups of labor with the extent of unionism of the groups,

$$\sigma^2_{\log R} = (\bar{B}\sigma_p)^2 + \sigma^2_L, \tag{61}$$

where $\sigma^2_{\log R}$ is the variance (squared standard deviation) of the log R among all groups, σ_p is the corresponding standard deviation of extent of unionism, and σ^2_L is the variance of the residual effects, L. In chapter ii (p. 39), I argued that the correlation between extent of unionism, p, and the residual effects, L, among all *industries* in the economy has probably been small. If so, then the dispersion of the relative wage effects of unionism among industries may be approximated from estimates of the *average*, $\bar{B}$, the dispersion of extent of unionism among industries, σ_p, and the dispersion, σ_L, among industries in the residual effects, L.

In chapters v and vi, I have estimated the order of magnitude of the unionism coefficient, $\bar{B}$. In this chapter, I estimate the dispersion, σ_p, of extent of unionism among industries. In chapter viii, I estimate the residual variance, σ^2_L, and the total variance, $\sigma^2_{\log R}$. I shall treat quite briefly in this chapter and the next the dispersion in extent of unionism and in the relative wage effects of unionism by sex, occupation, locality, and size of establishment.

VII.2. GROWTH OF UNIONISM IN THE LABOR FORCE AS A WHOLE, 1900–60

In chapter ii, I defined the average extent of unionism, $\bar{p}$, in the labor force as a whole as the ratio of the total employee compensation of workers represented by unions to the total employee compensation of all workers. The best approximations to this measure that we have available in long historical series are ratios of the total number of union members to the total number of workers in the economy as a whole, as in Table 72 (for detailed description and appraisal of the extent of unionism estimates presented in this chapter, see sec. vii.5).

The denominators of the percentages in Table 72 are estimates of the annual average number of persons engaged in production in the U.Se economy, excluding only persons in military service. The number of.

TABLE 72

NUMBER OF UNION MEMBERS AS A PER CENT OF NUMBER OF PERSONS
ENGAGED IN THE CIVILIAN ECONOMY, 1900–1960*

Year	Per Cent[a]	Year	Per Cent[a]	Year	Per Cent[a]
1900.	3.2	1920	12.3	1940	17.8
1901.	4.0	1921	12.3	1941	19.5
1902.	4.7	1922	9.8	1942	18.9
1903.	6.3	1923	8.3	1943	23.7
1904.	6.8	1924	8.2	1944	25.9
1905.	6.4	1925	8.0	1945	27.0
1906.	5.8	1926	7.7	1946	25.9
1907.	6.2	1927	7.8	1947	25.6
1908.	6.5	1928	7.5	1948	24.4
1909.	5.8	1929	7.3	1949	25.0
1910.	6.0	1930	7.5	1950	24.3
1911.	6.5	1931	7.8	1951	26.1
1912.	6.6	1932	7.8	1952	25.8
1913.	7.2	1933	6.8	1953	26.8
1914.	7.2	1934	7.3	1954	27.6
1915.	6.9	1935	8.2	1955	26.5
1916.	6.9	1936	8.5	1956	26.8
1917.	7.5	1937	14.6	1957	26.5
1918.	8.5	1938	17.4	1958	26.7
1919.	10.0	1939	18.5	1959	26.1
				1960	25.6

* For sources of data underlying this table, see the appendix to chap. vii (sec. vii.5).
a For the years 1900–1929, the number of union members includes Canadian members of unions with headquarters in the United States and some other members outside the continental United States; for the years 1930–60, Canadian members are excluded.

persons engaged in production is the sum of (a) full-time equivalent employment of wage and salary workers, (b) active proprietors of unincorporated businesses working more than half-time in their establishments, and (c) unpaid family workers, regardless of age, working at least fifteen hours per week.

The estimates of the annual average number of union members, numerators of the percentages in Table 72, are those of Leo Wolman for the years 1900–29 and the U.S. Bureau of Labor Statistics for 1930–60. These estimates in all years include a small number of union members employed outside the continental United States and Canada, and the estimates for 1900–1929 also include Canadian members of unions with headquarters in the United States. All of the estimates exclude members of independent unions that are strictly local in character.

Even for what they purport to measure—the fraction of the persons engaged in production who were union members—the percentages in Table 72 undoubtedly contain some significant errors, particularly in the year-to-year movements. Furthermore, the figures in Table 72, even if accurate, may differ from extent of unionism, $\bar{p}$, for two reasons: (a) the average number of *union members* may differ from the average number of *workers represented by unions* and (b) the average annual compensation of union workers may differ from the corresponding average annual compensation of nonunion workers. These problems are discussed in the appendix to this chapter (sec. vii.5). There is some evidence that the measured or reported number of union members has been more stable cyclically than the number of union workers, somewhat less evidence that, apart from these cyclical differences, the number of union members has been about the same as the number of union workers. Available data also suggest that *within* detailed industries, such as those of Table 76 in the next section, the mean annual compensation of nonunion workers commonly may have exceeded that of union workers in the last one and one-half to two decades. This would tend to make the 1953 figures in Table 76 for the more highly unionized industries a bit too high as estimates of extent of unionism. However, for all industries taken together, these compensation differences were probably approximately offset by the general tendency for union workers to be disproportionately located in industries in which the mean annual compensation of union and non-union workers taken together was relatively high.

With these qualifications, the figures in Table 72 may be interpreted as indicating the approximate level and the broad movements of the extent of unionism in the labor force as a whole. In the sixty years spanned by the table, there were only two periods, one ending in 1904 and the second beginning in 1936 and ending about 1944, of rapid and *permanent* growth in extent of unionism. From 1904 to 1935, extent of unionism was on a plateau at a level of approximately 6 to 8 per cent, except for a bulge at the end of and immediately following World War I. Since 1944, extent of unionism has been on a second plateau of about 25 to 30 per cent.

There is a suggestion in Table 72 that the "trend" of extent of unionism in the civilian economy as a whole since 1953 or 1954 may have been a slightly declining one. (The increase in extent of unionism from 1953 to 1954 shown in the table was a result of a recession decline in the number of persons engaged in production rather than an increase in reported union membership; thus the increase in extent of unionism shown may be simply a reflection of the cyclical rigidity of reported union membership figures discussed in the appendix.)

In the next section, I show that the industries in which unionism was most extensive in this period were the mining, contract construction, manufacturing, transportation, and communications and public utility industries. Although there were divergent trends of employment within this group of industries, relative employment—number of persons engaged in production in this group divided by number of persons engaged in production in the whole civilian economy—has been declining since 1953 [see col. (4), Table 73]. Indeed, the peak relative employment in this group (Group *a*) was reached in 1943–44. Relative employment in 1953 was about 3 per cent below this peak and relative employment in 1960 was 8.6 per cent below that in 1953. Thus the flatness of the series in Table 72 since 1943 reflects, in part, a declining relative weight of the more highly unionized industries, offsetting increasing extent of unionism, within industries. [The *fixed weighted* average extent of unionism shown in col. (3) of Table 73 rose approximately 20 per cent from 1944 to 1957 and does not show a decline from 1953 to 1958].

However, it has not been true in the past that really large changes in extent of unionism in the economy as a whole occurred as a result of changes in relative employment among industries. The relative employment changes have not been large enough. The truly large change in extent of unionism which occurred, mainly in the period 1936–44, came about through the spread of unionism to previously poorly organized industries (see Tables 74 and 76 in the next section) and occupations.

In my judgment, the main cause of this spread of unionism was the intellectual revulsion against free markets which in the Great Depression became New Dealism and led to the National Industrial Recovery Act, the Wagner Act, and to interpretations of existing law in a manner more favorable to unions. In contrast, no comparably important changes in public policy toward unions took place either in the thirty-year period beginning about 1904 or in the period since the late 1930's.

In the last half-century there has been no significant trend in relative employment in what are now the more highly unionized industries that would lead one to predict much of a change in extent of unionism in the next decade. It is more hazardous to predict the course of public policy toward trade unions. In recent years there has been considerable sentiment favoring the regulation of trade union affairs; the Taft-Hartley and Landrum-Griffin laws have been enacted at the federal level, and "right-to-work" laws have been passed in some of the states. This movement to regulate unions as public utilities may very well continue and produce more legislation. However, I interpret the point of view which favors such trade union regulation, not as a departure from, but as a part or logical consequence of, the point of view that led to the Wagner Act. I doubt that more legislation in the mold of the Landrum-Griffin Act will seriously affect the extent of unionism. Of course, an economic upheaval—a long and deep depression, a protracted war, a great inflation—could make this prediction quite erroneous.

VII.3. THE LOCUS OF UNIONISM AMONG INDUSTRIES

Table 73 presents estimates of the ratio, expressed as a percentage, of the number of union members to the number of persons engaged in production in each of the two large industry groups:

Group *a* [col. (1)], mining, contract construction, manufacturing, transportation, communications, and public utilities; and
Group *b* [col. (2)], all other industries except the military.

The numerators of the ratios in columns (1) and (2) are the same as those for columns (1) and (2) of Table 51 in chapter vi. The denominators in all years are the U.S. Department of Commerce estimates of the number of persons engaged in production by industry.

Column (3) is the fixed weighted arithmetic mean of the figures in columns (1) and (2), with the weight for each industry group equal to the number of persons engaged in production in the industry group in 1929. [The relative weight for Group *a* is the 1929 figure in col. (4).] The series in column (3) differs from that in Table 72 for the following reasons:

1. The estimates of the number of union members used in Table 73 differ from those used in Table 72.
   1929–32: Table 72 estimates 3 to 7 per cent higher than Table 73 estimates.
   1933–34: Table 72 estimates 5 to 11 per cent lower than Table 73 estimates.
   1935–36: Little difference.
   1937–41: Table 72 estimates average 29 per cent higher than Table 73 estimates.
   1942–46: Table 72 estimates average 14 per cent higher than Table 73 estimates.
   1947–58: Table 72 estimates average 5 per cent higher than Table 73 estimates.
2. The estimates of the number of persons engaged in production in the civilian economy in Table 72 were approximately 2 to 3 per cent higher than those in Table 73.
   The combined effect of these two factors would make the extent of unionism series in Table 72 differ from that in column (3) of Table 73 as shown below.
   1929–32: little difference.
   1933–34: Table 72 about one percentage point lower than Table 73.
   1935–36: little difference.
   1937–46: Table 72 about two to five percentage points higher than Table 73.
   1947–58: Table 72 less than one and one-half percentage points higher than Table 73.

TABLE 73

NUMBER OF UNION MEMBERS AS A PER CENT OF NUMBER OF PERSONS ENGAGED
IN PRODUCTION, GROUPS *a* AND *b* AND ALL INDUSTRIES, 1929–58*

YEAR	PER CENT, UNION MEMBERS OF PERSONS ENGAGED			RELATIVE EMPLOYMENT IN GROUP *a*[c]
	Group *a*[a] (1)	Group *b*[a] (2)	All-Industry Average[b] (3)	(4)
1929.........	15.4	1.7	7.1	0.391
1930.........	16.4	1.9	7.5	0.374
1931.........	18.6	1.9	8.4	0.348
1932.........	20.3	2.0	9.2	0.322
1933.........	19.1	2.0	8.6	0.322
1934.........	21.4	2.0	9.6	0.331
1935.........	21.3	2.1	9.6	0.335
1936.........	21.7	2.2	9.8	0.339
1937.........	28.5	2.9	12.9	0.355
1938.........	33.1	3.3	14.9	0.328
1939.........	33.1	3.6	15.1	0.343
1940.........	34.5	3.8	15.8	0.356
1941.........	35.7	4.0	16.4	0.392
1942.........	37.7	4.1	17.2	0.424
1943.........	41.0	4.4	18.7	0.446
1944.........	45.3	4.9	20.7	0.443
1945.........	48.3	5.4	22.2	0.422
1946.........	48.8	6.1	22.8	0.413
1947.........	49.9	6.5	23.5	0.421
1948.........	50.4	6.6	23.7	0.421
1949.........	51.8	6.6	24.3	0.405
1950.........	49.2	6.7	23.3	0.414
1951.........	49.8	6.8	23.6	0.426
1952.........	50.4	6.9	23.9	0.426
1953.........	52.1	7.0	24.6	0.432
1954.........	52.8	7.1	24.9	0.418
1955.........	51.6	7.2	24.6	0.419
1956.........	50.9	7.3	24.4	0.419
1957.........	52.0	7.4	24.8	0.414
1958.........	54.0	7.5	25.6	0.396
1959.........	...	...	...	0.399
1960.........	...	...	...	0.395

* See appendix to chap. vii (sec. vii.5) for sources.
  [a] Group *a* consists of the mining, contract construction, manufacturing, transportation, communications, and public utilities industries; Group *b* consists of all other industries except the military.
  [b] Fixed weighted mean of cols. (1) and (2); relative weight for group *a* is 0.391.
  [c] Number of persons engaged in production in Group *a* industries divided by total number of persons engaged in production in the civilian economy.

3. The series in column (3) of Table 73 is a fixed weighted average; that in Table 72 is a variable weighted average. The ratio of the variable weighted average to the fixed weighted average in any year is approximately the same as the ratio of the figure in column (4) for that year to the 1929 figure in

column (4). The series in column (4) shows the *relative* number of persons engaged in production in the Group *a* industries—the ratio of the number of persons engaged in production in these industries to the total number of persons engaged in production in the civilian economy.

The estimates, in columns (1) and (2) of Table 73, of extent of unionism in the large industry groups *a* and *b* have all of the defects of the economy-wide figures in Table 72, plus the additional one that the allocation of union membership by industry is subject to error. The basic membership figures underlying both Tables 72 and 73 are available generally only by union. Unfortunately, each of the largest unions (and many of the smaller ones) characteristically has members employed in a good many industries. There are relatively few industries, for example, that do *not* employ members of the Teamsters Union. The errors in classification of union membership by industry are undoubtedly much less for the very broad industry groups of Table 73 than for the more detailed industry groups of later tables in this section, but even in Table 73 these errors surely have not been entirely eliminated.

Although the figures in columns (1) and (2) are somewhat imprecise estimates of the extent of unionism in industry groups *a* and *b*, there can be little doubt that throughout the period 1929–58, and particularly in the last half of the period, unionism was quite unequally distributed among industries. If there were no dispersion of extent of unionism among industries *within* either Group *a* or Group *b*, then the dispersion (standard deviation) of extent of unionism among all industries could be estimated from the data in Table 73 by the following formula:

standard deviation = (col. 1 minus col. 2) $\sqrt{\text{col. 4 minus square of col. 4.}}$

This formula leads to the following estimates of the standard deviation of extent of unionism among industries: 1929, 6.7 percentage points; 1939, 14.0 percentage points; 1949, 22.2 percentage points; 1953, 22.3 percentage points; and 1958, 22.7 percentage points. These are *underestimates* of the standard deviation of extent of unionism among all industries because they ignore dispersion of extent of unionism within Groups *a* and *b*.

For example, in 1929 the extent of unionism in manufacturing, which employed about three-fifths of the persons engaged in production in Group *a*, was only about half as large as that for Group *a* as a whole, and the communications and public utilities industries were almost completely nonunion. In contrast, the extent of unionism in each of mining, construction, and transportation was roughly double that for Group *a* as a

TABLE 74

NUMBER OF UNION MEMBERS AS A PER CENT OF NUMBER OF PERSONS ENGAGED
IN PRODUCTION BY MAJOR INDUSTRY DIVISION, SELECTED YEARS*

Major Industry Group	1929 (Lewis)	1939 (Troy)	1953 (Troy)	1953 (Lewis)	1956ᵃ (BLS)	1958ᵃ (BLS)	1960ᵃ (BLS)
All civilian industriesᵇ...	7.0	14.7ᶜ	26.4ᶜ	26.6	29.1ᶜ	29.1ᶜ	28.0ᶜ
Agriculture, forestry, and fisheries.............	0.0	0.0	0.1	1.0	1.3	0.6	1.0
Mining	27.4	63.6	61.5	50.1	59.9	81.3	82.0
Contract construction...	30.8	47.7	57.8	50.5	50.3	57.7	54.2
Manufacturing.........	8.3	22.8	41.9	46.2	51.6	53.2	51.9
Transportation, communications, and public utilities............	21.6	47.9	76.7	70.2	79.7	82.5	79.1
Transportation.......	28.8	n.a.	n.a.	77.3	94.9	103.5	96.9
Communications and public utilities......	0.4	n.a.	n.a.	55.0	50.3	45.3	46.8
Trade, finance, and services............	1.3	4.2	7.6	7.5	8.9	8.8	8.4
Wholesale and retail trade	0.6	n.a.	n.a.	9.1	6.9	6.6	6.3
Finance, insurance, real estate.........	0.6	n.a.	n.a.	4.1	1.9	3.7	2.4
Services	2.3	n.a.	n.a.	6.1	13.9	13.5	13.1
Government and government enterprisesᵇ...	8.4	11.1	11.6	16.4	13.2	14.1	13.7

* See appendix to chap. vii (sec. vii.5) for sources.
ᵃ Includes Canadian and a small number of other members of U.S. unions employed outside the continental United States.
ᵇ Excludes work relief and military.
ᶜ Includes a small number of union members not allocated by industry.

whole. Thus in 1929 there was about as much dispersion within Group *a* as there was between Group *a* and Group *b*.

Table 74 gives estimates of extent of unionism in 1929, 1939, 1953, 1956, 1958, and 1960 that are comparable in concept to those of Tables 72 and 73, but for a more detailed industry breakdown than that of Table 73. The denominators of all the figures in Table 74 are the U.S. Department of Commerce estimates of the number of persons engaged in production by major industry division. The numerators in all years are corresponding estimates of the number of union members. The union membership estimates for 1956, 1958, and 1960 were made by the U.S. Bureau of Labor Statistics and were based on the Bureau's union surveys in these years. (The 1956 survey was the first one in which the Bureau asked the unions which were surveyed to report the distribution of their membership by industry.) The membership estimates for 1939 and one of the two sets of estimates for 1953 were made by Leo Troy and were based chiefly on union membership data collected by the National Bureau of Economic Research. The membership estimates for 1929 and

TABLE 75

PER CENT DISTRIBUTION OF PERSONS ENGAGED IN PRODUCTION
AMONG MAJOR INDUSTRY DIVISIONS, SELECTED YEARS*

Major Industry Group	1929	1939	1953	1956	1958	1960
All civilian industries[a]	100.0	100.0	100.0	100.0	100.0	100.0
Agriculture, forestry, and fisheries	20.0	18.7	9.6	8.9	8.7	7.9
Mining	2.2	2.0	1.5	1.4	1.2	1.1
Contract construction	5.0	4.2	6.2	6.6	6.5	6.5
Manufacturing	23.0	22.8	28.4	27.0	25.3	25.5
Transportation, communications, and public utilities	8.9	6.9	7.2	6.9	6.6	6.4
Transportation	6.6	4.9	4.9	4.5	4.2	4.1
Communications and public utilities	2.3	2.0	2.3	2.3	2.4	2.3
Trade, finance, and services	34.6	36.9	36.8	38.3	40.0	40.6
Wholesale and retail trade	17.0	18.9	20.0	20.3	20.7	20.9
Finance, insurance, real estate	3.4	3.5	3.8	4.2	4.5	4.6
Services	14.1	14.5	13.0	13.9	14.8	15.1
Government and government enterprises[a]	6.4	8.6	10.5	10.9	11.8	12.1

* See appendix to chap. vii (sec. vii.5) for sources.
[a] Excludes work relief and military.

the second set of estimates for 1953 are my own; they are based on a large number of sources, of which the most important were the estimates of membership in individual unions prepared by Leo Wolman and Leo Troy.

The differences between the 1929 and the 1939 estimates of extent of unionism by industry division and between these estimates and those for 1953, 1956, 1958, and 1960 surely reflect, in the main, real changes in extent of unionism more largely than errors in measuring extent of unionism. On the other hand, the differences for given industry divisions among the 1953, 1956, 1958, and 1960 estimates consist principally of differences in the way different persons have allocated the membership of unions by industry. Some of these allocation differences are large; they testify to the unsatisfactory state of our knowledge regarding the distribution of unionism among industries. (In the appendix [sec. vii.5], I have attempted to ferret out the sources of some of these allocation differences.)

Throughout the period 1929–60 the extent of unionism was low in the agriculture, forestry, and fisheries; wholesale and retail trade; finance, insurance, and real estate; services; and government and government enterprises industry divisions. The growth in extent of unionism in this sector of the economy from 1929 to the 1950's accounted for only about two to three percentage points of the twenty-percentage-point rise in extent of unionism in the economy as a whole. The manufacturing and communications and public utilities industry divisions also had low extent of unionism in 1929, but in the 1950's their extent of unionism was approximately twenty percentage points above the average for the economy as a whole. The growth of unionism in these two industry divisions accounts for half the total growth in extent of unionism in the economy as a whole. Thus only about one-third of the total growth in extent of unionism is explained by the increased extent of unionism within the three industry divisions—mining, contract construction, and transportation—which were the most highly unionized in 1929 and earlier years.

The standard deviation of the extent of unionism estimates for the ten industry divisions in Table 74 is 9.6 percentage points for 1929 and 22.5 percentage points for 1953 (Lewis estimates). In computing these standard deviations, the extent of unionism figure for each industry division was weighted by the corresponding relative number of persons engaged in production shown in Table 75. These standard deviations are surely underestimates of the true dispersion, σ_p, of extent of unionism among detailed industries, in 1929 and 1953, because they exclude dispersion of extent of unionism within the industry divisions. Table 76 contains my estimates of the ratio, in per cent, of the number of union workers to the number of persons engaged in production in 1929 and 1953 in each of the approximately seventy industries into which the U.S. Department of Commerce divides the economy in reporting national income by industrial origin, excluding only the military and work relief industries. These estimates are derived from the same basic data as the Lewis estimates for 1929 and 1953 in Table 74. The ratios in Table 76, even more than those in Tables 73 and 74, are subject to the hazards of estimating union membership by industry from fragmentary information.

Except for contract construction, which is shown in no more detail in Table 76 than in Table 74, Table 76 confirms the presence of dispersion in extent of unionism within the industry divisions of Table 74, especially within manufacturing and mining. Within manufacturing in 1953, for example, the figures in Table 76 range from eighteen to eighty percentage points and their weighted standard deviation is eight percentage points; within mining in 1953, the dispersion is even larger: the range is seventy-three percentage points and the weighted standard deviation is thirty-two percentage points.

The weighted standard deviation of all of the percentages in Table 76 is 12.4 percentage points in 1929 and 24.7 percentage points in 1953. I suspect that even these figures may underestimate the true dispersion in

1929 and 1953 of extent of unionism among detailed industries. There were many hints in the materials used to construct the estimates in the table that there was rather large dispersion within some of the industry groups, especially in the manufacturing industry division. These materials, however, were of insufficient quality, in my judgment, to warrant constructing more detailed estimates than those given.

I constructed Table 76 mainly in order to estimate the standard deviation of the extent of unionism among its industry headings rather than to provide myself and others with data on the extent of unionism in particular named industries. Thus, although I believe that the standard deviation of the figures in the table differs by no more than about five percentage points from the true standard deviation of extent of unionism among the industry headings, I suspect that some of the individual figures in the table may err by as much as twenty percentage points.

The doubling of the dispersion in extent of unionism among industries from 1929 to 1953 implies that the *growth* of unionism in this period was quite unequally distributed among industries. Thus five metal manufacturing industry groups—iron and steel and their products, including ordnance; machinery, except electrical; electrical machinery; transportation equipment, except automobiles; and automobiles and automobile equipment—account for almost one-third of the twenty-percentage-point rise in extent of unionism in the economy as a whole. In 1929 the average extent of unionism in these five industry groups was almost exactly the same as in the economy as a whole. These groups, together with contract construction, food and kindred products manufacturing, the railroads, and the telephone and telegraph industry group, explain almost half the increase in extent of unionism in the economy as a whole from 1929 to 1953.

The standard deviation of the extent of unionism among industries estimated for 1953 from Table 76 is only slightly less than half as large as the largest conceivable standard deviation of extent of unionism among industries. (The largest conceivable value of the standard deviation is 50 per cent.) I am confident that the true dispersion of extent of unionism in the 1950's was slightly larger than half the maximum, making another doubling of the standard deviation in future years not quite possible. Indeed, even if the average extent of unionism in the economy were to increase substantially in the future, the standard deviation of extent of unionism would not increase appreciably unless the increase in the average extent of unionism were to consist much more largely than it has in the past of the unionization of supervisory and staff (non-production) employees in industries in which production workers were

TABLE 76

NUMBER OF UNION WORKERS AS A PER CENT OF NUMBER OF PERSONS
ENGAGED IN PRODUCTION BY INDUSTRY GROUP, 1929 AND 1953*

INDUSTRY GROUP	PER CENT	
	1929	1953
Farms..	a	a
Agricultural services, forestry, and fishing.................	a	12
Metal mining..	3	68
Anthracite mining..	80	75
Bituminous and other soft-coal mining....................	30	86
Crude petroleum and natural gas..........................	1	13
Non-metallic mining and quarrying.......................	12	30
Contract construction..	31	51
Food and kindred products..................................	4	44
Tobacco manufactures..	12	57
Textile mill products...	3	30
Apparel and other finished fabric products...............	28	52
Lumber and timber basic products........................	12	20
Furniture and finished lumber products...................	3	29
Paper and allied products....................................	2	45
Printing, publishing, and allied industries................	23	37
Chemicals and allied products..............................	a	39
Products of petroleum and coal............................	a	67
Rubber products..	a	54
Leather and leather products...............................	12	39
Stone, clay, and glass products............................	9	44
Iron and steel and their products, including ordnance......	5	57
Nonferrous metals and their products.....................	4	46
Miscellaneous manufacturing...............................	3	18
Machinery, except electrical................................	13	45
Electrical machinery...	12	56
Transportation equipment, except automobiles.............	a	52
Automobiles and automobile equipment...................	a	80
Wholesale trade..	a	4
Retail trade and automobile services......................	1	11
Banking...	a	a
Security and commodity dealers, brokers, and exchanges....	a	3
Finance, n.e.c...	a	a
Insurance carriers..	a	a
Insurance agents and combination offices.................	a	8
Real estate..	2	11
Railroads..	33	95
Local railways and buslines.................................	36	74
Highway passenger transportation, n.e.c..................	a	58
Highway freight transportation and warehousing..........	25	63
Water transportation...	16	74
Air transportation..	a	51
Pipeline transportation......................................	a	50
Services allied to transportation...........................	22	59
Telephone, telegraph, and related services................	1	68
Radio broadcasting and television.........................	a	50
Utilities, electric and gas...................................	a	41
Local utilities and public services, n.e.c..................	a	a
Hotels and other lodging places...........................	2	20
Personal services...	6	19
Private households...	a	a

TABLE 76—*Continued*

INDUSTRY GROUP	PER CENT	
	1929	1953
Commercial and trade schools, employment agencies........	a	a
Business services, n.e.c................................	a	a
Miscellaneous repair services and hand trades............	a	a
Motion pictures.......................................	15	21
Other amusement and recreation.......................	21	23
Medical and other health services......................	a	a
Legal services..	a	a
Engineering and other professional services..............	a	1
Educational services, n.e.c............................	a	a
Non-profit membership organizations....................	a	a
Federal general government, civilian....................	11	15
Federal government enterprises........................	65	79
Public education......................................	a	2
State and local general government, nonschool............	1	11
State and local government enterprises..................	a	30

* See appendix to chap. vii (sec. vii.5) for sources. This table appears in my "The Effects of Unions on Industrial Wage Differentials" in National Bureau of Economic Research, *Aspects of Labor Economics* (Princeton: Princeton University Press, 1962), p. 233.
a Less than 0.5 per cent.

relatively highly unionized. The unionization of production workers in industries in which these workers were mostly nonunion, on the other hand, would tend to equalize the distribution of unionism among industries and reduce the standard deviation.

VII.4. DISPERSION IN EXTENT OF UNIONISM BY OTHER CLASSIFICATIONS OF THE LABOR FORCE

I have not attempted to make estimates of the distribution of unionism among occupations and other classifications of the labor force that are comparable to those given above for industries. The estimates by industry in Table 76 were laboriously pieced together from fragmentary and, often, impressionistic evidence. The detailed quantitative information we have on the distribution of unionism by occupation, especially by occupation *within industry*, is even scantier. We do know, to be sure, that, on the average, within industries the degree of unionization of non-production (office) workers is low, both absolutely and compared to that of production (plant) workers.[1] Furthermore, within many industries in

[1] See Toivo P. Kanninen, "Coverage of Union Contracts in Metropolitan Areas," *Monthly Labor Review*, LXXXV, No. 7 (July, 1962), 747–50. This article reports U.S. Bureau of Labor Statistics estimates of union contract coverage in 1960–61 for plant and office workers by broad industry division and region. The estimates were based on sample surveys of medium and large-size establishments in the manufacturing, trade, transportation and public utility, finance, and services industry divisions in

which the production workers are organized by craft there are undoubtedly substantial differences among the crafts in degree of unionization. Thus the average dispersion in extent of unionism among occupations within industries is surely large, quite possibly as large as the dispersion in extent of unionism among industries.

The extent of union organization among males in recent years was about twice as great as that for females:

Year and Sex	Union Members (Millions)	Civilian Labor Force (Millions)	Extent of Union Membership (Per Cent)
1956, male..........	14.9	48.6	30.7
1956, female........	3.4	21.8	15.6
1958, male..........	14.7	48.8	30.1
1958, female........	3.3	22.5	14.6
1960, male..........	14.7	49.5	29.8
1960, female........	3.3	23.6	14.0

The union membership figures are U.S. Bureau of Labor Statistics estimates based on its labor union surveys.[2] The estimates include Canadian members of unions with headquarters in the United States, but exclude members of AFL-CIO federal labor unions and local industrial unions.

---

eighty metropolitan areas. Workers were considered as being covered by a union contract if they were employed in establishments in which the majority of workers were covered by collective-bargaining agreements. The estimates of collective-bargaining coverage by industry division were:

INDUSTRY DIVISION	COLLECTIVE-BARGAINING COVERAGE (Per Cent)	
	Plant Workers	Office Workers
Manufacturing..........................	79	12
Transportation and public utilities........	95	65
Wholesale trade.........................	56	9
Retail trade............................	39	17
Finance...............................	...	3
Services...............................	56	11

In my judgment, these figures exaggerate the economy-wide average within-industry difference between plant and office workers in extent of union organization. Extent of unionism tends to be greater in large cities and establishments than in small ones, so that the above estimates are biased upward for both plant and office workers. The upward bias, however, is probably more serious for plant workers than for office workers.

[2] See its labor union *Directory* for 1957, 1959, and 1961, Bulletins 1222, 1267, and 1320, Tables 1 and 5.

The labor force estimates are those of the Bureau of the Census.[3] Women, to a considerably greater extent than men, are employed in the industries and occupations in which the degree of unionization is below the average for the economy as a whole. These differences between the sexes in the distribution of their employment by industry and occupation surely account for most of the above differences in extent of unionization by sex.

Within industries and occupations there are undoubtedly both regional and community size differences in degree of unionization. Leo Troy has estimated the extent of unionization of nonagricultural employees by state (including the District of Columbia) for 1939 and 1953.[4] His estimates for 1939 ranged from 4.0 per cent (South Carolina) to 41.7 per cent (West Virginia); for 1953, from 8.3 per cent (North Carolina) to 53.3 per cent (Washington). The corresponding weighted (by nonagricultural employment) standard deviations of his extent of union organization estimates were 7.5 (1939) and 10.0 (1953) percentage points. In both years the extent of union organization was markedly lower in southern and rural states than in others.[5]

The standard deviations of the extent of union organization of nonagricultural employees among the states surely understate considerably the standard deviations of extent of union organization of all employees, both agricultural and nonagricultural, among all *cities* in the United States for two reasons: (a) they exclude all dispersion *among cities within states* and (b) both in 1939 and 1953, agricultural employees were almost entirely nonunion. Although some of the dispersion in the state figures was probably the result of differences among the states in their distributions of employment by nonagricultural industry, I suspect that in both 1939 and 1953 the standard deviation of extent of unionism *among cities within industries* was nearly as large as the corresponding standard deviation of extent of unionism *among industries*.

There is also much evidence that unionism is centered disproportionately in the large establishments within industries and localities. For example, Table 77 shows the U.S. Bureau of Labor Statistics estimates of union contract coverage in eighty large metropolitan areas in 1960–61.[6]

[3] *Statistical Abstract of the United States: 1961*, Table 269.

[4] *Distribution of Union Membership among the States, 1939 and 1953* (National Bureau of Economic Research, Occasional Paper 56, 1957), Table 4.

[5] U.S. Bureau of Labor Statistics estimates of extent of collective-bargaining coverage in metropolitan communities in the 1950's have consistently shown a positive correlation between community size and degree of unionization and a considerably lower than average degree of unionization in southern cities. See, for example, the data shown in Table 77 and in more detail in the article cited in n. 1 above.

[6] Table 77 is a portion of a table (Table 2) included in the article cited in n. 1 above.

TABLE 77

Union Contract Coverage of Plant Workers in Metropolitan Areas,
by Size of Establishment, Industry Division, and Region, 1960–61
(Per Cent of Workers Covered by Contract)

Employment in Establishment	Manufacturing				Nonmanufacturing			
	North-east	South	North Central	West	North-east	South	North Central	West
Under 100......	57	37	57	69	50	14	49	55
2,500 and over..	91	87	95	93	85	71	69	99

The sample surveys from which the figures in Table 77 were derived covered no establishments with fewer than fifty employees and in twelve of the largest areas excluded manufacturing, public utility, and retail trade establishments with fewer than one hundred employees. Thus the contrast between small and very large establishments in union contract coverage undoubtedly would have been even sharper had it not been for these exclusions.[7] On the other hand, part of the establishment size differences in union contract coverage are probably the result of differences in the industry composition of the establishment size classes.

VII.5. Appendix: Description and Appraisal of the Extent of Unionism Estimates in Chapter VII

In chapter ii, I defined the extent of unionism, p, in an industry as the ratio of the total employee compensation of union workers to the total employee compensation of all workers in the industry. Unfortunately, compensation data by industry rarely separate the compensation of union workers from the compensation of nonunion workers. It is necessary, therefore, to estimate extent of unionism from employment data. Let p' be the ratio of the number of union workers in an industry to the total number of workers in the industry and k the ratio in the industry of the mean compensation per head of nonunion workers to the mean compensation per head of union workers. I shall refer to p' as the extent of collective-bargaining coverage and to k as the nonunion/union compensation ratio. It follows from the definition of extent of unionism, p, that

$$p = p'/(k + p' - p'k). \qquad (a)$$

It is apparent from equation (a) that the extent of collective-bargaining coverage exceeds or falls short of the extent of unionism as the nonunion/union compensation ratio exceeds or falls short of unity, unless the

[7] Notice that all of the figures in Table 77, with one exception, are above the average extent of unionism in the economy as a whole (see Table 72). The major reason for this is that the BLS surveys underlying the table covered only medium- and large-size establishments in large communities in the United States.

industry is completely nonunion or is completely unionized. Furthermore, the difference between extent of unionism and extent of collective-bargaining coverage in principle can be quite large: thus, for example, if k were 3.0 and p' were 0.5, p would be only 0.25. Therefore, even though available data do not permit precise estimation of the nonunion/union compensation ratio industry by industry, it is highly desirable to obtain at least a rough notion of the range of error in using p' as an estimate of p.

Table 78 contains estimates of p' and p for each of the manufacturing industry groups. The industry classification scheme followed in the table, except for combining ordnance and miscellaneous manufacturing, is that of the 1945 edition of the *Standard Industrial Classification Manual* (U.S. Bureau of the Budget). These estimates were made in the following manner:

Column (2), estimates of extent of collective-bargaining coverage, p': the product of (a) U.S. Bureau of Labor Statistics estimates of the per cent of *production* workers covered by collective-bargaining agreements and (b) the ratio of total production-worker employment to total employment of both production and nonproduction workers. The source of the percentages (a) is H. M. Douty, "Collective Bargaining Coverage in Factory Employment, 1958," *Monthly Labor Review*, LXXXIII, No. 4 (April, 1960), 345–49, Table 1. The source of the employment ratios (b) is U.S. Bureau of the Census, *1958 Census of Manufactures, Preliminary General Statistics*, MC(P)-1, December, 1959, p. 4. The estimates in column (2) assume that unionization of nonproduction workers in manufacturing industries was of negligible importance in 1958.

Column (3), estimates of extent of unionism, p: computed by means of equation (a) above with p' from column (2) and the values of $(k + p' - p'k)$ estimated as the ratio of the mean annual earnings of all employees to the mean annual earnings of production workers. The mean annual earnings figures for 1958 were computed from the *1958 Census of Manufactures, Preliminary General Statistics*, MC(P)-1, p. 4. These estimates of p assume that (1) the mean annual earnings of *union production workers* in each industry was the same as the mean annual earnings of *nonunion production workers* and (2) unionization of nonproduction workers was negligible. The means and standard deviations for all manufacturing industries are weighted, the appropriate weights being estimated from the data.

In estimating column (3), I assumed that the mean earnings of union and nonunion production workers were the same. There is much fragmentary evidence that (a) within the industry groups of the table the detailed industries which were more highly unionized were also industries which, historically, have had higher earnings than the average for the group and (b) within the detailed industries the union production workers tended, on the average, to have occupational and other characteristics which would make their earnings higher than the average for all produc-

TABLE 78

COMPARISON OF ESTIMATES OF EXTENT OF COLLECTIVE-BARGAINING COVERAGE
WITH ESTIMATES OF EXTENT OF UNIONISM, MANUFACTURING INDUSTRIES, 1958*

INDUSTRY (1)	ESTIMATES OF EXTENT OF		RATIO OF COL. (2) TO COL. (3) (4)
	Collective-Bargaining Coverage (2)	Unionism (3)	
Food and kindred products	45.4	40.3	1.13
Tobacco manufactures	56.0	51.4	1.09
Textile mill products	27.1	24.6	1.10
Apparel and related products	51.9	46.2	1.12
Lumber and wood products	38.0	35.7	1.06
Furniture and fixtures	40.6	36.4	1.12
Pulp, paper and products	60.6	55.4	1.09
Printing and publishing	39.8	37.7	1.06
Chemicals and products	42.6	37.1	1.15
Petroleum and coal products	65.8	60.8	1.08
Rubber products	62.2	57.3	1.09
Leather and leather products	44.4	39.3	1.13
Stone, clay and glass products	62.4	57.9	1.08
Primary metal products	71.6	66.4	1.08
Fabricated metal products	54.4	48.7	1.12
Machinery, except electrical	48.2	43.4	1.11
Electrical machinery	51.7	44.7	1.16
Transportation equipment	62.8	56.3	1.12
Instruments and related products	34.8	29.8	1.17
Miscellaneous, including ordnance	43.6	36.1	1.21
Mean, all manufacturing	50.4	46.4	1.09
Standard deviation, all manufacturing	11.06	10.42	1.06

* All estimates are in per cent.

tion workers in the industry. For these reasons, I doubt that extent of collective-bargaining coverage leads to overestimates of the mean and standard deviation of extent of unionism among manufacturing industries in as large ratios as those indicated by Table 78.

Column (4) of Table 78, the ratio of column (2) to column (3), is equal to the ratio of the mean annual earnings of all employees in each industry group to the mean annual earnings of production workers in the group. The unweighted mean of the ratios in column (4) is 1.11. I have also estimated similar ratios for eleven nonmanufacturing industry groups in 1958 as follows:

Industry	Ratio	Industry	Ratio
Metal mining	1.08	Contract construction	0.88
Anthracite mining	1.08	Railroads	1.10
Bituminous coal mining	0.91	Local railways and bus lines	1.00
Crude petroleum and natural gas production	0.98	Wholesale trade	1.23
		Retail trade	1.06
Non-metallic mining and quarrying	1.05	Electric and gas utilities	1.06

The numerators of the above ratios are the U.S. Department of Commerce estimates of mean annual earnings per full-time equivalent employee given in *Survey of Current Business*, XXXIX, No. 7 (July, 1959), 37. The denominators are the U.S. Bureau of Labor Statistics figures on average weekly earnings per production or nonsupervisory worker multiplied by 52. The source of these BLS figures is *Employment and Earnings*, V, No. 11 (May, 1959), Table SC-1. Comparison of these ratios with those in Table 78 suggests that, on the average, extent of collective-bargaining coverage may overestimate extent of unionism less among nonmanufacturing than among manufacturing industries.

The preceding discussion leads me to the following conclusions, which I would apply, at most, only to the last two decades. In individual industries and industry groups, extent of collective-bargaining coverage probably more frequently overestimated than underestimated extent of unionism, and in some instances, the differences in both directions may have been substantial. The all-industry standard deviation of extent of collective-bargaining coverage may have been larger, but I doubt that it was as much as 5 per cent larger, than the corresponding figure for extent of unionism.

These conclusions do not imply the further conclusion that the all-industry *mean* extent of collective-bargaining coverage was larger than the corresponding *mean* extent of unionism. Both means are weighted. The weight for each industry in the first is the ratio of total employment in the industry to total employment in all industries; the weight for each industry in the second is the ratio of total employee compensation in the industry to total employee compensation in all industries. The second weight will be larger than the first in an industry in which the mean annual compensation per employee in the industry exceeds the corresponding all-industry mean. By and large, the industries that were most highly unionized in the 1940's and 1950's had substantially higher than average mean annual compensation per employee. For this reason, the all-industry mean extent of unionism may have exceeded the corresponding mean extent of collective-bargaining coverage, even though in every industry the reverse was true. For example, the employment weighted mean of the 1953 figures in Table 76 is 26.6 per cent and the corresponding compensation weighted mean approximately 31 per cent, about one-sixth larger than the employment weighted mean. (The compensation weights used were approximations derived from U.S. Department of Commerce data.)

Before the late 1930's the union workers within industries in which there were any union workers to speak of consisted disproportionately of workers in skilled trades. Hence it is more likely for this period than for the last two decades that extent of unionism exceeded extent of collective-bargaining coverage both within industries and for the all-industry mean and standard deviation. But this, together with the preceding paragraph, implies that the large increases which occurred, mainly in the period 1936–44, in the extent of collective-bargaining coverage within industries and in the mean and standard deviation of extent of collective-bargaining coverage may exceed the corresponding increases for the extent of unionism measure.

All of the estimates of extent of unionism presented in the text of this study are estimates of extent of collective-bargaining coverage and therefore contain the defects discussed above. Furthermore, in the main, the numerators of these estimates are based on union membership data rather than data on the number of workers, both union members and others, represented by unions in collective bargaining.

All data on union membership ultimately stem from the unions themselves. The two chief compilers of these data have been the U.S. Bureau of Labor Statistics and the National Bureau of Economic Research. Both have attempted to measure, union by union, the average annual number of dues-paying members. Unions, however, do not have a uniform conception, which does not vary from one compiler to another or over time, of the "dues-paying" member. Some union reports of membership have included, others have excluded, unemployed persons, those in military service, involved in work stoppages, or retired from the labor force. Furthermore, from time to time some unions have overstated and others have understated their actual membership, and many unions have reported to compilers what are obviously quite rounded estimates of membership. In some instances, unions have refused to report their membership to compilers and the compilers were forced to resort to secondary sources. Also, it was not until 1957 (in the Bureau of Labor Statistics union survey of that year) that unions were asked to report the distribution of their membership by industry as well as their total membership. Finally, there was no systematic assembling of membership data on a current basis by either the Bureau of Labor Statistics or the National Bureau of Economic Research before the 1920's or in the years 1935–47. For both periods, estimates of union membership rest on historical documents of uncertain accuracy. It is not surprising, therefore, that the union membership estimates, particularly those for individual industry groups, of the National Bureau and the Bureau of Labor Statistics are not the same and that both compilers warn users that their estimates do not measure precisely either the number of union *members* or the number of union *workers*.

The paucity of data on the number of workers covered by collective-bargaining agreements makes it very difficult to judge the extent to which reported union membership figures err as estimates of the number of union workers. In its surveys of union membership for the years 1956, 1958, and 1960, the Bureau of Labor Statistics asked each union to report both its membership and the approximate number of workers covered by its collective-bargaining agreements. On the basis of the union reports, the Bureau estimated that in these years the total membership of all U.S. unions was almost exactly the same as the total number of workers represented by these unions in collective bargaining (see the Bureau's *Directory of National and International Labor Unions in the United States, 1957*, Bulletin 1222, p. 16, the *Directory, 1959*, Bulletin 1267, pp. 15–16, and the *Directory, 1961*, Bulletin 1320, p. 55). This is weak evidence, since for many unions, perhaps most of them, the best estimate of the number of workers they represent is their estimate of their membership, or vice versa. However, for the year 1958 the Bureau of Labor Statistics also estimated the number of workers covered by collective-bargaining agreements in *manufacturing* industries from sample surveys of employing establishments that were conducted quite independently of its union survey for 1958. The estimated number of union workers based on the establishment surveys differed by less than 1 per cent from the Bureau's estimate of the number of union members in manufacturing industries based on its union survey (see *Monthly Labor Review*, LXXXIII, No. 4 [April, 1960], 349). This evidence, though only for manufacturing in a single year, provides some basis for believing that accurate union membership counts *for large industry divisions* do not differ seriously in level from corresponding counts of the number of union workers.

There are three grounds for believing, however, that typically union membership counts may be less responsive than corresponding counts of the number of employees represented by unions to short-run variations in employment in union bargaining units. First, the Bureau of Labor Statistics union surveys have shown that unions have usually included unemployed members in their reported membership figures (*Directory, 1959*, Bulletin 1267, pp. 13–14; *Directory, 1961*, Bulletin 1320, pp. 51–52). Second, although unionism has been disproportionately located in industries whose employment was most sensitive to business cycle fluctuations, the cyclical variations, in per cent, of reported aggregate union membership, in the economy as a whole and in large industry groups, characteristically have been smaller than the corresponding variations in employment. This has produced fluctuations in the ratio of union membership to employment that are contracyclical to the variations in the denominator employment figures. Third, the time series for individual unions contain many examples of short-run rigidity of reported union membership: unchanging or only slightly changing membership figures in two or more consecutive years of rapidly changing employment.

The preceding discussion has dealt, in general terms, with the kinds of defects which all or most of the estimates of extent of unionism presented in this study may have. The balance of this note describes and appraises the estimates in chapter vii table by table.

Table 72.—For the years 1900–1953, the denominators of the ratios in Table 72 are John Kendrick's estimates of the average number of persons engaged in production in the U.S. civilian economy. These estimates were taken from his "Productivity Trends in the United States," mimeographed manuscript, National Bureau of Economic Research, June, 1959, Table A-VI. The denominators for the years 1954–58 are extrapolations of the Kendrick series, using the Department of Commerce estimates of the number of persons engaged in civilian production (*U.S. Income and Output*, Table VI-16, and *Survey of Current Business* [July, 1962], p. 29). The extrapolations were made by multiplying the Kendrick figure for 1953 by the index numbers, 1953 = 1, of the Commerce figures for 1954–58.

The number of persons engaged in production, as defined by Kendrick, differs in concept from the number of persons in the labor force, as defined by the U.S. Bureau of the Census, in that the first, but not the second, (a) includes unpaid family workers less than fourteen years old, (b) excludes unemployed persons, and (c) counts each part-time employee as less than one full-time employee. The denominators in Table 72 in the period 1947–60 were 1 to 8 per cent lower than the Bureau of the Census estimates of the labor force.

The estimates of the annual average number of union members, numerators of the ratios in Table 72, for the years 1900–1929 are those of Leo Wolman (*Ebb and Flow in Trade Unionism*, Table 5) adjusted in the year 1929 to include the membership of the Trade Union Unity League (*ibid.*, p. 144). Wolman's estimates of union membership are based on the annual reports of the Executive Council of the American Federation of Labor, proceedings and other publications of individual unions, and correspondence with union officers. Wolman's figures in all years include Canadian members of unions with headquarters in the United States. Exclusion of the Canadian members would reduce the ratios in Table 72 for the years 1900–1929 by approximately 5 to 6 per cent, or, in most of these years, by less than half a percentage point. (This statement is based on the estimates of the number of Canadian members of U.S. unions made by the Department of Labor of Canada in its annual report on *Labor Organization in Canada*, various issues.)

The numerators for the years 1930–60 are the U.S. Bureau of Labor Statistics estimates of the annual average number of union members (see the Bureau's "Union Membership as a Proportion of Labor Force," a multilithed table dated February, 1960, and its "Union Membership, 1960," a release dated November, 1961). They include a small number of union members employed outside the continental United States and Canada, but exclude Canadian members of U.S. unions. The Bureau's estimates of the number of members of unions affiliated with the American Federation of Labor and the Congress of Industrial Organizations (CIO) for the years 1930–47 are based almost entirely on the convention proceedings of these union federations. For 1930–34, the BLS estimates of the membership of independent unions are those of Wolman (*op. cit.*, Table 35) adjusted to include the membership of the Trade Union Unity League; for 1935–47, they are based on fragmentary data. The Bureau's estimates of total membership (including Canadian) of U.S. unions for the years 1948–60 derive from its mail-questionnaire surveys of unions. It should be noted, however, that for 1948, 1949, and 1950 the Bureau's estimate of total membership was given only as the midpoint of a range from 14.0 million to 16.0 million and for 1951 and 1952 as the midpoint of a range from 16.5 million to 17.0 million. The Bureau's estimates of the number of Canadian members of U.S. unions were those of the Canadian Department of Labor, except that for the years 1954, 1956, 1958, and 1960 the estimates derive from the Bureau's union surveys.

The principal source of error in the BLS figures is in its estimates of the membership of unions affiliated with the CIO in the years before 1948. The estimates of CIO membership before 1948 are based mainly on unsupported statements and reports of CIO officials regarding total membership of affiliated unions or gains in membership from one year to another.

Table 73.—The denominators of the extent of unionism ratios in columns (1) and (2) of Table 73 are the Department of Commerce estimates of the number of persons engaged in production by industry (see *National Income*, 1954 ed., Table 28; *U.S. Income and Output, 1958*, Table VI-16; and *Survey of Current Business* [July, 1962], p. 29).

The numerators of the percentages in columns (1) and (2) are the same as the numerators of the percentages in columns (1) and (2) of Table 51 in chapter vi. See the appendix to chapter vi (sec. vi.4) for the sources and methods of constructing Table 51.

The estimates of extent of unionism in Table 73 for industry Groups *a* and *b* agree very well with corresponding estimates which may be computed from Table 74 as the following comparisons show:

Year	Table	Group *a* (Per Cent)	Group *b* (Per Cent)
1929.........	73	15.4	1.7
1929.........	74	15.3	1.6
1939.........	73	33.1	3.6
1939.........	74	32.8	3.9
1953.........	73	52.1	7.0
1953.........	74 (Troy)	50.6	7.1
1953.........	74 (Lewis)	50.9	8.1
1956.........	73	50.9	7.3
1956.........	74	56.3	8.5
1958.........	73	54.0	7.5
1958.........	74	59.7	8.7

The 1956 and 1958 figures from Table 74 include Canadian members; exclusion of these members would reduce these figures by about 5 to 6 per cent, bringing them close to the corresponding figures from Table 73.

Tables 74 and 75.—The denominators of the ratios in Table 74 are the U.S. Department of Commerce estimates of the number of persons engaged in production by major industry division, excluding persons engaged in military service and in work relief (see the sources of the denominators of Table 73). The percentage distributions of these denominators among the major industry divisions are given in Table 75.

The numerators of the 1929 and 1953 (Lewis) figures in Table 74 are my estimates of the number of workers represented by unions in each of the major industry divisions in these two years. These numerators are based on Table 76 and are described below in the discussion of that table. The numerators of the 1939 and 1953 (Troy) ratios are Troy's estimates by industry of the number of dues-paying union members (see his *Distribution of Union Membership among the States, 1939 and 1953*, Table 6). Wherever possible, Troy based his estimates on the financial records of unions; where these records were not available, the membership figures were estimated from reports of union officers, information obtained in correspondence with unions, and from voting representation at union conventions. Troy's report of his estimates does not state how he allocated the membership of unions among industries.

The numerators of the 1956, 1958, and 1960 ratios are Bureau of Labor Statistics estimates derived from mail surveys in which each union was asked to report both its annual average dues-paying membership and the distribution of the membership by industry (see the Bureau's labor union *Directory, 1957*, Bulletin 1222, Table 7; the *Directory, 1959*, Bulletin 1267, Table 7; and the *Directory, 1961*, Bulletin 1320, Table 7). These BLS estimates, unlike those for 1929, 1939, and 1953 in Table 74, include Canadian members of U.S. unions. (Exclusion of the Canadian members would lower the all-industry ratio for 1956 in Table 74 to 27.5 per cent, that for 1958 to 27.4 per cent, and that for 1960 to 26.3 per cent.)

Although there is a general family resemblance in Table 74 among the 1953, 1956, 1958, and 1960 ratios, some of the differences between my estimates for 1953 and the other four sets of estimates are so large that they require some explanation. Consider first the differences between the 1953 (Lewis) estimates and those of the BLS for 1956, 1958, and 1960. The latter include non-U.S. members (principally Canadian) of U.S. unions. Exclusion of these union members, I estimate from data in the BLS reports (*Directory, 1957*, Appendix D; *Directory, 1959*, Appendix C; *Directory, 1961*, Appendix C), would reduce the 1956, 1958, and 1960 figures in Table 74 by approximately the following amounts in percentage points: mining, six to eight; manufacturing, three; construction, four to five; transportation, six to eight; and other industry divisions, less than one. After this 'adjustment, the BLS figures for manufacturing and contract construction differ from the corresponding 1953 (Lewis) figures by 10 per cent (five percentage points) or less.

Except for mining and transportation, I doubt that a significant part of the remaining differences is a result of the tendency, discussed earlier, for reported union membership figures to be somewhat rigid against changes in employment in union jurisdictions. In both mining and transportation, however, there were large declines in employment between 1953 and 1960 that may have led to significant overstatement of the number of union members employed in these industry divisions in 1956, 1958, and 1960.

INDEXES OF THE NUMBER OF PERSONS ENGAGED IN PRODUCTION (1953 = 100)
(Department of Commerce Data)

Industry	1956	1958	1960
Mining	97	85	81
Anthracite coal	58	46	32
Bituminous coal	81	68	58
Transportation	96	87	88
Railroads	87	71	65

Even absolute rigidity of reported union membership figures to these declines in employment, however, could not explain all of the remaining differences for these two industry divisions between my estimates and those of the Bureau of Labor Statistics, although for the transportation division the differences would be reduced to about 10 per cent. However, it is very likely that the BLS *membership* figures for the mining division overestimate the average number of *employed workers represented by unions* in that division. Internal evidence in the BLS reports indicates that its estimate of the number of members of the United Mine Workers in the mining division was at least 310,000 in 1956, at least 440,000 in 1958, and at least 420,000 in 1960, although, according to the Bureau (see *Employment and Earnings Statistics for the United States, 1909–60*, Bulletin No. 1312, p. 13), the average annual employment of production workers in coal mining in 1956 was about 213,000, about 175,000 in 1958, and about 149,000 in 1960. If it is assumed that the BLS estimate of the number of union members in the mining division was too high, *as an estimate of the number of workers represented by unions*, by 97,000 (310,000 minus 213,000) in 1956, by 265,000 (440,000 minus 175,000) in 1958, and by 271,000 (420,000 minus 149,000) in 1960, the resulting Table 74 ratios for the mining division are 48.7 per cent in 1956, 46.5 per cent in 1958, and 44.5 per cent in 1960. My estimate for 1953 was 50.1 per cent. A declining average extent of collective-bargaining coverage in the mining division from 1953 to 1960 would not be surprising in the light of the declining employment in coal mining relative to employment in the mining division as a whole.

Although not all of the unions surveyed by the BLS reported distributions of their membership by industry, the BLS allocations of membership by industry for 1956, 1958, and 1960 depend principally on allocations made by the unions themselves. I judge that a good many national and international unions, however, know, or at least will report to others, only somewhat rough distributions of their membership by industry. Indeed, in the 1956 survey the BLS asked of the unions (*Directory, 1957*, Appendix B) only this:

Indicate the approximate percentage of all union members working in estab-
    lishments in each of the following broad industry groups:
    Manufacturing
    Mining and quarrying (include crude petroleum and natural gas production)
    Contract construction (building and special trade)
    Transportation (include railroads, truck and water transportation and allied
        services)
    Telephone and telegraph

Public utilities (electric, gas, and water)
Trade (wholesale and retail)
Finance and insurance
Service industries (include hotels, laundries and other personal services, repair services, motion pictures, amusements and related services, hospitals, educational institutions, non-profit membership organizations)
Agriculture and fishing
Government: Federal, State, and Local

                                                                       Total

The language used in the 1958 and 1960 questionnaires (*Directory, 1959* and *Directory, 1961*, Appendix B) differed only (a) in requesting some industry detail within the manufacturing division and (b) in adding "classification not available" categories for manufacturing and non-manufacturing.

The approximateness of the reported industry distributions may account for the somewhat erratic behavior of the BLS estimates for agriculture, mining, construction, transportation, communications and public utilities, and finance. More importantly, since its questionnaires provided no further information to responding unions on the industry definitions they were to follow than is indicated above and requested only "approximate" industry distributions, I conjecture that the industry definitions actually followed by the responding unions differed significantly and systematically from the Department of Commerce definitions (*National Income*, 1954 ed., p. 66) which underlie my estimates in Table 74. In particular, the following departures from the Department of Commerce definitions seem likely to be significant:

1. *Transportation:* classifying union truck drivers under this heading although employed in other industries; classifying union members employed in government transportation enterprises under this rather than the "government" heading.

2. *Wholesale and retail trade:* in addition to 1, classifying union members employed in eating and drinking places and in automobile repair services and garages under the service industry heading instead of retail trade.

3. *Communications and public utilities:* classifying union members employed in radio broadcasting and television under the service industry heading rather than this heading.

4. *Services:* in addition to 1, 2, and 3, classifying union members employed in public education under services rather than government.

5. *Government and government enterprises:* in addition to 1 and 4, classifying other union members employed in business-type government enterprises under a private industry heading rather than government.

If these conjectures regarding differences between the industry classification scheme underlying my estimates and that underlying the 1956, 1958, and 1960 figures are correct, adjustment of the latter for the classification differences, I estimate, would change them by roughly the following amounts:

> *Transportation:* lowered by about 10 per cent.
> *Wholesale and retail trade:* raised by roughly 50 per cent.
> *Communications and public utilities:* raised by about 5 per cent.
> *Services:* lowered by about 30 per cent.
> *Government and government enterprises:* raised by 10 to 15 per cent.

These adjustments, together with those discussed in preceding paragraphs, would bring the BLS ratios in Table 74 close to the corresponding 1953 (Lewis) ratios.

Consider now the differences between the Lewis and Troy estimates for 1953. They are mainly differences in the distribution of union workers or members among the industries rather than differences in the totals distributed. Furthermore, I judge that, except possibly for the government and government enterprises heading, the differences do not stem from differences in underlying industry definitions.

The largest difference in percentage points between the Troy and Lewis estimates for 1953 is that for mining. Here I am confident that Troy's union *membership* figure overestimates the average *number of union workers employed* in the mining division in 1953. All of the estimates I have seen—those of Wolman and Troy, the BLS membership surveys in 1956 and 1958, and other sources—put the annual average number of union members or union workers employed in the 1950's in mining, other than coal mining, in a range from about 150,000 to about 200,000. The annual average number of production workers employed in coal mining in 1953 was about 274,000. It is well known that coal miners were not completely unionized in the 1950's. If they were 95 per cent unionized, the annual average number of union coal miners in 1953 was about 260,000. This leads to an estimate of no more than about 460,000 union workers employed in the mining division as a whole in 1953, about 51 per cent—compared to the Troy ratio of 61.5 per cent—of the 896,000 persons engaged in mining in 1953.

It is not possible to show in the same way as for mining that the Troy figures for contract construction and for transportation, communications, and public utilities are also overestimates. Notice, however, that the Troy ratio for construction is not only higher than the Lewis ratio for the same year, it is also higher than the BLS figures, which include non-

U.S. members. (The average of the BLS ratios for construction, after exclusion of non-U.S. union members, is slightly lower than the 1953 Lewis ratio for this industry division.) Similarly, the 1953 Troy ratio for transportation, communications, and public utilities is higher than the 1953 Lewis ratio and slightly higher than the average of the BLS ratios after excluding non-U.S. members from the latter. Furthermore, if my appraisal of the BLS union membership estimates for transportation is correct, the average of the BLS ratios for the transportation, communications, and public utilities group, after exclusion of non-U.S. members, is too high by about four to five percentage points.

Thus, although the evidence is not conclusive, it does suggest that the Troy figures overestimate the annual average number of union workers employed in mining, contract construction, and the transportation, communications, and public utilities group in 1953 and, correspondingly, underestimate union workers employed in the manufacturing sector.

Table 76.—The denominators of the percentages in Table 76, except for eight industries in 1953, are the Department of Commerce estimates of the number of persons engaged in production. Because of changes in industry definitions, the Department has not published estimates for the following manufacturing industries for the years beginning in 1948 that are strictly comparable to those for 1929–47: lumber and timber basic products; furniture and finished lumber products; chemicals and allied products; products of petroleum and coal; iron and steel and their products, including ordnance; machinery, except electrical; electrical machinery; miscellaneous manufacturing; and nonferrous metals and their products. (The industry classification scheme followed in Table 76 is that of the Department of Commerce, except that for the above eight industry groups the definitions are those of the 1942 rather than the 1945 edition of the *Standard Industrial Classification Manual,* in order to make the 1953 figures in Table 76 comparable to those for 1929.) For these industries I have extrapolated the Department of Commerce series for 1929–47, using data from the Department of Commerce, the U.S. Bureau of Employment Security, the Bureau of Labor Statistics, and the Bureau of the Census.

In the main, the numerators of the 1929 percentages are Leo Wolman's estimates by industry of union membership in 1929 (*op. cit.,* Appendix Tables I, V, VII, VIII, and IX). Relatively minor modifications of his basic data were made, chiefly the exclusion of Canadian members, using data from the Department of Labor of Canada (annual report on *Labor Organization in Canada*). Since the industry groups in Wolman's study are somewhat broader than those of Table 76, it was necessary to allocate union membership by industry within his groups according to the classification scheme of Table 76. This allocation was based on information obtained from union journals and proceedings and studies of trade unionism in the 1920's. (In a few instances this information also led me to reallocate union membership among Wolman's industry groups.)

The estimation of the numerators for 1953 in Table 76 was enormously more difficult than for 1929. Three factors account for this greater difficulty:

1. The much greater tendency for unions, particularly the large ones, to have collective-bargaining agreements covering workers in more than one of the industry groups of Table 76;

2. The relatively few industry groups in which, according to the authorities, extent of unionism was negligible; and

3. The absence of any systematic study of extent of union membership or of collective-bargaining coverage in the economy with as much industry detail as that of Table 76, coupled with the presence of a great mass of materials with conflicting implications for extent of union membership or collective-bargaining coverage in particular industries and industry groups.

What I set out to estimate for each industry group in Table 76 was the number of workers represented by unions in 1953. In making these estimates, I followed two routes, which differ from each other in terms of the type of information used:

1. The "route 1" estimates derive from data on the membership of or number of workers represented by individual unions in particular industries and in all industries. The most frequently used sources of information on the total U.S. membership of individual unions were the unpublished estimates for 1953 by Leo Wolman and Leo Troy and the estimates from the BLS union surveys as reported in its labor union *Directory, 1953, 1955,* and *1957.* Since the great majority of union workers belong to or are represented by unions each of which has collective-bargaining agreements in more than one industry, these estimates (and those from other sources) of the *total* U.S. membership served mainly as benchmarks: the total for a particular union of the industry-by-industry estimates of its membership should conform reasonably well to the level set by the benchmark. Only where the preponderance of the evidence indicated that all save a negligible fraction of a union's membership was employed in a single industry, was the union's *total* U.S. membership used as an estimate of the number of workers represented by it in the industry.

The information used to estimate the number of union workers or members of particular unions in each of the industry groups came from a wide variety of sources: the unpublished Wolman-Troy study; the Bureau of Labor Statistics union surveys, its *Current Wage Developments* series, and articles in its *Monthly Labor Review*; trade union proceedings and periodicals, and correspondence with some of the unions whose membership distributions by industry proved most difficult to estimate; business, trade, and popular periodicals; correspondence and interviews with economists who have studied unionism in particular industries; such standard statistical sources as the *U.S. Census of Population* and the BLS monthly *Employment and Earnings*; and, most of all, article and book-length studies of unions and of unionism in particular industries. In the last category the two most consistently helpful sources were Florence Peterson's list of the leading unions by industry (in her *American Labor Unions* [New York and London: Harper & Bros., 1945], pp. 276–85), and Neil Chamberlain's distributions of collective-bargaining units among unions within industries ("The Structure of Bargaining Units in the United States," *Industrial and Labor Relations Review*, X, No. 1 [October, 1956], 19–20). These sources of information were subjected to one other check in addition to that mentioned above: information was regarded as unacceptable if it implied that the extent of collective-bargaining coverage in a particular occupational or industrial category exceeded 100 per cent.

2. The "route 2" estimates were based on information regarding either (a) the number of union workers or members employed in particular industries or (b) the extent of collective-bargaining coverage in particular occupations and industries. The chief sources of information used in making the route 2 estimates were: the Bureau of Labor Statistics *Monthly Labor Review* and its *Wage Structure* studies; trade union proceedings and periodicals; business, trade, and popular periodicals, including newspapers; and other articles and books on unionism in particular industries. In general, the information of this second type was more fragmentary in character than the information used to construct the route 1 estimates.

With few exceptions, the various sources of information consulted yielded somewhat different estimates of the number of union workers by industry. The numerators of the 1953 figures in Table 76 represent my judgment of the central tendency among these estimates for each industry group.

I have made estimates of the extent of collective-bargaining coverage in as much industry detail as in Table 76 only for 1929 and 1953, and I know of no other comparably detailed estimates, except for the manufacturing sector, for these or other years. The BLS estimates of union membership by industry in 1956 (*Directory, 1957*, Table 7), except for dividing the communications and public utilities division into two components (telephone and telegraph, public utilities), have no more industry detail than is shown in Table 74. There was slightly more industry detail in the corresponding BLS estimates for 1958 and 1960 (*Directory, 1959, 1961*, Table 7): manufacturing was broken down into eight industry groups.

The Bureau of Labor Statistics has made estimates, however, of the average number of production and related workers employed in 1958 in manufacturing establishments in which the majority of these workers were covered by collective-bargaining agreements (*Monthly Labor Review*, LXXXIII, No. 4 [April, 1960], 345–49, Table 1). These estimates were based on establishment reports obtained from a probability sample covering about 6,500 manufacturing establishments. The figures in column (2) of Table 79 are the same as the 1953 percentages for the manufacturing sector given in Table 76. The figures in column (3) are the ratios, in per cent, of (a) the BLS estimates of the number of production and related workers employed in 1958 in manufacturing establish-

TABLE 79

COMPARISON OF LEWIS AND BUREAU OF LABOR STATISTICS ESTIMATES OF EXTENT OF COLLECTIVE-BARGAINING COVERAGE, MANUFACTURING, 1953 AND 1958*

INDUSTRY GROUP (1)	EXTENT OF COLLECTIVE-BARGAINING COVERAGE (IN PER CENT)	
	1953 (Lewis) (2)	1958 (BLS) (3)
All manufacturing............................	46	49
Food and kindred products.....................	44	47
Tobacco manufacture..........................	57	55
Textile mill productss.........................	30	27
Apparel and other finished fabric products........	52	52
Lumber and furniture group....................	24	38
Lumber and timber basic products[a].............	20	...
Lumber and wood products, except furniture[b]....	...	37
Furniture and finished lumber products[a].........	29	...
Furniture and fixtures[b].......................	...	40
Paper and allied products......................	45	60
Printing, publishing, and allied industries........	37	40
Chemicals and allied products..................	39	41
Products of petroleum and coal.................	67	60
Rubber products..............................	54	60
Leather and leather products...................	39	44
Stone, clay, and glass products.................	44	60
Metals and metal products group...............	55	61
Iron and steel and their products, including ordnance[a]................................	57	...
Nonferrous metals and their products[a]..........	46	...
Primary metal industries[b].....................	...	71
Fabricated metal products, including ordnance[b]..	...	53
Miscellaneous manufacturing group.............	18	38
Miscellaneous manufacturing[a].................	18	...
Miscellaneous manufacturing[b].................	...	40
Instruments[b]................................	...	34
Machinery, except electrical....................	45	47
Electrical machinery...........................	56	48
Transportation equipment group................	65	61
Transportation equipment, except automobiles...	52	...
Automobiles and automobile equipment.........	80	...

* For sources, see text.
a Defined in accordance with 1942 edition of *Standard Industrial Classification Manual*.
b Defined in accordance with 1945 edition of *Standard Industrial Classification Manual*.

ments in which the majority of production and related workers were covered by collective-bargaining agreements to (b) the Department of Commerce estimates of the number of persons engaged in production in 1958 (*Survey of Current Business* [July, 1959], p. 37). [The BLS study from which the numerators of column (3) were taken is the same as that underlying the extent of collective-bargaining coverage figures in column (2) of Table 78.]

Comparison of columns (2) and (3) of Table 79 is an uncertain check on my estimates in column (2) because:

1. The dates of the two sets of estimates are different. Data on employment and union membership suggest, however, that for the industry groups of the table, the changes in extent of collective-bargaining coverage between 1953 and 1958 were small.

2. For industries employing about one-fourth of the persons engaged in production in manufacturing in 1953 and 1958, the industry classification scheme underlying the 1953 figures (the 1942 edition of the *Standard Industrial Classification Manual*) is significantly different from that for the 1958 figures (the 1945 edition of the *Manual*). The differences in industry classification, however, are not large enough to explain the large differences between the figures in the two columns for the lumber and furniture group and the miscellaneous manufacturing group.

3. The numerators of the figures in column (3) are not (i) the average number of workers covered by collective-bargaining agreements, but (ii) the number of production and related workers employed in establishments in which the majority of production and related workers were covered by collective-bargaining agreements. Let p^* be the fraction of the production workers in an industry employed in establishments in which the majority of production workers are covered by collective-bargaining agreements and p' the extent of collective-bargaining coverage of all production workers employed in the industry. Given no more information than p^*, we can estimate p' no more closely than: $1/2\, p^* \leq p' \leq 1/2 + 1/2\, p^*$. Furthermore, the differences between (i) and (ii) in principle could be quite large, large enough to account by themselves for the differences between columns (2) and (3) of Table 79.

However, the differences between the two columns for the lumber and furniture group; paper and allied products; stone, clay, and glass products; and the miscellaneous manufacturing group are so large that, despite the preceding reservations, they suggest I may have underestimated the extent of collective-bargaining coverage for these industry groups in 1953. These groups employed about one-sixth of the persons engaged in manufacturing in 1953.

For the period 1941 to 1946 the Bureau of Labor Statistics annually published estimates of the proportion of "wage-earners" employed under collective-bargaining agreements (these appear in the *Monthly Labor Review* issues of May, 1942, February, 1943, April, 1944, April, 1945, April, 1946, and May, 1947). The estimates were reported in rather more industry detail for the manufacturing sector than those of Table 79. The tabulation for 1946 (*Monthly Labor Review*, May, 1947, pp. 765–69), for example, listed fifty-three manufacturing industries by title and covered other manufacturing industries which were not explicitly named.

Unfortunately, none of the published reports of these BLS studies of extent of collective-bargaining coverage state the industry definitions used, and the industry titles are unsure guides since in many instances they differ from those used elsewhere by the Bureau. Furthermore, the industries were classified into rather broad classes (under 20 per cent, 20 to 39 per cent, 40 to 59 per cent, 60 to 79 per cent, and 80 to 100 per cent) according to the estimated per cent of wage-earners under collective-bargaining agreements. In addition, I strongly suspect that the estimates are, on the average, too high. I have made the following rough check on the 1946 tabulation:

I assumed that, on the average, production workers in manufacturing were no less highly unionized in 1953 than in 1946. I then estimated the number of production workers covered by collective-bargaining agreements in 1953 in each manufacturing industry by multiplying the *midpoint* of the 1946 extent of collective-bargaining coverage class for the industry by the average number of production workers employed in the industry in 1953 (*Employment and Earnings* [May, 1959], Table SA-2). There were many problems of matching industry titles in the 1946 tabulation against those used for the 1953 production-worker estimates. In cases of doubt, I classified industries in the 20 to 40 per cent unionism class, since the 1946 tabulation stated that the extent of collective-bargaining coverage was at least 20 per cent in every manufacturing industry. The estimates of the number of production workers covered by collective-bargaining agreements in 1953, derived from the 1946 tabulation, were thus conservative in two respects: (a) no allowance was made for increases in extent of collective-bargaining coverage between 1946 and 1953; (b) for industries for which the 1946 tabulation was ambiguous, the lowest extent of collective-bargaining class recognized for manufacturing industries was used. Nevertheless, the resulting estimate of the total number of production workers covered by collective-bargaining agreements in all manufacturing industries in 1953 was 9.42 million, or 54 per cent of the persons engaged in manufacturing in 1953. This figure is 17 per cent higher than my estimate for 1953, higher by 10 per cent than the BLS estimate for 1958 in Table 79, and higher than the BLS figures in Table 74, although these include Canadian members.

The Bureau of Labor Statistics discontinued this series of estimates of collective-bargaining coverage by detailed industry after publication of the estimates for 1946.

VIII

Dispersion in the Relative Wage Effects of Unionism among Industries

VIII.1. INTERINDUSTRIAL DISPERSION IN THE RELATIVE WAGE EFFECTS

THIS CHAPTER brings together the data in chapters v and vii to estimate the order of magnitude of the dispersion of the relative wage effects of unionism among groups of labor, chiefly industries, in the United States.

In each industry, the index, R, of the effect of unionism on the average relative wage of the industry at a particular date is a weighted average, with extent of unionism (p) weights, of similar indexes, R_u and R_n, for the union and nonunion labor employed in the industry (equation 9):

$$\log R = p \log R_u + (1 - p) \log R_n.$$

If there were no differences among industries in either the indexes R_u or the indexes R_n, then in every industry R_u would be equal to the all-industry average, $\overline{R}_u$, for union labor and R_n would equal the all-industry average, $\overline{R}_n$, for nonunion labor. But then equation (9) reduces to equation (31)

$$\log R = \overline{B}(p - \overline{p});$$

that is, the logarithm of the index, R, then would be proportional to the excess of the extent of unionism of the industry over the average extent of unionism in all industries. The factor of proportionality, $\overline{B}$, is the unionism coefficient, the logarithm of the index, $\overline{R}_u/\overline{R}_n$, of the effect of unionism on the average wage of all union labor relative to the average wage of all nonunion labor.

If equation (31) were a good approximation, it would be very simple to estimate R for every industry from the estimates of $\overline{B}$ and $\overline{p}$ given in earlier chapters, provided, of course, that the extent of unionism of the industry also were known. The studies of unionism and wages discussed in chapter iii strongly suggest, however, that the effects of unionism on the relative wages of union labor have varied considerably among industries and that, therefore, equation (31) may yield rather imprecise estimates of R for some industries. For example, I have estimated that $\overline{B}$ was approximately 0.10 to 0.15 and $\overline{p}$ was about 0.25 in the late 1950's.

277

These figures and equation (31) imply that $100(R - 1)$ would be approximately 8 to 12 per cent for a completely unionized industry. Both men's clothing manufacturing and bituminous coal mining were highly unionized in this period, yet for the first industry I have estimated that $100(R - 1)$ was about zero in 1956–57, while the corresponding estimate for bituminous coal mining, on the other hand, was about 45 per cent.

That the distribution of the relative wage effects of unionism among industries cannot be calculated with great precision from estimates of $\overline{B}$ and extent of unionism, p, by industry does not imply that in this context these data are necessarily either useless or misleading. Turn to equation (11′):

$$\log R = \overline{B}(p - \overline{p}) + L$$
$$L = p(\log R_u - \log \overline{R}_u) + (1 - p)(\log R_n - \log \overline{R}_n).$$

The "residual effect," L, is that part of the total effect, $\log R$, which is not strictly proportional among industries to the excess extent of unionism, $p - \overline{p}$. If, as I have argued in chapter ii (p. 39), the residual effects are probably poorly correlated with extent of unionism among industries, then equation (11′) implies that

$$\sigma^2_{\log R} \cong (\overline{B}\sigma_p)^2 + \sigma^2_L, \tag{61}$$

where σ is the standard deviation among industries of the variable indicated by the subscript. This approximation—equation (61)—divides the total variance of the relative wage effects of unionism among industries into two components: $(\overline{B}\sigma_p)^2$, which is the part of the variance that is correlated among industries with extent of unionism; and σ^2_L, the variance of $\log R$ that is not correlated with extent of unionism.

The estimates of $\overline{B}$ in chapter v (Table 50) were: 0.15 to 0.20 in 1923–29; greater than 0.25 in 1931–33; 0.10 to 0.20 in 1939–41; 0.00 to 0.05 in 1945–49; and 0.10 to 0.15 in 1957–58. The extent of unionism data in chapter vii indicate that σ_p was about 0.12 to 0.15 in 1923–33; 0.25 to 0.30 in 1945–60; and roughly midway between these two ranges in the late 1930's and early 1940's. These two sets of figures yield the following estimates of $\overline{B}\sigma_p$: 0.02 to 0.03 in 1923–29; greater than 0.03 in 1931–33; about 0.02 to 0.04 in 1939–41; 0.00 to 0.015 in 1945–49; and 0.025 to 0.045 in 1957–58. Since the residual variance, σ^2_L, surely exceeded zero throughout the period 1923–58, these estimates of $\overline{B}\sigma_p$ must be regarded as lower-limit estimates of $\sigma_{\log R}$.

To simplify the estimation of the residual variance, σ^2_L, I assume that the indexes, R_u and R_n, of the effects of unionism on the relative wages of union and nonunion labor by industry were distributed among industries independently of each other and of the extent of unionism, p.[1] The definition of the residual L in equation (11') then implies that

$$\sigma_L^2 = \sigma_B^2[\sigma_p^2 + (\bar{p})^2 + k(1 - 2\bar{p})], \tag{62}$$

where $\sigma_B^2 = \sigma_{\log R_u}^2 + \sigma_{\log R_n}^2$ is the variance of $B = \log(R_u/R_n)$ among industries and $k = \sigma_{\log R_n}^2/\sigma_B^2$. R_u/R_n is the index of the effect of unionism on the average wage of union labor in the industry relative to the corresponding average wage of nonunion labor.

Since 1945, both σ_p and $\bar{p}$ have been approximately 0.25. Substitution of these numbers into equation (62) yields

$$\sigma_L^2 = \sigma_B^2(0.125 + 0.50k). \tag{63}$$

The table below shows values of $\sigma_L^2/\sigma_B^2 = 0.125 + 0.50k$ for various values of the ratio k. Thus even if the variance among industries, $\sigma_{\log R_n}^2$, of the effects of unionism on the relative wages of nonunion labor were equal to the corresponding variance, $\sigma_{\log R_u}^2$, for union labor—in that event k would be 0.50—the residual variance, σ_L^2, would be only three-eighths as large as σ_B^2. Indeed, I think it is quite likely that $\sigma_{\log R_u}^2$ was several times as large as $\sigma_{\log R_n}^2$ and, therefore, that σ_L^2/σ_B^2 was closer to 0.125 than to 0.375.[2]

σ_L^2/σ_B^2	k
0.125	0.00
0.225	0.20
0.325	0.40
0.375	0.50

Relatively accurate measurement of σ_B requires good estimates of B for a large, random sample of detailed industries. Unfortunately, the estimates of B that I have been able to derive from the earlier studies reviewed in chapter iii are few in number and, I suspect, are a biased selection from the whole population of industries. Some of the estimates are for occupations and others for groups of industries rather than for detailed industries. Furthermore, much of the dispersion among them may reflect errors of estimation rather than real differences in the relative wage effects of unionism.

[1] The assumption that R_u and R_n were distributed independently of each other and of the extent of unionism, p, is a stronger assumption than that the residual L was uncorrelated with p.

[2] See the discussion in chap. ii, p. 23.

TABLE 80

ESTIMATES OF B BY INDUSTRY

"Industry" (1)	Estimate Date (2)	Section of Chapter iii (3)	Estimate of B (4)
Contract construction....................	1939	5	0.180
Bituminous coal mining..................	1956–57	6	0.424
Men's clothing manufacturing............	1956–57	9	0.000
Local transit...........................	1958	11	0.117
Hotels.................................	1948	3	0.076
Paints and varnishes, footwear cotton textiles, and auto parts manufacturing............	1950	7	0.000
Wooden furniture, hosiery, and women's dresses manufacturing..................	1950	7	0.068
Barbers................................	1954	8	0.174
Commercial air transportation............	1956	10	0.242
Seamen................................	1950's	12	0.179
Rubber tire manufacturing...............	1936–38	4	0.130

Column (4) of Table 80 shows estimates of $B = \log(R_u/R_n)$ which I have derived from the studies in chapter iii.[3] For each "industry," the estimate of R_u/R_n used in the table is the most recent estimate (or midpoint of estimate range) given in Table 49 of chapter v, except that if the most recent numerical estimate fell in the period 1945–49:

1. It was excluded if there was no estimate for any other date;

2. If there were higher estimates for other dates after 1935, the highest of these estimates was used instead of the 1945–49 figure.

(Thus the estimates for physicians and for steel manufacturing were excluded and for rubber tire manufacturing the 1936–38 figure was used instead of the estimate for 1945–48.) Column (2) shows the date or period to which each estimate refers and column (3) the section of chapter iii containing the supporting data. The variety of dates probably contributes to the dispersion of the figures in column (4).

The weighted (by estimated employment in 1957) standard deviation of the figures in column (4) is 0.092. This figure is biased downward as an estimate of σ_B because it ignores dispersion within some of the broad "industry" headings of the table, especially contract construction. On the other hand, the figures in column (4) undoubtedly contain some large errors as estimates of B in recent years; these errors probably bias the dispersion strongly upward. Thus the calculated standard deviation, 0.092, is a quite crude estimate of the dispersion of the B's among industries in the recent period.

[3] The estimate for contract construction is the weighted average of the separate estimates for skilled building craftsmen and common building labor.

The variance, $\sigma_B^2 = \sigma_{\log R_u}^2 + \sigma_{\log R_n}^2$, of the B's surely consists mainly of dispersion in the effects, R_u, for *union* labor rather than in the effects, R_n, for nonunion labor. If, as I think likely, $\sigma_{\log R_n}$ was no more than half as large as $\sigma_{\log R_u}$, then k in equation (63) was 0.2 or less. It follows from this equation that if σ_B was 0.092 and k was no greater than 0.2, then the residual standard deviation, σ_L, was less than 0.044. The minimum value of σ_L permitted by equation (63) when $\sigma_B = 0.092$ is 0.032. The estimated value of $\bar{B}\sigma_p$, given earlier in this chapter, was 0.025 to 0.045 for 1957–58. Insert these estimates of σ_L and $\bar{B}\sigma_p$ in equation (61); the resulting estimate of $\sigma_{\log R}$ for the recent period is 0.041 to 0.063. That is, the estimated dispersion (standard deviation) among industries in the effects, R, of unionism on their average relative wages was about 4 to 6 per cent, or, roundly, 5 per cent.

For the period 1945–49, I have estimated that $\bar{B}\sigma_p$ was less than 0.015. Only seven of the studies (Rees, steel manufacturing; Greenslade, bituminous coal mining; Lurie, local transit; Scherer, hotels; Craycraft, barbers; Sobel, rubber tire manufacturing; and Lewis, physicians) provide data from which I have been able to derive estimates of B for this period. These estimates suggest that σ_L was no greater than 0.025. Hence I estimate that the dispersion in the relative wage effects of unionism among industries in 1945–49 was no more than half as large as it was in the latter part of the 1950's.

The standard deviation of the relative wage effects of unionism among industries is a type of average of the numerical values of these effects.[4] Since these values surely differ among industries, the standard deviation

---

[4] The standard deviation, $\sigma_{\log R}$, is the *quadratic* mean of the numerical values, $|\log R|$, of the relative wage effects of unionism by industry. The arithmetic mean of the $|\log R|$ is the *average* or *mean* deviation. Denote the mean deviation by $M_{|\log R|}$. Then

$$\sigma_{\log R} = \sqrt{M_{|\log R|}^2 + \sigma_{|\log R|}^2},$$

where $\sigma_{|\log R|}^2$ is the variance of the *numerical* values of the relative wage effects of unionism. Since the $|\log R|$ differed among industries, $\sigma_{|\log R|}$ was greater than zero. Therefore, the standard deviation, $\sigma_{\log R}$, of the *algebraic* values of the relative wage effects, $\log R$, was surely greater than the arithmetic mean, $M_{|\log R|}$, of the *numerical* values of the relative wage effects. That is, if the standard deviation of the relative wage effects was 5 per cent, then the "average"—meaning the arithmetic mean—of the numerical values of the relative wage effects was less than 5 per cent, probably about 4 per cent.

Furthermore, as I state in the text, the distribution of the numerical values of the relative wage effects was probably positively skewed. In this event, the median of the numerical values of the relative wage effects was probably less than the arithmetic mean of these numerical values and, therefore, less than 4 per cent.

could not be 5 per cent unless the relative wage effects, taken numerically, in some industries were less than 5 per cent and in some others greater than 5 per cent. On the basis of the data in Table 49 of chapter v and Table 76 of chapter vii, I judge that the majority of workers were employed in industries whose average relative wages have been raised or lowered by unionism by no more than about 4 per cent.[5] But these data also suggest that the distribution of the relative wage effects among industries is somewhat positively skewed, with effects in some industries as large as 20 per cent or even larger. The payroll of these industries, however, must have been a quite small fraction of the aggregate compensation of the whole labor force.[6]

What are the industries in which the relative wage effects most exceeded 5 per cent? It is much easier to say that there *were* some than to name them. As Table 49 shows, the extent of our knowledge of the effects of unionism on relative wages by detailed industry is very limited. Moreover, as I have stated repeatedly, the figures in that table are subject to errors of estimation which may be quite large. The data suggest that the list of industries in which the effects were large, compared to 5 per cent, includes bituminous coal mining, some of the skilled building trades in some cities in which the trades were highly unionized, possibly barbering in some cities, and, doubtfully, commercial air transportation, local transit, and ocean shipping. The information in Table 49 on air transportation, however, covers only the airline pilots, and they comprise a small fraction of the employees of the industry. Furthermore, according to Table 76, only about half the employees in commercial air transportation were unionized. Similarly, the information for ocean shipping covers only East Coast seamen, and for both the seamen and local transit the estimate ranges are wide.

There are many other industries which are highly unionized: most of the metal mining industries, anthracite mining, the railroads, some of the trucking and warehousing industries, automobile manufacturing, basic steel manufacturing, meat packing, petroleum refining, the manufacturing of men's and boys' suits and coats, and others. Some of these probably should be added to the above list. A high extent of unionization, however, is not sufficient for a large positive effect of unionism on relative wages, as the example of men's and boys' suits and coats manufacturing (chap. iii, pp. 97 ff.) shows.

[5] See n. 4 above.

[6] As an arithmetic matter, the fraction could not have exceeded 6 per cent if the standard deviation was 5 per cent.

VIII.2. OTHER DIFFERENCES IN THE
RELATIVE WAGE EFFECTS OF UNIONISM

Fragmentary information on the occupational distribution of unionism indicates that the interoccupational dispersion of extent of unionism is large, perhaps even larger than that among industries. Furthermore, the studies of unionism and wage differentials which have dealt with occupations suggest that there are substantial differences in the relative wage effects of unionism among equally unionized occupations: notice the variability in Table 49 among the estimates of the index R_u/R_n for common building labor, skilled building craftsmen, barbers, East Coast seamen, physicians, airline pilots, local transit motormen, and the skilled and unskilled labor groups in Goldner's study. Thus the dispersion in relative wage effects of unionism by occupation very well may be as large as that among industries. I strongly doubt, however, that interoccupational dispersion is twice that by industry. Moreover, part of the over-all dispersion in relative wage effects by occupation is accounted for by differences in relative wage effects among industries. Nevertheless, I suspect that the average interoccupational dispersion of the relative wage effects *within industries* is also substantial, of the same order of magnitude as the interindustrial dispersion.

The distribution of the relative wage effects by occupation, like that for industries, is probably positively skewed, with a small fraction of the labor force employed in occupations in which the relative wage effects exceed 20 per cent.

About 15 per cent of the females and 30 per cent of the males in the labor force are union members. If there were no differences by sex in the average relative wage effect of unionism among either union workers or nonunion workers, then these extent of union organization figures, together with the estimate of $\bar{B}$ (0.10 to 0.15) for 1957–58, imply that unionism has raised the average wage of males by about 1.5 to 2.25 per cent relative to the average wage of females. That is, unionism has raised the average *relative* wage of males by about 0.50 to 0.75 per cent and lowered the average *relative* wage of females by about 1.0 to 1.5 per cent. However, in the occupations in which, according to the studies in chapter iii, the impact of unionism on relative wages has been greatest—coal miners, commercial airline pilots, skilled building trades, seamen—the ratio of female to male employees is very close to zero. Thus the above figures may understate somewhat the gross dispersion of relative wage effects by sex. If the average relative wage effect for women were the same as that estimated for *nonunion* workers—a minus 3 to a minus 4 per cent—the average relative wage effect for males would be a plus 1 to a plus 2 per cent.

These rough estimates of the gross difference between the sexes in the relative wage impact of unionism, of course, are not standardized for differences between males and females in their distributions of employment by industry and occupation. The average difference in relative wage effects between males and females within the same industry and occupation is surely much smaller even than the gross difference, which would make the standardized difference very small indeed.

We know from incomplete evidence that within industries and occupations there is considerable dispersion in extent of unionism among localities and regions and establishment size classes; unionism tends to be less extensive in small establishments, small cities, and the South. These disproportionalities in the distribution of unionism suggest that the relative wage effects of unionism have also been smaller in small establishments and cities and the South. Estimation of the magnitude of the dispersion of the relative wage effects by these characteristics and others, such as color and age, however, requires data on extent of unionism and unionism–relative wage studies that are not currently available.

VIII.3. What Factors Account for the Differences in Relative Wage Effects?

Up to this point, I have been concerned with measuring differences in the relative wage effects of unionism rather than trying to explain what causes the differences. The studies reviewed in chapter iii indicate that the effects of unionism on the relative wages of *union* labor differ considerably from one union jurisdiction to another. What factors account for these differences? For example, have craft unions, especially those representing skilled workers, been more effective than industrial unions? Among highly unionized industries, has concentration of output among relatively few producers tended to make the relative wage effects larger than they otherwise would be?

For these questions, the evidence provided by the studies reviewed in chapters iii and iv is, in my judgment, quite inconclusive. The largest estimates of relative wage effects (R_u/R_n) are for bituminous coal miners, an industry with little concentration of output whose wage-earners have been represented by an industrial union, the United Mine Workers. The next largest, for men's and boys' suits and coats manufacturing, are also for an industrial union–unconcentrated industry combination, but the high figures for this industry hold for only a brief period, and since

World War II the estimated relative wage effects of unionism therein have been nil. Third from the top are the estimates for the airline pilots, highly skilled workers represented by a craft union bargaining with a regulated industry in which output is concentrated among relatively few large firms. The estimates for skilled building tradesmen, represented by craft unions, rank fourth. Building construction is characterized by small concentration of output among firms. And so on through the short list of industries and occupations for which the studies in chapter iii provide relative wage effect estimates.

That only one of the top four estimates is for a "concentrated" industry seems to indicate that unions do better in bargaining in industries with low concentration of output, but such a conclusion surely does not follow if less than one-fourth of the "industries" in the economy are characterized by relatively high output concentration. Note in this connection that of the eighteen "industries" dealt with in the chapter iii studies, only four—rubber tire manufacturing, basic steel manufacturing, local transit, and commercial air transportation—are "concentrated" and that for one of these the only estimate available is for 1945–48. In any case, the ambiguities in counting "industries," the small size and likely selection biases in the sample of industries covered in chapter iii, the differences in dates of the estimates, errors of estimation, and the need to control for factors other than output concentration[7] rule out a positive finding. Nor do the aggregative studies in chapter iii settle the issue. Both the Garbarino (see sec. iv.3 of chap. iv) and the Bowen-Levinson (sec. iv.6 of chap. iv) data, to be sure, suggest that output concentration tended to decrease the relative wage effect for union labor. However, I do not regard this result as a definitive finding on the question. Similarly, the estimates are ambiguous with respect to craft *versus* industrial unionism and skilled craft *versus* unskilled craft unionism.

Answers to these and like questions regarding the factors that produce dispersion in the effects of unionism on the relative wages of union labor will require much additional empirical research on the impact of unionism in industries and occupations for which relative wage effect estimates are not now available.

[7] Was the relative wage effect for airline pilots high because of output concentration, or was it that the industry is a regulated one, or because airline pilots are highly skilled and are represented by a craft union, or was it the combined effect of some of these and still other factors?

IX

Effects of Unionism on Relative Wage Inequality

IX.1. DISPERSION OF WAGES AMONG INDUSTRIES

COLUMN (1) of Table 81 shows the standard deviation of relative average annual full-time compensation per wage and salary worker, 1929–58, among the approximately seventy industry headings (excluding military and work relief) for which the U.S. Department of Commerce reports national income and its components by industry of origin. Columns (2) and (3) are the absolute money and absolute real counterparts of column (1). The series underlying the table are the same as those from which I constructed Table 54 in chapter vi, and the standard deviations are computed with the same fixed weights used in Table 54. (The 1929 and 1958 average annual full-time compensation figures for each industry heading are given in Table 82 below.)

Absolute money wage dispersion, column (2), increased in all except five of the twenty-nine years covered by the table and in 1958 was more than three times as great as in 1929. The upward trend in real wage dispersion was less great, but the standard deviation of real wages in 1958 was almost twice that of 1929.

My main interest, however, is with the relative wage dispersion figures in column (1). Throughout the whole period 1929–58 the amount of relative wage dispersion was quite large.[1] Furthermore, only a small part of the observed dispersion was transitory. In general, the industries whose relative wages were high in any one of the thirty years also had high relative wages in the other years: the standard deviation among the industry groups of their thirty-year average relative wages was 28.6 per cent, which is only slightly lower than the thirty-year average, 30.1 per cent, of the figures in column (1). Thus the interindustrial relative wage structure was a highly stable one in the sense that the correlations among industries between relative wages in one year and relative wages in another year were very high.

The structure was also fairly stable in a second sense: there is no trend

[1] The standard deviations in col. (1) are probably biased upward by errors of measurement in the relative wage figures from which they were computed and by differences among industries in relative full-time hours worked per man per year. On the other hand, they are biased downward by their exclusion of relative wage dispersion among detailed industries within the broad industry headings used by the Department of Commerce.

TABLE 81

DISPERSION OF AVERAGE ANNUAL FULL-TIME COMPENSATION
AMONG INDUSTRIES, 1929–58

	STANDARD DEVIATION OF		
YEAR	Relative Wages (Per Cent)[a] (1)	Money Wages (Current Dollars)[b] (2)	Real Wages (1947–49 Dollars)[c] (3)
1929.	29.6	445	608
1930.	29.9	437	612
1931.	32.1	442	680
1932.	35.1	424	725
1933.	34.4	389	704
1934.	33.4	391	684
1935.	33.1	407	693
1936.	33.0	427	720
1937.	31.8	439	714
1938.	32.4	443	734
1939.	31.9	449	756
1940.	32.1	463	773
1941.	32.0	501	796
1942.	33.1	589	845
1943.	31.7	637	861
1944.	29.4	641	853
1945.	26.6	610	793
1946.	24.1	587	704
1947.	24.2	649	679
1948.	24.9	717	697
1949.	25.4	755	742
1950.	26.5	829	806
1951.	27.7	933	841
1952.	28.0	993	875
1953.	28.7	1,068	934
1954.	28.9	1,108	965
1955.	29.7	1,192	1,041
1956.	30.5	1,287	1,107
1957.	30.9	1,365	1,136
1958.	31.5	1,448	1,173

[a] See text for source. The figures in col. (1) appear in my "The Effects of Unions on Industrial Wage Differentials" in National Bureau of Economic Research, *Aspects of Labor Economics* (Princeton: Princeton University Press, 1962), p. 338, Table 3.
[b] Col. (1) multiplied by col. (4) of Table 54.
[c] Col. (2) divided by U.S. Bureau of Labor Statistics index of consumer prices (1947–49 = 1.00).

to speak of in column (1). On the other hand, some of the short-run changes in relative wage dispersion were large: the standard deviation rose by almost one-fifth from 1929 to 1932, declined by more than one-fourth from 1942 to 1946, and increased by almost one-third from 1946 to 1958.

IX.2. THE IMPACT OF UNIONISM ON THE DISPERSION OF AVERAGE RELATIVE WAGES AMONG INDUSTRIES

To what extent was the relative wage dispersion among industries a result of relative wage effects of unionism? As the measure of the effect of unionism on relative wage dispersion among industries, I use the difference, $\Delta = \sigma_{\log v} - \sigma_{\log v_o}$, between the standard deviation of the logarithms of relative wages, v, in the presence of unionism and the standard deviation of the logarithms of relative wages, v_o, in the absence of unionism. Since the index, R, of the effect of unionism on the relative wage of an industry is the ratio v/v_o, and, therefore, $\log v_o = \log v - \log R$, it follows that

$$\sigma_{\log v_o} = (\sigma^2_{\log v} + \sigma^2_{\log R} - 2r_{vR}\sigma_{\log v}\sigma_{\log R})^{1/2}, \tag{64}$$

where r_{vR} is the simple correlation among industries between $\log v$ and $\log R$.

If the correlation, r_{vR}, were perfect and positive, then $\Delta = \sigma_{\log R}$. Similarly, if the correlation were perfect and negative, then $\Delta = -\sigma_{\log R}$. However, if the correlation is not perfect, $|\Delta| < \sigma_{\log R}$.

Columns (1) and (2) of Table 82 give the figures on average annual full-time compensation per wage and salary worker for 1929 and 1958 by industry group. These figures are the same as those used to compute the standard deviations for 1929 and 1958 in Table 81. Columns (5) and (6) show for each industry group, for the two years 1929 and 1958, the ratio of total employee compensation of wage and salary workers in the group to the corresponding total employee compensation of all industries included in the table. The numerators of the employee compensation ratios in columns (5) and (6) are also the numerators of the average annual full-time compensation estimates in columns (1) and (2). The standard deviations, $\sigma_{\log v}$, of the natural logarithms of the figures in columns (1) and (2) are:

  1929: 0.324, with 1929 weights from column (5) of Table 82;
  1958: 0.326, with 1929 weights from column (5) of Table 82; and
  1958: 0.278, with 1958 weights from column (6) of Table 82.

These logarithmic standard deviations are close to the standard deviations of relative wages for the same years in column (1) of Table 81.

In chapter viii, I estimated that in recent years the standard deviation, $\sigma_{\log R}$, among industries of the logarithms of the relative wage effect indexes R was about 0.04 to 0.06. In 1929, the value of $\sigma_{\log R}$ was probably somewhat smaller, since the dispersion in extent of unionism among industries in 1929 was about half as large as that in the 1950's. Thus it is quite clear that even if the correlation among industries between relative wages and the relative wage effects of unionism were very high, the level of relative wage dispersion among industries shown in Table 81 must be accounted for mainly in terms of factors other than unionism.

TABLE 82

AVERAGE ANNUAL FULL-TIME COMPENSATION OF WAGE AND SALARY WORKERS
BY INDUSTRY, 1929 AND 1958; EXTENT OF UNION ORGANIZATION
OF WAGE AND SALARY WORKERS BY INDUSTRY, 1929 AND 1953*

INDUSTRY	AVERAGE ANNUAL FULL-TIME COMPENSATION (Dollars)		EXTENT OF UNION ORGANIZATION (Per Cent)		WEIGHTS	
	1929 (1)	1958 (2)	1929 (3)	1953 (4)	1929 (5)	1958 (6)
Farms..........................	379	1,484	0	1	0.025	0.012
Agricultural services, forestry, fisheries......................	906	3,773	0	24	0.002	0.002
Metal mining...................	1,645	5,934	3	70	0.004	0.002
Anthracite mining...............	1,754	5,043	80	80	0.005	0.000
Bituminous coal mining..........	1,312	5,790	30	88	0.012	0.005
Crude petroleum, natural gas......	2,050	5,970	1	14	0.006	0.007
Non-metal mining, quarrying......	1,432	5,170	12	32	0.002	0.002
Contract construction............	1,712	5,352	48	72	0.050	0.060
Food and kindred products........	1,523	4,856	4	45	0.031	0.029
Tobacco manufactures............	986	4,022	12	58	0.003	0.001
Textile mill products.............	1,161	3,608	3	30	0.029	0.014
Apparel, finished fabric products...	1,366	3,402	29	53	0.021	0.016
Lumber and timber basic products..	1,180	3,800	12	21	0.014	0.008
Furniture, finished lumber products	1,412	4,151	3	29	0.012	0.008
Paper and allied products.........	1,532	5,557	2	45	0.009	0.013
Printing and publishing...........	2,021	5,507	23	38	0.024	0.019
Chemicals and allied products.....	1,691	6,459	0	39	0.013	0.023
Petroleum and coal products......	1,938	8,662	0	67	0.005	0.008
Rubber products.................	1,608	5,669	0	54	0.006	0.006
Leather and leather products......	1,335	3,586	12	39	0.010	0.005
Stone, clay, glass products........	1,580	5,326	9	45	0.012	0.011
Iron and steel and their products...	1,765	6,223	5	58	0.042	0.048
Nonferrous metals and products....	1,674	5,729	4	46	0.011	0.010
Miscellaneous manufacturing......	1,579	5,083	3	18	0.009	0.013
Machinery, except electrical.......	1,843	5,962	13	45	0.028	0.037
Electrical machinery.............	1,672	5,760	12	56	0.017	0.027
Transportation equipment........	1,760	6,463	0	52	0.005	0.026
Automobiles and equipment.......	1,819	7,024	0	80	0.019	0.018
Wholesale trade.................	2,083	5,803	0	4	0.067	0.068
Retail trade, including auto services	1,418	3,747	1	14	0.118	0.114
Banking.......................	2,037	5,185	0	0	0.015	0.013
Security, commodity dealers, etc...	3,188	8,227	0	4	0.008	0.003
Finance, n.e.c..................	1,977	5,834	0	0	0.005	0.005
Insurance carriers..............	2,293	4,768	0	0	0.016	0.016
Insurance agents, etc............	2,000	5,251	0	11	0.005	0.005
Real estate.....................	1,629	3,645	3	15	0.009	0.007
Railroads......................	1,791	6,394	33	95	0.065	0.025
Local railways, bus lines.........	1,721	4,934	36	74	0.009	0.002
Highway passenger transportation..	1,377	3,918	0	69	0.004	0.003
Highway freight and warehousing..	1,322	5,727	38	78	0.007	0.017
Water transportation............	1,287	7,081	16	76	0.004	0.004
Air transportation...............	2,624	6,785	0	51	0.000	0.004
Pipeline transportation...........	1,927	6,760	0	50	0.001	0.001
Services allied to transportation....	1,441	5,134	22	61	0.005	0.004
Telephone and telegraph..........	1,416	5,124	1	69	0.015	0.016

TABLE 82—*Continued*

INDUSTRY	AVERAGE ANNUAL FULL-TIME COMPENSATION (Dollars)		EXTENT OF UNION ORGANIZATION (Per Cent)		WEIGHTS	
	1929 (1)	1958 (2)	1929 (3)	1953 (4)	1929 (5)	1958 (6)
Radio broadcasting and TV.......	2,513	7,192	0	52	0.000	0.002
Electric and gas utilities..........	1,615	6,277	0	41	0.015	0.015
Local utilities, public services......	1,152	4,200	0	0	0.001	0.000
Hotels and other lodging places....	1,103	2,909	2	28	0.008	0.006
Personal services................	1,224	3,197	9	29	0.015	0.011
Private households..............	732	2,150	0	0	0.034	0.014
Commercial and trade schools, etc. .	1,700	4,302	0	0	0.001	0.001
Business services, n.e.c...........	2,287	5,291	0	0	0.007	0.014
Miscellaneous repair services	1,831	4,805	0	0	0.002	0.003
Motion pictures.................	2,183	4,378	16	22	0.006	0.003
Amusement and recreation........	1,277	4,352	25	29	0.006	0.004
Medical and other health services...	927	2,820	0	0	0.008	0.016
Legal services..................	1,378	4,052	0	0	0.002	0.002
Engineering, other professional services	2,314	6,595	0	2	0.002	0.006
Educational services, n.e.c........	1,321	3,638	0	0	0.006	0.008
Non-profit membership organizations.................	1,723	3,844	0	0	0.012	0.012
Federal general government, civilian	2,062	5,959	11	15	0.011	0.040
Federal government enterprises....	1,943	5,560	65	79	0.011	0.013
State, local general government, nonschool...................	1,589	4,326	1	11	0.036	0.042
Public education	1,483	4,712	0	2	0.032	0.039
State, local government, enterprises	1,609	4,655	0	30	0.003	0.006

* See text for sources.

More precise calculation of Δ requires estimation of the correlation r_{vR}. For 1958, I made two estimates of this correlation. The first estimate covers twelve of the "industries" included in Table 80 for which I was able to calculate estimates of both the relative wage, v, and the index R: construction, bituminous coal mining, men's clothing manufacturing, local transit, hotels, rubber tire manufacturing, paints and varnishes manufacturing, footwear manufacturing, cotton textiles manufacturing, barbers, airline pilots, and seamen. I calculated the estimates of log R from the equation

$$\log R = pB + \log R_n, \tag{65}$$

with log R_n set equal to zero.[2] The estimated values of B are those in Table 80. The sources of the estimates of p are listed below.

[2] There are no estimates by industry of the indexes R_n. I therefore assumed that log R_n was not correlated with log v in the sample of industries. This assumption is equivalent to that made in the text.

Construction: column (4), Table 82, figure for "Contract construction."

Bituminous coal mining: column (4), Table 82, figure for "Bituminous coal mining."

Local transit: column (4), Table 82, figure for "Local railways, bus lines."

Hotels: column (4), Table 82, figure for "Hotels and other lodging places."

Barbers: from Craycraft's study of barbers.

Airline pilots: assumed to be equal to unity.

Rubber tire manufacturing: from the sources underlying Table 76.

Seamen: column (4), Table 82, figure for "Water transportation."

(It was not necessary to estimate p for the other industries, since for them the estimated value of B was zero.) I estimated log v for 1958 from the data in column (2) of Table 82 and the sources from which this column was estimated.[3]

The simple correlation between log v and log R in this sample of twelve industries was 0.63.[4] This correlation, together with the figures for $\sigma_{\log v}$ and $\sigma_{\log R}$ given above, yields the estimates of $\sigma_{\log v_o}$ and Δ for 1958 in Table 83.

TABLE 83

ESTIMATES OF $\sigma_{\log v_o}$ AND Δ IN 1958

Weights	$\sigma_{\log R}$	$\sigma_{\log v}$	$\sigma_{\log v_o}$	Δ
1929.........	0.06	0.326	0.292	0.033
1929.........	0.04	0.326	0.303	0.023
1958.........	0.06	0.278	0.244	0.034
1958.........	0.04	0.278	0.254	0.024

In the second estimate of r_{vR}, I assumed that the correlation among industries between log v and log R was the same as the correlation between log v and extent of unionism, p. For the purpose of calculating $\sigma_{\log v_o}$ and Δ, this assumption is equivalent to assuming that

$$\log v_o = \log v - (p - \bar{p})\sigma_{\log R}/\sigma_p, \tag{66}$$

where $\bar{p}$ is the average extent of unionism among all industries. I calculated log v for 1929 and 1958 for each industry heading in Table 82 from the average annual full-time compensation figures in columns (1) and (2) of the table. Columns (3) and (4) show estimates of extent of union

---

[3] For airline pilots and barbers, however, the estimates of average annual compensation were based on the studies from which the estimates of B for these occupations were drawn.

[4] In calculating this correlation I weighted the observations for each "industry" by the total compensation of wage and salary workers employed in the industry.

organization of wage and salary workers, by industry group, in 1929 and 1953. In calculating log v_o for 1958 by equation (66), I assumed that the extent of union organization in 1958 differed little, industry by industry, from that in 1953. For both 1929 and 1958, I set the value of $\sigma_{\log R}/\sigma_p$ at 0.2.[5]

Table 84 shows the standard deviation, $\sigma_{\log v_o}$, among the industry headings of Table 82, where log v_o was calculated for each heading from the data in that table according to equation (66). The resulting values of Δ for 1958 are a bit lower than those in Table 83. For 1958, the correlation, r_{vR}, between relative wages and the relative wage effects of unionism implied by the figures in Table 84 is 0.50 to 0.58; the value of r_{vR} implied by the table for 1929, however, is only about 0.2.

TABLE 84

Estimates of $\sigma_{\log v_o}$ and Δ Calculated from Table 82
by Equation (66), 1929 and 1958

Year	Weight	$\sigma_{\log v}$	$\sigma_{\log v_o}$	Δ
1929.......	1929	0.324	0.320	0.004
1958.......	1929	0.326	0.300	0.026
1958.......	1958	0.278	0.256	0.022

The statistics in Tables 83 and 84 indicate that in the recent period, unionism may have made the relative inequality of average wages among industries, as measured by the standard deviation of relative wages, two to three percentage points, or about 6 to 10 per cent, higher than it otherwise would have been. The corresponding effect in and near 1929 probably was less than one percentage point (2 per cent). In the light of the data in Tables 49 and 50 of chapter v and in Tables 73, 74, and 75 of chapter vii, it is likely that unionism increased the inequality of relative wages among industries by about two percentage points (6 per cent) in the late 1930's and early 1940's, but by no more than one percentage point (4 per cent) in 1945–49.

IX.3. Unionism and the Relative Inequality of Wages among All Workers

That unionism has increased the relative inequality (as measured by the coefficient of variation) of average wages *among industries* in recent

[5] For 1958, this estimate of $\sigma_{\log R}/\sigma_p$ was based on the value, about 0.05, of $\sigma_{\log R}$ estimated for recent years in chap. viii and the estimate, approximately 0.25, of σ_p for 1953 made in chap. vii. I assumed that the value of $\sigma_{\log R}/\sigma_p$ in 1929 was the same as that in 1958.

years by roughly 6 to 10 per cent does not imply, of course, that unionism must also have increased the relative inequality of the distribution of wage and salary income (on a full-time equivalent basis) *among all individual workers* by 6 to 10 per cent, or even increased the latter inequality at all. The relative inequality of wages among all workers depends on both the relative inequality of average wages *among industries* and the average relative inequality of wages of individual workers *within industries.* Therefore, in principle, unionism could have reduced the all-worker inequality by reducing the average inequality within industries by more than enough to offset the increase in inequality among industries.

In a popular picture of unionism, collective bargaining has reduced relative wage inequality within the more extensively unionized industries by (a) raising the wages of unionized production workers relative to the higher wages of nonunion nonproduction workers, (b) equalizing occupational wage rates among firms within and between localities in nationwide collective-bargaining agreements, (c) reducing occupational relative wage differences within firms by across-the-board cents-per-hour wage increases, and (d) eliminating or reducing interpersonal wage differences within occupations. This picture may fit some industries producing for a national market whose wage-earners are highly organized by industrial unions.

On the other hand, consider the commercial air transportation industry, about half of whose employees are represented by unions on a craft basis. I have estimated that in 1956 the average relative wage of commercial airline pilots was 21 to 34 per cent higher than it would have been in the absence of pilot unionization. The annual earnings of commercial airline pilots in 1956 averaged about $12,000, more than double the average annual full-time earnings of all employees in the commercial air transportation industry. Furthermore, there were large differences in salary among the airline pilots in 1956. Thus it is by no means obvious that unionism has reduced, rather than increased, relative wage inequality within the air transportation industry.

Air transportation, of course, employs only a small fraction of all union workers in the economy. About one-eighth of all union workers, however, are employed in contract construction. Construction workers are represented by numerous craft unions, collective bargaining typically is conducted on a locality basis, and there is some tendency for unionization to be more extensive among construction workers in large firms, large cities, and outside the South.[6] Moreover, Sobotka's study of the

---

[6] This tendency is not peculiar to construction. As I pointed out in chap. vii, there

building trades suggests that the relative wage effects of unionism in this industry group may have been much larger for skilled than for unskilled workers. Similarly, the popular picture does not appear to fit barbering, the printing, publishing, and allied industries, and the entertainment industries.

Thus even within the more or less highly unionized industries unionism probably has had mixed effects, reducing relative wage inequality in some industries and increasing the inequality in others.

Within industries in which the degree of unionization is low, the effects of unionism on relative wage inequality are mainly the indirect results of relative wage changes caused by unionism elsewhere in the economy (see chap. ii, pp. 19 ff.). I see no reason for expecting that within these industries the average change, either reduction or increase, in relative wage inequality has been more than trivial. Over half the wage and salary employees in the economy, I judge, are employed in industries in which less than a fourth of the employees are covered by collective-bargaining agreements. Most of these work in industries in which the degree of unionization is close to zero.

The preceding paragraphs suggest that the majority of employees work in industries within which unionism has had a negligible impact on relative wage inequality. The remaining minority are divided in uncertain ratio between industries (a) within which unionism has increased relative wage inequality and industries (b) within which unionism has decreased relative wage inequality. But this, in turn, implies that the average increase in relative wage inequality within the industries (a) in which unionism has increased inequality, or, alternatively, the average decrease in inequality in industries (b) in which unionism has decreased inequality would have to be quite large to change the economy-wide average *within-industry* relative wage inequality by as much as, say, 5 per cent.[7]

---

is a general tendency for unionism to be concentrated disproportionately within industries in large cities outside the South. This disproportionality probably works toward increasing relative wage inequality within industries.

[7] For example, assume that:

a. Half the labor force is employed in industries within which unionism has had a negligible impact on relative wage inequality, 20 per cent in industries within which unionism has increased relative inequality by 5 per cent on the average, and the remaining 30 per cent in industries within which unionism has reduced inequality;

b. In the absence of unionism the average within-industry relative wage inequality in each of the three groups would have been the same.

Then in the group of industries within which unionism has reduced inequality, the amount of reduction would have to exceed 22 per cent in order to reduce the average within-industry inequality by 5 per cent.

In the preceding section I estimated that unionism has increased the inequality of average relative wages *among industries* by about 8 per cent. If, in addition, unionism has changed the average relative wage inequality *among workers within industries* by less than 5 per cent, then I estimate that unionism has changed the relative inequality of the distribution of wages *among all workers* by less than 6 per cent.[8]

I conclude tentatively that the impact of unionism on relative wage inequality among all workers has been small—under 6 per cent.[9] The direction of the effect, on presently available evidence, is ambiguous.

[8] The data in Table 85 in n. 9 below suggest that the standard deviation of relative wages on a full-time equivalent basis among all workers was less than 75 per cent in 1958. The standard deviation of average annual full-time compensation among industries was about 32 per cent in 1958 and would have been, I estimate, about 8 per cent lower in the absence of relative wage effects of unionism. If the standard deviations of relative wages within industries were uncorrelated with average relative wages among industries, then:

a. If unionism reduced the relative inequality of wages among all workers by as much as 6 per cent, it must have reduced the average within-industry inequality by more than 8 per cent;

b. If unionism increased the relative inequality of wages among all workers by as much as 6 per cent, it must have increased the average within-industry inequality by more than 5 per cent.

[9] Table 85 compares the relative inequality of wages among all workers with the relative inequality of average wages among industries in the period 1945–58. The coefficients of variation in col. (3) are the same as those in col. (1) of Table 81 in the text. Col. (1) shows estimates of the coefficient of variation of annual wage and salary income of persons fourteen years of age and over with wage and salary income. Assume that over the period 1945–58, unionism had *no* effect on the average inequality of relative wages *within* industries, but caused the relative inequality of average wages

TABLE 85

RELATIVE WAGE DISPERSION AMONG INDUSTRIES AND AMONG ALL WORKERS, 1945–58
(Coefficients of Variation of Wage and Salary Income in Per Cent)

Year	Persons, Aged 14 and over, with Wage and Salary Income (1)	Full-Year Wage and Salary Workers (2)	Industry Average Wages (From Table 81) (3)
1945	80.7	...	26.6
1946	...	...	24.1
1947	74.3	...	24.2
1948	77.3	...	24.9
1949	76.7	60.5	25.4
1950	75.9	...	26.5
1951	76.5	...	27.7
1952	77.7	...	28.0
1953	84.8	...	28.7
1954	86.2	...	28.9
1955	86.9	...	29.7
1956	87.9	...	30.5
1957	87.7	...	30.9
1958	90.4	...	31.5

among industries to increase by about 5 per cent more than it otherwise would have between 1945 and 1958. Then this effect would cause the coefficient of variation of average wages among industries to rise by a bit less than 5 per cent relative to the coefficient of variation of wages among all workers. This is almost exactly the amount by which the ratio of col. (3) to col. (1) increased between 1945 and 1958. The data in Table 85, by themselves, are very inconclusive evidence, of course, that unionism was not a significant factor tending to change the economy-wide average inequality of relative wages within industries.

The figures in col. (1) overestimate the coefficient of variation of "full-time" wage and salary income among all workers, since the income distributions from which they were computed included, without adjustment, the wage and salary income of part-time and part-year workers. The figure in col. (2) is the coefficient of variation of wage and salary income of wage and salary workers in the experienced civilian labor force who worked 50–52 weeks in 1949. This coefficient of variation is 21 per cent lower than the figure for 1949 in col. (1).

The coefficients in col. (1) were computed from income distributions reported in various issues of Bureau of the Census, *Current Population Reports: Consumer Income.* The source of the income distribution underlying the figure in col. (2) is Bureau of the Census, *U.S. Census of Population: 1950,* IV, *Special Reports,* Part 1, chap. B, Occupational Characteristics, Table 23. All of these income distributions were open ended at the highest income class. I "closed" the open end by fitting a Pareto curve to the data for the top income classes.

Index